*How to be very very lazy in*

# Marseillan

## and a lot of Languedoc

by Laurence Phillips

im rint

# To the very special people of Marseillan

And with many thanks and raised glasses to:
*family, friends, and neighbours in Marseillan and beyond; with many of whom the reader shall be on first name terms by the final pages; and remembering Armand, fellow diner and fellow traveller in many adventures. To local historian M Albert Arnaud for an inspiring entrée and the occasional nudge; la famille Henri for countless evenings and mornings of memories and photographs; and to all mine hosts and dining partners over the years*

*And for professional help, courtesy and so much more to the Mairie of M Yves Michel, to M Jean-Michel de Courthezon, Mme Afrae El Hadrami and her excellent team at Marseillan's Office de Tourisme, Mme Banq and her fellow Marseillan librarians, Mme Patricia de Pouzilhac of the Comité Régional du Tourisme Languedoc Roussillon, Mme Sabrina Lucchese of Hérault Tourisme, and M Samuel Vannier of the Voies Navigables de France and their many colleagues in cities, towns and villages across the region.*

Published by imprint illyria books

© copyright Laurence Phillips 2011
© Maps (pages 394-398) copyright Ville Marseillan
© Map (page 399) copyright Région Languedoc Roussillon (adapted imprint illyria)
Cover design and illustrations © imprint illyria 2011

First published 2011
Revised and updated reprint June 2012

ISBN 978-0-9558247-1-5

Printed and bound by CPI Antony Rowe, Eastbourne

## im/rint illyria books
### London
www.imprintillyria.com

# Contents

---

**REGULAR UPDATES ON LINE**
visit www.LazyFrance.com

Visit our website before travelling for updates to listings in your guide. Download or print to ensure that your copy of the book always has the latest addresses.

# How to use this book

## Symbols in listings pages

 Mainline rail station

 Bus service from Marseillan

 Tram stop (Montpellier)

|3| **B2**  Map reference (see pages 394-399)

All Marseillan and Marseillan Plage addresses have the postcode 34340

€     Menus start under 15 euros
€€     Menus start around 20-30 euros
€€€     Menus start over 30 euros

**L**     Lunch
**E**     Evening

Restaurant set-menu prices are based on evening meals. Lunches are often cheaper, with many Marseillan establishments offering slightly limited (if smaller) midday meals from €12-16, even when regular rating is €€. Often, top gastronomic restaurants will have an "affordable" *prix-fixe* lunch in a lower price band – this may be the best way to sample a top flight *Michelin* meal at half what you'd pay in the evening. Opening hours and days (Especially in Marseillan) change with the seasons. Prices correct at the time of writing, but fluctuate and should be regarded for comparative purposes only. Key symbols give an approximate idea of budget. For entry prices at museums and attractions, check websites or telephone in advance.

In the unyoked humour of our idleness, it still takes many months to indulge in as many meals as are numbered herein. And with delays of appetite and capacity compounded by vagaries of publisher and *humeur du chef*, inevitably some meals and prices (though hopefully not too many addresses), have changed since the napkin left my lips. So please piece out our imperfections with your grace, as a wine is only ever as good as its last summer and a meal as its last clean plate.

This could never be an exhaustive guide to Languedoc Roussillon. It is a private carnet of addresses, favourite places and reminiscences of happy days and weeks spent in a land that will always drip-feed its secrets at its own measure. It has taken two and a half millennia to create and would surely take as long to fully understand. So apologies if your favourite corner is not to be found within these pages: and congratulations; you got there first and may keep it as your private secret just a little longer. Life in the Languedoc is a work in progress and, since each of us travels at a particular pace, I simply share my journey so far.

Laurence Phillips
Marseillan 2011

lolly@laurencephillips.com

# Introduction

The ochre yawn of an improbable sunrise.
The silver blue splash of an impossible dawn.
The whisper of a vagrant wind and the caress
of a well-seasoned sun getting into its stride.
The plish-plash of a daybreak returning fishing boat.
And the full-throated taunt of a strutting mallard
at the exuberant swooping of early swallows and swifts,
And the audacious flights of the lagoon's flamingos.

I T IS MORNING IN MARSEILLAN VILLAGE; the church tower shakes off the vestiges of sleep as the bell chimes the ish. The clock always strikes the ish in Marseillan: two minutes to the hour, maybe two minutes past. Or perhaps both. One thing is certain: when the clock strikes eight, you know that either it was eight o'clock not so very long ago or it will be eight o'clock quite soon.

It is morning in Marseillan Port and the castanet clink-clank of the rigging on the boats tied up in the safe haven of the little harbour acknowledges the *vent du jour*, today's unique breath of refreshing wind:

Perhaps the *marin* blowing the moist breath of the Mediterranean or the *tramontane*  that cuts crisply through narrow *ruelles* of the historic centre of the village, bringing fresh mountain air down to the coast, and reminding young and old alike that we all own elbows. To be followed perhaps by a *mistral* to turn heads and furrow brows, reinventing the day's weather at the slice of noon

Whichever wind blows today, it promises a balm for the sunshine that graces the village some 300 days each year, and speeds early morning cyclists and pedestrians on their way to buy fresh baked croissants and baguettes from the *boulangerie.*

The day starts with warm bread and piping hot coffee. Yet, from the first promise of the morning to the last benediction of the wee small hours, every peal of the clock's negligence brings new diversions, tastes and sensations. The infinite variety of myriad private nothings: Perhaps a platter of oysters freshly gathered from the lagoon and savoured at a quayside table, with a glass of the village's crisp and fresh white wine, Picpoul de Pinet.

Maybe a sensual surrender to the savours and flavours of so many secret herbs that make up the unique *Noilly Prat* vermouth, stilled, matured and sun-ripened in waterside warehouses. The tasting and tour is a Marseillan must. Or perchance, a slosh and swirl and a slurp in the cool of a wine cellar, as *vignerons* share their newest wines safely shielded from 40-degree summer sunshine outside.

Then again, as the sun relinquishes its strength, one might always see out the afternoon in chocolate with syrupy crepes and ice cream sundaes, or toast the long evening with a *pichet* of refreshing rosé, on a tiny terrace scraped from the roofspace of a steep little village house, or the balcony of an apartment by the waterfront, or yet a quayside café table.

Play the menu game as you check out the mouth-watering selection of fresh fish from the étang at one of a score of village restaurants. Catch of the day, sea bass, bream, sole and some of the best seafood in all France.

Meanwhile Marseillan has much to distract you between glasses and mealtimes: Listen to a concert between the cool white walls of the church of Saint-Jean-Baptiste; nibble olives and crunchy garlic cloves, barter for ceramics and pick up something for lunch at the market on Tuesday morning; go fishing from the breakwater; walk alongside a stranger's dog up to the lighthouse at the mouth of the Canal du Midi; or take a trespasser's picnic to a poppy-freckled meadow. Pick up *Gallé* glass, *Limoges* plates, art deco lamps or some vintage magazines at Languedoc's favourite *brocante* flea market; discover the eccentric local sports or the simple pleasures of a boat trip on the still waters of the lagoon; make for the 12-mile stretch of sandy beach that runs from Cap d'Agde to Sète; catch a travelling circus show pitching overnight camp outside the village or admire the skills of local artists and craftsmen in their workshops.

At the end of another perfect meal and another perfect day, take time to stroll down to the waters edge and watch the silver moon rise above the twinkling lights of the Mont St Clair across the bay.

There is so much more to see in this blessed corner of Languedoc, but no need to make time for it today. When swallows sweep in the morning, the *tramontane* exhales its way down the rue Emile Zola and the church clock remembers to chime the new ish; tomorrow is another day.

# Marseillan
## in Languedoc

*A little history and just enough geography to be getting on with*

Poussière de soldats, cendre de troubadours,
    Pendant mille ans notre âme en ta glèbe est entrée,
Tes roses sont mes sœurs, et tes vignes dorées
    Du sang dont bat mon cœur se gonfleront toujours.


The dust of soldiers, ash of troubadour
    Your soil our soul a thousand years defines.
Your roses, my sisters, and your golden vines
    With blood of my heart-beat fulfilled ever more."


- "Marseillan" by Achille Maffre de Baugé (1855-1928)

# Once upon a time and place

ONCE UPON A TIME in Marseillan is a story of buccaneers and true independent spirits, of a fisherman risking all to save a damsel in distress, of adventurers and farmers, of winegrowers and revolutionaries, of poets and feminists and the secret of James Bond's favourite tipple. *Il etait une fois à Marseillan* begins many a tale of a delightfully contrary human spirit, zest for life in the slow lane, leading gently to a recounting of simple recollections of human nature.

I have been flirting with France since boyhood, and claim as treasured conquests the full-on *affaire* that is Paris and a positively Leporellian *catalog e questo* from the eternal *jeunesse* of Lille in the north to that bashful dowager Menton at mimosa and lemon season. Yet my favourite location for trysting and dalliance with the country is here in the still gloriously unspoilt Languedoc Roussillon. Way down south and turn right before you get to the commercialised Riviera:

Roussillon is succulent fruit trees, and coastal villages to inspire Matisse; Languedoc is rugged rosemary- and thyme-scented mountains, ruined castles, noble cities and saltwater lagoons. Winding its way through the undulating landscape of hills and rivers, cathedrals and endless vineyards, through Languedoc and beyond, is the tree-lined Canal du Midi linking the Mediterranean to the Atlantic - one of the most evocative images of the land. And where the Canal, after strutting magnificently through town and country, past ramparts high and vistas green, concedes eventually to shed its awning of leafy boughs and settle down in calm contemplation of the good things in life; so I too discovered the simple pleasures of *la vie Marseillanaise*.

A village surrounded by vines and lapped by the waters of a lagoon brimming with oysters and seabass, with a weekly market offering delicious fruits, olives and the aromatic herbs of the south of France and two dozen mouthwatering restaurants. The perfectly proportioned little port, a canal-like inlet of the lagoon, is a confection of wine warehouses, homes and café tables untainted by brash branding. Crowning a crest of treetops and terracotta, the belfry of the parish church with its caged bell leads the visitor to the historic centre of the village; cobbled and alleyed, where centuries huddle cheek by jowl in shaded timelessness.

I was not the first, and will certainly not be the last, to embrace this place. Nor, probably was anyone ever the first to set foot here. When the adventurers that lazy historians and media soundbiteurs call ancient Greeks (most likely Phoceans) discovered this settlement on its vast open waterway running parallel to the Mediterranean coast, in those days a veritable inland sea from the Rhône to the Hérault estuaries, they encamped by the port. Yet others had already been squatting in makeshift huts around what is now the port Tabarka; simple fishing folk living on the marshlands. Romans inevitably followed, as the port grew, and a fortified town evolved.

Through all the years, the constant in so many changing regimes, when France's political fortunes blew from the *Porte d'Agde* to *the route de Montpellier* with the fickle volte-face of prima donna winds, has been the special blend of contrariness and simple integrity that mark out the *Marseillanais* themselves. So Marseillan managed to be both Revolutionary and Christian at once; as other communes sacked churches during the Terror, turning altars and naves into stables and warehouses, Marseillan augmented her Eglise Saint Jean Baptiste, grabbed new rights of free citizenship and went to Mass. When Marseillan was the first community in the new Republic to erect a statue of the Marianne, symbol of France, in a public square, she was depicted not as the helmeted warrior immortalised on a million stamps and coins, but holding scales of equality and the declaration of the *Droits de l'Homme*. Townsfolk have always managed to progress a knight's move away from the courses dictated for them by their masters. Thus, as local historian Albert Arnaud recounts, at the waning of the 19th century, when the town planted its fine *Esplanade*, a grand public space, lined with trees for shady strolls and leisurely promenades, protected from the harsh glare of the Midi sun, it did not become the timeless essential centre of Marseillan's social life. The novelty wore off and the locals stayed away, grumbling *"Elle est trop loin, trop ventée, poussiéreuse..."*, it was too far away, too windy and dusty, they complained.

Instead, they chose the wide pavement outside the then-new post office (now police station) on the boulevard Lamartine for their *passegiata*. Here, on *"le trottoir"* pretty girls in their finery would walk past equally well-dressed boys, time and again, to elicit glances enough to lead to arm in arm strolling on subsequent evenings.

This very Mediterranean ritual that runs through the heart of the Midi from the Cours Mirabeau in Aix to the Allées Riquet in Béziers is a latin tradition and never the sole prerogative of youth. All ages like to see and be seen, and even a generation that no longer feels the imperative to seek a mate would be happy to sit, watch, nod and whisper. So it was, on this stretch of pavement, that *le tout* Marseillan would always gather, once the sun was past its strength, to take the air and breathe in the heady *bavardage* of village life. The strolling ground ran from cafés closer to the Mairie, along the pavement down to the square where stands the theatre, and back again.

The circuit was an essential part of the Marseillan day, and locals would talk about going out for an hour or so to *"faire le trottoir"*. These social saunters continued through two wars and up until the 1960s when the town bowed to the wisdom of its citizens and spruced up the rest of the boulevard Lamartine, planting kerbsides to give the main road the feel of *les Allées*. And so, naturally, within a very short time, the people moved elsewhere for their evening *rendezvous* – mostly indoors, with the newly popular television and an early evening date with Mireille Matthieu, Claude François and other fashionable songsters.

Today, a strategically chosen table at a café or restaurant on the quays serves for people-spotting; ex-pats at market morning café tables, compare their shopping and swap paperbacks; locals, in the evenings, loiter in the glass doorway of that same Marine Bar, one eye on the sports channel, another keeping look out for passing acquaintance, still barely yards from the original *trottoir*, and of course, though times may change, people come and go, there is always *la Grille*, the railings by the Mairie (itself, once a popular café) always the very conduit and *carrefour* of public opinion. *Plus ça change,* and whilst tradition, *patrimoine* and the old way of doing things have to the French the unquestionable divinity of maidenhead; street signs and place names may change with impunity. There is surely not a place de la Liberté in France that has not formerly been known as the place de la République having ditched the original monicker place Royale. Similarly, how often have we all wandered down mediaeval rues Emile Zola, Marechal Foch or Jean Jaurès without considering what the street might have been called in the many generations of its existence before its 19th or 20th century namesake was even conceieved. For the record: Marseillan's rue Emile Zola, threading the old village before decanting into the main place Carnot, has also been known as rue de l'Ancienne Mairie (since the last (3rd) town hall was housed at number 7) But it has known many appellations as one of twin axes of the original fortified village, the other managing three names in one year *(see page 34)*.

Names change, and that is a fact of French life and maps. But place Carnot, ever Marseillan's heart, is still referred to as the Place Couverte. It was renamed in honour of the popular president Sadi Carnot, whose regard locally was probably not universal since (this came up in conversation with artist Jean-Claude Chabrol one morning when we were setting scene of some of his canvasses of buildings along the canal) popular Marseillan conviction is that the assassination of the president was plotted in the old stone fishing shacks at Les Onglous opposite the lighthouse *(see page 42)*.

This is the seductive lure of Marseillan: In a village built on stories and storytelling, tales passed *bouche à l'oreille* are ever more savoury than those founded on hard dry facts and served on a platter of indigestible dates.

I am not writing a formal history of Marseillan. That has been done far better by many illustrious writers whose work is championed in the closing pages of this handbook. I make no excuses; I offer no apologies and this volume comes with neither guarantees nor legally binding provenance. My stories shall be shared with you in much the same way as they reached me; in anecdote and recollection, confidence and explanation, from the warm and witty folk of this special place Those villagers who shared their inherited gossip with me would be first to shrug off a request for back-up, and even the most respected historian can admit that the events of such a century at such a place might have occurred somewhere quite different at another time altogether.

So instead of an annotated chronology and threat of a spot test for those not paying attention at the back, we'll share legends of the vines when we visit the vineyards, old family recollections may spill out at a restaurant, a seafarer's yarn be tripped by a view of the port, and our special heroes will be recalled on a day in the country or a trip to a neighbouring town. Each time in its place; each tale in its setting; and each personality recalled wherever life was lived at its best.

# Marseillan's Timeline

## The Struggle for Identity

| | |
|---|---|
| 6$^{th}$ c BC | Marseillan settled by the Phoceans |
| 5$^{th}$ c BC | Celtic invasion |
| 3$^{rd}$ c BC | Volcae in Nîmes took control of Marseillan |
| 2$^{nd}$ c BC | Volcae ousted by the Roman colony based in Narbonne |
| 118 BC | Via Domitia road links Rome and Spain |
| 52 BC | Marseillanais provide military support to Julius Caesar |
| 49 BC | Town becomes Roman *Messalum* under the consul Fabius |
| 5$^{th}$ c AD | Invasion by Vandals, then Visigoths |
| 720 | Marseillan devastated by the march of the Saracens |
| 737 | Vineyards and all crops destroyed in Charles Martel's scorched earth policy that successfully evicts Saracens. |
| 787 | Charlemagne gives Marseillan château to Bishop of Agde |
| 850 | Marseillan becomes a *cité seigneuriale* |
| 930 | Scythians from the Middle East invade Septimanie |
| 933 | Raymond Pons, Count of Toulouse, wins back the region |
| 11$^{th}$ c | First formal hospital established |
| 1139 | Raimond 1er Trencavel becomes *propriétaire* of Marseillan |
| 1170 | First consulate of Marseillan |
| 1187 | Bishops of Agde take on the seigneurie of Marseillan |
| 1209 | Ravaged by Simon de Montfort's knights templar |
| 1218 | Pope excommunicates "all the men of Marseillan" |

## Finally French

| | |
|---|---|
| 1229 | Marseillan finally joins the Kingdom of France |
| 1241 | The town builds its fortifications against invasion |
| 1310 | Covered market opens |
| 1348 | 60% of the population die during the great plague, which returns in 1361, 1375, 1572, 1628 and 1629 |
| 1563 | The Consulate of Marseillan wins right to self govern. |
| 1600 | Marseillan builds a working and trading port |
| 1609 | Sanctuary to *Morisque* Muslims fleeing Spanish Inquisition |
| 1642 | Ailing King Louis XIII stays in Marseillan |
| 1654 | Molière and his troupe perform in Marseillan |
| 1683 | Canal du Midi (Canal Royal) opens |
| 17$^{th}$ c | Church rebuilt, and four penitent brotherhoods established |
| 1709 | Cholera and famine ravage the town |
| 1789 | French revolution – Marseillan unaffected by the "Terror" |

# Years of Innovation

| | |
|---|---|
| **1790** | February. First municipal elections in Marseillan |
| | Jean Charles Baille d'Astier voted Mayor |
| **1791** | Town divided into ten sectors and first town plan created |
| **1802** | Ramparts and fortifications pulled down |
| **1813** | Joseph Noilly creates France's first vermouth |
| **1819** | First school for girls run by the Sisters of Saint-Maur |
| **1822** | Saint Jean-Baptiste church returns to Roman Catholicism |
| **1831** | First public school for boys and girls |
| **1856** | Les Onglous station opens (railway vetoes name *Marseillan*) |
| **1870** | Le Château du Port built by wine merchant Jean Voisin |
| | Women permitted to drink in bars and cafes |
| **1876** | Phylloxera blight devastates Marseillan's vineyards |
| **1878** | Marianne statue erected: the first in France |
| **1881** | Replanting of the vines |
| **1897** | Marseillan finally gets its railway station |
| **1907** | 1000 Marseillanais join Béziers wine-grower riots |
| **1914** | The town establishes welfare payments for poor families |
| **1915** | Hospital for wounded soldiers founded. |
| | Marseillan-born Général Roques becomes commander of French army; appointed war minister, awarded Grand Croix de la Légion d'Honneur in 1916 |
| **1919** | The Mairie moves to its present site |
| **1920** | Theatre opens |
| **1931** | Market hall built next to the church |
| **1935** | Marseillan's wine co-operative formed |

# Modern Times

| | |
|---|---|
| **1942** | German occupation of Marseillan |
| **1944** | Canal de Pisse Saumes opens étang to the sea |
| | 22 August Marseillan liberated, Germans retreat |
| **1947** | Holiday resort created at newly named Marseillan Plage |
| **1953** | Marseillan station closes 20 years after last passenger train |
| **1958** | Summer floods wreak havoc in the town and vineyards |
| **1960** | General de Gaulle visits Marseillan Plage and meets an old companion in arms |
| **1961** | Winegrowers revolt once again |
| **2010** | New beach road between Marseillan and Sète |

# What to see in Marseillan

**Allée du Général Roques**
avenue Victor Hugo [3] **B2**
The first face you see as you step up to this esplanade is
not that of a flat-capped *pétanque* player, nor a group of
young friends hanging out in the shade, but the bust of
Pierre Auguste Roques, the high-flying general and
politician who gave France *l'avion*. His story begins in the
family home (look for the plaque on **boulevard Jean
Bertouy**, just behind the left bank of the port); but his
glory belongs to the skies of France and beyond. Born in
1856, he had a distinguished military record as an army
engineer during the latter part of the 19th century and by
1909 was the youngest army chief in his country's history.
Yet it was in the early 20th century that he gained fame and
*reclame* as founder of the *Armée de l'Air*, France's air
force, and as government inspector of aeronautics in 1910.
He may not have invented the aeroplane, but it was he
who chose the French word *avion* as a replacement for the
original gallicised term *aéroplane*. Army commander at
the start of the First World War, he became War Minister
in 1916, was awarded the grand cross, his fifth and highest
level of the *Legion d'Honneur*. After the armistice, he
received the *Medaille Militaire* from the state and a sword
of honour by Marseillan. He died in 1920 and the
promenade in the village was renamed in his memory, as
was a street in Paris' 16th arrondissement.

A symbol of the merchant prosperity of the town, the
*Esplanade* or *Promenade* was landscaped and planted
during the *Belle Epoque* for citizens of the town to parade
in their Sunday best. After the inauguration in 1893, the
park had a mixed reception *(see page 13),* but the shade of

tall trees is a blessing in the heat of the summer. Whilst the regard of a hero graces the main entrance from the avenue Victor Hugo, the war memorial (*see photo, page 94*) is a powerful emotive depiction of the orphans of conflict, three children stepping up to a lectern, carrying the belt and cap of a soldier father, killed in battle. A *boulodrome* hosts regular serious *pétanque* contests, summer circuses often pause here and it is not unusual to see llamas tethered to trees. The streets around the *Esplanade* are lined with traditional *Maisons Vigneronnes* and the small building behind the park is a former public bathhouse – later a library and youth centre. Opposite the park, **Salle Paul Arnaud**, a converted wine warehouse, is a community centre named for a 20th century mayor (1982-89).

### Ancien Couvent des Récollets (Eglise St Roch)
rue de l'Hôpital [1] A/B2

With so many religious orders clustered in such a compact area, it is no wonder that Marseillan was well known for its social care. Nuns established schools for girls and boys well before the state took on the duty of educating the young. There had been hospitals in Marseillan since the 11th century when crusader knights of St John of Jerusalem set up a ward around Les Onglous, and some historians suggest organised health care may have started almost 200 years earlier. The main hospital stood in the centre of Marseillan, on what is now the rue Emile Zola (*see **Third Mairie**, page 45*). Beyond the fortifications, a modest chapel also welcomed sick and weary strangers. Alas, by the 16th century, the 300-year-old church had been destroyed by successive religious wars. In 1613, the Frères Récollets, followers of St Francis of Assissi, proposed establishing a convent safely within Marseillan itself. Originally known as the *Coventu San Francesi Marsiliani*, this convent of St Francis of Marseillan incorporated its **church of Saint Roch** with a chapel dedicated to Saint Sauveur, whose patronage is credited with several minor miracles in Marseillan: Local raconteurs declare that, within a few years of the chapel being founded, the saint's spiritual intervention calmed a crazed mule that had grabbed 9-month old Catherine Hérail, saving the baby from certain death. And it was widely believed that supplication rescued Marseillan from the plague that ravaged nearby villages in 1629. The Faubourgs Saint Joseph and La Fontaine districts remained relatively untouched by the epidemic. Away from the drama of miracles, the Convent had more constant quiet success in tending to the sick and the poor and offering support and shelter to the needy and hospitality to travellers passing through the region. Since Chaucer first blew the whistle on life on the road and mediaeval bishops published excellent (and deliciously revealing) handbooks for party animals on a quest, so

18

pilgrimages were essentially the tourist industry of their times. A favourable criticism of a church, the suggestion of a minor miracle or merely an informed tip-off regarding decent hospitality could determine routes to shrines across Europe, and sway the fortunes of towns on the *chemins religieux* pilgrimage trails.

By the 17th century, pilgrims could overnight at the *Couvent des Frères Récollets* of the *Eglise Saint Roch*. Marseillan received glowing reviews from religious chroniclers, who wrote of a lively and bustling settlement and trading post on the *étang* and canals, with a healthy and tolerant attitude towards its religious orders. The welcome here was that of family and friends, according to Père Chrysostome Gaufredy, writing in 1680.

Ten years earlier, Paul Riquet, having selected Marseillan as terminus of his great Canal project, came to pray at the *Eglise Saint Roch*. Observing the poor state of the vaulting, the engineer designed a solution and personally oversaw restoration work. In gratitude, monks added his name to a list of souls in their care, sealing a close relationship between the father of the Canal du Midi and this little church at the back of the village. In the months that followed, Riquet continued to work on the improvements, and the name Riquet was incorporated in the panelling.

By the Revolution, the religious order had left Marseillan, and the 1790s saw the convent sold as a saltpetre workshop making gunpowder for the military, and eventually repurchased by the town as a hospice, becoming the main hospital when the Mairie moved to rue Emile Zola. From time to time, the Eglise Saint Roch would deputise for the main Parish Church of Saint Jean Baptiste. As the convent became a hospital and church school, so the chapel became absorbed within the main establishment and in 1954 it was finally deconsecrated and closed down. It became Marseillan's old people's home until the new *maison de retraite* opened on rue Victor Hugo on the cusp of the 21st century. Of this eventful history, little remains; some church treasures donated to the parish church (*see page 28*). All that stands now, on the rue de l'Hôpital, is but one ornate door of the Eglise Saint Roch, a reminder of Marseillan's "other" church.

**Bell Tower** (*see* **Eglise St Jean Baptiste**)

---

**DID YOU KNOW?**
When village roads are renamed in French, they often keep their original Occitan or *patois* names, which give a clue to the original French version. Check out the rues Goudet, Charles Reboul, Emile Zola and Achille Baille.

---

## Boulevard Jean Bertouy [2] A2

Now a quiet residential street, with large family houses, shuttered from public gaze, the boulevard Bertouy is a sleepy alternative to the busier boulevards and avenues that link the village to the bustling cafes and restaurants of the port. Yet, for centuries this was *rue du Port* and *av de la Marine*, main route from the centre to the commercial trading world of the quays. Side roads fanned out southwards to the main port and north to a fishermen's quarter around the old *Port des Nacelles*, with wineries on rues de la Crabe and 19 Mars and the *Labrousse* distillery rue Edouard Adam until 2005.

On this road of *vignerons* and *pêcheurs*, Jean Bertouy, much-loved Mayor of Marseillan since 1886, died in his family home on 19 May 1913. The street was immediately renamed in his honour. Son of a humble boatman, who died, crushed under the weight of a 600 litre barrel of wine when Jean was a few months old, Jean was raised by his mother and studied hard, eventually securing a place at the prestigious *Ecole des Arts et Metiers* in Paris. A promised brilliant career never materialised since the young Jean became dangerously ill and returned to Marseillan where he worked as secretary to the Mairie. Vociferous advocate of universal education and campaigner for a steam tram link between Marseillan and Agde, he was elected Mayor when 38 years old, and held the post for the rest of his days.

The council might well have chosen to rename the street the *boulevard des Grands Hommes*, since it has been home to many a hero: Just before the Boulevard sweeps a right-angle towards the quayside and the main road changes its name to the rue Suffren, two plaques mark out neighbouring homes. Number 13 was home of air-force founder and war minister General Auguste Roques (*see page 17*). The General found greatest fame, yet the family gave many more lives to France, five other sons are listed on the war memorial in the Church. The house next door, number 11, honours another pioneer of aviation, and scion of the Roques. The General's nephew, Pierre Deley, born here in 1893, had a distinguished career as a fighter pilot during the Great War. Fame came in peacetime, however, as founder of France's first civil airline, *Les Lignes Latécoère*. With fellow air ace, Antoine de St Saint-Exupery, author of the classic fable *Le Petit Prince*, he created the airmail service, forging postal links firstly between France and Spain, then on to Casablanca, Dakar and on to South America. He was part of a legendary Andes rescue mission. Deley founded Santiago's airport and after World War Two was Air France's representative in Chile and Argentina. He retired to Marseillan in 1952 and died here in 1981. Neither house is open to the public. But you may see family tombs in the cemetery. General Roques, as a national hero, is interred at *Les Invalides* in Paris.

**Cave Cooperative**
quai de la Résistance   **[2] B2** (*see page 98*)

**Chapelle des Pénitents Bleus**
place Miramond **|1| B2**
In the 16<sup>th</sup> and 17<sup>th</sup> centuries, religion became something of a growth industry for Marseillan. Politicians and merchants, whilst gearing the day job towards Mammon, were still keen to hedge their bets with enough contrition, atonement and devotion to get their chosen camels through the eye of any needle. As the church itself was restored to glory, so a quartet of religious brotherhoods of penitent monks took up residence in the village, charged with praying for the eternal souls of their sponsors. In its heyday, Marseillan boasted orders of black, grey, and white friars, and the Blue Pénitents settled here on what is now the place Miramond in 1596.

This delightful square, a riot of geraniums in summer, and just wide enough to hold the shade of a spreading plane tree, was not known by that name at the time.

Various incarnations have stronger echoes of the penitent past – *place de la Punition* being amongst the addresses to make a modern sales-conscious estate agent shudder in resignation. More familiarly referred to as the *Plan St Jean*, the name reflects the statue of Saint John the Evangelist poised in a gothic niche by the remaining window above the archway and gate that are the last vestiges of the **Chapelle des Pénitents Bleus** on the façade of the house in the corner of one of the prettiest little squares of the *centre historique*. This is the final remnant of these religious buildings. The brotherhood was dissolved around 1720.

There is even less to see of the other orders, that once colonised a swathe of the village, the length of rue Vedel. At the junction of rue Michelet, and there is nothing to show that this was home to the Pénitents gris. The top of the street opens to the former hospital and convent building of the Frères Récollets *(see page 18)* on rue de l'Hopital, and the road decants into the place Carnot, once home to Pénitents Noir.

## Château (or Maison) du Bayle
place Carnot [1] B2

To most casual visitors, this narrow house in the corner of the town square is known for its gastronomy at the restaurant *La Table d'Emilie* (*see page 273*). Nevertheless, whilst creations on each plate may threaten to eclipse even the gothic vaulting of the ground floor dining room, the house itself is one of Marseillan's prized glories.

Some sources call this the *château*, some the *maison*, of the diocesan bailiff, charged with running the town on behalf of the count-bishop of Agde. Beautiful proportions from the flamboyant first floor window to the regimented neatness of upper stories. Until the modernisation of the shop next door, the side of the building revealed a magnificent staircase, showpiece of the home of the Marquis de Montalet.

Since the days of the Seigneur bishops, Maison du Bayle was home to the celebrated Maffre Baugé family. The clan's local influence can be judged from its grand marble war memorial in the church. Most famous son was poet Achille Maffre de Baugé, born in 1855, whose poignant lines on his home town (from '*Terre d'Oc*', *see page 10*) are painted above the entrance to the restaurant. He was last in a long line of notable Marseillanais to enter and change public life from within these walls. His father's family tree fairly dazzles with luminaries: not merely the mayor who commissioned the Marianne, but renowned female troubadour Clara d'Anduze and even a pope (Alexander III).

Politicians and soldiers have born the name Maffre, but none wore it so brilliantly as the poet, whose first hand experience of the 1914-1918 conflict gave him, like fellow Marseillan writer Justinien Baudassé, the perspective of a French Sassoon, Brooke or Owen, and whose life, after the Great War, was never to return to normal. One local historian, showing me the house, talked of despondency in later life that led to him to find solace in gambling. In riper years, he was a familiar fixture by the place de la République, the moustachioed old-timer, sitting on a white stone bench at the *Grille*, invariably surrounded by children, transfixed by his storytelling; master wordsmith spinning tale after tale of Marseillan past. How fitting that the village school should be named in his honour.

Throughout his life, he was a passionate champion of the old language. History categorises him as one of the masters of Occitan and he counted himself a friend and colleague of the great Provençal writer and activist Frederic Mistral. Yet, in his mother tongue, French, and as a poet himself, he had the indefinable touch of genius. His works still have the power to thrill and inspire; the simplicity, truth and honesty of the language of the balladeer found in the works of such successors as poet Jacques Prevert, and singers Brel and Brassens.

Aged 19, he moved to Paris and published his first anthology *Dièzes et Bémols*. A steady stream of books flowed until *Terre d'Oc* in 1908. His final work *Le Promontoire* was published shortly before his death in 1928. He had an easy and seductive style, whether penning homage to Lord Byron or reflecting on the seas that had shaped his village's character and history: comparing the waves to "a horse driven mad by the wind; lashing its reins on the rocks of the Cap and the dunes of the sands and rearing up a foaming mane." Anyone who has stood in the port of Marseillan at the turn of the wind as it whips a storm over the waters will recognise these images, minted 130 years earlier.

A contemporary declared that Achille Maffre de Baugé was defined by the poetry and passion of youth "It is essential that the human soul speaks poetry when it wakes and reason when it retires" As to his own writing, that tribute to Marseillan remains engraved on the façade of his house. His books are long out of print, but, as he wrote in 1880, "My philosphy is summed up in two words - *Toujours Français* - and let the wind carry away my pen if I ever think otherwise. For me, life is too short; I do not have the time to lie."

### Château d'Eau (Water Tower)
avenue de Pomérols [3] B1

The concrete water tower that rudely upstaged the church's *clocher* as landside Lorelei on the horizon for those approaching Marseillan across the vineyards experienced a true renaissance in the 21$^{st}$ century, reborn not merely as part of the civic infrastructure, but as a work of art.

Once upon a time, a *Glacière* stood nearby, at the junction of the routes de Florensac and Pomérols, where now iconic "pencil" road crossings mark the schools district. Now that every home has a fridge, the ice house is no more. Still, its younger neighbour, the *Château d'Eau*, remains. Every town, every village, has its water tower: a vast container suspended above the fields, assuring water pressure for farmers and village houses alike. The makeover of this particular tower was one of the popular *grands projets* of Mayor Williams Merric's regime: a grand mosaic on the skyline, celebrating the bounty of the *étang* amid the treasures of the soil.

Architect and designer Marnix Verstraeten was invited to transform the edifice. Verstraeten proposed cladding the tower with a great collage of oyster shells. Representing the maritime history of the port and village, this beacon of mother of pearl *caché* shimmers in the ever changing light, reflecting sunrise and sunset, skimming clouds and watery sunshine in a glistening wave that seems to flicker and glisten from dawn to moonrise.

Under the supervision of another architect, Luc de Kerpel, and ten experienced shell artists, a team of 30 toiled for six weeks between March and May 2007 until they had covered all 2000 square metres of the tower with the designer's patterns in the form of a seascape of waves. High winds and spring *mistrals* made the task of completing around 30 square metres each day a noble challenge for the team, who worked on 24 separate sections to create an *oeuvre* that would stand the tests of climate and time.

Each of 200,000 shells, harvested from restaurants around the Basin de Thau had been prepared for the worst: Every shell was rinsed and soaked in special baths to avoid damaging the finish, finally lain out in the sun to dry naturally over several days. Once all had been placed around the tower and the mosaic complete, two coats of varnish were applied, ready for the official unveiling by the mayor on 9 May. Twenty-three metres high, and over 18 metres in diameter, the ultimate in designer shell-ware perches high above the village on bright blue pylons: bringing horizon and waters ever closer to the *terre* of Marseillan

## Château Ermengaud
rue Achille Baille [1] B2
First thing's first: If you are expecting a mini Carcassonne or visual echo of the Loire, prepare to be disappointed. No ramparts, drawbridges nor moats to be found in the back streets, mere yards from the market place. Even the motte and bailey *castrum* of earliest times is subdued by centuries of town planning, cobbles and modesty. In other words, as the police *cliché* whenever they roll out the yellow tape at any crime scene "nothing to see here, mate".

Many visitors peer hopefully at the walls of the house at the corner with its promising turret and grand mural of the Etang de Thau at the time of the ancient Greeks, but they are looking in the wrong direction. What seems to be the façade of a row of terraced houses on the other side of the road is Château Ermengaud, official residence of the *Seigneurs de Marseillan.*

Originally built as a fortified stronghold, the cellars go back to the 11th century and an underground passage to the church was in good order until flooding only a few years ago. The place, now private homes, is occasionally opened to the public on September's Heritage Weekend. Aerial photos reveal the scale and scope of the closest thing Marseillan has to a palace – a courtyard garden presenting a green secret oasis in the intensely built historic centre.

Most famously, King Louis XIII stayed here in 1642, returning from war with his Spanish in-laws, and commissioned a staircase for the house, embossed with royal *fleur de lys*. It is claimed that Molière too passed through the doors to give a command performance.


## Château du Port
quai de la Résistance  **[2] B2**
If you talk of the *Château* in Marseillan, most people will not think of the feudal residence of the old town, but of a little slice of Paris served at the end of the quai de la Résistance . One of the quartet of iconic buildings that announce Marseillan to visitors (the others are the church belfry, the water tower and the lighthouse at Les Onglous), the architecture is pure *Grands Boulevards*, a chunk of metropolitan sophistication on the Mediterranean.

Built around 1880 for Marseillan's leading wine merchant Jean Voisin, in deliberate echo of the imposing residences on Baron Haussmann's new Parisian boulevards, it proved a powerful symbol of the village's 19th century role as global player on the international wine and spirit circuit. Voisin not only sold drinks, he imported raisins from Greece to make *Passarilhas*, a speciality wine for export, Passarilhas. In honour of this two-way traffic, the street next to the *Château* was named rue de Corinthe.

For many years, it served as an hotel, with a sweeping staircase and ornate fireplaces to belie its low price and 2-star rating. The hotel offered unmatchable views across port and village from balconies of the lofty bedrooms and suites on first and second floors, and an even better vista from smaller mansarded windows of *chambres des bonnes* in the attics. The ground floor was independent home to one of the first bars and restaurants on the port, initially a family affair and latterly part of the stable of Languedoc eateries by local-twins made Michelin-starred good, Jacques and Laurent Pourcel (*see page 255*). Most recently, the dining room was taken over by an up and coming restaurateur from Beziers.. The *Château* was fully renovated and returned to its original identity as a private home in recent years, although the restaurant remained a self contained entity at street level, made over after the building was damaged by fire in November 2003.

**Le Christ de la Croix de Mission**
place Général Guillaut  [1] B3
This spot, by the bell tower is the third official location for the town's statue of Christ. Originally a huge cross stood on what is now place de la Republique on the spot now occupied by the **Marianne**. It spent many years of its post-revolutary era on a stone pedestal in the less controversial location of the **Cimetière Vieux** on boulevard Roqueblave, the first cemetery to be built away from the church itself. In the late 19th century, it was decided to move the Christ and its cross to a new site in the centre of Marseillan and the fittest men in the village were recruited to carry the 8-

metre long monument. However, less than 300 metres of the journey, the heavens opened and a spectacular storm saw the mission cut short and the convoy rushed for shelter at number 41 boulevard Pasteur, by the impasse de la Belle Scribotte. As rain poured down and lightening flashed, the project was abandoned and the cross left to rust where it fell and many years later the remains of the statue, by now missing an arm, were rescued from the cross and stored in the church crypt. A century after the storm, it was decided to restore the Christ to a new cross on the place Général Guillaut.

The sculptor Christian Vidalier (*see* **Place Pradet** *page 41*) was commissioned to restore the statue, and he used his own arm as a model for the replacement. The renovated Christ de la Croix de Mission was formally unveiled on 26 June 1994.

26

**Church** (*see* **Eglise Saint Jean-Baptiste**)

**Cimetière Vieux (Old Cemetery)**
boulevard Marcus Roqueblave [1] B1
Just a few yards from the first roundabout into town and next door to the youth centre a double flight of steps leads to the old cemetery gates. When Marseillan got rid of its original churchyard on place de l'Eglise, graves were disinterred and replaced by these family tombs and ossuaries beyond the then town walls. The cemetery opened in 1781 but soon proved too small and was extended before the end of the century. By 1856, the town built its second cemetery (see below) around the corner on the main road to Montpellier. Inevitably, as no new funerals were held here, the older graveyard soon fell into disrepair and today it remains overgrown and mostly forgotten, amid 21$^{st}$ century rumours of redevelopment. The **Christ de la Croix de Mission** stood here until its ill-fated journey back to the village in the 19$^{th}$ century.

**Cimetière Neuf (New Cemetery)**
avenue Gabriel Peri [1] C1
One of the prettiest and most poignant walks in Marseillan is behind the high walls of the "New Cemetery", especially towards the end of the year when the allées and pathways of this lovingly tended and uplifting necropolis are a vibrant carpet of colour. November 1 is the day French families remember their dearest departed with pots of chrysanthemum, and for weeks these blooms add brightness to the dappled shade.

This is not a gloomy graveyard, but a celebration of *Marseillanais* past and present. The names on the often ornate tombs are recognisable from shop-fronts and letterheads of today's villagers. Branches of the Maffre and Baudassé clans, Vidals, Negrous and Banqs, a real sense of community, as you pass tributes and reflections on the uncles and aunts, parents, grandparents and cousins of those people who sell you your bottle of wine or basket of oysters.

The French custom of personalising marble, granite and basalt memorials means that many graves are illustrated with enamelled photographs of those who have passed on. Never more poignant than on the huge memorial to sons of the village lost to World Wars and later conflicts. More than the painful roll of names, the same family frequently cited line after line after line, an entire generation slaughtered on the fields of France, from Verdun in the East to Flanders in the North; studio photographs of teenagers posing proud in their uniforms make them ever more real to the casual visitor who recognises in the glint of an eye, the wry wit of a mischievous smile, or the defiant jut of a chin the lads playing in the park this morning, the *jouteur* or *capaleteur* taking a tumble in the port in July, or the salutation of a fellow *Ricardier* at the counter of the Marine Bar last night. These are the faces of Marseillan.

Sometimes personal effects may be placed alongside the flowers. A pair of jugglers' clubs or a photo of a motorbike remind us that peacetime too has its youthful casualties. This cemetery is well tended. A rack of watering cans poised for the approach of visiting relatives. As you walk along the lanes of the lost, but never forgotten, bright slices of living sunlight dazzle glimpses of hazy sails on the étang. A pause between remembrances and a glance over the vineyards and the oyster park, across the water to Bouzigues, Balaruc and the Mont Saint Clair; reminder of the respect Marseillan has for its past, reserving for the departed the finest view in town.

**Clocher (*see* Eglise Saint Jean Baptiste)**

**Eglise Saint Jean-Baptiste (Parish Church of St John the Baptist)**
place Général Guillaut [1] B3
(parish information 04 67 77 21 87)
A commanding neoclassical façade may dominate the square, but walk around the building to touch centuries of gothic and Romanesque incarnations then step inside the church for a treasury of Marseillan's heritage: Architectural reminders of devotion and authority; gilding and artworks from periods of prosperity; simpler reminders of harsher times.

Marseillan managed to avoid the vandalism that Revolution inspired elsewhere. Christianity remained part of daily life, there was no rush to the tumbrills, and whilst many towns demolished their eclesiastical *patrimoine*, Marseillan actually added to its sacred heritage, with a daring raid on the nearby Cistercian Abbey of **Valmagne** (*see page 194*) to capture and save its stunning multicoloured 18th century altar. The state was selling off its newly acquired religious buildings and contents to the highest bidders, but locals were determined to keep their religious birthright. Marseillan had been associated with the 12th century abbey since its founding and the unorthodox "liberation" of the altar at a time when there was a very blurred line between deconsecration and desecration is still a matter of pride amongst some older village families. This green marble altar now has pride of place in the parish church and was listed as a national monument in 1951, alongside the organ and bell tower.

Alas, the 163 steps to the top of the belfry are rarely opened to visitors (September's Heritage Days being the exception, when the stunning views across the region may be admired, and you understand the importance of the tower as a wartime lookout point).

The 19th century organ is a beauty and there for the dropping of jaws, whether it is being played in concerts or services or merely admired for its decorations – three statues of Notre Dame de La Tribune, Saint Barthelemy and Saint Roch, all predate the pipes and whistles of the instrument.

Music, both sacred and quotidian, is at the heart of church life. Sunday Mass still attracts a respectable congregation and Christmas can be standing room only. In fishing and farming villages, benediction and hymns still thread the calendar. When flowers are strewn on the étang in memory of lost sailors, the day begins with a packed church service and the statue of Saint Peter hoist high on shoulders of fishermen as Mayor, civic dignitaries, parish priest (perhaps even the Bishop) parade from prayer to port (*see page 86*). Sometimes concerts, classical, jazz, gospel or even rock bring a wider audience to the church. Check the notice boards outside the church and Mairie for forthcoming attractions. The beauty of the building and its treasures are never more vivid than with a soundtrack of an organ recital or the soaring voice of a Russian baritone.

Much to appreciate and savour as you explore: Smaller chapels each have their own treasures and symbols votive and varied. Most stunning is the Chapel of the Virgin to the right of the choir. Best seen when morning daylight from the east floods the niche with a burst of brilliant iconic colour. The 2-metre high marble Madonna and Child dates from 1610. It is said that soldiers in the wake of the Revolution used the statue for target practice and shot away her arm and Christ-child. The Bishop of Béziers commissioned its restoration and the new model for the infant Jesus is said to be the son of a local aristocrat and benefactor, which is why, rather than the conventional babe in arms, Marseillan's Virgin cradles a toddler. A decade after the guillotine, *noblesse* still obliged.

The Chapel of the Sacred Heart has artwork featuring the four apostles. The choir's five stained glass windows depict life of St John the Baptist.

You might take a crash course in French church architecture just walking around the building, although little remains for the untrained eye to notice of the original Romanesque church, but for a few stones at the base of the tower and choir.

The omnipresent church tower actually dates from 1839 and was inspired by that of the Collegiale St Jean in Pézenas. From behind the original 13th century hexagonal base, a 36-metre tall square bell tower, with its clock facing the village centre, is crowned by the traditional iron cage of the *Midi* allowing the strong wind to blow through without causing damage. The bell famously tolls the "ish" from here, and locals have many theories as to why it firsts sounds the hour a couple of minutes before a second rendition. Some say that it rings twice because capriciousness of the breeze might carry the sound away from waiting ears; one parishioner was assured by her priest that the first chimes were for the Virgin Mary and the second for mere mortals; another told me that he thought the second toll was a reminder to fishermen. A respected historian and chronicler of Languedoc lore, declared the first bell was a warning to those who might be busy chatting when the chimes begin to then listen more carefully the second time and count the hour. I prefer the theory that with a population well into the *3eme age*, the bell reflects short term memory issues by pealing the senior moments.

Whatever the motive, the bell tolls just once on the half-hour, causing gentle confusion to light sleepers who might hear a single chime three times between midnight and 2 am and still be none the wiser as to the time!

The first bell, launching this tradition of chiming the approximate hour and the precise half hour, weighed a ton and was so heavy that it threatened to bring down the tower itself. A smaller bell was commissioned and rang from 1851 until the Franco-Prussian War of 1870 when it was removed to be melted down for cannons. The third bell, paid for by public subscription and created in Villedieu–Les-Poelles in Normandy, has tolled above the village ever since 1877.

That first stone church, built in the last decade of the 11th century, replaced a simple wooden chapel that survived the predicted Armageddon of the year 1000, but not the ravages of wind and weather of the century that followed. Less than 200 years later, constant political and religious wars of these uncertain times brought fresh destruction. So, in the second half of the 13th century, work began anew on the seven walled gothic choir that still forms the core of today's *église*. Foundations for an hexagonal bell-tower was erected soon afterwards, even if the full project would not be realised for another 600 years (*see panel above*). By the early 17th century, a fresh remodelling resulted in the present nave and a staccato programme of works saw improvements initiated and halted according to political will, with a rush of improvements scheduled in the 20 years before the revolution – when, unsurprisingly, the project was abandoned once again. Fresh renovations began in the 1820s, with intermittent interruptions as funding and materials were diverted to secular projects. However, the neoclassical façade and freshly restored nave were eventually unveiled a few years before the tower. During various periods of closure, Marseillan's second church, **Eglise St Roch**, in the hospice hosted parish duties. Some artworks and statuary (notably the figures of St Roch and Saint Philomena), a marble stoup and reliquary were moved to the main church when the St Roch was deconsecrated in the 1950s.

Of course, church building is never a finite project, and even the 21$^{st}$ century brings change. The roof was recently replaced (builders found traces of the original Romanesque masonry in the walls), restoration work continued on a 17$^{th}$ century gilded wooden statue of the Virgin Mary and, in 2005, the imposing great oaken doors, by now riddled with woodworm, were removed, replaced by a modern glass entrance behind simpler wooden doors.

Village life continues just outside. Before the inauguration of the indoor market **halles** next door, the northern wall was a fish market, with fishermen's wives selling their husbands' fresh catch from buckets, baths and baskets alongside the church. Now, in summer, restaurant's set up tables in the shade of that same wall for alfresco dining. And Tuesday morning's market fairly wraps itself around the building. Christmas week sees alpine chalets and a yuletide fair outside the main doors.

Unlike many churches, Marseillan's Eglise is open most days, offering tranquil sanctuary for reflection even in the height and heat of summer.


**Eglise Saint Roch** (*see* **Ancien Couvent des Récollets**)

**La Fabrique** (*see* **Place de l'Eglise**)

**First Mairie**
impasse Carnot [1] B2
Tucked away in the alley behind the *Pharmacie Bastide*, and all but masked by the impedimenta of a neighbour's air-conditioning, is the beginning of a tour of Marseillan's civic history. Not much remains of this very first town hall, other than some letters and numbers carved in stone above a doorway, but the *Maison Commune*, home to the council, and its municipal archive, predates even the establishment of the role of Mayor. The door originally opened into a 14$^{th}$ century building, between the **Eglise St Jean Baptiste** and the **Château du Bayle**. Already pretty run down when selected for the role, the house was rebuilt in 1587. You may still make out the town

emblem carved into the local black volcanic stone. Within a heart shape are the letters CC (standing for *Corps Consulaire*) and the date. Council chamber and offices occupied the first floor, since at street level the building housed the *boucherie close,* official civic butchers, the only place licensed to sell meat: until the Revolution, a trade governed by church and politicians. When the building again fell into disrepair, the town hall moved opposite the covered market, complete with its *boucherie* and three gaols (one for criminals, another for political prisoners and the third for people held on civil charges). Nothing remains of that second Marie, which served from the late 17th century until after the Revolution.

**La Grille** (*see* **Hotel de Ville**)

**Halle Aux Oiseaux (bird collection)**
Office du Tourisme
avenue de la Méditerranée, Marseillan Plage [4] A2
Many guidebooks to Languedoc and countless websites still recommend this museum as one of three attractions (with **Noilly Prat** and the **Marianne**) of Marseillan, despite the fact that it closed down years ago.

The original **Halle aux Oiseaux** occupied the first floor of the market hall in the village (*see below*) from 1994 until it had to make way for the new library in 2006. Several hundred stuffed birds from around the world had been donated to the town by Monsieur Alain Bort. Three generations had amassed the collection and many rare exhibits, complete with meticulous hand-painted backdrops, dated from the 19th century. A small part of the collection, featuring species of birds to be seen around the Etang de Thau, has been re-housed at the tourist office in Marseillan Plage and forms part of a permanent exhibition of lagoon life, including displays of oyster farming and winegrowing. An eclectic programme of shows by local artists complements the main gallery. Admission is free.

**Les Halles (Indoor Market)**
place 14 juillet [1] B3
When the walls of the church garden **La Fabrique** were demolished in 1910 (*see* **Place de l'Eglise**) a grand new public square was formed between place de l'Eglise and boulevard Lamartine. This became the favoured location for strolling circuses and fairs who would pitch tents here much in the way they still occasionally favour place Pradet and the allées Rocques. The square even became Marseillan's original cinema, as itinerant cinematographers would screen their projections here. A tradition continued locally by the

Estirac-Constant family who set up the village's first cinema in a tent before opening a purpose-built cinema. Nowadays, "uplifting" film shows are held in the theatre.

However it was the coming of a modern indoor market in the 1930s that gave the new space its proper identity. The original market place of Marseillan was around the corner on the **place Carnot** where the covered market stood since 1310. The fish market was moved from the main market over the years, as customers and fellow traders complained of the smell, and so fishwives would sit outside the church hawking bream, eels and mussels.

In 1937, this purpose built closed market building was erected, with counters for fresh fish, market garden fruit and veg, meat and dairy produce. Renovated in 1994, the official covered market opens during the week, but is busiest on Saturday morning and Tuesday, where it acts as a hub for satellite food stalls and vans. Upstairs, the municipal *médiathèque* is a modern library, with internet access available for card-carrying residents. The library took the name of the long demolished **Fabrique** and replaced the **Halle Aux Oiseaux** bird museum, which has since moved part of the collection of stuffed birds to a gallery at the tourist office (*see page 32*). *For more on local markets, see page 244*

### Hospitals (*see* **Ancien Couvent des Récollets**)

### Hotel de Ville (Town Hall)
rue Général de Gaulle [1] B2/3
Publicly given the grand urban title of **Hotel de Ville**, but universally known as the *Mairie,* this is the fourth official home to the town council and stands at the centre of the village, poised between the original crossroads of the mediaeval town and the boulevards that redefined Marseillan in the 19th century. The location has a powerful resonance for the *Marseillanais*, since on one side it looks towards the **place Carnot**, hub of village life and marketplace for 700 years, and on the other to the place de la République, the original *Grille* public meeting place and, in pre-war years, the avenue de la Gare.

Marseillan had enjoyed a pretty good 19th century - apart from the wine blight, of course - with its new middle class finding unimagined prosperity. Business was good, the canal and railways a boon to trade, and new boulevards around the historic centre offered spacious light and open living accommodation in *maisons vigneronnes*, with working garages on the

33

ground floor, but boasting living accommodation upstairs akin to the *maisons parliamentaires* of great cities. Little wonder Marseillan felt its municipal home should be the finest house in the town. A grand 18$^{th}$ century *maison de maitre* of a distinguished family was the ideal choice. Charles Rey was also *châtelain* of the **Château de Richemont** (*see page 72*) and had agreed the sale back in 1899. With the traditional dragging of heels that had marked the changeover to the **Third Mairie**, the paperwork was finally completed in 1919, at the price quoted in the previous century.

Of course, in true French style, the name of the main road (from boulevard to market place) would be changed from the original *Grande Rue* to *rue de la Mairie*. A short lived appellation, but not the briefest: In 1941, the street became known as *rue du Marchecal Pétain*, but political wind of change followed the *tramontane* and by 1944, signs for *rue de la Marie* were taken out of mothballs once again; allegiances finally swivelled with the *Vichysoise* title duly eclipsed by the eventual redesignation as *rue du Général de Gaulle* at the end of the year.

The grand old house has kept up with demands of a growing and thriving municipality: flags fly from balconies, notices of births, deaths and marriages posted on boards (where people tut and shake their heads and mutter "That's no age" should anyone pass away before the age of 90) and news of the state of the water in the lagoon, programmes of events in the theatre and election results might be consulted and digested before being ruminated upon with like-minded neighbours by the ironwork on the corner.

This *Grille* is the forum of Marseillan. Old timers sit on benches in the morning; youngsters in the evening lean against the ironwork, skateboards upended, bikes akimbo; and dogs lay patiently at their masters' feet in the afternoon, summer-hot heavy tongues on ever-cool paving stones, resigned to the fact that it will be a long conversation before the constitutional *promenade* might be resumed. In election years, parties paste their posters onto metal screens in front of the railings.

The site had long been the core of life. The area to the side, bounded by the famous *Grille* was for many years the smart *Café de la Grille*, where prosperous and well-dressed families would pass the afternoon, taking a turn about the terrasse in their Sunday best, as working classes clustered around tables of smaller establishments across the square beyond the railings (*see page 137*). In the *Mairie* itself, regularly refitted and refurbished since the 1970s, a grand staircase lends an air of occasion to any visit to the planning office or mayoral parlour. By the stairs, a display of antique relics

34

*Gathering at the Grille*

rescued from mud, marshes and waters of Marseillan's past, cannon and terracotta and even a remnant of the second *Arbre de la Liberte*, planted on Place Carnot in 1848, give a tantalising hint of history.

*See also* **First Mairie** *and* **Third Mairie**

## Jeu de Ballon

rue du Perron, bd Pauline Bouisson [1] C2

Today this is a landscaped slip-road car park, first impression of Marseillan as you turn left into town from the vine-lined road from Mèze and Montpellier. But, for 250 years until 1950, it was the sporting centre of town. Now named for philanthropist Pauline Bouisson who bequeathed her fortune to the town when tempers were still frayed after 1907's winegrowers revolt, it was for years *place du Jeu de Ballon*.

Why such sparse windows on the façades of the houses? Until recent years, the wall was originally fenestration-free, as its role evolved from rampart to something akin to a squash court. *Jeu de ballon* is the generic term for the sports that elsewhere evolved into tennis: *pelota* (usually associated with the Basque country) *jeu de paume*, a version of real tennis played with hands rather than rackets, and the traditional Languedoc passion of *tambourin*, when the ball is struck with small drums, all on the fixture list. Modern day ball games continue a couple of hundred yards away at the tennis courts (*chemin de l'Abattoir* and *chemin des Parcs*). The site previously home to Marseillan's main abattoir, where private butchers (once the state monopoly was lifted) took animals for slaughter).

## Lighthouse (*see* **Pointe des Onglous**)

35

## La Marianne
place de la République [1] B3

This is where church finally ceded authority to state, when place de la Croix de la Mission was officially renamed place de la République in 1878, as mayor Henri Maffre announced that a new statue celebrating the Third Republic would be financed by public subscription and built on the spot where once had stood the imposing village cross.

In the aftermath of the Revolution, France had determined that its seal of state should bear the features of a woman representing the liberty of the people. Marianne is that symbol of France, her image defined anew by each generation and minted on coins and stamps. In the age of glamour, her face has been modelled on actresses Brigitte Bardot, Catherine Deneuve and singer Mireille Matthieu.

However, Marianne has never been a slave to convention and political correctness: When Laetitia Casta, the fashion model was anointed face of France, she promptly upped sticks and moved to live in London, tax breaks and Eurostar links proving irresistible. And earlier, when artist and film maker Jean Cocteau was commissioned to create a bust of Marianne for the Mairie at the seaside town of Menton, people remarked on her uncanny resemblance to the male movie star Jean Marais, his one-time lover. Most recently, a 2009 poll to choose the next Marianne saw First Lady Carla Bruni-Sarkozi narrowly pipped at the post by comedienne Florence Foresti. Italian rock-chick First Ladies not yet recognised as natural heirs to Joan of Arc and her ilk.

Celebrity culture had not yet come to the fore when, with habitual shrewd foresight, Marseillan decided that unlike most effigies of the period, its statue would be carved in stone. Too many bronze and cast iron monuments had been sacrificed to the war efforts over the years, dismantled, melted and reborn as armaments; therefore a stone figure stood a better chance of surviving into the next century.

Fittingly, when sculptor Taillefer unveiled his imposing Marianne on 1 November 1878, she was no warrior maiden of tradition, as found elsewhere in France, no bare breasted revolutionary of Delacroix's tableaux, but a sober and modestly-garbed intellectual, a free thinking libertarian in the ubiquitous Phrygian bonnet of freed roman slaves, armed not with weaponry, but scales of justice and the declaration of human rights. A feminist of her time for a 19th century Marseillan, which had pioneered education for girls and allowed women to drink in bars.

In 1990 the state confirmed Marseillan's stone Marianne as the oldest in any public square in France. Today, after a gentle wash and brush up in 1989 and again in 2005, the thinking woman's face of a nation stands head and shoulders above her younger celebrity rivals as role model, and national treasure.

Today the square itself is a comparatively quiet spot (apart from the traffic), but once was the bustling heart of café culture, lined with bars and dotted with tables (*see page 137*). The town hall railings remain a hub for gossip and political activism (*see page 34*)

**Mairie** (*see* **Hotel de Ville** *and also* **First Mairie** *and* **Third Mairie**)

**Maffre de Baugé** family house (*see* **Château du Bayle**)

**Maison du Bayle** (*see* **Château du Bayle**)

**Noilly Prat**
place Noilly **[2] A2** (*see page 49*)

**Place Carnot**
**[1] B2**
This square was not always the global capital of retail pharmaceuticals it may appear today. Where now flashes the ubiquitous green cross at the corner of the rue Emile Zola, once stood an old-fashioned general store, magical emporium of infinite variety. Until 2002, Monsieur Bardou's *Aux Deux Passages* could equip a modern kitchen with the latest white goods or furnish a player of pétanque with a magnet on a string to pick up his boules without the effort of bending over. Still, even now, the little *Spar* grocery, a brace of bakeries, the *maison de la presse* and a handful of small independent shops, selling flowers, knitting wool, watches and jewellery

augment the two grand *pharmacies*, around the square. And the tributaries of the main drag remain the key shopping streets of the centre, serving the community from fish and fruit shops, butchers and *patisseries* to modern high-tech businesses. Before the relatively recent development of boulevards around the village centre, this crossroads of the rue Général de Gaulle with the rue Emile Zola was the principal *axe* of Marseillan.

At the heart of this hub of free enterprise stands the covered market, the **Place Couverte**, within the Place Carnot. This covered market built of black volcanic stone from Agde has been the secular meeting place of Marseillan since 1310. Whilst the church, its gardens and outbuildings dominated the next square, here ordinary citizens might meet and mingle on market days and public holidays. The roof provided shade for traders and a canopy for dancing. It is even said to have served as a makeshift stage when Molière's troupe of players came to town in 1654. The simple wooden roof was replaced in 1808 with a more sophisticated affair. Look closely at the pillars on each corner and you'll see traces of low stone counters on which traders would once display their wares, tripe and meat, just like the shelves outside the oldest *echoppes* in the centre of Pézenas. These effectively closed in the hall, which had open entrances on each side. When the modern market *Halles* opened next to the church in the 20th century, fresh-food traders moved to the new building and so the market's arcades were opened up in 1984 as the cobbled square itself was re-laid.

Today's covered market hosts a summer art contest, when amateur and professional painters spend a day interpreting local scenes as gawpers lean over shoulders and squint at easels with a critical eye. Best of all, the arcades are closed in each December as the square is transformed into a living nativity crèche, with life-sized figures blending biblical and bucolic tableaux, as live donkeys, lambs and fowl wander amongst various scenes of the Holy Family in the stable and the village blacksmith at his forge.

The imposing market building rather steals the attention, but look behind the arches and tubbed olive trees to see one of the most impressive historic buildings in town. Home to the restaurant *La Table d'Emilie*, this is the **Maison du Bayle**, architectural jewel of old Marseillan.

As one of the twin centres of merrymaking, the square would share party duties with place de la République (more recently, the church square and Pradet have joined the rota). It is also a symbolic site of record. After the Revolution, successive *Arbres de la Liberté* were planted here in 1792 and 1848. The modern name is that of President Sadi Carnot, assassinated by a local baker *(see page 43).*

**Place de l'Eglise**
place Général Guillaut and place 14 Juillet [1] B3
Place de l'Eglise is not a name you'll read on a map of Marseillan, yet paradoxically it still finds itself on every programme of events and summer merry-making. The large space between the church and the boulevards is officially two squares, the new **place 14 Juillet** bounded by the Marine Bar, police station and market hall and the original **place de l'Eglise** in front of the church itself.

Officially called the **place Général Guillaut**, the former church square was renamed for a local hero of the Résistance. Born in 1895 and decorated for bravery during the First World War, Joseph Ulysse Justin Guillaut was a successful career soldier and served with distinction in the Second War until France signed its armistice with Germany. Officially demobbed, he became a Résistance leader in 1942, was arrested by the Gestapo in May 1944 and executed by the SS in the forest of Castelmaurou, outside Toulouse, on 27 June. He was just 49 years old.

There are other streets and even military buildings across France named for this hero, but this place brings the hero back to the bosom of his home town: the true heart of Tuesday morning's street market that trails hats and gloves along the boulevard, spills delicious foodie aromas from Les Halles and will sell you anything from a new shirt to an olive bush, tempting dried herbs to a well thumbed Catherine Cookson, before decanting into the original market place around the corner in place Carnot.

On what is now something of a piazza in the centre of the village, beneath new-laid cobbles, replacing a tarmac carpark, and fresh-planted saplings succeeding 60-year-old trees, was the original parish graveyard, the path to prayer lined with tombs, headstones and fenced-off family plots, with steps from the cemetery to the church itself. The 18th century saw remains from those graves removed to ossuaries and a **cemetery** constructed outside the town walls.

The church, its bell-tower the symbol and *phare* of Marseillan (*see page 30*), still stands on what was once a grand ecclesiastic complex that dominated what is now an open square from the boulevards to the centre of the Village. As well as the **Church of Saint John The Baptist**, this enclave was sealed off from the rest of Marseillan by a presbytery and the austere walls of **La Fabrique**, commissioned by the 17th century bishop of Agde, Louis Fouquet. This Fouquet may not have been an *éminence grise*, but his family were several shades closer to royalty and national power.

Brother Nicolas was Louis XIV's controversial finance minister, eventually arrested by d'Artagnan (of *Three Musketeers* fame) and imprisoned for life. Bishop Louis's contact book did not run to such thrilling names as his high spending *château*-building brother, who numbered Versailles' landscape artist Le Notre amongst his contractors, nonetheless, *La Fabrique* was host to the parish council office, and a seminary run by the Agde diocese, and had its own grand walled garden that stood alongside the even larger *Jardin du Presbytère* until 1910, when the new law separating church and state allowed the council finally to demolish the buildings and high walls to create the place du 14 juillet. The name *La Fabrique* was revived in the title of the 21$^{st}$ century *médiathèque* on the original site of the garden.

**place Général Guillaut** (see **place de l'Eglise**)

**Place du Pradet**
avenue de la Marine [1] C3
Still referred to as "*Champion* car park", not for a much-loved sporting hero, but after the forerunner to the edge-of-town *Carrefour* supermarket, this square (also called **place du Théâtre**) on avenue de la Marine is the site of the *Pradet* pasture which separated village from port and used mainly as grazing land until after World War Two, since frequent flooding made it unsuitable for vines. The area began to be developed in the 20$^{th}$ century as no-man's-land between the two settlements gradually diminished. For generations, traffic to and from the quays would make its way along the rue du Port (now **boulevard Bertouy**) but the replacement of the ramparts by wide boulevards of grand private residences in the 19$^{th}$ century led to the extension of boulevard Lamartine to the water with a line of trees: the avenue de la Marine.

The first major development was the **Theatre**, one of the last Italian style playhouses in the region. Originally conceived in 1911, the project was shelved with the coming of war and finally opened its doors in 1920 nearly a generation after the *Belle Epoque* fashion for entertainment that had inspired the project. In later years the theatre took the name of Henri Maurin, mayor from 1963-1973 and a great supporter of the arts. There is no fixed seating in the theatre, making it a versatile space for meetings and exhibitions as well as performance. The annual programme of events includes the regular *Jazzinade* jazz concerts (*see page 362*) children's shows and touring productions of plays as well as documentary film shows.

Opposite stood the public weigh station where all manner of crops, timber, even horses could be placed on the scales. In the late 1920s the station moved closer to the port itself, where the garden of the **square 8 Mai 1945** now stands. Nowadays, truckloads of grapes are weighed at the entrance to the cave co-operative, smaller quantities in the produce aisle of that new supermarket! Until the 1970s, vineyards reached the far side of the Pradet. These were replaced with the **Centre Commercial**, a strip-mall of small shops, pizza counter, café-bar and hairdressing salon and the original *Champion* supermarket. The village post office moved to its present site here, with the tax office and the main free car park.

Next to the theatre is the *boulodrome*, where all generations play *pétanque* under the shade of tall trees. The *boulodrome* also serves as an additional music venue in summer, with concerts on a temporary stage against the theatre wall and a bar counter set up to keep the party swinging.

The single storey villa and its garden next to the *boulodrome* was the family home of Louis Boudou (mayor from 1989-93; distinguished scion of a long line of *bataliers*, who had lived and worked in the port for generations). A neighbour on avenue de la Marine was celebrated 20th century sculptor and artist Christian Vidalier, whose varied public works include the restoration of the **Christ** statue next to the **Eglise** and the design of the roundabout in front of the theatre. The artist's house and garden can easily be recognised by the totem pole, exotic sculptures and Heath Robinsonian creations in the front garden. This is however a private home and not a gallery; so please do not ring the bell nor lean over the garden wall.

**Place du Theatre** (*see* **place du Pradet**)

**Pointe des Onglous Lighthouse**
chemin du Canal du Midi
This is the quiet unassuming spot that marks the end of a dream and the beginning of an assassination. Walk past the **Noilly Prat** estates and take the waterside trail alongside the promenades of Belle Scribotte and Belle Bouche until you come to a mini roundabout, where the main road turns inland. A little pathway, the hemin du Canal du Midi, continues along the shore. And there you'll find the most modest of Marseillan's icons, the little red and white lighthouse, the **Phare de la Pointe des Onglous**. Standing on the short eastern jetty projecting into the waters of the Etang, it marks the beginning, or end, of the **Canal du Midi** *(see page 343)*. The long avenues of leafy  trees all the way from the Atlantic have thinned on the final kilometre or so, as the canal juts into the Etang de Thau, but the lighthouse stands just across the water on Pointe des Onglous as warning to inexeperienced or unlicenced boatmen not to enter the lagoon.

It is strictly forbidden to travel beyond this point at night, or when the wind blows a Tramontane, Mistral or Grec above force 4. The dangers of bringing a canal boat into the Etang were realised as early as 1755, when plans for a warning lamp were first drawn up. No one could agree on a traditional lighthouse, so the project was abandoned and, to compromise, a triangular white stone column, known as a *Pyramide*, was erected at the point where the still waters of the canal met the capricious étang.

*Pointe des Onglous*

Similar stone edifices were established at the various ports between Les Onglous and Sète. However, since the *Pyramide* was of no use in fog or outside daylight hours, a traditional lighthouse was finally built on a rocky jetty at the dawn of the 20$^{th}$ century. You can get a closer look by either ringing a bell by the little basin along the canal to call the tiny ferryboat tub that leads to the port on the opposite bank, or you may walk the length of this initial stretch of the waterway, past silent fishermen and dog-walkers to the **Pont du Maire** by the *Domaine de la Baronne* and cross for the long stroll back to the **Port des Onglous.** This is Marseillan's forgotten fifth port and a plaque measures the metres along the canal to the first lock at Bagnas (4,742m), to Sète across the étang (20,000m) and to the lighthouse itself (540m). Once the terminus for canal trade, port buildings these days are home to *Les Glenans* sailing school which organises regattas and courses during the year; the distinctive red and white sails are familiar sights the length of the lagoon.

Around the tumbledown shacks on the opposite bank, legends thrive. It was here, according to local lore, passed *bouche a l'oreille* father to son, that Sante Geronimo Caserio a 20-year-old Italian baker, living in Sète, is said to have met up with fellow anarchists in the spring of 1894. His plot hatched at the mouth of the Canal, Caserio travelled to Lyon where France's President Sadi Carnot was to give a speech. Caserio described the events of 24 June: "I heard the *Marseillaise* and the cries of *Viva Carnot!* I saw the cavalry. I understood that the moment had come and I held myself ready. On seeing the President's carriage I drew my dagger and threw away the sheath. Then, when the carriage was passing close by me, I sprang forward, supported myself by resting my left hand on the carriage, and with my right hand buried the dagger in the President's breast." Defiant to the last, the young assassin was dragged to the guillotine, where his last words might have been a message to his fellow conspirators of Les Onglous *"Coraggio cugini! Evviva l'anarchia!"* ("Courage, cousins! Long live anarchy!")


## La Pompe
impasse de la Pompe [1] C2

One of the few remaining village water pumps can be seen in this alley behind the old **Jeu de Ballon**. Find another (less complete), at the end of **rue Auber** ([1] B2). Most old houses had their own wells and pumps in the ground floor garage space, with running water, like electricity, very much a post war luxury in local homes. Locals attribute the celebrated longevity of the population to the lack of mod cons and amenities. With no refrigeration (since the ice house closed in the mid 19<sup>th</sup> century – *see page 23*), and no tap water until recent years, food had to be freshly bought and prepared daily, and with so many steps to climb from pump or well to kitchen, fresh air and exercise came as standard with a healthy Mediterranean diet of red wine, fresh fish, olive oil and vegetables.


## Le Porcheron
rue du Porcheron [1] B2

This archway, on your left as you wander up the rue Emile Zola, is more than a quaint architectural feature linking two houses across the little side street. Like many more recent renovations, it owes much to Marseillan's popularity with foreign incomers.

The British officially discovered Marseillan at the end of the 20<sup>th</sup> century, but at least one of their countrymen may have had the town on his to-do list around 650 years earlier. Edward The Black Prince, having already won the Battle of Crécy and besieged Calais on his warrior *tour de France,* headed south in 1355, intent on annexing much of Aquitaine and Languedoc.

Fearful of the English giving Marseillan the same treatment as Calais (where citizens had been reduced to eating their pet dogs before the infamous surrender that later inspired Rodin's famous sculpture), the Bishop of Agde commissioned fortifications on what is now rue Vedel and a stone doorway within to shut down the city against possible attack. This archway is the last vestige of those defences.

44

**Prison** (*see* **First Mairie** *and* **Third Mairie**)


**Le Théâtre Henri Maurin**
avenue de la Marine [1] C3 (*see* **Place du Pradet**)


**The Third Mairie**
7 rue Emile Zola [1] B2
Officially designated the third Mairie, this is actually the fourth building to serve as town hall, since between the second Mairie on the square falling into disrepair and the politicians getting their act together to organise the building of the new base in rue Emile Zola, the council had had to move into a temporary home in a presbytery on place de l'Eglise, where it squatted unmarked for more than a decade.

A long time coming, the official move had been planned for the best part of half a century, but local and national political upheaval managed to keep the project on ice for longer than anyone had anticipated. The chosen site was a former hospice and hospital. Mayor Maffre had actively lobbied for the hospital to be moved from its central site, arguing that housing sick and diseased people so close to the market place could be a health risk for all concerned. Eventually, patients moved out and politicians took their place in 1816, together with archivists to keep the paperwork up to date and prisoners to fill the nice new cells in the basement. The delay meant that the stones from the original **Porte d'Agde** from the ramparts, demolished as part of the town's expansion, could be used to build a thoroughly modern Mairie, good enough to last a full century.

The final move to the present **Hotel de Ville** took place after the Great War, in 1919. Since then the building on rue Emile Zola descended into disrepair once again and now smart new public housing has been built on the site. However, the original doorway has been preserved.


**Reserve Naturel du Bagnas** (*see page 47)*

# Parks & Gardens

With the exception of Parc Gaujal, dogs are welcome in all Marseillan Parks. Owners should clean up after their pets, and a supply of bags with a dedicated bin may be found by the entrance to each park. Discover children's play areas and sports facilities at Tabarka and Boudas, and *boulodromes* on **allées du Général Roques** and **place du Pradet**. The wildlife reserve around the lagoon is an unmissable treat. Alternative bracing walks include the Promenade pathway along the Etang from the main port to the **lighthouse**, and the *allées* of the **New Cemetery**.

**Allée du Général Roques**
avenue Victor Hugo [3] **B2** (*see page 17*)

**Parc Gaujal**
boulevard Pasteur [1] **C2** ; rue du Faubourg St Pierre [2] **A1**
08.00-17.30 (Oct-Apr); 08.00-19.30 (May-Sep)
This is a traditional Victorian park, ideal for trundling a proper old-fashioned pram, in the time-honoured fashion of nannies on the place des Vosges or Kensington Gardens. Dogs and bikes are not allowed and children should be on their best behaviour in this formal walled garden with its Mary Poppins style wrought iron gates. Leaf cover is practically factor 50 so dense is the foliage that makes this the antidote to sunworshipping on the plage. A lovely shady spot for sitting down with a good book on a summer's afternoon.

**Parc de Tabarka**
rue 19 Mars 1962 [2] **B1**
On the road from the *port des Nacelles* to the oyster sheds, where for generations fishermen have strewn their nets outside makeshift shacks is now a purpose built leisure park for families. The corner between **Port Tabarka** and the **Madeline St Jean** wine warehouses remains fishermen central, with the modern container successors to the original sheds forming a new clubhouse. The main park has been reclaimed from a former municipal campsite and is a well-maintained garden and playground right on the very banks of the étang itself. A first-rate skate park is very popular especially on Wednesday afternoons, with pipes, pyramids and ramps, a magnet for all ages. Other swings and climbings and a basketball court may also be found

at the port end of the park, with equipment for younger children discretely positioned away from the teenagers' space. Of course, boys will be boys, and no amount of state of the art sports equipment will completely detract from the forbidden lure of diving off jetties and roofs in the port itself. One perennial summer crime is to make a ramp out of old crates and ride a bicycle at speed landing in the water. A plastic bottle tied to the back of the bike helps in retrieving the cycle for the next Eivel Kneivel recreation. Now organised watersports can be enjoyed with **Kithau** kitesurf and wake park with its clubhouse and jetty and teleski style winch for waterski stunts with or without a kite. Further along the park, picnic tables and benches have magnificent views over the water. The park leads to **La Plagette**, lagoon bank where locals have always tiptoed through seaweed and rocks, and risked a harmless sting or two, in order to have a dip, and where, with the up-marketing of the quarter in 2009, truckloads of sand are now tipped onto the shore at the beginning of the season to create a more visitor-friendly beach for sunbathing.

### Parcours de Santé du Boudas
Chemin de la Belle Bouche
Keep following the main road as it veers away from the promenade and the étang by the **lighthouse** and it will take you to a new exercise area on a mound overlooking the canal and wetlands favoured by egrets and wading birds. Here is an exercise circuit for power-walking, fitness and generally enjoying an open-air workout. Outdoor gym equipment, bars, rings and frames to punctuate your routine and paths for joggers and mountain bikers. There is also a basketball court.

### Place du Pradet
avenue de la Marine [1] C3 (*see page 41*)

### Réserve Naturelle Nationale du Bagnas
Domaine du Grand Clavelet, route de Sète
04 67 01 60 23
www.adena-bagnas.com
The tourist office may be home to the remaining exhibits of the defunct **Halle Aux Oiseaux** (*see page 32*), but a around 250 species of wild birds may be discovered, living, breathing and thriving just a few hundred yards away from the exhibition. Marseillan has a noted nature reserve at the far Southern end of the lagoon - close to the flock of flamingos you will pass on your way to the beach.

The flamingos are the best known of the many species that live or pass through these protected wetlands each year. Home to black storks to larks, herons to osprey, this remarkable habitat has been nurtured and guarded since 1983. More than 560 hectares of reed beds and tamaris, sand dunes and salt marshes from canal to coast. Whilst there are roadside lay-bys for the optimist observer to park up near the vines and settle down with thermos and fieldglasses, the reserve is not generally open to the public.

However, you may discover the wildlife in the company of a ranger for just €5 (accompanied children, free). Book in advance, as the escorted walks are usually only organised for a minimum of 5 people. Some midweek and Saturday morning rendezvous (details published each month at the Marseillan Plage and Agde tourist offices) and in July and August, there is a weekly magical sunset stroll through the area, from 7 or 8 pm until nightfall. Catching the dusk flight of the flamingos or a final shimmer of improbable blue light as kingfishers return to their nests is an unforgettable experience. Binoculars are provided. Wear appropriate footwear.

The rendezvous point is the *Domaine du Grand Clavelet*, on the route de Sète - follow the **Agde** sign from the Marseillan Plage roundabout, where it is always worth checking out the exhibition to remind yourself what to look out for later on. For other nature walksand excursions from here, see **Agde**.


**Square du 11 Novembre 1918**
[2] A2
Named for the Armistice Day marking the end of the Great War, this is the elder of twin parks at the top of the port. Mature palm trees provide shade for equally ripe villagers to sit on renewed benches and take the air. Mornings on market day may see widows and their dogs having five minutes respite between shopping and lunch chores; afternoons the flat cap brigade smokesand converses in silence.


**Square du 8 Mai 1945**
[2] A2
Across the road, this smaller garden, named for the ending of the second major conflict, has never quite grown into itself. Schoolchildren may occasionally plant a symbolic sapling, but essentially it remains a small open space, which in summer, festooned with strings of light bulbs, is the new venue for the Thursday evening "midnight" craft market, from 7pm until late in July and August.

# Noilly Prat

1 rue Noilly [2] A2
04 67 77 75 19   www.noillyprat.com *Escorted visits in English or French*
May-Sep 10-11, 14.30-18; Mar-Apr, Oct-Nov 10-11, 14.30-16.30 Cl: Dec-Feb, 1 May

GO STRAIGHT TO THE QUESTION no-one quite likes to ask: you don't pronounce the LL but you do pronounce the T. As unlikely a linguistic pairing as the French Monsieur Noilly with the English Mister Prat, and as happy an association as the secret blend of 20 herbs and spices, two local wines and a dose of Mediterranean sunshine that produce the world's most upmarket vermouth, *le vrai* Dry of a proper Martini and living legend of Marseillan Port.

Our first day in Marseillan: we had lunched by the water and seen sunlight catch copper cuves of *Noilly-Prat* showroom across the port. So we crossed the harbour and took the tour. Inside the lofty warehouse, the air is cool and welcome chill, a moist sweetness to catch the breath, and flavoursome tangy kiss on the lips: the taste of a tradition dating to 1813; when Joseph Noilly created the first French vermouth. And the taste of success, from 1855; when Joseph's son Louis and English son-in-law Claudius Prat set up the family firm to market the drink. Four years later, Claudius died, followed shortly by Louis, so it was left to widow Anne Rosine Prat to run the company for four decades and create a global brand leader.

Sacks of nutmeg and cloves, Tunisian orange peel, French camomile and Sri-Lankan cinnamon hint at the confection, but nowhere will you find the recipe. Shadows shade confidences inside, but as wide doors are flung open to a grand courtyard behind the *chai*, secrets turn to shock. Decades of distillery and winery tours have taught me the golden rule: barrels need shelter in cellars, in the cold and in the dark. Here in brightest, relentless summer sunshine, bask Soviet row upon endless Mayday row of barrels. A battalion of sprinklers twist turn and spray seasoned wood, as Picpoul and Clairette wines slow-cook to sherry ripeness. This is the *enclos*: where casks are exposed to four seasons of sun, wind, frost and rain, evaporating 8% *le part des anges*. An echo of past conditions when wines braved the elements on the high seas from the étang's bourne to the New World. Nurtured by veteran cellar-master Jean-Louis Mastoro, who adds *mistelle* grape juices and spices brought to Marseillan across every sea and every ocean; the wine macerates in cathedral barrels of a Chamber of Secrets for 3 week's *dodinage*. Finally, pressed to concentrate and remove sediment, convalescing in oak for 6 weeks, before decanting into 4 million bottles.

Abiding image of the tour: brilliant light and passionate heat after cool sanctuary of the shade. Lingering flavour is the tasting before visitors are let loose in the shop. The white (*Dry*), universally acknowledged the finest by chefs and barmen; compared to the human soul by Somerset Maugham; red (*Rouge*) an Italianate vermouth, for export only, but mixed in equal proportions to make local apéro *Marseillanais*; and exclusive syrupy zinger *Ambrée*, only available in the village: amazing in or with desserts, like extra-dry white, adds genius to cooking.

# Walks and Tours

## Marseillan's History

French language tours of the old centre of the village meet outside the Mairie at 10 am in June and September. In peak season the rendezvous is the Tourist Office in Marseillan Plage, and the guide begins telling the story of the village on the minibus into town. The walk concludes with a visit and tasting at the Cave Coperative in the port. Free, but reservations essential through the Tourist Office on 04 67 21 82 43. Fridays.

The English language guided tour of Marseillan is led by local resident and keen historian Mike Worsam. Meet outside 11 bd Lamartine ([1] **B3**) at 10.30. No charge, but charity donations appreciated. Wednesdays www.marseillanhistorique.info 04 67 77 38 64. Another tour in English takes in the historic port area. Same rendezvous. Selected Thursdays.

## Self-guided stroll

In 2010, Marseillan created a heritage walk highlighting the principal sites of the village. 14 illustrated panels featuring a map and information in four languages (French, English, German and Occitan) line the walk. Allow 15-30 minutes to complete the circuit. Start outside the brasserie *O'Soleil* on the quai Antonin Gros to read about **The Port**. Then walk up av de la Marine to the **Theatre Henri Maurin**, continue along bd Lamartine to the **Marianne** at place de la Republique, then turn back along along rue Général de Gaulle for the **Hotel de Ville** on your left, **place Carnot** and **Maison du Bayle** on your right. then turn right again ito the impasse Carnot for the **First Mairie**, turn around, cross the square and walk up rue Emile Zola, looking right for the **Third Marie** and **Porcheron** and continuing to rue de l'Hopital for the door of the **Couvent des Recollets** and former church of **St Roch**. Another about turn, back down rue Emile Zola to the place Miramond and **Chapelle des Penitants Bleus**, then rue Ledru Rollin, right into rue Galilee and continue to bear right into the rue Achille Baille and the former **Chateau**. Carry on to the place Carnot and walk to the church square, place Général Guillaut to view the **Christ de la Croix de la Mission** on the corner with rue Charles Reboul then return to visit the **Eglise St Jean Baptiste** and its listed altar. *(More information on these and other sites on the circuit on pages 17-45)*

# Flavours of Marseillan

### Walking with the winegrowers
Rendezvous around 9am outside the Cave Cooperative in the port ([2] B2). The 3km walk through the vines is escorted by a local winemaker. The visit finishes with winery tour and tasting. Price €5. Reservation essential on 06 71 23 16 70 or through the tourist office on 04 67 21 82 43. Weds from mid-June til September's harvest and selected Spring and Autumn dates. Some weeks, a Friday tour departs from the co-op's Agde branch on boulevard du Soleil, for a 3-5 kilometre stroll through vineyards from the banks of Hérault to the Canal du Midi. A summer walk from Cap d'Agde takes in a museum visit. You may need a car to drive to the start point and take you back to the *cave* for a tasting session, but lifts may be arranged in advance.

### Noilly Prat (*see page 49*)

**Les Saveurs de Marseillan** is a day presenting every taste of village and port. Meet in the port at 9.45 on Thursday mornings from mid June until the end of August for a day of discovery of the flavours of the village. Visit the **Noilly Prat** cellars, stop by **Annie Castaldo**'s oyster and mussel farm for a seafood lunch before meeting Marseillan's maitre chocolatier **Emmanuel Servant** in his kitchens (*see page 251*) and rounding off the afternoon with a wine tasting in the cellar of the **Madeleine Saint Jean**. Reservation essential on 06 08 06 84 43. Price €16 adults, €6 for children 5-12 years.

## Nature walks

**Réserve Naturelle Nationale du Bagnas** (*details page 47*)

**Walking in volcano country**. A guided ramble through the volcanic land around Agde, taking in the wildlife of the Mont Saint-Loup and the cliffs of Le Cap d'Agde. Bring stout and sturdy walking shoes and a stick if required. Meet up at the **Domaine du Grand Clavelet** in Agde. Free. Selected dates, year round. Information on 04 67 01 60 23.

## Exploring the back country

Coach trip from the tourist office, visiting the back country lakes and hill-top villages. Weekly in peak summer. Cost is around €8. Precise itinerary varies each season, but a perfectly gentle way to discover the country behind the popular coast. Details from the tourist office on 04 67 21 82 43.

HARD BY the blink of the harbour light, a little jetty nudges *Anjodi*, the narrow boat fêted for its role in Rick Stein's television *Odyssey*: with her cargo of fine wines and a chef's imagination and manifest of those with the time and means to cruise at an intimate pace, *Anjodi* sounds a basso profundo farewell, setting off on the week-long expedition along the Canal du Midi. Next week, her berth-right is taken by a sister, *Athos*, and on days in between other barges may squat overnight.

*Habitués* of the ports know the regular arrivals and even the most time-worn boatman scraping barnacles from his hull in the boat yard will glance up for the approach into harbour of an old friend: A houseboat dog back from the morning baguette run will bark a greeting to a familiar jib; and when *Pollux* unfurls her sails to take afternoon trippers to a mid-lagoon anchorage for their lazy picnic and swim, a wave from above a paperback at a café table will recognise each sortie or return.

Best loved of all is **Jusq'au Bout**, an old wooden sailing boat, as much a Marseillan icon as any architecture. With its flamboyant rigging, conspicuous barrel of rum and skippered by a white-bearded seadog from your favourite yarn, her homecoming from any excursion is a private occasion for the heart and soul. Moored beyond Tabarka's boatyard in summer, or occasionally on the main quay should the weather turn tempestuous, *Jusqu'au Bout* is justly named, since her every arrival, if only from Sète, across the water, feels as though she has weathered the South China Seas, rounded the Cape and routed the Barbary hordes.

Truly loved, and very much part of the community, she gets involved in local life: playing a starring role in *son et lumière* pageants; leading the flotilla from the port on the *Fête du St Pierre*; even on one memorable evening staging an unheralded opera recital against her red sail. Much photographed, she may tart herself for each passing camera looking to frame the perfect shot of the Mont Saint Clair, she nonetheless remains a lady and a siren, unleashing a secret Raleigh or Ransome within every lifelong 11 year-old boy.

# The Port of Marseillan

THE VIEW IS THE MONEY SHOT. It is the Lorelei, the roper and the clincher. It disarms the unsuspecting visitor, reels you in for lunch and wins your heart for life. Vista-hardened travel writers and journalists surrender to the charms of Marseillan the minute they hit the port. *The Sunday Times* described it as "like St Tropez before Bardot", *The Guardian* went further, enchanted by "low level houses, laced with wrought-iron balconies and splattered with flowers", and hailing the "undeniable frisson" and "early Riviera vibe".

The truth is that, after centuries in the wine trade, and having survived a post-war reality check, the principal export of the port of Marseillan is love at first sight. This perfectly proportioned slender channel is almost certainly the last unspoilt authentic port on the French Mediterranean. Despite the trending of bistros and cafes, no *CocaCola* sign dwarfs the menus and you may yet find a simple piece of fish to please Elizabeth David; Picpoul and oysters still reign supreme. Even larger cruisers, on shared mooring with simple tubs, retain a touch of wood, brass and make-do-and-mend; not the bright white brash *arriviste* glare of a millionaire's marina.

*Rive Gauche* (known to mapmakers as Quai Antonin Gros) fuels appetites along a string of tables, blackboards and potted plants. A mannered jungle of chalked-up *plats du jour* and *formules du midi,* ripe with promise and heady with intermingled scent of coffee, herbs and spices, echoes to the hum of satisfaction and tintinnabulation of ice cubes in *Ricard* and *rosé*, counterpoint to the whipped slap of halliard on mast. At the turn of our millennium, terrace tables perched on the water's edge, plates borne from kitchens across the way. Alas, a mayoral edict exiled waterside terraces back to the shop fronts. On *Rive Droit* warehouses and homes with shuttered windows and basalt-framed garage doors outnumber restaurants by the *arrière port*, and this quai de la Résistance remains home to *Noilly Prat*, the wine co-operative and the harbour's signature building, *Château du Port*: pirate flag on the roof, brasserie tables spread neatly on the quayside - perfect vantage point for enjoying summer sports *Lou Capelet* and jousting (*see page 81*).

Pleasure is served: fireworks set off from the stone-clad breakwater on Bastille Eve, mid-August and New Year; summer jazz by the winery, whilst swallows loop and swoop twilight manoeuvres from nests under the eaves; autumn's *vin primeur* is uncorked yards from the harbour master's elegant *Capitainerie* – claimed by some as the smallest in France.

The harbour light on the opposite bank, with its benches for reflection, becomes a music venue in holiday season: when Marseillan Plage comes into town to enjoy a celtic festival, a local rock band sets up stage or travelling musicians moor on the little jetty to launch an itinerant salsa concert from a barge. But along both quays, raise your eyes above the sedentary charms at street level and the silhouette of the port denies the past hundred years.

In the second half of the 19<sup>th</sup> century, the port was in its prime and was considered the second port of Hérault. Wharfs, warehouses and garages lining the quays, were the *chais* of wine merchants, distillers, and independent vignerons making sweet wine and aperitifs for export. Just as the village *maisons vigneronnes* had huge garages for family farmers to house carts and *cuves*, behind the port's big double doors, more ambitious businesses stacked stock for loading onto boats, and the ground-floors of private homes might be cooperages; demand for barrels and huge *demi-muid* vats keeping tonneliers such as the Navarres and Banqs busy for generations. Successful wine merchants would even have a couple of barrel makers permanently on the payroll; major players, such as *Noilly Prat*, dependent on casks for production; employed as many as 22 coopers simply to meet demand.

Other trades grew around the success of the wines. A merchant navy almost eclipsed the traditional fishing fleet. An administration class emerged, *fonctionaires* and tax collectors to render unto Caesar (or Napoleon III) anything between the *negociant's* cut and the *part des anges*. More visibly, once simple little *nacelles* were exiled to the Port Tabarka, broader sails of cargo ships now ined each bank of the cut. Boatmen loaded casks of wine to ship across the étang to the Mediterranean trading post at Sète or along the Canal du Midi to the Atlantic and new markets in a New World. Postcards from the 1880s show the port in its heyday: the grand new Château du Port iconic symbol of the prosperity of its *maitre* wine merchant Jean Voisin, whose name flows fluently through many tales of his century; *futs* and *tonneaux* stacked on the quays; lines of boats, sails furled, awaiting the next turn of the wind and the gusts to send them on their way.

Since Marseillan scents change in the market and fortune as cannily as the old-timer predicts a mistral on the morrow and the north-easterly of noon, and as some boatmen upgraded from fishing tub to freight ship, so in 1913 Monsieur Bardou added a 20-horsepower motor to his sailing boat *St Etienne,* to steal a march on the fickle flightiness of the winds.

Rummaging through family photos of just one house, at the corner of rue Edouard Adam and quai Antonin Gros, reveals just such a talent to adapt. The building served first as a barrel maker and store, then, when the ice-house closed down to make way for schools in the 19th century, sold ice collected from Agde's **Glacière** (*see page 148*) to fishermen and villagers, before becoming a private home. It is now host to an expanded *Taverne du Port* and weather vane, reflecting the harbour's new role in the leisure industry of waterfront dining and pleasure trips.

Wise men concur that Marseillan's story begins with the port, even if they may not always agree the original settlers' route (some reckon they sailed up the estuary of the Hérault, crossed Bagnas marsh to reach the étang; others have Massaliots arriving via the Grau de Pisse Saumes). The *Cadarache* hillock, on the western shore, caught the eye, and so the earliest boats berthed in what was to become the port of Marseillan. This confluence of *grau* and tributary was more fishing harbour than trading port for its first millennium. Originally developed around Tabarka, behind the main modern port, it occasionally proved strategic naval haven during the Roman era, finally meeting the outside world in the 13th century, when Marseillan's rulers, keen to develop trade links, struck a deal with Lunel's Jewish merchants to transport wine and olive oil from the port. Despite inevitable taxes on cargo, Marseillan became port of choice for other towns and villages in the area, Florensac and Bessan choosing to trade cereal here rather than the bigger Mediterranean docks at Agde.

By the commercially focused 17th century, the main port took over from Tabarka's muddy shores In 1680 Riquet's Canal Royal opened infinite new mercantile possibilities and the *arrière port*, the distinctive slim harbour by today's brasserie *O'Soleil*, developed specifically to accommodate long narrow boats that would travel on the new waterway between two seas.

Marseillan's position at the end of what was later to become known as the Canal du Midi was recognised with funding from the King's financier Colbert. Not necessarily an altruistic act of *noblesse oblige*, since there was something fishy about the deal. Centuries before oyster farming, the *étang* was known for sardines and mackerel. Pickled in brine and crammed in barrels, these prized exports were subject to duty and Royal Excise men were stationed in ports around the Thau. Years of wrangling over double taxation followed, since all cargo from Marseillan to Sète was obliged to be held over in a bonded warehouse before leaving for the Med.

100 years on, formalised quays usurped crude banks and landing stages. These were then known as the *quais nord-est* and *sud-oeust*. Grand plans for developing the commercial port took a knock when the phylloxera blight all but destroyed France's wine trade in 1876 *(see page 96),* and public funding marked for the project diverted to deal with the agricultural crisis.

The north-easterly *rive gauche* had already been properly paved in the 1860s. Once the post-blight wine trade had been revived, the council put pressure on the other bank's two major employers, Noilly and Voisin to smarten up their side of the port. Businessmen converted marshland, built 1000 square metre warehouses, and constructed proper roads. Jean Voisin's revamp included his landmark *Château*, his finances during the recession boosted by a sideline importing Greek dried raisins to make fortified wines; a process eventually banned in 1900.

*Belle Epoque* expansion of the working port saw the breakwater, 50 metres off shore, extended to protect a growing harbour, *musoir* jetties on each quay jutted proudly into the étang, until the docks boasted 600 metres of moorings. Beyond the ports, a new *pyramide* marker buoy beacon warned of treacherous rocks just below the water line, and business managed to survive the first half of the 20th century, although the eventual arrival of the railway took a lot of business away from the waterfront.

Distinctive and stylish green and red harbour lights, planned before the German occupation of the region, were unveiled and switched on in 1951. They are painted with the town's name in French and Occitan.

Yet, even as the new beacons flashed their welcome, warning signs could be read for the future of the port. In their first year, lights regularly guided 12 familiar boats plying the route between Marseillan and Sète. Year by year the numbers declined until the very last craft on the run was finally retired in the 1960s, as freight took to the roads.

Rather than vegetate, local authorities actively courted pleasure port rank. Marseillan became an early haven for self-catering holiday boats emerging from the Canal du Midi. There were no restaurants to begin with until the ground floor of the *Château* shared its kitchen and bar, and the *Taverne* wine shop across the water offered traditional meals to showcase a *Corbières* or *Faugères*. A bar, *La Belle Scribote*, opened in the *arrière port* and, from late 1990s more restaurants and cafes gradually appeared in place of the shuttered garage doors of the old buildings on the quays.

**Capitainerie**
quai de la Résistance  [2] B2
04 67 77 34 93; 06 12 20 35 35
Sep-Jun Mon – Fri: 08.30-12.00, 13.45-17.30; Sat: 08.30-12.00
Jul-Aug every day 08.30-12.00, 15.00-19.00
Contact the harbour master for information, advice and mooring reservations for all three ports of Marseillan Ville

**Cave Cooperative** quai de la Résistance  [2] B2 (*see page 98*)
**Château du Port** quai de la Résistance  [2] B2 (*see page 25*)
**Noilly Prat** place Noilly [2] A2 (*see page 49*)

**Port de Plaisance**
quai du Toulon [2] B2
In 1975, Marseillan officially adopted *Port de Plaisance* status and soon welcomed more than the original blue and white Canal du Midi "bumper boats" as committed yachtsmen disparagingly call them. Self-catering motorboats still pass through and overnight if lucky enough to get a mooring. It soon became clear that the harbour would need to attract long term residents. Now the largest port on the étang, the new marina on quai du Toulon, beyond the *rive droit* has piers serving 230 vessels up to 15m, from sea-going yachts to a genuine wooden Chinese junk. Managed by the Capitainerie (*see above*), it provides mains water, electricity and wifi, and can also offer short-term berth to 30-metre canal boats in the main port. A nautical centre hosts watersports clubs and sailing associations, all conveniently located between a winery and a brewery!

**Sailing Clubs:**
**Aviron Marseillanais** 04 67 77 23 69
**Cercle de voile de Marseillan** 04 67 77 65 22 www.cvmarseillan.com
**Les Voiles Marseillanaises** 06 20 08 43 24 voilesmarseillan.free.fr
**Atouvents** Sail with a skipper (*see page 66)* 06 20 08 43 24

**Watersports**:
**Ski Nautique Club** (*waterskiing*) 04 67 77 60 55; 06 11 62 83 48

## Port Tabarka
rue des Pecheurs [2] B2

The quaint Port Tabarka, is where traditional *chalut* fishing boats berth overnight before heading out to the oyster tables in the lagoon. They lie alongside 120 dayboats and basic dinghies whose masts pierce the skyline against the stunning backdrop of the Mont Saint Clair for each gilded dawn and silvery sunrise.

A tranquil'scene, and the prettiest view in town; the timelessness of Tabarka where sounds of a summer evening come from the dusk cries of crickets and swallows, calls of optimistic seabirds following a late returning fishing boat and the gentle tinkle of the breeze teasing the rigging of vessels safely moored for the night. Nightfall heralded in more stentorian timbre as the harbour's colony of *canards en liberté* mallards quack each family in to the safety of the pier, until silent darkness finally filters through the flitter of wings of pipistrelle bats circling the port lights.

Daybreak brings dog walkers heading to the new park by the harbour wall and gentle awakening of a residential neighbourhood of fishermen, winegrowers and retirees. The occasional hardy swimmer will haul himself from the waters to the breakwater and an amateur angler primed with rod and hope seek purchase and vantage on a rock by the harbour mouth. On rues des Pecheurs, Chantiers and Suffren, traditional warehouse conversions stand cheek by joist alongside new-build homes with unmatchable views. Yet this recently colonised quarter is arguably the oldest part of Marseillan. Here the ancients founded a colony that became a village that became a trading empire. Only when the union of money, engineering and political influence in the 17th century determined more formal delineation of the ports, did the town decide fishing boats belonged here and merchant ships required the main basin as their own. This harbour was known for many years simply as the *Refuge des Nacelles*, after the distinctive little boats, masts and sails akimbo, that landed mackerel and mussels, eels and clams on the marshy shore to be carted up to the village for fishermen's wives to sell against the north wall of the church.

Unlike its wharf-lined sister, this port was defined by the elements and the caprice of the waters. Maps from each generation show differing outlines and banks blurred by silting, a squelch from shore. Even in the 20th century, boats moored as far back as the line of warehouses that currently house the barrels of Madeleine St Jean's winery on rue 19 Mars, and old photographs on the wall of the *Glacier* restaurant in the village show the port a hundred yards or so behind the current boardwalk. That basin is now a field where fishermen spread nets in the sunshine and light fires for barbecues; muse

*Quality time at Tabarka*

and mooch and share tall stories around their huts (in reality a hamlet of containers). These cabins are HQ to *Le Loup Marseillanais* fishing and social club that plans occasional public boat trips and barbecues. Tabarka has a long tradition of *cabanons*. Just as fishing families settled the beaches before Marseillan Plage became a resort, so the lane from the main port to the oyster parks was ever lined with sheds and shanties from old planks and metal sheets. In 1891, the strip of land beyond Tabarka was officially licensed to the fishing community for their *cabanons*, and garage doors in nearby streets even now may be retreats where men chew the fat, sip and smoke in bonding communion, whilst patient mongrels at their feet take sabbatical from *la chasse*.

The field replaces twin rows of purpose-built concrete garages on the waterfront with proper terracotta roofs, demolished to make way for an *aire de carénage* where the crane hauls boats from the water for a good scraping of barnacles or paint job, and waste products are treated. Plans for the boatyard date back to the 19th century when a long-lobbied-for *radoub* opened to ensure craft were fit for purpose. That first yard soon proved too small for demand, and by 1935, the port itself fell into disuse. Not until the Hérault *département* commissioned new boardwalks and refurbished the stone walls was the dedicated yard finally opened. At the same time, conversion of an abandoned campsite into a family friendly park *(see page 46)*, development of a new type of tourism (initially self-catering in smart private port houses, then the conversion of an empty warehouse into a chic *résidence-hotel* on the waterfront) led to the area's makeover. Now the *Kithau* kite surfing wakepark has further energised the area. A new lagoon road and pavement linked both ports, a *plagette* introduced between park and oystersheds. Happily, gentrification has not gone too far: nothing can stop a distinctive marine whiff from the étang on the path between the ports when the wind changes; nor over-prettify the waste ground in front of the *carénage* zone, where for three years the village re-enacted its musical pageant of *La Belle Scribote* (*see page 90*), and summer music festivals were regular events!

**Capitainerie** (*see page 57*).
**Kithau** *(Kitesurf-wakepark)* 06 87 07 11 93 www.kithau.com
**Le Loup Marseillanais** 04 67 00 07 57
**La Madeleine St Jean** The last private winery in the port (*see page 102*).


**Port des Onglous**
Canal du Midi *(see page 42)*


**Port Départemental des Mazets** (seafood port)
route des Parcs
*(Take the lagoon road beyond Port and Parc Tabarka towards the tennis courts or drive along the unfortunately named chemin de l'abbatoir from the cemetery on the Mèze road. Then follow route des Parcs or chemin de Fontaurie.)*
Back in 1941 oyster production in Marseillan began to be formalised. Since roman times, seafood farming had long been a matter of gathering mussels and diving for clams. Youngsters could earn cash in hand for a good haul, often sold informally in bars and on street corners. But the new oyster industry established in neighbouring Bouzigues by Louis Tudesq in 1925 *(see pages 176 and 296)* was a marine bandwagon not to be missed, and now 800 farmers work the entire étang. In the decade that saw tourism hit the sea shore, so the Marseillan found a replacement for its declining wine freight and traditional fishing business. This port, managed by Marseillan on behalf of the *département*, is no tourist site, but a working agricultural zone, harvesting oysters from tables in the water, bringing the catch on conveyer belts from jetties to be sorted, packed and sold. No collective infrastructure, each producer runs for his own pier and facilities. The port is responsible for quality control and maintaining the eco-system. See exhibitions on fishing and farming at the **Tourist Office** (*see page 74*) and at Bouzigues' **Musee de l'Etang de Thau** (*see page 176*) and learn about the management of the

waters at Meze. Visit the port to buy oysters and mussels directly from producers, to dine in restaurants overlooking sheds and beds or to take part in a *brasucade* summer seafood barbecue. Guided tours of are usually followed by a tasting session.

**Mas Azaïs** 33 parc à Huitres
04 67 77 68 58
Grand *brasucade* Tue, Thu & Fri in season at 12 noon (*see page 267*)

**Annie Castaldo: Ultra Marine** chemin de Fontaurie
06 08 06 84 43; www.castaldo-aquaculture.fr
Organised visits/tastings. Also featured in day-long *Saveurs de Marseillan* excursion, featuring vermouth, wine and chocolate tours (see page 51)

**Mas Roucairol** chemin des Parcs
04 67 77 23 81; www.huitres-bouzigues.fr (groups only)

**La Grande Bleue** chemin de Fontaurie
06 60 82 20 60; www.conchyliculture.com
Mon-Fri 09.00-15.00
Guided visits, tasting/wine included, €6. Disabled visitors welcome.

**La Ferme Marine** route des Parcs
04 67 76 14 59; www.lafermemarine.com
Fashionable dining room and huge waterfront terrace above the oystersheds of *Les Plats Thau d'Occi* (*review page 267*)

Other oyster producers – *see pages 251-2*

**Port de Marseillan Plage  [4] B2**                              (*see page 69*)
(Capitainerie) 04 67 21 99 30; 06 12 20 35 45
(Capitainerie hours) Sep-Jun Mon – Fri: 08.30-12.00, 13.45-17.30; Sat: 08.30-12.00; Jul-Aug every day 08.30-12.00, 15.00-19.00
At the mouth of the original Grau de Pisse-Saumes, the Mediterranean marina has 220 permanent moorings, with four berths for casual visitors. Port to the region's oldest purpose built holiday resort, sports and leisure base, and host to Marius' 'same-day boating licence' training centre.

**Top Fun** (*chandlers etc*) 04 67 21 98 44
**Aviron Marseillanais** (*sea fishing*) 04 67 77 23 69
**JPA Activités** 04 67 01 62 70
**Yacht club** 06 11 94 78 14
**Jet ski** 06 09 33 64 97 www.marseillan-jet-ski.com
**Permis Bateau Commandant Marius** 06 09 09 52 30

Boat hire:
**Dolphin Nautico** 04 67 21 85 69 www.dolphin-nautico34.com
**Marseillan Marine** 04 67 77 38 32
**Blue Pearl** 06 27 07 14 21 www.location-bateau-marseillan.com

# The Etang de Thau

IS IT A LAKE, IS IT A SEA; was it created by Mother Nature or by pioneering ancient engineers? For centuries, historians, scientists and the wise men of the south have put forward theories as to the birth of the Etang de Thau. Most agree that the headlands of Sète and Agde are remnants of two volcanic eruptions that spilt fiery foundations into the Golfe de Lion. Perhaps they created the lagoon, when first the Volcan Saint Clair and then the Volcan Saint Loup were roused from their slumbers on the sea bed, with a belated hurrah from Brescou way off shore.

Whatever shaped this special lake, legend has always muscled in to blur its history, just as mists and fogs obscure the view of Sète across the bay. My favourite yarn tells of our own private Atlantis. Some chroniclers tell of a cataclysmic disaster, a flood swallowing the lost city of Thau beneath the waters. They cite archaeological finds at the northern end of the lagoon, barnacles clinging to remnants of classical architectural chunks. What a metropolis it must have been. Such a pity no one wrote about it at the time.

Sceptics argue these architectural teasers were but remains of an aqueduct feeding the Balaruc spa, and that Romans divided the waters from the sea. The truth is, earlier empire builders had already discovered the place, and the Etang was known centuries before Romans conquest. Perhaps myths were moulded by diving fisherboys telling tales of what lay beneath the calm surface. Those waters still hide France's most beautiful protected park.

When 21$^{st}$ century editors of *Paris Match* magazine first saw stunning images offered to them by globetrotting wildlife photographer Laurent Ballesta, they did not believe that these were pictures of France, so vibrant and vibrant the colours of exotic plants and vivid-hued sponges just yards below the surface of the Etang. Graceful parades of seahorses, as emblematic of the Thau beneath each barnacled hull as are the pink flamingos above the waterline; colonies of shimmering fish glide through the nacre mouldings of the seabed, bewitching enough to turn sane minds toward the myth of a lost civilisation.

Some 19 kilometres long, from *Les Onglous* to Sète's *Aiguille de l'Angle,* and just three to five wide, the Etang de Thau has been hub of civilization for two millennia. The abundant stock of its waters and fertile soil on its shores has guaranteed self-sufficiency for Marseillan and its neighbours through siege and political turmoil and fostered a seam of independent spirit and healthy disrespect for authority that runs through the story of its people: A self-contained lake for fishing, its *graus* (such as *Pisse Saumes*, more recently channelled into a formal canal at Marseillan Plage) access the wider sea and outside world, and a long sandy shoreline stretches from Sète and beyond Agde. The étang lends itself to the will of those who live on its banks. When oyster farming was introduced on *la Côte Bleue*, so wider sections of the lake might lay a panoramic buffet-spread of tables; when Riquet decanted his canal, Marseillan could develop a working trading port in safe harbour, free from the exposure of open sea; by the shallow marshes and southern *gourgs*, salt might be harvested, traces of the former *salins* remain; and when two rival communities emerged in Sète, they shared the fishing rights, Italians from French, the sea from the *étang*.

Variously described as a lake or an inland sea, the Etang de Thau is quite shallow, averaging 9-10 metres, only 3-4 metres by Marseillan. However, between Bouzigues' oyster park and Balaruc's beach lies the *Fosse des Abysses*, a modest abyss but 30 metres deep and 200 metres in diameter.

Yet only a fool would judge the étang by its dimensions. It is broader than its width and far more profound that its depths; above all, much wilder than the beauty of its wildlife. On a clear day, one may well be able to see plainly to the Mount across the bay, but never forget that this is no mere pond, but a sea in microcosm. When mists descend, suddenly as they will, the loneliness of the boatman is palpable; mariners may be trapped even a mile from shore. Holiday boats chugging twixt Canals of the Midi to the Rhône-Sète may be barred from crossing, and recent chroniclers, such as Terry Darlington in his best selling *Narrow Dog to Carcassonne,* speak with trepidation of a first time crossing of this micro sea. Winds may churn the waters, a millpond turn on a whim, and even experienced sailors brought down by its power. We've seen rescue boats called out and not just for the disorientated amateur, and the spirit chills, even in summer's heat, when helicopters and planes circle in the forlorn hunt for a lost soul. The tragedy of the widespread superstition that keeps so many fishermen from learning to swim, aand claiming the life of a young *pêcheur,* stays long in the memory.

Respected and appreciated, the Etang de Thau is nonetheless a welcoming host, and a boat trip with an experienced skipper is an unmatchable experience. Glimpsing Marseillan's village from the water is to see it in perfect proportion, terracotta rooftops crested by green tree coronets, skyline pierced by the church tower and underscored over undulating countryside by the *châteaux d'eau* of lakeside communities.

Iconic flamingos, once winter visitors like the blacknecked grebes, now are year-round residents at each tip of the étang, alongside avocets, herons, egrets, stilts and tawny pipits, and joined at breeding time by flocks of terns and in the off-season by ever more varieties of gulls.

Water temperatures vary from 7 degrees in winter to 24 in summer, and the seasons determine the seasoning, salt-water from June until January, and fresher, milder brackish the rest of the year. Gentle shallows are there for the paddling and perhaps a cautious dip, Mèze has a charming little beach, tucked behind the main port, striped bathing huts and café tables, an *Hulot* holiday in miniature. Bouzigues has a similar shore. A late arrival to the ranks of étang *plagettes* was that of Marseillan Ville itself, which tagged a sandy shore to the side of the newly groomed Parc Tabarka in time for *Le Figaro's* full feature on the chic allure of 'village' rather than 'resort' Marseillan. The Paris press went somewhat overboard, listing the small bathing zone as among France's top 30 beaches, a claim to choke even its most charitable supporter. Sands need be imported and poured on the shore each season. By winter, marsh coast weeds and reeds triumph and a trek to water is best undertaken wearing a pair of crocs. Nonetheless, local families have long enjoyed their Sunday *bord de l'eau* experience here, and generations of Wednesday afternoon schoolchildren ever hurled themselves off the rocks of Tabarka.

Phocean geographers first listed the lagoon as part of their new territory. A second-century Roman chronicler described the étang as part of a chain of inland waterways and lakes linking the Alps to the Pyrenees. The writer recorded a colony of modest huts where Marseillan was beginning to establish itself on the water separating Iberians from Ligurians.

Of all the settlements on its shores, the *étang* has been kindest to Marseillan: Those Roman pillars that first nurtured oysters in the waters of Bouzigues eventually came crashing down; and in the 16<sup>th</sup> century the ramparts of Mèze were likewise rent asunder by the force of the elements: our new millennium saw the phenomenon of the inverted woodland: what seemed like an entire forest, ripped from the soil of the Rhône, swept out to sea and thrown back ashore on the long Lido beach with such force that trees embedded themselves upside down in sand and stood with vintage root branches outstretched, clutching buffed and polished rocks from another land; an eerie lifeless leafless grove that stood until bounty hunters with saws had hewn their way through this midwinter gift of free firewood.

*Oystermen on the Etang*

Through the years, Marseillan's port and village suffered little by comparison. Sure, every couple of winters will bring house-high waves crashing over port walls, and barely a season passes without an ill-secured fishing boat battered and grazed into retirement; the *Taverne du Port's* menus have photos of Thau breakers lashing the roof of the *entrepot* where now stands *Residence Rive Gauche;* and widows of the quarter reminisce of the year the rocks of the Tabarka wall came rolling up rue des Pecheurs on a tide of waters, "for all the world like sugar cubes on a tumbled tea tray".

Yet, the houses on the quays still stand, the village goes about its business, protected, and never threatened, by the waters.

Historian Jean Fayet quotes a poet, who wrote "Marseillan spreads itself between the azure sheet of her étang and the woven web of her vines. This peaceful spread mirrors, in its shimmering undulating reflection, the houses of the village"

Another writer, Achille Maffre de Bauge (*see page 22*), spoke of the view, of looking out at sails "framed by the waves and the sun, as our souls and our eyes glide towards the gilded horizon on the wings of the gulls".

65

But for how long will Marseillan enjoy this protection?

For, whilst its origins are lost in legend, the Thau, with its seasons of eels and breeding *daurade*, its underwater park of flora and fauna, flocks of flamingos that congregate in the *gourgs* of its shallows and schools of seahorses that frolic in the depths, the railway line across the isthmus that sends night trains from the second to the right and straight on till morning, may be on the verge of another dramatic metamorphosis.

The new coast road from Sète to Marseillan Plage, Europe's most ambitious sand-moving scheme, with new dunes, fresh landscaping and the redefining of the Lido beaches, was created for a reason: Scientists studying rising sea levels and weather conditions, erosion of the beaches and dunes came to a chilling conclusion. Should the project to reconstruct the strip between the twin headlands fail, then, by 2050, the lagoon will be consumed by the sea, the étang will be no more and Marseillan could become the premier port on the *Baie du Thau*.

**Atouvents** quai de la Résistance   |2| B2
06 20 08 43 24; http://atouvents.free.fr
If you have neither boat nor mooring of your own at Marseillan, you may still spend a morning or afternoon sailing on the étang with your own private skipper. Perhaps dropping anchor to swim, with mask and snorkel for a glimpse of the secret garden under the water; maybe fishing for your supper; certainly with a picnic to toast the unforgettable views of Marseillan from the lagoon. Albert, Gérard and Jean-Claude welcome guests aboard their sailing boats Pollux, Sunny and Inca. Buy an annual membership valid until March 31 for €30 per person; €50 for a family or group of 3; €65 for up to 5 people and your first afternoon out is free. Then, pay only €10 per person, each time you fancy a half-day on the water or €18 for a full day. Under 12s €5.

**Sightseeing Boat trips** Excursions on glass bottomed boats leave from the Grand Canal at Sète, other tour boats from Agde
**Sailing Clubs & Schools** *(see page 374)*
**Ports** at Marseillan, Mèze, Bouzigues, Balaruc and Sète
**Access to sea** Canal Piss Saumes and port of Marseillan Plage.
Alternatively via Sète –check opening hours for raising and lowering the bascule bridges. 04 67 46 34 36.
**Weather reports** posted daily at Capitaineries or call 08 36 68 08 34.
**Emergencies** 04 94 61 71 10; Gendarmerie Brigade Nautique 04 67 30 07 24.

# When the wind blows

A S THE LAND OF OZ IS RULED BY ITS WITCHES, so Marseillan is defined by its winds. Visitors from other worlds where a gust *du jour* may be described as bracing at best and blustery at worst cannot fail to be impressed by the arched eyebrow of the *batalier* who sniffs the air and looks across a mirror calm lagoon, and declares we'll not see the Mont St Clair from lunchtime until the weekend.

Serious student and hardy boatmen may rattle off maybe two dozen appellations from all points of the compass. The rest of us might learn that the *Tramontane* that whips and scolds us through narrowest *ruelles* from village to port has a prodigal welcome on its return after a week or more of the humid compress of the *Marin* sea-breath that lingers, laundry dank and damp even when the sun is at its height, and tangs the tongue with the salt of mariners' yarns

But fishermen and wine-growers know the taste, trail and provenance of each nuance of the breeze. The *Tramontane* is the north wind that defines the rawness of winter as it blows through rows of vines lining the route de Mèze; yet, should it arrive from the fields of Pomérols and Florensac, it may veer towards the path of a north-westerly *Mistral* (not to be confused with its namesake that ransacks the Rhône), cold, strong and ruthless, banishing clouds far out to sea. Older sailors have country names for the winds. *Mistral* is the *Magistrou*; *Tramontane* the *Tramountana*.

When they speak of *Lou Gregaou*, they refer to *Le Grec*, sneaking the length of the étang from the north-east, beyond Balaruc and Bouzigues, bringing warm rains and, in summer, even less welcome attendant biting bugs and midges. The current that rushes in from the east, where sun rises over Mont Saint Clair, is the aptly named *Levant* (or *Lou Lebant*) and its closest neighbour is the bane of the laundress, the *Marin Blanc*, sometimes known as *Mer à Levant*, blowing over clear water between the headlands. A cluster of gusts, *Vents du Mer* and *Demi Mer* take their turn across the sea and over the Lido pages, and the most southerly sea breeze is gentle and refreshing *Labeche Midi*, known to the Occitan as *Labech Miejournaou*, and to the poet and the sea dog as *Le Vent des Dames*.

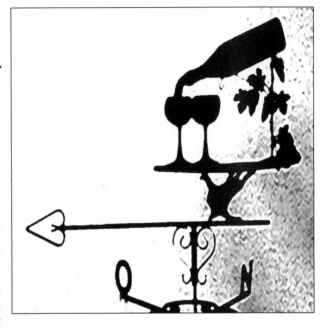

*La Girouette: chasing the winds at the Taverne du Port*

The south-westerly moisture heavy wheeze panting along roads from Agde is the *Ponant* or *Garbin*, and, following the coastline from the border, *Vent d'Espagne* is sister to *Bélard* puffing to town along the Bessan road and best known as the *Narbonais*, showing up after the *rentrée* for an occasional dramatic late summer or early autumn storm. *Vignerons* have a weather eye for the *Narbonais*; skilled in timing their harvest to avoid its squals.

Sometimes a mad whirl of a wind will whistle through town for never much more than a week, rattling the rigging in the port, toppling plant pots and dustbins in a tempestuous tantrum, such as *Les Vacaliaux* showing up around Eastertide in a mad bust of energy after so much Lenten restraint. The winds that follow through until Maytime and the begining of summer have the names of saints: *Georges, Marc, Vital* and *Jean l'Evangéliste*, but it takes a lifelong local to know one from the other.

Should you be fortunate enough to be one in three; listen to the ancient mariner. The men who plough the waters have always had the last word when it comes to talking about the weather. Indeed, one Roman visitor to Marseillan spoke of the Etang de Thau and its many moods as inspired by the power of the elements: The town's fortunes having thrown it amongst many other cultures: Celtic, Viking and Greek, the chronicler wrote that the people named their waters the Thau either after Thor (Norse god of thunder) or Taurus (the wild bull of the heavens).

# Marseillan Plage

**M**ARSEILLAN MAY BE on the Etang de Thau, but there is no doubt whatsoever that Marseillan Plage is on the Med. This seasoned seasonal beano of landscaped holiday is an endless expanse of sandy beaches backed by dunes and lapped by rippled sea, separated from the étang by the railway line and palm-fringed strips of bars and photo-menus, primary coloured treats and Day-Glo lilos.

Once a place of toil, where men worked vines, hauled nets and raked salt. Yet, thanks to a wartime scorched earth policy, a visionary social reformer and the generosity of Mother Nature, Languedoc's first purpose-built holiday resort rose from the ashes of World War Two.

These days, fish are beached by anglers, and any trawling is of a social nature: at midnight foam parties under the stars, volleyball on the beach or encounters in the dunes. With karaoke soundtrack and fuelled by family-sized cauldrons of *moules-frîtes*, avenue de la Méditeranée is where shoulders glow and stingle with after-sun balm in the hours between flopping and bopping. This is unashamedly, proudly and successfully a family holiday resort. Myriad camp sites boast activity programmes to put a cruise-ship to shame. Water chutes and splash parks for kids and rum cocktails garlanded with coloured paper for parents turn estates along avenue des Campings, route de Sète and beyond into self-contained virtual resorts.

The main drag promises trike hire and happy hours, nightclubs shoot laser welcomes to the skies and a fun-fair sends shrieks and squeals across the étang with each thrust and roll of its giant swings and big wheel. Daytime diversions of paint-ball, karting or riding out to the wetlands vie with a packed programme of circuses, monster-truck shows and *torro-piscine* (family-safe alternative to the *corrida*) that could almost eclipse the sea. Rock, pop and folk concerts pepper the summer diary, and strolling bands blast from bar to bar during festive fireworks weeks around 14 July and 16 August. The tourist office handles everything from troubleshooting to selling tickets to events and attractions and is home to temporary art shows. Other exhibitions held opposite, at the Cave Co-operative, site of weekend brocante flea-markets.

But there is a *plage* in the title and several beaches in reality, and the *raison d'etre* for the destination lives up to its billing. For many, the *Lido*, a long 18-kilometre stretch of soft sand from the canal to Sète is summer Mecca. Dotted with lifeguard huts along the old beach road (now that traffic is relocated back along the railway line), this was once screened from public view by a wall of RVs and camper trucks. Mid-June 'til September a carpet of factor-fiftied flesh lies basted for toasting; the rest of the year an unspoilt spread of virgin *sables* for dog walking, horse riding, kite flying and beachcombing, the miles delineated by gnomic anglers, rods planted at an obeisant angle to gentle wind-driven waves.

But this run of beach, pampered to the east by private bars, marquees and thick mattresses, is not Marseillan Plage, which actually begins at *plage Robinson*, hugging the canal, served by hotels and shielded by the port, a firm favourite with locals. The *plage d'Honneur* is closest to amenities and the full back-up of the resort, whilst the *plage Rieu's* sands pace the avenue des Campings and continue south-westwards towards the Agde frontier. It is a typical Mediterranean beach; where drink and snack vendors pick their way amongst the fallen in the no-man's-land between a quartet of first-aid stations and occasional beach bars with sun-beds. Volleyball and beach football tournaments take place all season, sensation seekers kite-surf, jet-ski and hire boats and a diving school caters for all ages. Meanwhile, the budget-conscious bucket and spade brigade embark on a rolling programme of sand castle building to landscape each family group.

Various sections of the beach are adapted for disabled vistors: *Faciroule* matting paths for wheelchairs, *Audioplage* guided swimming routes for the blind and rental of special trikes to take physically challenged bathers right into the sea (*see page 377*). Buffered by dunes and stamina, the beach eventually gives way, even in summer, to that sense of space and nature that is the hallmark of the long off-season. The naturist zone runs up to the Cap, and a notice indicates when clothing is "optional" (as in "frowned-upon") and common sense tells you which sections are for families, which for gay men and which (*see* **Cap d'Agde**, *page 148*) are libertine in practice.

Whether the lure is hedonism or merely skin-tone, the defining feature of the entire landscape for four months of sundaes is a vast expanse of epidermis: honed and toned or free range and flowing; nipped, tucked and liposucked, or contoured undulation of Rubenesque abundance. Yet, little more than half a century ago, things were very different.

*Salins* around *graus, gourgs* and marshes, vines behind dune reeds, fresh fish virtually surrendering to the shores, this was the larder beyond the Thau. The *Compagnie des Salins du Midi's* saltworks at Quinzieme, Bagnas and the Cap provided backbreaking work for villagers. When harshest winds lashed rough skin raw, salt rich air made the chore even more painful. For centuries past, the effort of evaporating and raking had yielded the wherewithal for sardines and mackerel to be preserved, packaged and packed off by sea and canal to export markets, salt boosting the economy of the village and the coffers of the taxman at the same time.

Since the Middle Ages, fishermen who worked the étang in winter would summer on the sea's wide beaches. Under tents imagineered from sails and masts, entire families lived on the sand, welcome breezes tempering relentless sunshine, bonfires toasting the pick of the catch. Everyone, from grandparents to children, press-ganged to walk heavy nets into the shallows and trawl and haul fresh fish to land.

By the 20<sup>th</sup> century, an Atlantic vogue for paddling, begun when Empress Eugenie discovered Biarritz, had spread Medwards. For four weeks from 15 July, Marseillan families left cool dark houses in narrow village streets to join fisherfolk on the sands. They too set up home-made *tentes rustiques*, youngsters helping lug nets as commuting fathers cycled three miles back to the day job. Sundays, after church, friends and family from inland villages would visit and the beach reverberate to sounds of parties and picnics. *Plat du jour* the length of the sands: *Pairolada*; fish poached in seawater and served with greenery garnered from the dunes. These were the first summer vacationers and early on canny entrepreneurs spotted a market. Bakers improvised *dépôt de pain* counters and some enterprising café owners even built makeshift beach bars during the month-long exodus. One July, the *Tour de France* cycled beside the dunes and Parisian press photographers thrilled to the sight of a rough and ready canvas and bamboo camp by the sea; pictures appeared in newspapers and fashionable magazines. Come August, villagers returned home, sands abandoned to fishermen who continued casting *filets* on the waters until autumn: but for a few nets drying on the sand and wisps of cigarette smoke rising from a canvas shelter, no sign of life from sea to étang.

Today, with serried concrete balconies, rented mobile homes and family-run campsites crammed twixt railway line and coast; it is hard to conceive that all this was once one *domaine*: park of the *Château de Richemont*, probably the only true fairy-tale holder of the title *château* Marseillan has ever known. An elegant palace at the heart of a wine estate, home to the Rey family, whose townhouse in the village is today's *Mairie*. Surviving images on postcards show a veritable Versailles of *parterres* and pathways, ornate statuary, fountains and flowerbeds and, of course, regimented ranks of vines. The family entertained lavishly at this summer palace, and to the east stood a grand belvedere: imposing seaboard gateway for family and guests, to step onto the beach bypassing the summer camp hoi polloi. No one took umbrage at the grand display of wealth. According to Albert Arnaud in his pictorial history, one local wag merely named his more modest home *Château de Piètremont.*

Razed to the ground by German troops in 1944, so they might string coastal defences against allied invasion, nothing remains of *Richemont*, its buildings, nor of the world of space and tranquillity that it represented. Exit the occupying jackboot; enter the march of progress. Visionary mayor, Andre Filliol saw wasteland as an opportunity to boost Marseillan's fortune in the tradition of pioneering social reform. A new form of tourism, a new breed of tourist, a new type of summer holiday lay ahead. After all, if the village's working families had enjoyed endless miles of sandy shore each year, what about factory workers from Lyon, Clermont Ferrand and beyond or families from the hinterland?

Filliol argued that neither marketing nor development may shift millionaires from their favoured playgrounds of Cannes and Nice, so why not create holidays that do not turn on five-star hotels with braided and betassled commissionaires pocketing half a week's wages in every tip and spin of a revolving door. Before the War (and eventual deportation to Dachau), reforming Prime Minister Léon Blum had calmed national industrial action in 1936 by instituting mandatory paid holidays for French workers.

In 1945, Filliol reasoned that, even with a minimum wage, traditional Med resorts  would be out of reach of the common  man with  the right and wherewithal to spend a week at the seaside. He persuaded the council to buy Richemont's land from Madame Voisin (by now, Marsellan's two wine dynasties had united in marriage and *La Voisin* was also officially Madame Charles Rey), and set to work creating an independent town designed for holidays. The designation *Marseillan Plage*  was adopted in 1947 and *Les*

*Onglous* station renamed for the tourist trade. Temporary shanties, home to displaced post-war Marseillanais folk, were demolished, and work began on 130 municipal holiday chalet "bungalows". A civic camp site opened and the rest of the land parcelled and sold to developers of rival accommodations.

In two years between conceiving the project and getting hold of the land, the mayor had worked out a basic town plan. He saw a central area of shops, restaurants and amenities, a place for dancing and entertainment, an esplanade along the seafront, jetties and piers for boats and a fishermen's quarter along the Grau de Pisses Saumes so that *Marseillanais* might continue working the sea. The *Grau* had been deepened by the Nazis as an anti-tank defence, and so that became formalised as a Canal, informally named by the locals after their former occupiers: *Canal des Allemandes*.

Remarkable foresight. Today's avenue de la Méditeranée and its tributaries are now crammed with restaurants, cafes and bars; a bustling market place and church, with summer facilities from post office to fire station and *gendarmerie*; the port is now a marina; and night clubs and discotheques throb nightly when bars wind down: Summer brings a huge funfair and year-round bargain hunters flock to the flea-markets. Since the resort developed a lagoon's breadth from the village, historic Marseillan has been preserved. Three hotels, countless apartments and a range of campsites from pitch-and-pay to almost theme-park quality mean that a good 40,000 visitors from France and across continental Europe and Scandinavia spend their summers on what was once an abandoned wine estate. In 2012, Mayor Yves Michel unveiled a new palm-tree-lined ramblas-style esplanade, complete with oyster styled fountain designed by Richard Salles. Not a penny on the rates for the makeover, it was financed by selling off the original municipal campsites, badly in need of improvement, to private operators. Even the pleasure port by *Hotel Richemont* smartened up with the old *Capitainerie* and public toilets converted into a stylish new beach restaurant and bar *Marina Bay*, with €15 lunch menu and superb views on and over the sands.

**Tourist Office** avenue de la Méditerranée; 04 67 21 82 43 |4| A2 *see page 369*

**Bakers**
**Les Airettes** 185 chemin de l'Airette; 04 67 21 86 21|4| A2
**Azzo Pains** 396 av des Campings; 04 99 43 02 06 |4| A3

**Banks**
**Dupuy de Parseval** avenue de la Méditerranée; 04 67 21 97 62 |4| A2
**La Poste** avenue de Richemond; 04 67 21 97 18 |4| A2
**ATM cashpoints**  avenue des Campings |4| A3      chemin de Pairollet |4| A3
                   avenue de la Méditerranée |4| A2   Office de Tourisme |4| A2

**Doctor** 251 chemin de l'Airette; 04 67 21 99 66 |4| A2
**First Aid** poste secours central, plage d'Honneur; 04 67 21 96 41 (15/6-15/9) |4| B2
**Flea Markets** Parking Cave Co-operative/ Tourist office |4| A2 *see page 244*
**Harbourmaster** *see* **Capitainerie** *page 61*
**Launderette** Espace Le Phocéa |4| A2
**Market** place du Marché |4| A2 *see page 244*
**Petrol Station** Station Campus, Ancienne route de Sète |4| A2
**Pharmacy** CC 2000, rue des Commerces 04 67 21 96 31|4| A2
**Police** Gendarmerie, rue des Goëlands; 04 67 21 90 59 (Jul, Aug) |4| A2
**Post Office** La Poste, avenue de Richemond; 04 67 21 97 18 |4| A2

**Supermarkets**
**Spar,** Chemin de l'Airette; 04 67 2197 65 [4] A2
**Epicerie Magique** avenue de la Méditerranée; 04 67 21 82 11 |4| A2

**Accommodation** *see page 380*
**Restaurants** *see page 275*
**Bars** *see page 140*

**Activities**

*For sports (Jet-ski, diving, tennis, boating etc.) see page 374*

**La Ferme Enchantée**
route de Sète |4| A1
06 27 12 17 60 www.lafermeenchantee.com
Open daily (school holidays); Wed, Sat, Sun (term time) 10 – 18
Pony rides for the under 12s, a children's quad track, bouncy castles and a petting farm. Accompanied pony rides in the park for €5; Over-sixes can test the quad track at €6 for 8 laps, €8 for 12 or €10 for 16.

**Karting de Marseillan**
zone de loisirs du Prieur [4] A1
04 67 01 65 06 www.kartingdemarseillan.fr
Jul Aug 11-01 daily; Apr-Jun, 1-15 Sep, Autumn half-term 14-19 daily; Sep 15-30, Oct, 1-15 Nov 14-19 Sat Sun. Closed 15 Nov-Mar
The 5x600m track is a major feature of the new road system by the fair and flea markets. Adult karts, kid's versions for 7-14s and *biplace* vehicles for one adult and a child above 5 years old. After 20.00 in summer, the track is adults only.

**Parc des Attractions**
zone de loisirs [4] A1
Mid-Jun – mid-Sep evenings only.
Some 40 sideshows and rides including big ferris wheel. Fireworks and half price discount evenings, see posters in village. Some attractions accessible for disabled.

**Le Petit Train de Marseillan Plage**
Resort tour linking the campsites and beaches with the main drag. 06 22 13 08 66

**Ranch La Camargue**
route de Sète
06 16 17 20 67 www.ranchlacamargue.fr
Bernard Molina came from Spain in the 1950s to raise thoroughbred Andalusian horses. Explore marshes, coast and St Loup slopes to see wildlife on an escorted trek. €18 (1 hour), €34 (2hrs), €45 (3hrs). Children's pony rides €8 for 30 minutes.

## Nightclubs

**Le Kry's Club**
zone de loisirs [4] A1 04 67 37 59 52 www.krysclub.com
Club 23-06; restaurant 22-05. Jun Sep daily; Oct-May Fri, Sat, Sun, hols
By the big wheel, a big discotheque for over-25s to party til dawn. Regular theme nights (often featuring go-go girls, boys and strippers). In the garden, **Le Dar Janna**, Arabian Nights themed restaurant, serves full meals way beyond midnight.

**Entrée Gratuite**
zone de loisirs [4] A1
04 67 39 59 52 www.lentreegratuite.com
Jul Aug 23-05. Closed Sep-Jun
Big brash open air bash next to Krys Club, with internet and radio spots plugging the biggest dance floor under the sky. Techno nights, mousse parties and general holiday bopping with soft drinks at €3; hard stuff from €7.

**Le Cassiopée**
447 avenue des Campings [4] A3
04 67 21 86 17 www.cassiopee-club.fr
Apr-end summer
Away from the leisure park, and just behind the beach, nightclub for the campsites.

# Other beaches to visit

**Agde**
Cap d'Agde, Le Grau d'Agde, La Taramissiere: 13 Beaches *(see page 157)*

### Les Aresquiers

Antidote to coastal resorts, few casual holidaymakers discover one of the most isolated spots on the coast with none of the usual concrete facilities. Nature reigns as this former military land is a protected site. Now the old barracks have gone, building of any kind is banned. Naturists share space with fully clothed, even muffled, dog-walkers, sunbathers and anglers. Here, you may imagine what the region was like before tourism. The main pebble and shell beach is where families tend to stop and picnic. To find your own space, park up by the canal and walk down to the shore.

### Argelès

Way beyond the local run from Marseillan and a castanet's click from the Spanish border, but this is one of the finest beaches in Languedoc, and if you are off to the Perpignan, Collioure or even Spain, this is the reward for good behaviour in the car. Main beach is pretty much family party time, but head to the northern stretch for space, as even the resort is kept from the shore by some nice landscaping. It is a true treat for the senses, the light is magical, the views of azure skies and blue seas are inspirational, especially set against the back drop of the Pyrenees, and the air filled with the scent of pine.

### Carnon Plage

Sandy beach between the fleshpots of Palavas and La Grande Motte. Well maintained, with kite-surfing and watersports. Popular with Montpellier's off-peak weekenders on sailboards. Attracts a young city crowd, with a good nightlife in summer, and close by **Le Grand Travers**.

### Corniche & Lido

The long Lido strip of fine white sand on the isthmus between Sète and Agde is the natural extension of **Marseillan Plage** and a main beach of choice for Marseillanais. As part of the biggest sand-moving operation since the days of the Pharaohs, the road has been pushed back to run by the main railway line; dunes raised to protect beaches from imminent erosion. Once views were obscured by a phalanx of caravans and camper vans. Now a run of organised car parks towards Sète includes **Villeyroy** for access to the promenade board walk, shops and facilities. In Summer: a string of luxury

*Private space on the Lido*

beach bars and restaurants with private recliners and mattresses for rent and moorings on the breakwater. Best known **Le Ola** (*page 332*), host to after-hours jazz-fest jamming. The northern run is Sète's *plage* at the foot of **Mont St Clair**: good beach for the port, with decent food and drink options close by.

**Espiguette**
Across the county line, in the Gard, *La Pointe de l'Espiguette* is a vast expanse of sand, backed by huge dunes. Visit the 27m lighthouse, **Phare de l'Espiguette**. Families stay close to car park, and amenities: *buvettes*, bars and beach sports. Further along, remember to take a bottle of water with you and you may explore for miles. Furthest from the road, find naturist, gay and more adult zones. Ideal for exploring the wetlands of the **Camargue** and **Aigues Mortes**.

**Frontignan - La Peyrade**
If you happen to be on the other side of Sète, have speedos in the boot and can't face the traffic keeping you from Marseillan, *voila*: a fully fledged blue-flag beach resort, for playing volleyball on pebble and sandy beaches or keeping a squinting eye on your kids across the top of a magazine. The town is known for Muscat wine, has a cultural programme of music and literary festivals, there is an underwater archaeology museum for those inspired by shipwrecks and it is on the summer water-jousting circuit.

## Plagettes on the Etang

See page 64 for more on the *étang plagettes* in **Marseillan, Bouzigues** and **Mèze**. The spa resort **Balaruc-Les-Bains** (*see page 160*) has a lovely long strip of beach on the south eastern coast: promenade lined with good restaurants and even a marked-out, fence-protected swim zone.

## La Grande Motte

Mass market beach with every facility from lifeguards to pizza a plastic ball's throw from the towel. Typical resort, marked by distinctive 1960 concrete pyramids, racks and stacks of apartments and casino nightlife. Thalassotherapy centre, golf course and sports facilities offer alternative diversions away from the beach. Real draw is *Le Grand Travers* (below).

## Le Grand Travers

Just as Paris reinvents itself as the seaside each summer with *Paris Plage* offering skiploads of sand along *les quais* so city poseurs may sport shades, sneers and beachwear without changing so much as a postcode; so this normally undistinguished 60's high-rise resort tacked onto *La Grande Motte* pulls off a pretty chic trick. For the fashionista who has everything, the ultimate beach accessory is "*Madame's usual table?*" as your regular big city restaurant, is transported to *les sables* for the duration. Between May and September, Montpellier's best restaurants up-sticks, kitchens and dining rooms and camp under canvas on the beach. Even the Pourcel twins, Michelin-garlanded godfathers of the cutting edge, who might not dismantle their *Jardin des Sens* flagship, ensure their popular brasserie **Compagnie des Comptoirs** (see page 312) heads for the coast. Hard by, the Pourcels have an even pricier chunk of beach-shack chic **L'Effet Mer** (www.effetmer.com). This offers €80-100 *à la carte* dinners, €35 Sunday brunch and a weekday midday menu at just under €20. Caviar works out at €39 and a glass of house champagne €12 if you want to impress. Evenings see ultimate Paris club DJ's taking the TGV south to host beach parties from the restaurant's bar. And there are temporary and permanent nightclubs close by the beaches – details in listings mags from tourist offices. Nearby **La Voile Bleue** (www.lavoilebleue.fr) could give your *carte bleu* an even run for its money, but does offer a set lunch or saladed *charolais tartare* for under €20 for those not to be diverted from their fortunes by lobster and crab on the *carte*. All restaurants offer *transats* (literally deckchairs, but in reality more like well-upholstered divans) to be reserved in advance). Come autumn's cut off date, these glamorous hangouts prove as ephemeral as their A-list punters, and trackies, hoodies and extendible dog leads replace that fabulous Diane von Furstenberg off-the-shoulder one-piece and the Prada wrap.

## Maguelone

Of the capital's beaches, Maguelone ticks more boxes than most for anyone seeking an escape from commercialised resorts. Many people prefer to drive away from the facilities at the main entrance to the beach (sunbed rental, cocktails and pay-and-display parking) leave the car and wander through the dunes to sleepier sands. Like much of the coast, there is a naturist presence, but areas of nudism are easily indicated by buttocks without bright white bits, and the modest may avert their gaze before contours become distinguishable from flesh tones. Bounded by wildlife reserves, bordered by scrub, with seabirds and marine life all around, Maguelone is as likely to welcome naturalists as naturists. *La plage* is essentially a 12km strip of sand running across the Etang de l'Arnel and salt marshland between modern settlements at Palavas and Frontignan. Hard to imagine this was once one of the seven most important cities of the south. All that remains of mediaeval grandeur is a Romanesque cathedral, quietly slumbering amid dunes on the *presqu'île* amongst the wetlands, and certainly worth the hike to visit.

**Palavas les Flots**
Montpellier sur Mer: a brash busy resort, beach dwarfed by ranks of flats and hotels, it even features a revolving restaurant! Once a fishing port, now a holiday industry with children's attractions and a packed programme of events from *joutes* to *corrida* and concert and cabaret at arena and casino featuring such international stars as Charles Aznavour.

**Portiragnes**
Rather nice and unassuming stretch of the coast, with usual showers and amenities close by, yet no sense of a mass market destination. A pleasantly dated feel, clean and neat but not over-maintained. With low-level holiday homes hidden from view, a holiday resort from another age. (*see page 223*)

**Serignan**
Another old-fashioned beach where nature trumps artificial diversions. Less flashy, more rural, with rough grassy hillocks behind the sands to hide civilisation: simply bathing, lazing and views. *(see also page 231)*

**Valras**
Béziers' local plage is where a city crowd comes after work or school. Sandy beaches, divided into smaller sections to protect against erosion. All facilities: kids clubs, good range of cafes and eateries. Towards Serignan is a naturist area; town end best for traditional holidaymakers.

**Vias**
A modest strip of sandy shore, backed by bamboo and grasses to screen real life, so though the road has usual pizza, chicken, snack and glace options and enough outlets selling as much brightly coloured plastic a family could desire from the beach all you are aware of are sands, sea and views along the coastline. *(see page 241)*

# Fresh alternatives:

## Lake, Spa and River bathing

**Pont du Diable,** Saint Guilhem le Desert
Just before you reach Saint Guilhem and Demoiselles caves the road swings to the left and on your right you glimpse the improbable sight of a beach halfway up a mountain. The River Hérault flows fast and wide here (you may rent canoes to take on the challenge) and both banks open to superb summer beaches. Bring a blanket or towel (because it is stony) and a parasol (because early birds grab all shady spots beneath trees) and a picnic (because the snackeries at St Guilhem are just too touristy and its not worth the drive). Good paddling here, though strong swimmers who can handle the current, find deeper waters downstream. *See page 225*

**Barrage des Olivettes**, Vialhan
A village beyond Roujan for picnic and swimming half an hour inland. The dam flooded a valley to create a reservoir and is responsible for quite a strong current to mark these deep waters for strong swimmers only - not recommended for family idlers. Shady trees, picnic benches for view-gazing over bread and pate. Teenage hang out on term time Wednesday afternoons, otherwise a peaceful spot outside school holidays.

**Lac d'Arques**
In Cathar country far from Marseillan: when it gets too hot on the coast, we head to the hills and hide out in the region's barely-known ski-resorts of the Pyrenees Audoises: Camurac and Belcaire. *En route*, turn left at Limoux, head to the hills and Cathar castles (*see page 357*) . There is a VVF holiday village, so peak summer is busy. But when leaves begin to turn (and rival New England for colour), stop by the lake for a dip in gorgeous waters.

**Lamalou-les-Bains**
(*see page 186*)

**Lac de Salagou**
(*see page 229*)

*Salagou in autumn*

# Lou Capelet, the saint and the jousters

## Marseillan's fêtes and traditions

## Lou Capelet

IT WAS A SUMMER BEFORE the *Château du Port* became fashionable. Patricia yet sashayed curvaceous elegance between waterfront tables, Charley held court by the door; their daughters pressed into service to wait on the holiday crowd. The last coffees had been sipped, credit cards slipped and the kitchen now closed until evening: and I lingered on the terrace, nursing a glass of *Les 3 Poules* rosé. Rooting and tooting *peña* brass rent the air and a rag-tag procession of schoolboys in white t-shirts led the way for sailor-suited men, aglow with the radiance of *pastis*-fuelled *camaraderie*, to follow the band, Mayor and Miss Marseillan herself to the grandstand on the far quay. With port moorings cleared of leisure craft, a *peniche* swung across the width of the harbour. Aboard the barge, a ship's mast poised athwart a wine barrel, thrust at a sharp angle over and above the water. This was the *bigue*, for the *capelet*, or *course à la bigue*: challenge of the greasy pole, that on two days each summer sorts the men from the boys, 18 metres of slippery wood to make heroes of pals in a triumph of hapless equilibrium over dubious sobriety.

From my vantage point, wine glass topped up through the afternoon, I watched my first *capelet*, and cemented a love affair with the eccentricity and bold spirit of Marseillan.

*Triumph: the second hat*

Since then, every year come July 14 and August 16, I have joined the quayside throng as the day follows the familiar pattern: that parade of contenders, main event at five proceeded by a children's challenge. Ere the barge swerves into place, fork-lifted volunteers slap on tallow and soap to make the mast as slippery as possible. At the tip of the *bigue,* a *baton* crowned by a beribboned straw hat perches perpendicular; two metres closer, the second hat and stick. Players board the *barge,* line up behind the mast, *tricoleur* flags held proudly aloft. The band shifts from carnival jig to the *Marseillaise* and all stand for the anthem. Let the games commence.

A tradition dating back long before the Revolution, *lo capelet* in Occitan, *le capelet* in French (the t sounded either way), rules are simple: players take turns running the pole in a bid to snatch the hat. In reality, slipping and sliding on the grease, the ignominious plunge into cold water on a hot day as inevitable as the cheers at each fall from *grasse*. Oboe fanfare and drum roll of anticipation heralds every attempt, just as good natured groans dismiss each failure. Once all have made a first stab, the brass strikes up a jaunty tune and the roll call begins anew for round two. And so it goes until the first hat and pole are captured and all dive into the water to congratulate the victor, then regroup to attempt the second, final *chapeau.*

To yells of *"Allez, allez, allez!"* and the reedy encouragement of hautbois and drum, every trail hailed loudly, every near success greeted with mass intake of breath and every splash applauded: the commentator reports *le premier pas* on the painted blue or red stripes at the hat end of the pole, the nearly-does-it first abortive grab-and-slip, the lunge to plunge, and finally the victorious snatch and dive when the hat emerges from the water atop its *baton* amid man hugs and air-punches in the scramble to the basalt steps. Both hats claimed, the triumphant march back to the village is a chaotic affair of digression, congratulation and celebration.

Children, with their low centre of balance, fare best; tiddlers traditionally triumphant. The athlete in his prime makes August's game a true sport, played by fit lads 18-30 years old. Yet, sometimes over-confidence trumps perfect balance and a casual saunter, with debonair wink leads to a plummet but a fingertip from glory. Sometimes dignity flails as a fallen hero grips the bar on his way down, clings on, sliding as far as possible to palm away soap and ease a successor's path, before surrendering to a dunking. Different fun at July 14's derby affair, when paunchier troupers in their 30s and 40s take to the pole. Heavyweight contenders land astride the bar, as the letters IVF loom large in the prospects of anxious wives and girlfriends.

The veterans' Bastille Day challenge is a relatively recent addition to the programme (like the children's warm up events). Sometimes old-hands return to the *bigue* to perform a burlesque routine in full drag as an *entr'acte* between first and second hats of August's *capelet* proper.

Nobody knows for sure when the game began, but all have a theory. Similarities to a military sport in Honfleur, lead some to hazard a link to the 11th century Norman Conquest of the Med; others suggest naval training exercises from the age of the *Marine Royale* (one prominent local communist visibly blanched when I used the R-word). Marseillan is now the only place the *course* is still run, although the game was originally played all along the coast. Frederic Mistral wrote of seeing men run the pole in Cassis in 1850, whilst the first printed report of Marseillan's sport was in the 1890s. Besides whispering 1767 as year of "*la catastrophe*", the history of the *capelet* is a story without dates, albeit annotated with heroes and legends. For most of the 19th and 20th centuries the 21-metre *bigue* itself was the story: rescued from the warship *Rhône*, shipwrecked with 320 men aboard off the Marseillan coast on its return from Algeria. The crew survived, as did the main mast that was brought out every August, even after its tip snapped off (reducing the run to 17 metres 30 centimetres). In 2007, the *Rhône bigue* was retired and replaced with an 18-metre version.

Champions become folk heroes. Grab a hat and you'll rarely have to buy your own drink. Decades on, people still speak of Réné Cabal seizing both *chapeaux* in his first two runs, and of Joseph Danis running the pole *en sabots*. One veteran recounts seeing the father-in-law of rocker Johnny Hallyday "touching" the first hat. Thus legends are born.

During my first afternoon in the port, skies turned unseasonably grey, clouds grew black, the rains came, and thunder rumbled ominously close as forked shards of lights flashed and slashed at the étang. Spectators fled to shelter of cafes and porches, and shirts on *capaleteurs* aboard the barge were wetter than those of their fellows still floundering in the water. Still, the men ran the *bigue*, battling driving rain, risking lightning aiming ever closer to the mast. The first *chapeau* still unclaimed: all to play for and the devil take the danger. As I retreated to the Château doorway, an *espresso* appeared at my side and Charley's voice muttered: "*Ils sont vraiment meshugeneh, non?*". Midsummer, in the driving rain, watching yet another valiant foolhardy hero poised to run a race contrived by the navy of a long defunct monarchy, 900 miles from home, and a Frenchman was confiding to me in Yiddish about a game with an Occitan name – *Vive Lo Capelet.*

## Jousting on the water

As summer sun dazzles from fresh white paint and laundered shirts, two boats, one red and one blue, approach each other along the narrow channel of the port. To clarion of hautbois and tambour, the sportmen raise their lances in salute. This is the first pass, a gentleman's nod to over 700 years of chivalry. As the boats cross, the combatants shake hands. Next time, courtesies will be thrown to the wind and one unfortunate consigned to the indignity of a tumble into the water.

Marseillan Port's "other" game is Languedoc's principal water sport. First played by 13th century crusaders at Aigues Mortes awaiting fair wind to the Holy Land, water jousting, or *les joutes nautiques,* has been a tradition in Agde since 1544 and Sète's honour roll inscribes every victor since a 1666 match celebrated the completion of the Canal du Midi. Even now, August's *Saint Louis* final in Sète attracts scores of thousands of spectators, the game rivalling rugby in the public's affection.

Two white *rames,* emblazoned in red or blue, are powered by ten muscular oarsmen. At the bow, musician-mascots in bright straw boaters; astern, the *bigue*, a broad ladder, leads to the *tintaine* platform, two metres high. Here stands the jouster; *confrères* perched below, covering their heads with *pavois* wooden shields, as the boats approach for combat. Lance poised, 2.8 metres of steel tipped painted wood, each man lunges to topple his opponent into the water. Crowds cheer as a quayside brass band strikes up lively tunes between passes, serenading each splash and triumph, whilst a motorboat chugs out to rescue the loser's battered shield and lost lance.

Every town, each club, has its traditions. But there is always a blue team and a red team. Blues in 18th century Sète were bachelors, reds married men; in other contests, dockers versus fishermen. As in any sport, the event might be a grudge match; one Marseillan umpire's decision challenged by the loser, who swam furiously to the quay and dragged himself ashore, white strip dripping wet, to vent his anger at the judges' table. Most spectators regard the event as a good-natured romp, and public allegiance may be fickle (as the teams "changed ends" midway through a contest in Agde, so capricious schoolchildren on the river bank unblushingly swapped the chant of "*allez les bleues*" to "*allez les rouges*").

A solidly manly sport, the only women on the boats will be playing oboes or drums; on the one occasion I saw a female competitor, she knocked her male opponent into the water to cheers and a not-bad-for-a-girlie compliment from the (male) commentator. The voice from the tannoy then suggested that the point should not be counted, and lets-leave-the-game-to-the-boys. Joan of Arc, Eleanor of Aquitaine, even Ellen MacArthur notithstanding, true feminism has yet to make its mark on the waters of the Midi.

*Let battle commence*

The region boasts 16 clubs, so plenty of matches to enjoy in Marseillan's port in July and August. Besides genuine league games, extra events for tourists have motors replacing the rowers. Other bouts are staged at the canal in Marseillan Plage, and every week a contest is to be caught on the river Hérault at Agde or Grau d'Agde or along Sète's Grand Canal, ever lined with grandstands for the Saint Louis finals. Each club fields four teams: heavyweights, middleweights, juniors and seniors. Veterans provide the best entertainment, but money changes hands on the outcome of the heavyweight tournaments. Check out Sète's museum displays *(see page 238)* or read the full rules online at www.joutes.fr

For afternoon matches in Marseillan, arrive early to grab a café table and order a *pichet* to toast each tumble, or jostle along a front row bench on the quay. Otherwise, you'll know when the event begins as fugue of oboe, cheering and unmuted oompah echoes through the village.

# With Saint Peter to the étang

To the blaring of Charpentier's prelude *Te Deum*, and under the benign regard of an archbishop and parish priest, a procession of *matelots* in blue and white striped jerseys mingles along the aisle of the church in sauntered march. Hoisted high on their shoulders is a small wooden boat festooned with flags, and filled with flowers around a carved statue of a Saint Peter who bears an uncanny resemblance to Pavarotti. Behind them, as they emerge into needle sharp June sunlight, the Mayor in his jacket, clergy, epauletted naval men, shirt-sleeved dignitaries and parishioners, follow as the parade regroups to follow the band along the boulevard down to the port.

This is the *Fête du Saint Pierre*. Bemused tourists sipping coffee on the quay pause twixt cup and lip as *tricouleur* flags bat shadows across glittering trumpets and the wooden saint is lifted aboard a waiting pleasure craft, crammed with VIPs. The boat slips its mooring; in its wake a flotilla of smaller tubs and dinghies and *Jusqu'au Bout* in full red sail. Beyond the breakwaters, pause for benediction as the priest honours sailors and fishermen whose lives were claimed by the sea. Wreaths then strewn on the water and the band toots and blasts the *Marseillaise* and, in a moment of stillness, all aboard salute the lost souls of the Etang de Thau.

# A year en fete

**Regards des Femmes**                     *early March*
2 weeks of exhibitions, concerts and shows for International Women's Day

**Fête du Printemps**                     *late March or early April*
Maitre Pierre and the miller's dance, *see page 91.*

**Carnival Parade**                     *Easter Sunday*
With rooting and tooting; floats, bands and majorettes, procession through
the port, bd Lamartine and av Victor Hugo (*see page 91*). The parade
returns for August's Marseillan festival and visits Marseillan Plage in July.

**Remembrance Day 1945** *(see page 93)*          *8 May*

**Fête de l'Europe** Concert and aperitif.          *9 May*

**Journée de la Résistance**          *27 May*
Honouring local wartime heroes of the French Résistance . *See page 93.*

**Roadside Beach party**                     *mid June*
The first Harley bikers rally of the year at Marseillan Plage: a weekend of
shiny chrome and well worn leathers. Grand concert on the Saturday night.

**Fête de la Musique**                     *21 June*
Legacy of legendary culture minister and *bon vivant* Jack Lang, when
musicians give free concerts in village, town and city squares and sites.
Worth a trip to Béziers, Montpellier and, especially, Sète. In Marseillan,
Jazzinade (*see page 370*) plays the quays or co-operative; others perform
on the place de l'Eglise stage, followed by dancing to live bands til late.

**Fête du Saint Pierre**                     *Sunday in late June*
*See page 86.* Procession to the church at 9.45, with a musical mass at 10
and the parade to the port at 11. Blessing of the waters at 11.30 and drinks
served on the allees Roques at 12.15.

**Bastille Eve**                     *13 July*
The festival begins on the 13th with a torchlit procession from the Mairie at
22h, fireworks in the port at 22.30, and a ball in the village from 22.45pm.

**Bastille Day**                     *14 July*
On the 14th, *Capeleteurs* parade from the Marie at 10h, with an official
ceremony at 11.30, followed by drinkies for all offered by the mayor at the
Grille. The under 14s' *Capelet* takes place at 15h followed by the veterans
at 17h. Ball in the village from 22h. *See page 81.*

**Les Joutes**                                    *15-18 July and late August*
Three-day tournament in July and special events in August. *See page 84*

**Fiesta Marseillan**                                              *late July*
An annexe to Sète's annual fiesta. Music, food and drink on the quays.

**Fête de l'Huitre**                                               *end July*
Grab a plate of seafood and a bottle of picpoul, squeeze onto a bench by
the water and enjoy a free concert in the port.

**Fête des Vacanciers**                            *late July or early August*
Tourists honoured with a best-of selection of local treats served in
Marseillan Plage. An art market, live bands and a late night ball and
fireworks, with evening jousting on the Canal de Pisse-Saumes.

**Fête de Marseillan Plage**                                  *early August*
Boat trips, Evening jousting on the canal, fireworks on the beach and
dancing in the streets.

**Les Quais de l'Art**                                        *early August*
For one night only, local artists set up easels and brushes in front of
restaurant terraces the length of quai de la Résistance   to show and sell
their canvases from 18h-midnight. Another version held at Marseillan Plage.

**Fête de Marseillan**                                  *week of 16 August*
Over five days, Marseillan parties. A ball or disco held night by either place
church, Marianne or Pradet. One evening sees fireworks in the port. The
main *Capelet* tournament (*see page 81*) is on the 16th, with the fittest young
men of the village taking to the pole at 17h for the annual trophy and title.
Teenage lads have a go at 15h. Pre-games events as on 14 July.

**Brescoudos bike week**                           *first week in September*
Officially at Cap d'Agde, but spilling over through the region, the biggest
gathering of Harley Davidsons and Goldwing bikes take over the region. On
Sunday, bikers drive from the Cap to Sète and it can take two hours to pass
through Marseillan Plage. www.brescoudos.com

**Journée des Associations**                 *2$^{nd}$ Saturday in September*
To mark the rentrée, scores of clubs, teams and societies set out their stalls
throughout the centre of the village in a bid for new blood. Be it genealogy,
sport, the arts or something more political, this is essentially a freshers' fair
for the *nouveau Marseillanais* or the freshly retired.

**Journées de la Patrimoine**                      *3rd weekend in September*
For two days each year, private and public buildings open their doors to the public for a rare chance to explore hidden treasures. In Marseillan, Heritage weekend could mean the old château in the village; further afield, discover palaces and chateaux. Details from the Mairie.

**Fête des Vendanges**                             *mid September*
Harvest festival on the port in front of the co-op. Grape sorting on long tables, convivial sipping and often some music too,

**Fête du Vin primeur** *see page 127.*            *mid October*

**Halloween**                                      *31 October*
Threatening to usurp the local tradition of 1 November and the sanctity of All Saints Day, when locals take chrysanthemums to the cemetery, Halloween now brings the inevitable costume party for village children.

**Armistice Day 1918** *see page 93*               *11 November*

**Marché de Noël**                                 *mid to late December*
The incongruity of alpine chalets on the Med for the evening gift market is now as normal a part of advent a la Marseillanais as the steam locomotive parked outside the Mairie. Garlands of lights link port to village, but star attraction is the nativity scene under the covered market. A crèche with live animals in the stable alongside the Holy Family. Baby lambs and donkeys nibble and nuzzle at visitors; partridges strut and chickens cluck around the Magi and Languedoc characters, *chasseurs, forgerons* and *vignerons*. Carols and contemporary concerts in church. Midnight Mass on the 24th.

**Reveillon Saint Sylvestre**                      *31 December*
New Year's Eve is the big bash. Sometimes celebrated with fireworks in the port. Always feted with a huge banquet. Restaurants have special menus and sell out early (usually priced €50-75). The town holds a grand banquet and ball at the Salle Paul Arnaud **[1] B2** with a top dance band. Advance tickets sold at the Boulevard café. Cap d'Agde and resorts run glitzy Vegas-style binges with male and female strippers. *Chacun son gout.*

Not forgetting ...

Les Floralies – when the town becomes a flower and plant market
Marseillankordeon – international music legends theatre & port - *page 370*
Fête St Jean – grand paella party on the Pradet
Convivencia – salsa party as the music barge moors in the port
Jazzinade – three superb soirees at the theatre *see page 370*

# La Belle Scribote

IL ETAIT UNE FOIS A MARSEILLAN, once upon a time, so the story begins and the *Marseillanais* retell their romantic saga of innocence lost and regained, of Barbary pirates, escape from a harem and of swashbuckling derring do. As Robin Hood is to Sherwood, the legend of *La Belle Scribote* is the stuff of Marseillan myth.

For four summers, this tale, hitherto traded round table or hearth, was shared with a wider audience in lavish *son et lumière* when, throughout the Williams Merric mayoralty, the story became a Broadway-style musical with a massive cast and special effects of almost Victorian excess.

The show involved some 150 villagers, with soloists, stunt horsemen and a camel. A tall grandstand of 1000 seats was set up in the Port Tabarka, the whole area covered with sand; modern fibre-glass motor-boats removed for the duration; in their stead, an extravagant set showing the port as in centuries past, a Spanish harem, and *Jusqu'au Bout* playing the role of pirate ship.

For a fortnight each summer, the quarter echoed to sounds of dress and technical rehearsals and a week of nightly performances as the sun set over the étang around 10pm and the first song began with twilight masquerading as dawn, when young girls heralded sunrise over the Mont Saint Clair. Music was in the French summer pageant tradition, like every Eurovision number you thought you'd forgotten, and once the finale was sung, bunting trailing around the port, fireworks and lasers illuminating the sky and the inevitable long and passionate speeches for the benefit of VIP politicos in the best seats, around 1200 spectators would skip through the barriers back to the main port and their cars. For me, the show was heralded by the return of Rita the camel, who passed time waiting for her cue, nibbling rosemary from our first floor terrace and confusing the dog. Her final visit was in 2008, when the show played its valedictory season before Tabarka was renovated and remodelled. There is talk of a revival one day, and certainly much of the set still exists – since the mocked-up well from the quayside scene sees service in December's nativity *crèche*. Meanwhile, the musical is digitally preserved for new audiences on DVD, available from the tourist office.

Without the benefit of amplification and well-primed chorus, it is left to villagers to tell their favourite tale in prose, and anyone in Marseillan could regale you with the yarn for little more than a *verre de Ricard* and a *pichet* of iced water. If some of the more academic-minded elders quibble at the provenance of the story, they'd never dare voice their doubts in public. *Scribote* belongs to the port of Marseillan as the Mermaid to Copenhagen.

Are you sitting comfortably? Then gather round and fill your glass: Marie was known to her friends, family and neighbours as Scribote. Abducted by Barbary pirates she was sold into slavery and the harem of the Caliph of Grenada. Jean Mas, her fisherman fiancé, determined to save her and the good Christian, gathered a band of sympathetic Muslim soldiers to find and rescue the lass. Among the Islamic adventurers was a Hali, a fearless fellow who saved Jean's life in many swashbuckling battles that ensued. Eventually, our heroes arrived at the Caliph's palace and, disguised as artists, offered their paintings to the women of the Harem. Marie recognised Jean's signature and the lovers plotted their escape. Jean smuggled in a spare smock and false beard, so Marie could flee dressed as a man. The couple sailed back to Marseillan in Hali's boat to return Marie to her family, then the two young men went off to slaughter the pirates, returning to a heroes welcome and double wedding, as Hali married Jean's sister, the "infidel" now a respected citizen of Marseillan. Time has spiced the legend with many variations: prayer and miracles, signs and wonders, feature in several versions, but the message of welcome and co-operation with outsiders is a feature of Marseillan's melting pot spirit to this day.

# The Miller's Tale

The other story-telling tradition of Marseillan is that of *Maitre Pierre et la Danse au Soufflets*, the tale of the Miller and the bellows dance: a tradition still enacted each spring to this day. Game and story date back to the days of the salt taxes. The *salins* around the étang were essential to the local economy, in both salting fish for export and lining the coffers of the tax man, since salt was subject to duty much as alcohol is today. 17th century customs men, convinced wily locals were smuggling salt, would stop and search dodgy characters. They were especially suspicious of Maitre Pierre the miller, grinding flour at the old mill behind the village (around today's avenues Chassefière and Victor Hugo), since moving so many bags around village and port would have been the perfect smugglers' ploy. But when Pierre was forced to open his sack, the wind rose up and the duty man was covered, not in illicit salt but fresh milled flour. Since then, Lent has been celebrated with a street party, one villager dressed as Maitre Pierre, with a handful of flour to throw in the breeze. This evolved into a slapstick tradition sprinkling water and flour on all and sundry. The miller's robe segued into a fantasy costume blending Napoleonic headgear with a harlequin suit! Over the years, participants used bellows and agricultural to ensure everyone got a good soaking or sprinkling. Briefly ditched in favour of an egg and flour throwing free for all, with shells crunched underfoot and a horrible mess everywhere, the Miller's dance and parade is now firmly re-established on the calendar. Maitre Pierre usually launches the *Fête du Printemps* sometime before Easter weekend.

Easter Sunday, the town takes to the streets once more for a grand procession of carnival floats, giant *paper-mâché* heads and tableaux, majorettes and marching bands, Rio-style showgirl costumes and a chariot carrying Miss Marseillan and her court. A ball or disco is held that evening.

Ay perdut ma Mestresso
    Mourriday de chagrin
        L'aymabé, é mé l'oon préso
            Lous Morous Sarrasins


To die of grief shall be my end
    I lost my fiancée
        I loved her ere the Saracen
            The Moor stole her away


- Complainte de La Belle Scribote (traditional)

# Lest we forget

THE BITISH TABLOIDS and one or two broadsheets might not mention the fact, since it could seriously dent a culture of xenophobia so essential when declaring war or facing an election, but 8 May is Liberation Day 1945, marked by the French with the same reverence that they and the rest of us also give to 11 November 1918.

In every town and village, shops and offices close so all may pay tribute to the heroes of WWII. This particular year, I made my way to the Mairie and at 10.50, mayor and town band marched in procession, followed by old soldiers bearing standards and wearing medals. Most remembrance seasons see the cortege wending its way to the memorial in the hilltop cemetery *(see pages 27-28)*. On this day, we walked to the monument on the Allées Roques. As we passed the retirement home, veterans and nurses nodded from the windows. On 19 March, victims of conflicts in Algeria Tunisia and Morocco take a similar path to gather by their new memorial at the end of the av Victor Hugo, by the route d'Agde roundabout.

Today's cenotaph is at the back of a leafy shady dusty park. The **Allées du Général Rocques**, where a game or two of *boules* is played ere sundown on a summer's evening, and the occasional llama tethered to a tree when the circus comes to town. A bust of the eponymous General graces the stately entrance to the allées, Marseillan has great respect for its heroes. Yet the town's emotional response to the reality of war stands in reserve back from the main road. Especially poignant, the statue depicts not military men of action but three war orphans, babe, toddler daughter and sailor-suited son, heads bowed in memory of a lost father. Veterans stood in two rows, flags held high, and three village policemen saluted. At two minutes to eleven we heard the Last Post. A minute's silence, broken, of course, by the *Marseillaise*. Old soldiers spoke of their gratitude to the allies from the US, Britain and the Commonwealth, and talked of the Résistance movement, first convened nearby in 1943. In Marseillan, that silence had also been tribute to the local men and women of the underground lined up and shot against the walls of so many parks just like this one. Each year, on this day and again on the *Journée de la Résistance* on 27 May, Marseillan recalls yet

*Marseillan's children mourn their lost heroes. The War Memorial on the Allées Rocques*

another local hero, perhaps naming a street, or maybe honouring a brave survivor. We salute Jean Moulin, brave man of Béziers remembered in every city in the land (*see page 174*); Joseph Guillaut, for whom the church square was renamed (*see page 39*). The mayor read a poignant speech by the Defence Minister, then, in his own words, spoke of European Ideals, human rights and the anniversary of reconciliation with Germany. Knowing that all across France men women and children would be paying respects to the heroes and victims of the past, valuing each sacrifice and mourning each tragedy, honouring the selfless actions of war and cherishing the true sanctity of peace, all the while the jeering voices of modern politicians and their acolytes chant jingoist slogans, hurling taunts across borders whilst ignoring the date on the calendar, I contemplated the fragility of truth. I receive many poison emails demanding a boycot of things French and weaving a myth of ingratitude to the Liberators of D-Day. Yet, on the soil that swallowed the blood of bigotry, the truth is spoken thrice yearly.

After the short but poignant ceremony we crossed to the Salle Arnaud village hall. Suddenly aware that holiday teeshirt and scruffy joggers though perfectly acceptable for the streets, might seem disrespectful in the hall, I waited outside. In the hall, tables were set with cutlery, wine, water: Marseillan puts some money aside each year so that those who come to remember in the traditional manner should dine and toast those who fell for *La Patrie*. Some come to raise a glass to those they had loved; for the rest of us, time to honour the men and women most, we never knew, and to whom Marseillan owes so much.

94

# Enjoying wine
# in Marseillan

WHATEVER YOU POUR into your glass in Marseillan, your first drink should be a toast to the wind. The very *Mistral* and *Tramontane* that plays havoc with your hair when you hurry to a noonday *rendezvous*, and that *Marin* and its allied saharan and greek gusts that season your lips when clouds play above the *étang*; all the winds of the Languedoc that tease mere mortals are fiercely protective of the dozen or so *cépages* of our endless vineyards lining our paths and *chemins* from the *Via Dometia* to the *autoroute,* the new-build *lotissements* to the marshlands behind the dunes.

These winds play their part in the alchemy of a unique microclimate that has nurtured the grape since first century Roman occupiers planted their vines by the Etang de Thau. Stony clay and lime soil works on the roots whilst 300 days of sunshine tend the fruit. Skittish yet insistent breezes keep disease at bay and cool vines during summer's hottest days. Accordingly, the wines of Languedoc would always grow without too much encouragement or nurturing. In their earliest centuries, quantity rather eclipsed quality as grapes simply happened and wine merely ensued. By the industrial revolution, whilst Marseillan's whites and *rosés* were being shipped off to cool the French colonies, the bulk of Languedoc's *gros rouge* plonk, cheap, rough and plentiful, was used to refuel factory workers. Whilst many wines over the centuries might have occurred rather than been cultivated, there has always been a hard core of aficionados to care about the finished product. By the 3<sup>rd</sup> century AD, the astute emperor Probus laid down a set of rules and production quotas for quality control in his Languedoc vineyards. Visit the roman villa in **Loupian** for a *clin d'oeuil* at the lifestyle and taste of an estate manager of the period. The region's turbulent political history played its part in disrupting the winegrower's routine, ravages of war and political decrees demanding that land be given over to food crops. However, since the Revolution, the fields of Marseillan flourished – convenience of a port for trade and invention of fortified wines for export advancing the local economy.

Then came the notorious blight of 1877: the 19th century *phylloxera* epidemic, when an all-destroying beetle wiped out much of France's winestock, did not spare the region, and the aftermath, grafting of hardier American stock to rebuild the vineyards, created a leaner, more business-conscious, industry. Many "lost" *cépages* were registered and saved at the national archive of the vine, **Domaine de Vassal** in Marseillan Plage (*see page 104*). In recent years, thanks to researchers at Vassal and a new generation of oenologists from some of Marseillan's oldest *vigneronne* families, some forgotten varieties and brand new parvenu hybrids, such as our home-bred Marselan, have joined immigrant Chardonnays from Burgundy and Viogniers of the Rhône.

But blight was not the only bump in the road to modern winemaking: Echoing to cries of *"Vignerons en colère"*, 1907 was the year of the winemakers revolt.

Since *phylloxera*, cheap imports of African wines had decimated the local market. At the same time, inferior wines were boosted with added sugar, as a cheap alternative to the real thing. Once government slashed duty on sugars, this all but crippled the revival of true winegrowing. Faced with ruin, the *vignerons*, led by café-owner Marcelin Albert, Robin Hood of the wine trade, took to the streets of Narbonne and Béziers. This local protest evolved from violent scuffles claiming at least six lives, to religious and political upheaval and almost brought down the government. The uprising led, a decade later, to the creation of France's world renowned *Appellation d'Origine Contrôlée* system.

When next you visit Narbonne, pause by the cathedral to read a memorial plaque to the victims of the violence that ensued when a regiment of the French army broke away and joined the protesting wine growers. It is said that a thousand Marseillanais, more than one-fifth of the local population, joined rallies in Béziers. Even after the dispute was resolved, feelings ran high, and local benefactress Pauline Buisson left the town 50,000 francs in order that the elderly might live together in harmony – you'll see her name immortalised on street signs as you drive into the village from the vineyard-lined route de Mèze.

On the centenary of the insurrection, minor outbreaks of civic disobedience erupted in town squares and railway lines across France *grace au Comité Régional d'Action Viticole*, whilst, in Marseillan, the story of the *evenements* of 1907 was retold in a charming musical at the theatre. Nonetheless, whilst the village's wine community embraces the present and the future with confidence, you may yet hear echoes of the spirit of Marcelin Albert in voices making speeches at wine festivals here and in towns and villages close by. Vineyards gracing all roads into Marseillan once reached the very edges of the boulevards of the village. In living memory, fields of ripening vines bordered the port itself, where now lies car park tarmac by the shops and post office at place du Théâtre. Planting may have been nudged back as the village expands, but it remains the foreground to every landed horizon. And every parcel of land tells a story. *Domaine de la Barronne*, oldest and one of the largest wine estates in Marseillan dates back to 1583 and stands by the *Pont du Maire* on the road down to Marseillan Plage. Marked out by its age-old trees along the driveway, the *domaine* is home to the oldest tree in Marseillan, the only cedar to have survived the German occupation of World War II.

Winemaking dictated the architecture of the village. *Maisons vigneronnes* are the definitive houses of Marseillan. The ground floor, with basalt framed garage doorways, once given over to cottage industry winemaking. Huge vats often incorporated into the very fabric of the building, and the vast space might be home to tractors and presses, barrels and bottles. A few producers still macerate, ferment, store and sell their wines at street level. Others may use the space to store tractors, even harvesting machines, but trundle their *grappes* in trailers along the lanes between the vineyards and along the boulevards Lamartine and Pasteur in late summer to contribute to the co-operative winery behind the quai de la Résistance.

Back in the 1930s, when scores of independent winegrowers united to form the first co-operative, even the smallest family business suddenly won equal access to the most modern machinery and methods of wine productions. According to shrewd local historian and commentator Albert Arnaud, the *vignerons* of Marseillan soon began to consider themselves as *viticulteurs*. With the opening of an impressive winery by the quayside, hard by the *chais* of *Noilly Prat*, on the very land once governed by the influential wine merchant Jean Voisin, so the quality of *les vins blancs et rosés de Marseillan* began to blossom. So much so that in 1937 wine from rue de Progrès was chosen to toast the launch of the Paris International Exhibition. In recent decades, the co-op has expanded and embraced into the fold fellow *vignerons* of Agde. From April until September, you may take a 2-3 hour walk through the vines, in the company of a *Marseillanais* or *Agathois viticulteur*. These *Ballades Vigneronnes* blend anecdote, sipping and plenty of fresh air and exercise – pretty much the perfect lifestyle. *See page 51*

The village finally has its *fêtes de vendange* and *vins primeurs*. In the past, other towns celebrated their harvest and bottling with greater fervour than Marseillan. But in very recent years, the bringing in of the grapes has been feted with picking and sorting on the quaysides, and the launch of the *vin nouveau* heralded with fanfare and feasting by the co-op (*see page 127*) . The second festival, in 2009, saw the announcement that the Terret grape, first variety to arrive at the co-operative at the start of the *vendange*, had finally emerged from the shadow of its better known neighbour *Picpoul*. The village thrilled to the news that the *Henri de Richemer Terret* had become the first wine from a humble co-operative to be recommended by the prestigious *Guide Hachette* wine bible.

Wine remains the very lifeblood of Marseillan and so many villages around the region. There is an indelible purple stain to the fingers and a 13.5° proof passion in the soul of the people. Artist Chabrol captured this in tableaux of the *vigneron's* life, rich colours of the wine and the heady *part des anges* scent of evaporation in the air reflected in his work.

And to take wine with the winemakers of Marseillan is truly to enter the village and its life.

# Cave Cooperative

**Henri de Richemer**
*Marseillan Ville*: 5 quai de la Résistance; 1 rue du Progrès [2] **B2**
*Marseillan Plage*: Route de Sète [4] **A2**
*Agde*: 2 boulevard du Soleil, 34300 Agde [5] **C2**
04 67 77 20 16 www.richemer.fr
At the smart modern visitor centre, new art gallery and shop right on the quayside of Marseillan, walk between vast vats towards the tasting room and discover what happens to the vast majority of the grapes that define the landscape of the Etang de Thau and its back-country. Around 450 wine makers from Marseillan and Agde, farming around 1500 hectares of vines around the etang, form the co-op named after merchant Henri Richet, who

sent the wines of Marseillan out to lands beyond the seas – thus the label **Henri de Richemer**. The cooperative in the port was founded in 1935, and Agde joined the label in 1998. Each year, combined yield of two towns produces a staggering 300,000 bottles of *Vin de Pays des Cotes de Thau, Vins de Pays de l'Hérault* and *Vin de Pays d'Oc*.

White wines account for around 80% of wine sold in Marseillan, but you'll find an impressive choice of reds and rosés as well. Whilst standard selections may be carried home in wine boxes or pumped into your own canisters in the time-honoured fashion, sheer diversity of bottled wine on sale in the modern showroom is a world away from the conventional image of the simple local co-op. As well as a dozen single variety options under the **Henri de Richemer** name, and an **Hippocampe** selection of blended wines, new labels for emerging markets can be discovered. **Terre et Mer**, launched in 2009, is a commercial branding of a newly fashionable *cépage*, under the slogan *"Vin de Terret, vin de la mer"*.

With shrewd awareness of the modern demand for a lighter wine (Languedoc wines are notoriously potent with 13.5° very much the norm). Since Béziers launched its *vin plume* for the lunching market during the *Feria* of 2006 (see page 108), Marseillan has worked on developing its own range. In 2010, the co-op unveiled three new wines under the title **Léger 11°**. The red is 100% Syrah, recommended for pizzas; a white, suggested for fish and seafood, blends Terret with Loire-like light touch of Sauvignan and Grenache and Cinsault combine in a peachy *rosé*, offered as an accompaniment to sushi – but equally ideal for people watching. At a more traditional strength, the **Tempête de Saveurs** label promises a blend of the fruits of veteran vines, matured in oak barrels. And there are now four sparkling wines: two whites and two *rosés*.

Regular art exhibitions are held in *caveaux* and shops, the quai de la Résistance entrance is backdrop to the annual wine festival in October as well as live jazz during the port's *Fête de la Musique* celebration in June. Marseillan Ville and Agde addresses are the alternating starting points of the regular *Ballades Vigneronnes* guided vineyard tours (*see page 51*). Facelifts for salerooms reflect changes within the business of promoting wines: An R&D lab to research new techniques, a profile-raising team with an eye on international operations, and a keen awareness of logos (seahorse and seashell images on the Richemer coat of arms given corporate oomph in publicity material): all very 21st century. But follow the Hansel and Gretel trail of dropped grapes during the first week in September and find yourself at the back of the co-op where the farmers drive through gates to a building easily recogniseable from pre-war photos; look at men riding tractors over the weighbridge, weather-worn faces leading rickety trucks, juice stained fingers reaching for a pack of cigarettes from a darned top pocket; and you know that whatever the marketing men are planning for tomorrow, *le terroir Marseillanais* is still in safe hands.


## Independent Winemakers in Marseillan


**Domaine Carayon**
place de la République [1] **B2**
04 67 77 26 68
Open Wed, Thu, Sat mornings only
If you've never tried feel-good factor 50, then you need to sit on a Marseillan terrace in early summer, at your side a glass topped up with chilled rosé and glistening with condensation, a bowl on your lap and a bag of freshly picked peas ready to shell . As you flick the petits pois from the pod with your thumb, sneaking an irresistible taste of the improbably sweet vegetables twixt sips of the local wine, there is very little that ready cash could buy to rival the moment. Pleasure comes from a one-stop shop on the place de la République, formerly thriving heart of Marseillan's wine trade. Just across the way from where Baudassé wine merchants once dominated the tiny square on the site of today's *Credit Agricole* bank, **Domaine Carayon** trades in more than their reds, whites and rosés when garage doors open for business, at the cave next to the Marie's *Grille*. Once they traded in Picardan, unseasoned yet ripened vermouth wine from Noilly, the secret of many a village family recipe, Now, alongside *picpoul* and *merlot*, which locals buy *en vrac* and visitors take home in smartly labelled bottles, are shelves stocked with farm honeys and local olive oils, and there are always crates of fresh picking from the market garden. Sweet melons and soft fruit in high season, strawberries in late spring, and, if you are very lucky, piles of garden-fresh petits pois, ripe for the shelling.


**Domaine des Charmettes**
route de Florensac
04 67 77 66 16 www.domainelescharmettes.com
Wine writers began talking about the **Domaine des Charmettes** in the early years of the new century, as *La Magdelaine* wines commenced tickling the

national nose and pleasing the critical palate. *Le Figaro* waxed lyrical on subtle blending of Languedoc stalwart *cépages* such as Grenache and Terret with the robust incomer Viognier to bring out the best of rich clay soil on slopes behind Marseillan. And *Guide Hachette* added its own murmur of approval. The Alcon family have worked the fields along the Florensac road since just after the last War, but it was not until the late 1980s that the family left the village co-operative to strike out on their own. Press acclaim was recognition for the work of the newest scions of the family, Eric and Nicolas, who, whilst respecting the back-breaking hard work of their grandparents, have studied the science of oenology and technology of modern production to create wines for the contemporary market. I've enjoyed both complex and teasing summer rosés and whites, including a smashing little belter of a *Grenache*. Tasting visits by appointment at cellars just by the "other" water tower on the road from Marseillan to Florensac.

**Domaine La Fadèze**
route de Mèze
04 67 77 26 42 www.lafadeze-vinsdulanguedoc.com
Closed Sun
Walking off a particularly long and hearty lunch, and keeping as close as possible to the lagoon, a stroll past the oyster sheds eventually leads you the well maintained courtyard of **La Fadèze**. Motorists get there quicker, the long way round by the Mèze road and turning off down a narrow vine-lined track. The *domaine* was originally called *"La Fadaise"*, colloquialism for a crazy novelty or bauble. However, when Georges and Guy Lentheric purchased the estate in the 1970s, they determined to take a serious attitude to business. And now three generations work the land, using modern techniques, with an eye on eco-friendly production. Grass strips between every four rows of vines filter pesticides and aid irrigation. Specialising in single *cépage* wines, fashionable with modern drinkers, the estate yields almost a dozen varieties from the commercial Chardonnay and Merlot to more traditional local Terret and Carignan. Good marketing sees Fadèze on many a wine list. Tours of the winery should be booked in advance.

**Domaine des Laux**
route de Marseillan, 34810 Pomérols
06 11 32 77 15 (phone in advance) www.domainedeslaux.com
If you have a birthday, wedding or celebration in the offing, then you might like to know that this Domaine will personalise wine labels for you, should you buy 24 bottles or more. The Laux family might have an almost biblical

tradition for punsters, turning Laux into *le vin*. No matter the *cépages* in their vats, they have a long association with the water: Dad, Jean-Louis, is a veteran water polo judge; daughter Caroline, a celebrated diver, whose young daughter is already no stranger to swimming; and sons Cyriac and Geoffrey are major figures in French water polo. Cyriac is a former international and Geoffrey has trained since the age of 8 and has represented France in European championships since he was 17. Currently, at the peak of his game, he still lends a hand with the family wine business. For years the family had sold the estate's full range both in bottles and wineboxes, including a popular, full and fruity rosé, from syrah grapes, and a picpoul. from a shop counter in the village, but in 2010 the domaine moved out of the rambling maison vigneronne that has been home and cellar to set up a new site on the road between Marseillan and Pomérols . Find the Domaine's stand in Sète's market hall (mornings except Mon and Thu). The old cave in Marseillan is now the sports bar *Le National.*

**La Madeleine Saint Jean**
Rue du 19 mars 1962 **[2] B2**
04 67 26 12 42 http://lamadeleinesaintjean.free.fr
At the **Madeleine Saint Jean** lessons of wine-making go far beyond the barrel and the bottle. The Banq family know a thing of two about growing wine, and just as they marry complex grape varieties to create their hearty reds and surprising whites, they have taken the best of each generation to create a modern winery with an eye alert to modern tastes and methods and a heart imbued with tradition. So when the younger generation studied the future and the world away from the village, the parents brought to them the wisdom of the past. The result, an evolving selection of wines that have seen several forgotten grape varieties, all but lost since the vine blights of the 19th century, and modern *cépages*, interwoven with old faithfuls we know and expect. Thus Cab-Savs and Syrahs of red wines, with regional stalwart *grenache*, share honours with such *arrivistes* as Arinarnoa, Egiodola and our very own Marselan – the only grape in France named for its birthplace. *Marselan* blent with Merlot for a popular red, and the widely appreciated **Cuvée du Père Joseph** uses this local variety to enhance Syrah and Grenache. Whitewise, a Viognier offers a robust riposte to the Languedoc summer, tangy and ripe in its own right, but tempered with Chardonnay and Sauvignon for **Cuvée La Maison Blanche** as alternative to ubiquitous Picpoul accompaniment to seafood harvested along the oyster road. Unusually, these cellars in the quiet port Tabarka also yield a *vendange tardive* from Viognier and Muscat grapes recommended for *foie gras* and as a special dessert wine.

**Vignobles Montfreux de Fages**
Domaine Haut de Bel Air, Route de Mèze
04 67 77 59 17 www.montfreux-de-fages.com
It was the hoopoes that first drew me to the vineyard behind the *Château de Bel Air* one Sunday afternoon, soon after I first came to Marseillan. Seeing the distinctive plumage of these and other birds among the vines brought the realisation that somebody was producing organic wines on the edge of the village. The somebodies in question were Guy Rambier, 5th generation vigneron, and industrialist and winelover Jacques Tournant. The men found a shared passion for nature an interest in organic farming. Away from Marseillan, they grow vines at the **Château Fon des Prieurs**, and here, besides the étang, they produce their Picpoul de Pinet.


**Domaine Morin-Langaran**
route de Marseillan, 34140 Meze
04 67 43 71 76
Summer 10-19; Winter 10-18. Closed Sun (Jan-Feb)
Technically not Marseillan: but just across the invisible boundary where wide open spaces of our own vineyards meet those of the commune of Meze. This is where we and other loyal customers spent that memorable Whit Sunday afternoon at the *brasucade* (*see page 336*). The domaine is a great detour for stocking up on last-minute foodie presents on the drive back to the airport. The estate is part of the *Bienvenue a la Ferme* project of farm shops and offers visitors guided visits of the production process of the domaine's wines. You may also loiter amongst delightful displays of locally produced tapenades, honeys, olive oils and jams to take home. A keen eye for passing trade means that there is ample parking for coaches as well as cars. Dogs are welcome and the place is wheelchair accessible. The Morin family's imposing farmhouse dates back to the 1930s but has the air of a grand French country house. The good range of wines on offer includes an innevitable choice of Picpouls, subtle differences for varying tastes.


**Domaine Les Prouilles**
1 rue de la Plage / 12 bd Pasteur [1] **C3**
06 62 22 57 31
www.lesprouilhes.fr
In the kingdom of the Picpoul, you knock on this door for a Chardonnay: A Chardonnay that some critics have suggested could hold its head high in Burgundy; a Chardonnay nurtured by the wetlands where the herons and flamingos fly. From the slopes between Marseillan and Agde, the closely

pruned vines are stung along wires, like espaliered fruit trees, the better to succumb to the sun and the winds. Georges and Marc Rouvière, whose family have grown wines in Marseillan since the aftermath of the phylloxera *affaire,* tend the vineyard on land granted by a roman emperor as pension to a worthy soldier. Taste the wine *en ville,* at restaurants or by visiting the cellars.

# A living archive

**Domaine de Vassal**
Centre de Resources Genetique de la Vigne
Route de Sète
04 67 21 91 81
www1.montpellier.inra.fr/vassal/index.html
Just as the ravages of phylloxera beetle began to rage through the vasty fields of France, so in 1876 did the Agricultural faculty of Montpellier University begin an ambitious project to salvage every variety of vine and create a unique archive for future generations. With the help of botanical gardens around the country and Paris' Natural History museum, work began and by 1949 the collection moved to its home in Marseillan Plage. The *Unité Expérimentale du Domaine de Vassal* is home to some 7000 examples of every known grape variety from France and some 40 other countries. Since the blight all-but obliterated many native species dating back to the romans and greeks, the Domaine hosts the very last seeds of wines not tasted for centuries. The site was chosen as soil contains less than 1% clay and is immune to parasites; thus original vines may be safely planted without being grafted onto foreign stock. A seedbank, 400 square metres of greenhouses and some 19 hectares of cultivated vineyards on the sandy spit between the Mediterranean and the étang create a unique environment where researchers cultivate forgotten cépages, experiment with creating brand new wine varieties to meet contemporary tastes and climatic conditions, and from where, from time to time, vines of yesterday might be reintroduced into the mainstream to contribute to the wines of tomorrow. Online resources are used by students of wine across the globe. Archive and library open by appointment only to outside researchers. Very occasional group visits to the estate are permitted.

# Detours and wine-tasting around the region

HIT THE ROAD, JACQUES, for there is little to compare with discovering a wine by the wayside. The map of France is threaded with *routes des vins*, from the Burgundy's Côtes de Beaune, where street signs read like a Mayfair sommelier's wishlist, to unmarked rural backwaters where getting lost is but prelude to bacchanalia. When driving down to Marseillan, or returning to ferry ports, with time on your hands enough to forgo the autoroute fast track, you may meander merrily through wine lands of Loire and Champagne, explore Côte du Rhône and Beaujolais, or bide a while at vineyards Bordelaises or Burgundian, depending on whether your whim is for the heavyweight gastronomy of Lyon on the western route, or the infinite variety of a digression through the patchwork *paysage* of the *cassoulet* and the sander.

Your way will be directed by officially sanctioned maps, perhaps well appointed signage, or by simply chalked notices advertising "*cave*", "*caveau*" or "*degustation*" – the last word once being delightfully mistranslated by the immaculately coiffured wife of a well-to-do landowner on the Côtes de Nuit, with the *maquillage* of a well-preserved seventies starlet who invited me to "be disgusting in my 'usband's cellar".

Other vignerons will share their particular philosophies and lore with you. In our own region, some may speak of the pull of the moon, others of conspiracy theories; in **Montpeyroux**, you might come upon a winemaker who declines to take a glass of his own wine with you, preferring to sip water – his explanation: a doctor once told him that the human liver takes three months to repair itself from serious damage, thus he drinks immoderately for nine months of the year, followed by the minimum required period of abstinence. Elsewhere, you could encounter a grower whose labels are symbols of family loss or great love, or another who hides coded anarchist acrostics in the descriptions of each *cépage*, perhaps even a poet elegising each new vintage.

Around the country, some detours have been commercialised. A few even feature special attractions to lure in more than hard core wine-lovers. In Bordeaux, *Château Pape Clément* offers a replica papal tomb to keep the family amused and in Reims, *Piper Heidsieck* has an out-and-out theme park ride with cars disguised as champagne corks whizzing through tableaux of Hollywood movie classics, a souvenir replica of the very ice bucket that Marilyn Monroe kept by her bed during her final illness and a gallery of celebrity Oscar-night photos in the tasting room.

Nonetheless, most *vignerons* leave entertainment duties to their wines, and it is only by visiting the fields where vines are grown and the cellars where they are made that the visitor will ever truly understand the peculiarly French concept of *terroir*. More than merely chemical composition of soil and meteorological facts of weather and climate, *terroir* is a wine's upbringing, both nature and nurture. You may be introduced to wine in the formal setting of a shop or a restaurant, but it is only by going to its home and meeting the family that you will ever get truly to know and understand what makes it tick.

Do not wait until your return travel plans are primed to be pumped from the inkjet to take in the designated wine destinations of France. When you are out and about, exploring countryside beyond Marseillan; whether nipping out to Montpellier or Béziers or a long run down to Perpignan or the *étangs* beyond Narbonne, take time to get to know more about that fabulous red you enjoyed in the port last night, or to get to know the individual characters behind such generic terms as Saint Chinian, Corbières or Faugères. See page 114. Map 5 at the end of this book hints at the wine areas.

A few likely diversions during your travels in Languedoc – this is no definitive list, merely a casual selection of possible pauses as you take to the road at a leisurely pace. Most *caveaux* are open for tasting and visits from mid morning until 12 noon and from mid afternoon until around 6pm, although some will close earlier and others remain open later. Since the working life of the vineyard takes priority over the conviviality of the tasting room, do telephone before making a special journey.

## Hérault

### Abbaye de Valmagne
34560 Villeveyrac [5] C2
04 67 78 06 09 www.valmagne.com
Valmagne is one of the area's must-sees. Best enjoyed during concert season, but always worth a visit for a swilling, sniffing and spending session. If your child is just starting secondary school, you could spend around €12 now on a bottle to open when the A-level results come through.

*Cuvée de Turenne*, named after the snappily monickered count Henri-Amédée-Mercure de Turenne who bought Valmagne abbey and estate in 1828. The new appellation *Gres de Montpellier* is worth laying down for a good 5 years or more, throaty Syrah and Mourvèdre blends ripen into a rich evocation of *fumoirs*, chesterfields and vintage bookbinding. For more immediate drinking pick up the *vin de pays Nonenque*, a whoosh of Viognier goes down a treat when you've a seabass or bream on the barebecue. It is named after Frère Nonenque, 16th century cellarman when the wines were produced by monks at Valgmagne. *See page 194.*

### Domaine de la Grangette
34120 Castelnau de Guers [5] C2
0 4 67 98 13 56 www.domainelagrangette.com
Closed Sun
We came for the art, but we left with a secret wine that we never knew existed. Domaine La Grangette, on the road from Polerols to Castelnau, is named for its historical role as the stables of Baron de Guers. Yet, despite having to produce fodder for the Baron's horses during the Middle Ages, the land has always managed to produce some excellent grapes. We'd been invited to the *vernissage* (private view) of an exhibition by Malcolm "Mac" Macdonald, a talented British-born artist based up the road in Pomérols. Once we'd tasted the provocatively named wines, we knew that we'd need to make space in the boot of the car.

The *Part des Anges* is a fabulous Syrah-Grenache that tastes almost mulled so winter-nutmeg and clove-like is the first whiff from the rim of the wineglass and the flavour clings to the the roof of the mouth until well-passed sipping time. And *l'Enfant Terrible* is actually an Enfant Cordiale, nicely balanced Picpoul with just enough of a zesty aftertaste to perk you up without giving your eyelids whiplash. But the *Enfant's* secret cousin was the revelation. First time we'd tasted the Piquepoul Noir and it proves a stunning rose. The variety has all but disappeared from the region, and it is good to get the chance to experience it.

### Château de Montpezat
34120 Pézenas [5] C2
04 67 98 10 84 www.chateau-montpezat.com
Closed Sun
There are still plenty of long haul snobs out there who raise a supercilious eyebrow when you talk of Languedoc wines, but two words tend to reset their foreheads to default. The names Robert and Parker usually do the trick.

For more than a decade the doyen of American wine critics has been dusting off his most evocative adjectives when it comes to writing about the wines of this historic estate on the Roujan road east of Pézenas. Cellar visits recommended if you are looking for wines for laying down. You'll appreciate the expertise to help you decide which of the reds you should keep and which wines to serve next weekend. Since 2009, the estate has adopted organic techniques.


**Moulin de Lène**
route de Fouzilhon 34480 Magalas [5] **B2**
04 67 36 06 32 www.moulindelene.com
Closed Sat Sun
I can remember my first taste of the *Cuvée Justine*, slipped between the honey rich *pelardon* salad and a grilled seabass, the distillation of a local summer in a glass of Côtes de Thongue was a memory waiting to be minted. Marseillan's noonday heat outside the restaurant was cooled by the blend of Chardonnay and a dash of Muscat. At the caveau, north of Béziers, with its smart contempory tasting room hewn from the old stone, meet the wines on their home ground, by the ruins of an old roman aquaduct. The traditional *Justine* that I prefer is also joined by a *Grande Justine* – with a generous helping of that woody casky flavour so beloved of Chardonnay merchants. Some very contrasting styles in the rosé selection also. And some reds worth taking time out to explore.


**Domaine de La Colombette**
ancienne route de Bédarieux, 34500 Béziers [5] **B2**
04 67 31 05 53 www.lacolombette.fr
I am not sure what gave me greater pleasure: the HM Bateman expression of horror on the faces of some of my traditional Marseillanais neighbours when I tentatively suggested we try the *Vin Plume* from La Colombette, or the delightful surprise of the wine itself. The truth of the matter is that *Vin Plume* was an innovation waiting to happen, and Béziers is nothing if not the cradle of *carpe dium*. The keen eye on the future that nurtured Riquet's canal, and once snatched the railway and seat of commerce from Pezanas, had spotted that business lunchers were pouring more Badoit than Merlot in their glasses in order to keep a clear head in the modern world of trade. Thus father and son team François and Vincent Pugibet created a wine with reduced levels of alcohol (a mere 9 degrees in a region where wine strength is numbered in the teens), but retaining a full clutch of flavours. We tasted it over lunch during Béziers' Feria season, and loved the headache-free

afternoon it gave us. Most recently we dropped by the Domaine (the location defies sat-nav and signage is a tease) to buy wines for a family party and were stunned at how well the plume holds its own against the traditional versions of the same cépages. Pugibet *père* replied to our surprise at the flavours, suggesting alcohol may often mask true flavour in wine just as salt does to good ingredients in cooking, the reduction in potency often releases unexpected zings and sparkles even in such predictable varieties as Chardonnay. The family has grown wine here for generations, but it was François Pugibet who chucked out tired old vines, vats and techniques and reinvented his land, even daring to plant Chardonnay in Langudoc soil. By 1995 Colombette had won the *Gault Millau* trophy for the world's finest Chardonnay. Two years later, son Vincent, who had been away studying in Bordeaux, re-joined the family firm, with the drive that led to the light-touch innovation. There is more than a *pomme alummette* on the *épaule* of the patriarch when the subject of the wine and restaurant establishment falls into the conversation, frustration at the attitude to novelty within the world of terroir. But it must be satisfying to see each of Colombette's *"folies"* gradually becoming standard practice elsewhere. The bulk of production here is nonetheless focussed on the full strength class acts. Visit the estate today, and, alongside the restraint of the *Plume*, find some belting single variety classics in all three colours. The mainstay of many a classy wine list, try them in situ under the tutelage of the modern masters. And don't be surprised at the next innovation. At the time of writing the Pugibets were on the verge of creating a full bodied red with zero alcohol (*see page 168*).

### Château des Estanilles
Lenthéric, 34480 Cabrerolles [5] B2
04 67 90 29 25 www.chateau-estanilles.com
You'll need to draw lots and victimise a designated driver before hitting the Faugères road to this old favourite domaine. The estate may now have a new master in Julien Seydoux, but the famous reds and rosés developed by Michel Louison remain potent as ever. The classic *Rosé M* (named for the Mourvèdre grape) packs one hefty punch at 15% proof. The more delicate AOC rosé, labelled *Tradition*, favoured by many sommeliers, weighs in at a respectable 13.5 and is a judicious blending of the big M with Cinsault and Grenache. Bottled in Spring, this has a respectable shelf-life and will not have lost its berry balance by the time you toast the first mimosa of the following year. Time your visit right, for in vintage years the domaine produces a worthy winter drinker *Le Clos du Fou*, a red Faugères AOC Syrah that comes into its own the Christmas after next when truffles, goose or game are part of the festive board.

**Château de La Liquière**
La Liquière 34480 Cabrerolles [5] **B2**
04 67 90 29 20 www.chateaulaliquiere.com
Closed Sat, Sun
*Les Amandiers Rosé* is probably my favourite Languedoc lunchtime tipple –
a truly refreshing rush of creamy summer fruitiness that never overshadows
the plate. Full and gently teasing, the mixture of Cinsault, Grenache
Mourvèdre and Carignan is the classic combo for a perfect AOC from the
flinty terroir of Faugères . The wine never purses your lips nor compromises
your smile. Worth the drive into the *arrière-pays* to discover the Vidal-
Dumoulin family's full and wide range of wines, including *Vrille d'Automne*
a *vendange tardive* for keeping and a red Carignan-Grenache drawn from
vines more than 100 years old.

**Domaine de Terre Mégère**
rue Jeu-de-Tambourin, 34660 Cournonsec [5] **C2**
04 67 85 42 85
Open Mon-Fri (pm only), Sat (am only)
It is more than 30 years since Michel Moreau changed pastures from his
Grenoble homeland to those of Cournonsec just beyond Gigean off the old
road to Montpellier. Plan A was to raise donkeys on the garrigue scrubland.
However, since the very nature of planning is to inspire blushes on
reflection, so history has determined that Monsieur Moreau will forever be
known for his fine Merlot and other award winning wines.. *Terre Mégère* is
the land of the shrew, and the Moreau taming of the shrew has resulted in
some tiumphant *Gres de Montpellier* and *Cotaux de Languedoc* bottles on
the world's wine lists. And to justify the eclipsing of the donkeys by the
vines, a quotation from Pliny the Elder is carved above the tasting table
*"L'homme doit au vin, d'être le seul animal à boire sans soif."*

**Mas Jullien**
34725 Jonquières [5] **C1**
04 67 96 60 04
Closed Sat, Sun. (open pm only, Jul Aug)
They say that you follow the song of the *cigalles* to find your way through
Jonquières to the Mas Jullien (where the crickets even feature on the odd
label), but you might even follow burgundian accents, since wine buffs from
the most prestigious region, where comments on Languedoc's wine are not
always the kindest, would never dream of passing through en route to St

Guilhem de Desert, without a pilgrimage to a living legend. Son of a co-operative farming family, Olivier Jullien began making his own wines on his own land apart from his parent's vineyard. A pioneer of the new generation that believed that the soil of the region could produce great wines, rather than mere plonk, his success catapulted him into the top flight of Languedoc's wine wizards. Prices for this wine, way above the popular conception of the rate for a local wine, but Mas Jullien produced not merely a great local wine, but very good wines by France's national standard. Jullien's wines are planted on the plateau of Larzac in well chosen parcels of land. An ongoing quest to find ever more perfect marriages between land and vine, sees the map of the estate shifting like the tide. Following the success of Olivier's venture, Jullien *père* has also since left the co-op to produce his own quality wines at the **Mas Cal Demoura**, now almost 20 years old. Most of the reds at Mas Jullien are for nurturing and anticipation, the bottles not relased for sale until they come of age, but *Les Etats d'Ame* is a younger Grenache blend (Syrah, Cinsault Carignan) for earlier drinking.

**Clos Bagatelle**
34360 St Chinian [5] **B2**
04 67 93 61 63 Closed Sun
For many, no visit to Languedoc is complete without the companionship of a good Saint Chinian. And the Clos Bagatelle is a good spot to get to know a classic. A true family vineyard, the business is now run by a brother and sister team, Luc Simon looks after the vines whilst his sister Christine is the wine-maker. The Simon family wines are respected far beyond regional borders, their 2008 *Cuvée Tradition* won a *Decanter* award for wines under £10 sterling, rich, ripe and spicy, with tannin to make the roof of your mouth withstand a Languedoc winter. The best of the reds is the *Gloire de Mon Père* – the name may be taken from Pagnol, but the wine is named for Christine and Luc's late father Henri. A worthy detour to discover where *patrimoine* meets *terroir*.

**Vinipolis**                                                    310
5 avenue des Vendanges, 34510 Florensac [5] **C2**
04 67 77 00 20
Open every day; bistro closes Mon and eves (except Sat)
The ultimate co-operative experience – enjoy a meal as you taste the range of wines. Where farmers meet the *Michelin* chefs and *terroir* meets high tech. *See pages 185 and 303*

# Aude

**Château Peyriac de Mer [5] B3**
24 Chemin Neuf, 11440 Peyriac de Mer
04 68 42 82 47 www.chateau-peyriacdemer.com
Open every day
The name of the village is probably familiar thanks to wines produced by the local co-op for budget supermarket chains, but the good stuff is produced in private winery such as this run by Kees Graste and Peter van de Ven who brought northern European wine-marketing know-how to the sandy, salted herb-rich shores of Corbières when they took over the *Château* a few years ago. Retaining a quality *oenologue*, they continue to nurture and develop some smacking good wines. First year, we had great fun exploring and tasting mystery bottles as unlabelled treats emerged from the cellars, but true delight has been in the evolving quality of delicious AOC, as well as some pretty fine *vins de pays*. Most unlikely scents created by this unique terroir on the southern slopes of Corbières, between Narbonne and the sea, coastal yet garrigue-like soil on the edge of Etang de Bages. One white whipped up memories of licorice allsorts and midget gems. Muscat is a dry white here, not at all syrupy, the 2010 redolent or elderflower and summertime, and AOC Corbières red 2006 had aftertaste of sucking on ripe cherry stones. USP is finding top wines in the bag-in-box rather than everyday plonk. Logic: no chance of air spoiling a started wine; bonus: a great way to carry wine in your luggage!

**Terra Vinea**
chemin des Plâtrières, 11490 Portel des Corbières [5] B3
04 68 48 64 90
Local wine co-op showcased theme park style. *See page 116*

**Domaine Antech**
Domaine de Flassian, route de Carcassonne 11300 Limoux [5] A3
04 68 31 15 88 www.antech-limoux.fr
Closed Sat, Sun
Blanquette de Limoux and its allied Crémant are royalty amongst sparkling wines. Predating Dom Perignan's official Champagne Eureka moment by generations. Even before the bubbles, wines around Limoux won decent reviews by roman writers, and local bubbly can be gentle and full flavoured. Euro-for-euro, a modest Limoux may knock spots off a budget high street champers. Roads leading into town lined with wineries, some bordering on factory status, but **Domaine Antech** is worth a visit for more than just a fix

of fizz. For there is another *methode champanoise* to discover here, and I don't mean bottle turning and cork-popping. Just as great Champagne houses were founded by powerful women (think of the widow Pomerey and la Veuve Cliquot), so this etablishment owes its fortune to generations of women winemakers. More than 100 years ago, Eugénie Limouzy was one of the first women winemakers of Languedoc; in the 1930s, niece Marguerite married local vigneron Edmond Antech and steered her domaine's fortunes. Now Marguerite's granddaughter Françoise is at the helm. A member of *Vinifilles,* Madame Antech-Gazeau is amongst a handful of women looking to bring a new approach to wine in the 21$^{st}$ century (*see page 120*). A tasting visit reveals *Cuvée Eugénie,* named for Françoise Antech-Gazeau's great-great aunt. The 2007 manages to be fresh fruity and creamy with enough minty citric sharpness to keep tastebuds on their toes. *Cremants* allow more creativity, since this recent appellation allows leeway from exclusive use of the Mauzac grapes that define a Blanquette, and so the unfortunately named Antech team have a free hand with Chardonnay and Chenin to perk up the mix. For a lighter gentle pink, almost blush, option, try the *Cuvée Emotion.*

## Pyrénées-Orientales

**Clos de l'Origine**
route de Lesquerde, 66460 Maury **[5] B2**
09 52 15 03 17
Marc Barriot is a man on a mission: ardent about organic farming and tradition, his vines are planted within the turning circle of a donkey (yes, THAT organic: just as secateurs are wielded by hand, so harvest panniers are borne on the back of a beast) and herbs and plants around each pied of the vines nurtures and with nature's nutrients to bring an authenticity to his harvest. To walk through fields with Marc, at the furthest corner of the region where Occitan meets Catalan, is to be infected by a passion for the possible, faith in potential and the knowledge at all dreams lie within the reach of a believer. Visits and tasting by appointment, as the man himself is as like to be halfway up a hillside when you drop by tending to his crops. *Les Quilles Libres* is a lively white *Vin de Pays des Côtes Catalane* and worth a try and the *AOC Cotes de Rouissillon Soif de Plaisirs* is a gem and a half, harvested by hand under a late summer moon, a practically heraldic mouthful of the flavours of the south and practically a who's who of the grapes that matter: Carignan, Grenache, Syrah, Mourvèdre and Cinsault.

**Château de Jau,** 66000 Cases de Pène, Rivesaltes **[5] B2** – *see page 324*

# Driving through the best labels

## Where to find the AOCs

OF THE 37 APPELATION D'ORIGINE CONTRÔLÉE wines of the region, Marseillan's listed labels bear the names Picpoul de Pinet and Coteaux de Languedoc. Lazy drives from Marseillan in most directions, including Montpellier, should rope in plenty more Coteaux de Languedoc. Should you head through Béziers, you'd best turn right (west) for Faugères then Clairette de Languedoc and or left to Saint Chinian and keep going east to the Minervois, en route to Carcassonne.

Drive south from Marseillan along the coastal etangs towards Narbonne and you'll catch La Clape (forgive me) and arrive in Corbières. Narbonne is the old roman crossroads and a drive westwards through Corbières would pass by the sparkling wines of Limoux and the AOCs of Cabardès and Malpère; whilst continuing along the coast down to Perpignan, you would drive through Fitou to reach the Côtes de Roussillon and Côtes de Roussillon Village, with Maury and Rivesaltes inland and Collioure and Banyuls on the shoreline before the Spanish border.

Travelling north from Marseillan, find more Muscat country around Frontignan, by Sète and again around Nîmes. Taking the old Montpellier road you pass through the Gres de Montpellier and you could turn north before reaching the city to explore the Terrasses de Larzac en route to St Guilhem le Dessert or drive on to find the wines of Pic Saint Loup. When as you cross over into the Gard discover the Costières de Nîmes straddling the Rhône wine region. Languecdoc has a growing list of recognised appellations and hundreds of uncategorised vins de table. In between there are well over fifty different styles of Vin de Pays d'Oc. Closest to home, those labelled Côtes de Thau may be found in the vineyards around the etang, and, driving inland, Bessan has its celebrated and eponymous rosé and the vineyards of the Côtes de Thongue yield some smashing little belters.

## Planning a lazy wine route

Hérault Tourisme produces some excellent free road maps of the departement, with wine-tasting detours clearly marked. www.herault-tourisme.com Otherwise contact or visit the local *Maisons des Vins*.

114

## Maison des vins des Coteaux du Languedoc

Mas de Saporta, 34 970 Lattes [5] C2

04 67 06 04 44 www.coteaux-languedoc.com

Closed Sun

In a old wine estate some, 400 local wines are available for tasting, help is on hand for route planning and you can even sit down to a traditional meal and have your wines explained to you. An excellent one-stop shop for sorting out wine excursions, since they carry info from other wine areas througout the region. Good for dropping by *en route* to the airport.

## Syndicat AOC Faugères

4 rue de la Poste, 34600 Faugères [5] B2

04 67 23 47 42 www.Faugères.com

For suggested walking routes and detours in Faugères and very informative pocket guides to the wine and winemakers. Choose between ten itineraries, with lists of good restaurants for lunch breaks.

## Maison des Vins de Saint Chinian

Av de la Promenade, 34360 Saint Chinian [5] C2

04 67 38 11 69 www.saint-chinian.com

Closed Sun (Sep-Jun)

Plan a driving or hiking itinerary and discover the wines of Saint Chinan in the house where Charles Trenet's father once worked as a notary. Tasting classes and trips to markets to learn how to buy food to flatter your wine.

## Syndicat Général de l'AOC Limoux

20, avenue du Pont de France, 11300 Limoux [5] A3

04 68 31 12 83 www.limoux-aoc.com

Learn the difference between Blanquette de Limoux, Crémant de Limoux and Méthode Ancestrale then collect maps and routes for a themed day or weekend exploring bubble country. As well as the religious and grape-growing topics, other excursions are wrapped around water-sports and fresh air and exercise.

## Syndicat général de l'AOC Malepère

Maison des Terroirs, Domaine de Cazes, 11240 Alaigne [5] A3

04 68 69 95 10 www.vins-malepere.com

With a good website for downloading routes before you set out in the general direction of Toulouse and points west, this is ideal for exploring the wild countryside beyond Carcassonne. Three options, taking in Cathar sites, the old Circulade villages and getting back to nature in the protected parkland are ideal for hikers and cyclists.

**Maison du Minervois**
Château de Siran, 34210 Siran [5] A2
04 68 27 80 00
Pick up interesting maps and themed drives, including pairings of wine and olive tasting sessions and wine cellars and abbeys.

**Le Temps de la Barriquaille**
35, quai des Tonneliers, Port Minervois, 11200 Homps [5] A2
04 68 91 29 48 www.lechai-portminervois.com
Closed Sun (am) Jul-Aug; Sat Sun Sep-Jun
Alternative source of information on the Minervois, exhibition hall and a shop, the centre is housed in a 19th century wine storehouse.

# Wine themed days out

**Terra Vinea**
chemin des Plâtrières, 11490 Portel des Corbières [5] B3
04 68 48 64 90 www.terra-vinea.com
Shop: 10-15 - 18.15. Visits: Mon – Fri: 13.45, 15.15, 16.45; Sun, hols: 13.45, 14.30, 15.15, 16.00, 16.45
One of those themed museum-entertainments that France does so well: Despite the slogan "*pôle régional de la civilisation du vin et des cultures méditerranéennes*", which sounds more like a thesis than a day out, this lures the kids with promising a plunge into the bowels of the earth. As you travel through an old gypsum mine (part theme-park train ride) you learn the history of man's civilising imprint on the Med and look at winemaking and gastronomy through the ages, plus some little tableaux about mining. Yet, the combination of plaster of Paris and fine wines proves greater than the sum of its parts. So after some ooh-ah moments with *son et lumière* preseentation in barrel-filled wine cellars, a reconstruction of a roman villa and a visit to lake some 80 metres below ground, you explore the wines of Corbières, as the attraction doubles as showcase to *Les Caves Rocbère*, home to Peyriac-de-Mer, Sigean et Portel des Corbières co-operative wines. The shop is a something of a foodie treat with tasting platters of local produce to savour in a restaurant open lunchtime only. Menus €10-20.

**Vinecole**
Domaine de Gayda, chemin de Moscou, 11300 Brugairolles [5] A3
04 68 31 64 14 www.vinecole.com
If you would rather do more than nod sagely, raise eyebrows and shrug when next you meet a vigneron in his *caveau*, then a crash course in aspects

of Langedoc wine may be a day well spent. Of course you could spend a residential week or more, learning at the red-stained feet of the masters, but a wine tasting session and or mini course at Vinecole gets you started and gives ideas for interesting questions for your own forays into wine country. From €30 for a 2-hour course, tasting your way through 8 key wines reflecting the distinctive appellations of Languedoc, under the tutelage of an English-speaking Master of wine, to a full day's basic training featuring a vineyard visit, sessions on the science, history, alchemy and passion of winemaking as well as the tutored tasting for €125; a range of courses feature mixing wine with food and a family option introducing children to the subtleties of grape varieties through non-alcoholic juices. All events are based on a wine estate near Carcassonne, and reservation is essential.

### Le Jardin de Bacchus
Les Vignerons de Pouzols [5] B2
route de Carcassonne (D5), 11120 Pouzols-Minervois
04 68 46 13 76 http://www.pouzols-minervois.com/la-cave/accueil_cave.htm
Closed Oct-Apr
Next door to the co-op of the village of Pouzols discover the grape garden with its 65 varieties - an open air museum of vines and winemaking. Explore the underground cellars with wine bottles and vessels from roman times to the 21st century. But best of all, come at 10 on a Wednesday morning in July or August, when (for €15) a local winegrower will escort you round the fields and cellars; you'll get a guided tour of the village and its church, then join the winegrowers for a barbecue and wine tasting.

### Domaine Bourdic
34290 Alignan du Vent [5] C2
04 67 24 98 08 www.domainebourdic.com by appointment only
Some people would consider selling their home, children or vital organs for the privilege of creating their own wines in a French vineyard. Happily, there is no need to slap a kidney on eBay these days, as a couple of kindly vignerons will be happy to let you develop your own *assemblage* for less than €100. Musicians Christa Vogel and Hans Hürlimann blend their twin passions by holding music festivals in their own vineyard, between Pézenas and Roujan. However, an earthier form of blending should be second nature and a key skill for a fine winemaker. Each year, the estate is opened to visitors when the vignerons reveal the secrets of the *assemblage*, the actual blending of grape varieties to create their distinctive wines. For €99, guests may learn how to mix *cépages* for themselves and even take home a bottle of their own creation. Email the domaine at info@domainebourdic.com for dates of forthcoming assemblage courses.

**Cité de la Vigne et du Vin**
Domaine INRA de Pech Rouge, 11430 Gruissan **[5] B3**
04 68 75 22 62
Something of a science museum for vinogeeks, with opportunities to discover vines and technology first hand, and enjoy hands on interactive stuff rather than theme-parkerie and cuddly mascots. Certainly a step up from the traditional barn with a tailor's dummy perched on some old family tools from the back of grandpere's shed. Serious stuff, part of the *Academie de Montpellier,* this is designed to inspire schoolchildren and students of the region to take up a serious carreer in winegrowing

La vigne en fleur dans les chemins
Faisait rever d'un presence
Quande la douceur du crepuscule
Figeait les rires des placettes
Mais elle ne voulait voir
Que le cote de ciel ou le soleil descend
Sur le chemin qu'il avait pris

The flowering vine in the paths
Dreams of the moment
When the gentle twilight
Freezes the frivolity of the fields
Yet she only wished to see
That corner of the sky
Where the sun would slip
To the path it had taken

- Marcel Barral, Marseillan (1909 - 1907)

118

# The Cépages of Languedoc

## Red grapes:

**Arinarnoa** modern 1950s variant on *Merlot*. Cherry ripe.
**Cabernet Franc** local answer to *Cabernet Sauvignan*, some gentle shades
**Cabernet Sauvignan**, a *bonne maman's* sneaky *gauloise;* smoky & jammy
**Carignan** hearty and spicy
**Cinsault** fruity mouthful - Languedoc classic
**Egiodola** invented in Marseillan, hybrid variety with fruitiness & little acidity
**Grenache** all brambles, roots and rich burnt sugar
**Mourvèdre** Languedoc and Catalan classic, musky and peppery.
**Marselan** plummy newcomer, truly native to Marseillan, "best of" *Cabernet Sauvignan* and *Grenache*
**Merlot** classic *Bordeaux* flavours of bad wolves & grandmother's hankie drawers
**Pinot Noir** imported full and fruity back up for *Crémant de Limoux* sparklers, and at the heart of 2009's "fake" wine scandal.
**Portan** *Grenache's* illegitimate offspring: strong and spicy
**Syrah** rich woodland ripeness, maybe even a hint of olives

## White grapes:

**Bourboulenc** original ancient Greek forerunner to *Clairette*.
**Chardonnay** tastes of vanilla, smells of the inevitable oak barrels.
**Chenin Blanc** fresh crisp and sharp with scents of tropical fruits.
**Clairette Blanche** classic Languedoc white; and bedrock of the *Noilly Prat* vermouth.
**Grenache Blanc** a light touch.
**Macabeu** floral Spanish stalwart.
**Marsanne** aromatic with a whiff of almond.
**Mauzac Blanc** orchard scents – sometimes blent with *Chardonnay* for fizz, and the keynote of *Limoux* bubbly.
**Muscat** (**Muscat à Petits Grains**, **Muscat d'Alexandrie**) this one actually tastes of grapes! Used mainly for dessert wines.
**Piquepoul** (*or* **Picpoul**) fresh light and dry local speciality for the sharp green crisp accompaniment to seafood.
**Piquepoul Noir** very rare old variety, makes a lovely rosé.
**Roussanne** honeyed smack of soft fruits.
**Sauvignan blanc**, scent of freshly mown grass and taste of ripe melon.
**Terret** crisp and dry emerging popularity.
**Tourbat Blanc** (aka **Malvoisie du Roussillon**) richness of stewed fruit.
**Ugni blanc** (better known as the raw material for cognac) sharp and dry.
**Vermentino** aromatic citric Corsican import.
**Viognier** the tang of a peach-stone with a hint of spiciness

# The Grapes of Marseillan & Languedoc

The signature white wine of Marseillan is without doubt **Picpoul de Pinet**. Grassy gold in colour and lip-smackingly tangy, its immortality assured by its harmonious relationship with the oysters of the *étang*. Of course the wine is also produced in nearby Pinet, as well as Pomérols, Florensac and Mèze. Whilst indelibly linked to the *terroir* of the Thau, the grape variety also pays a minor role, across the regional border in *Chateauneuf du Pape* wines. The grape itself is actually spelt **Piquepoul**, the wine appellation **Picpoul**. In the past couple of years, another local white grape has found itself on fashionable menus – look out for **Terret** wines. Among the reds to discover is **Marselan**: a modern hybrid introduced in 1961, the only wine grape in France to be named after a place. As well as reinforcing local wine lists, the **Marselan** is making a name for itself in the New World, and is big in India.

**Muscat** dessert wines are a regional speciality, mostly found in Roussillon, around Rivesaltes, Collioure and Banyuls, and in Languedoc at Frontignan, behind Sète, and the countryside close to Nîmes. Some local winemakers produce their own versions and a couple of the private domains create a *vendange tardive* "noble rot" fine wine to go with foie gras or sweet desserts.

The first French sparkling wines came not from Champagne, but the area around Limoux, where *Blanquette* and *Crémant* wines can often rival far better known bubbles. In recent years, Marseillan winemakers began producing their own fizz using predominantly **Chardonnay** grapes.

The most common varieties found in the fields around Marseillan are **Grenache, Syrah, Cabernet Sauvignan, Carignan, Chardonnay, Cinsault, Marselan, Merlot, Muscat à Petits Grains, Piquepoul, Sauvignon, Terret, Vermentino** and **Viognier**.

Over 30 *cépages*, grape varieties, are grown in the region (*see page 119*), and, whilst once Marseillan concentrated on producing whites and rosés for export, today's vineyards host a range of vines including some from far beyond the regional boundaries.

Marseillan's rosé wines tend to be made from **Cabernet Sauvignan, Cinsault, Grenache, Syrah** and **Marselan**.

---

A Woman's Place ... is in the cellar, and the field, and the boardroom

The image of the vigneron is a masculine one (*en colère* in 1907, weather-beatten in any vineyard), yet, in the tradition of Anne Rosine Prat (*see page 49*), Languedoc has its women winemakers. Visit **www.vinifilles.fr** to meet a dozen trailblazers in Hérault: from Valérie Tabaries Ibanez at Domaine Roquemale up the road in Villeveyrac to Véronique Etienne following in her mother's footsteps at the Château la Dournie in St Chinian. *See also page 113.*

---

# Le Vin Primeur
# est arrivée

**O**F COURSE, WE KNEW what to expect. We had done it before. In our very first autumn in Marseillan we had stumbled across our first *Primeur de l'Hérault festival* of the new wine. We had read the leaflet, passed the poster and squinted at the Michelin map to find **Nezignan l'Eveque** ([5]C2), another quaint spiral of a village, just twenty minutes drive and half an hour's misdirection from home.

The village had seemed deserted as we drove up the hill to the church and down to the shops, until we hit on the idea of following family groups to the edge of town where the communal wine cellars offered a glimmer of light in the autumnal gloom. There, between rows of huge concrete wine vats, long trestles were laden with canapes, seafood would soon be borne and - time would reveal - fruit flans would follow. Meantime, ranged on scaffolding a group of musicians, *Nuthin' But the Blues*, were giving soul and voice to song in proof that whilst France herself may not have given birth to the blues, she had provided a trusty and safe haven from the age of Le Jazz Hot through the decade of Le Jazz Cool to our own intemperate and uncertain times. Milling around were scores of locals and we family of four welcome outsiders, waiting for the speeches that would follow the first musical set.

Discourse duly followed, with passion, and assorted dignitaries spoke of *terroir*, of *patrimoine*, of pride in the fruits of our labours; of one little village's importance in a wider world; of clinging to the values of our forefathers in a world of fickle perfidy. With no direct citation, the speaker in his black shirt and piano-key tie evoked the spirit of the *vignerons en colère* of 1907, who had fought to the brink of death for the very vines that defined their lives. With the last harvest still a twinge in every back in the room, and the wine-soaked soil barely scrubbed from the fingernails, the townsfolk shifted impatiently for the first taste of the new wine that would determine the village's fortune for the year to come.

When the dark bottles with their bright russet-leaf labels were finally uncorked, the wines flowed, as steadily as the music played, dancing evolved from shuffled foot tapping to jumping jive and the night prepared to live on for a full winter in many memories.

So, yes, we knew what to expect when the following year's leaflet arrived the morning of the first *Primeur* fest of the season. A different we this time. Five of us. That is, two neighbours and their genially acquiescent poodle; me and my walking stick, which generates its own jigging and skittish identity at the merest suggestion of music and making merry.

*Depliants* and the internet had told us of at least half a dozen towns and villages hosting festivals on this first of many autumn nights of wine fêting. We opted for **Servian** (**[5] C2**). Organisers may have requested a modest door charge for the tippling, unlike the previous freebie, but the evening would encompass Thongue valley villages, including last year's winegrowers of Nezignan. And other events on the programme looked like formal banquets. And formal never suits the first evening chill of October.

So we hit familiar unfamiliar roads, those ill-signed country lanes that weave beneath the autoroute and along the river and canal banks and were soon at Servian. The car park at the cooperative seemed empty, so we left the car there and listened out for the sound of celebration.

Rooting and tooting blew on the breeze and a near-crowd of ordinary people flowed through flashes of multi-coloured minstrel wear. We decided to follow the motley, and fell in step with the sounds of euophonium, trombone, sax, claranet, banjo, drums tambour, catstanets and other unspecified strange squeaky-farty reed instruments of Slav music.

From the outskirts into and through the city centre, these pied pipers drew their followers, attracted by their cacophony and their garb. They wore striking modern interpretation of traditional jester-yester-wear: tabards, bonnets, caps and capes in natural linens, patch-painted in the muted pastels of vegetal hues.

And so we pursued, joined, blended and merged with the crowd through the streets. This is surely the only way to see an ordinary village, time to take in

122

the names on shop fronts, details of railings, to notice the modest building on the corner rejoicing under the title *Ecole de Musique*. Led by jaunty sounds of brass we took it all in at the measured saunter that denotes either France *en fête* or New Orleans in sprightly mourning.

The impression of having slipped into celluloid and found oneself printed onto a classic art house movie about French village life, was strengthened as we came to the end of our journey. We wound our way up the hill to the steps of the church. Not conventionally a beautiful scene, but perfection - another ideal opera set, tiny narrow alleys between the buildings, juxtaposed at improbable angles, would have served for the entrances and exits of a chorus of supernumaries; only the ensemble was already in place.

Behind us an ordinary *boulangerie*, smelling of burnt butter, and sugared crumbs; opposite, a tiny police station, just big enough to fit one well-nourished gendarme, the grand café with its *belle époque* murals and well-polished bar; then, facing the church, the smaller café, with chalked menus and the ghostly impression on the outside wall tracing the distinctive legend of *Dubonet*. Dominating that side of the road, the Hotel du Ville: as wide as a whisper and as tall as a republic, curves, carvings, arches, all the impedimenta of imposing grandeur squeezed into a shop's-breadth. Traces of lighting strings around three grand windows, suggested that after dark it would glow blue, white and red, in true patriotic style. But State was dwarfed by the grand edifice across the street, the village *église*. Each or any of the buildings, with the possible exception of the police station, could have hosted a wonderful evening, but the crowd today was, in contempt of question, gathered around the steps of the church.

The yellow stone of the vast flat frontage, relieved only by a gold leaf framed icon, was greedily drinking in the glow of the last droplets of sunlight before dusk, and, high above us, gargoyles looked down from a tall tower. Below, the band took its place at the side of the *église*, whilst on the steps were ranged sundry locals wearing orange scarves denoting membership of the town choir.

Behind them, two barrels stood at the church door, garlanded with vine-leaves and flowers, and into this Ruritanian frame stepped the elderly parish priest. Beaming like a benign cartoon white-friar, the old man took his place under the old swaying olive tree and began the benediction: the Lord blessed and was blessed by all the good gifts of nature, the vines, the grapes, the soil, the sun, the sky, the birds of the air and the creatures on the place beneath.

Then, with the practiced slip of intonation known to preachers the world over, the old churchman unleashed the crowd into the Lords Prayer.

Amid this sanctity, came the profane padding of a tabby cat. Suddenly startled by the chanting crowd into which it had emerged, it darted this way and that, finally scuttling across the church steps to sanctuary behind the wall. The terrier that a couple of minutes later followed in her wake trotted through regardless of human foibles and rites.

The choir then struck up with a hymn to the tune of Beethoven's Ode to Joy, followed by the seductive harmonies of an Occitan poem extolling immortality, and telling the odyssey of a snowflake. The quiet crowd, so secular for the rest of the evening, even possibly the rest of the year, had somehow filtered into devotional gratitude from the first involuntary genuflection during the prayer.

The glittering inscription above the door may have been in vernacular French, rather than the regular Latin, some people may have grown away from the Church and its rituals during the course of their adult and working life, but at this moment, the divinity that shaped their ends, working with the land, for the wine and against the elements, was celebrated with love and gratitude.

After the music died down, and the sun's strength with it, paper lanterns were distributed and we followed the band back through the streets to the co-operative's car park, where the choir once again regaled us with popular song. There, outside buildings housing presses, barrels, maceration tanks and bottling plants, surrounded by vehicles, and a stones throw from the local filling station, we noticed, with some alarm, a model bull, the civic totemic mascot, maybe wood, perhaps copper, possibly hide, and please, please not *papier maché*, being garlanded with fireworks.

The heavy creature was taken to the centre of the crowd, where it was lifted aloft and worn and borne by the town hero or village idiot, delete as applicable. His cohort, dragging on a short tether the blindfolded bull-costumed human torch, lit the touch paper. Then, far from retiring, he danced in front of the "Bull" who then charged into the crowd, fireworks, rockets, roman candles and assorted Catherine wheels flaring and soaring from its horns, rump and snout, golden showers spattered into the shrieking throng, as I idly mused how a country so fond of red tape and triplicate applications for the mere scratching of a nose, can have such a cavalier attitude to health and safety.

124

Whilst the village policeman nodded and smiled at the scattering masses, and I wondered if I was properly dressed for appearing on the TV news ("Merrymaking turned to tragedy in the South of France"), the crowd instinctively backed as far away as possible as the beast lurched towards us, firing its flatulent pyrotechnic extravaganza from every orifice nature might have granted it and plenty more man-made opportunities behind.

Even as our lips formed the mantra "No win, No fee", we could not help but admire the dance and the spectacle, though we gaped as much for the folly as the frenzy. The display seemed never ending, each time that we assumed that the bull had fired its last sky rocket, the horns would spin and fire like the iconic Bugs Bunny bullfighting cartoon. Eventually, the model animal was lain upon a table and its still flaming crown taken to a place of safety a few inches from a brand new and recently tanked-up BMW.

The sparks had brought more people to the co-op and we surged forward to the large shed where the wine was to be launched, a sign at the door asked for 3 euros for an engraved glass, our passport to unlimited wines to follow.

Dotted around the hall were clusters of barrels, holding a selection of the *primeur* wines from half a dozen villages. At the edge of the room was the buffet, covered in cling film. A dozen children scurried under tables, on errands from grown-ups, stacking paper plates, displaying leaflets and brochures and generally acting as shoemaker's elves during the obligatory speeches from local big wigs. Less inspiring than the previous year's exhortation to glory, pride and honour, the major politicians were tonight presumably playing the crowds of bigger towns; they followed the usual pattern of thanks and lists.

At the instruction to eat, drink and be merry, the *primeurs* of the Côtes du Thonge flowed and covers were whipped off seafood salads, massive platters of cold meats, pates and salamis. As sacks of baguettes were opened and bowls of mustard and mayonnaise distributed, we juggled full wine glasses with fuller plates, finding barrels or boxes on which to perch, as the folk band was replaced by a zany youthful jazzy rock combo, dressed in equally colourful costumes, and screeching parodies of the speakers through a megaphone. They proved excellent musicians, and totally charming company.

Civilised handshakes and cheek brushing as the two bands nodded acquaintance belied the skittish lunacy of their performance. They bowed their heads and charged through the crowds like a smiling rouge-cheeked invading musical militia, and wound their way through the munching sipping and supping party. At the end of their set, when they streamed out of the building, as flamboyantly as they arrived, the first clutch of musicians returned. By now, apple tarts and huge succulent bries had been added to the board, and, having sampled a red and a white, I was already on the *vin rosé*!

The repertoire of the remarkable band took in most of Europe and the Mediterranean, with some definitely African sounding charms followed by castanet clicking and then deep emotive central European folk song. I found myself standing bolt upright, stamping my feet and shouting "hoy" at the end of each phrase. Full four generations has my family been settled in Western Europe, yet this music has a fast track to the soul and it seems that DNA will out: even in rural Languedoc, you can take the boy out of the Baltic, but … as perceived wisdom has it …

One of the drums sported a car nationality sticker, BH, not the Boosey and Hawkes insignia we might have found on the trombone, but Bosnia Herzogovina, the clue to the only part of Europe that might comfortably manage to be both Latin and Slav. Soon the group bowed out and left the floor to their returning zany swinging colleagues, who provided a mellow if surreal moment, playing Cole Porter to the manner born, and singing *C'est Magnifique* through a megaphone.

The food would flow on, the music would continue to alternate between the two bands, and the wine showed no sign of being withdrawn, we left the party happy and contented that the townsfolk still had several hours merrymaking in them. This was only one of six festivals on the first night of five weeks of 50 celebrations of the new wines of the Hérault villages.

I had a flight booked for the morrow, my friends had the entire autumn spread before them, as generous a buffet of thanksgiving and celebration as anyone could wish for. Each evening, each town, each community, promising a party quite apart.

And just like the wines of Languedoc, we could be sure that no two festivals would be the same. We know what not to expect next year.

For next year, we would celebrate in Marseillan.

# Blessed are the winemakers
## Marseillan joins the primeur crew

"DRINK ALONE AND YOU ARE A LUSH; drink with others and it is Holy Communion". With wise words, and clad in chinos and ecclesiastic stole, Father Robert Martin slipped into benediction mode, blessing the first bottle of the *Millésime 2010* as "the work of man to create harmony amongst humanity. *Du siecle au siecle. Amen*". Then he turned to his audience and suggested that perhaps instead of *amen* he should have said *aux lèvres* (to the lips!).

Had you heard the church bell toll the sevenish, that chilly October evening, you might have dismissed as caprice any suggestion that it was syncopating a sombre rendition of *Let It Be* as prelude to a wake. Actually, the happy harmony of the belfry with a brass band pumping out Beatles' classics on the quayside was more in the order of a baptism. *Le Primeur de l'Automne est arrivé.*

Not the carnival atmosphere of some neighbouring towns; just a small tent and some trestles at the far end of the quai de la Résistance: the Château du Port now dark and closed for the off-season and empty chairs at the string of café-restaurants on the opposite quay. However, as the band *Bastid & Co* began to swing to the inevitable Saints marching in and garlands of light-bulbs in the marquee augmented the twilight, so waterfront tables were stacked with wine boxes and plastic cups, and stalls under the canopy awaited platters of seafood and *tielles* from the *Syndicat des Conchyliculteurs Marseillainaises* and piemakers' brotherhood *La Confrérie des 1001 Pâtes.*

Marseillan belatedly joined the roster of villages celebrating the *Primeur de l'Hérault*. Other communities had long used the launch as an excuse for a party (*see page 121*) but it was well into the first decade of the 21st century that Marseillan decided to inaugurate the *nouveau* with bunfight and fanfare at the *Cave Co-operative* in the port. By 2010, the shindig was also open to private wineries, domains of Fadèze and Madeleine Saint-Jean joining their *confrères* from Henri de Richemer. A respectable crowd in coats and hats had clustered in front of the small platform where a table glistened with trophies against the backdrop of the étang.

Although the Richemer *Primeur Blanc* had won a gold medal at the concours for new wines, these prizes were not for wine-making.

Just like school speech day, Mayor Yves Michel, after congratulating the *viticulteurs*, thanking the organisation *Traditions Marseillanaises* for reviving the festival and welcoming honoured guests, delivered handshakes and plaques to hardy cyclists who had peddled from Marseillan to Spanish twin town Caudette.

It was left to co-operative president Stéphane Hugonnet to ignite the political fireworks with a robust peroration in defence of wines, 'maligned' he said by Christelle Ballestero, TV presenter and journalist who had denounced as myth the healthy cardiovascular benefits of strong red Languedoc wine. Monsieur Hugonnet's passionate and scornful rebuttal was worthy of Marcelin Albert in 1907. To claims of wine being doctored with sugar, he retorted that Languedoc was the only region that expressly forbade such action, winning rousing cheers to set the ducks of the port to startled flight. It would have been a very brave Ballestero that would dare enter Marseillan that evening. Smoke could already be scented from the flaming barbecue around the corner Beside the Château, and in a town with such a strong agricultural heritage, pitchforks are readily accessible.

Fortunately, Père Robert Martin's jolly blessing, peppered with its witty *assemblage* of sacred and secular references, turned attention back from yesterday's media outrage and towards tonight's new vintage. Wine-boxes declared open, the surge began for plastic cups of rosé, red and a particularly citric and full-flavoured white. A fresh cheer rent the air when a massive tray of *brasucade* mussels was carried onto the quay and the band struck up Brassens' anthem of conviviality *Les Copains d'Abord*. Familiar songs, comfort food and brimful autumn-chilled fresh wine shared with friends and neighbours prove as good as any celebration of the nights drawing in.

The festivities in Marseillan do not yet take over the town, stuck out on a limb on the "other" side of the port. Posters and announcements only emerge in the few days before the event, so the *Primeur Marseillanais* does not have the full-blown party mood of Agde's Sunday morning celebration, where a costumed procession from the cathedral takes wine to the heart of the city. This is a more intimate affair: a *vin d'honneur* or *apéro entre-amis;* and that makes it a secret worth sharing.

# Touring the other tipples

**Noilly Prat**
1 rue Noilly, 34340 Marseillan
*See page 49*

## Perrier – fizz and passion in a bottle

Wines may be more than 13% proof, but when it comes to arousing passion, there is certainly something in the water just off the road between Montpellier and Nîmes. The **Perrier** spring has inspired plenty of emotion and sensation over the years. Even before Julius Caesar began carving up local vineyards as an early pension plan for officers, plenty of legionaires and fellow colonialists had been taking to and of the waters, the great Hannibal stopped by for a well-deserved drink in the 3rd century BC. So the gassy gush from the ground near **Vergèze** put the hamlet of **Les Bouillens** on the tourist map.

The fizzy stuff continued to woo passing trade, and when, in 1863, Napoleon III declared the spring officially a natural mineral water spa, bubbles became big business for the Granier family who owned the land. Since Napoleon and his Empress Eugenie were the trend-setters of their day, tingle-time in effervescent water developed into an aspirational A-list fad. Sadly, this was short lived. Fire destroyed the spa, the business crashed and it was not until the new owners leased the spring to a doctor from Nîmes that the sparkle returned to the place. By the turn of the 20th century, Dr Louis Perrier was bottling and selling this unique naturally carbonated water to the health conscious *nouveau riche* in the market for lifestyle products.

Dr Perrier needed a business partner and found just the man in St-John Harmsworth; yes, those Harmsworths, aka the Rothermere and Northcliffe clan. Whilst his older brothers were busy inventing the concept of outrage and launching their *Daily Telegraph* and *Daily Mail*, young St-John put his mind to selling water to the British Empire. He redesigned the bottle, inspired by the shape of Indian exercise clubs, and the world's restaurant bills have been a comfortable 10 euros plumper ever since.

If you still reckon that *terroir* and emotion are sole preserve of winemakers, you've not visited Vergèze where gas and water inspire the same outpouring of obsessive pride elsewhere evoked by *schiste* and and *calcaire* in the soil and *cinsault* and *carignan* on the vine. Perrier's USP was the fact the stuff came out the ground ready bubbled and full of fizz. I well remembered the

129

outrage when European dictats decreed that naturally carbonated mineral water fell foul of rules regulating quantities of gas for labeling purposes. The sort of ruling that sends the modern day descendents of the newspaper Harmsworths into front-page frenzy. So Source Perrier was compelled to develop techniques to remove gas from water, then pump the very same carbon dioxide back in under EU regulated supervision. The label was subtly altered from "*naturally carbonated mineral water*" to "*carbonated natural mineral water*".

There had also been a scandal when the drink was recalled from the world's supermarket shelves after a health scare involving chemicals found in the water. And in 1992 the brand was bought, lock stock and green bottle, by corporate giant Nestlé, owners of S. Pellegrino in Italy and many other world class waters. Then came Vergèze's 21st century version of the *vignerons* revolt, when locals got wind of a rumour that Nestlé was considering outsourcing production abroad. Considering the water had come from the same village spring at Les Bouillens since before Julius Ceaser had *venied vedied* or even *vicied* his first colony, and that the village name was Occitan for "bubbling spring", tempers rose. Words spoken and lawyers primed and after the best part of two years locals won their final day in court. In 2006, mayor René Balana told the world's press "*Tout le monde* has referred to *Les Bouillens* as *Source Perrier* for over 60 years. It's in the common language, so our case is solid. *Perrier* is our cultural, geographical and historic heritage." Thus, the spring and the district were renamed *Perrier-Les Bouillens;* a master stroke since it virtually afforded Perrier water the same *appellation* privilege as Champagne and the fine wines of Bordeaux. If what goes in the bottle is not made in the place called *Perrier*, you can't call it *Perrier*. Jobs, pride and vintage local tradition saved.

Hearts have not been the only organs inflamed by a passion for Perrier. Anyone who has ever seen "*La Main Perrier*", a notorious and deliciously audacious Christmas film advertisement, will not have been spared a single blush. Lock the kids in the spare room and surf to www.lamainperrier.com to see the ad on line. Just as the leggings of such cultural icons as David Cassidy and Jeremy Clarkson were born here in the region (*serge de Nîmes* cloth finding fame as denim), so the world's best known bottled water is literally on the map. And therefore is now on the tourist trail. So treat your designated driver, who has spent the past few days as noble voyeur and visit the Perrier estate and Château Harmsworth. Groups and individuals taken by coach to walk through the vast bottling halls and see the modern day production process. A video, museum of more than a century of iconic advertising and a tasting session at the visitor centre are all part of the 90 minute guided tour. But the highlight for many is a chance to spend time in the stunning gardens; a haven of lush greenery and perfect plating, pruning and design that is quite an unexpected treat in the dusty rugged landscape where the Hérault meets the Gard. Bring a picnic.

Whilst water employs some 1500 people from Vergèze, a few families still work the fields in the traditional manner; and if a tasting of fizzy water but a chaser to the hard stuff, follow local signs to *Vignerons de la Voie d'Héraclès*, local wine co-op, to try and to buy typical table wine. The station at Vergèze closes at the weekend.

**Source et Musée Perrier**
Les Bouillens, 30310 Vergèze |5| **D1**
04 66 87 61 01 www.perrier.com
Jul-Aug every day (reservation recommended);
Sep-June Mon-Fri (reservation essential) Closed mid Dec-mid Jan, May 1,

Also consider: an add-on trip to the nearby **Haribo** sweet factory & museum

**Le Musée du Bonbon** Pont des Charrettes, 30700 Uzès
04 66 22 74 39 www.haribo.com
Sep-Dec Feb-Jun: Tue-Sun 10-13, 14-18; Jul-Aug daily 10-19

## Ricard: the classic pastis of the South

Pastis, iconic drink of the South of France, forever *Jean de Florette* and Pagnol, French cinema and emblem of timeless time-off, was born in Marseille. The word comes from *pastiche*, a copycat, but safe, successor to banned *absinthe* that made the heart grow fonder but the mind go wander. And whilst pastis is forever associated with Provence, and vermouth is the child of the Languedoc, the traditions collide ten minutes from Marseillan where, alongside a *rosé* wine co-operative, **Ricard**, celebrated pastis of Marseille is made. It is in **Bessan** (|5| **C2**) that Paul Ricard's original secret formula from 1932 is closely guarded behind locked doors and high walls. Until a few years ago, a small visitors centre and shop let the public into the building but not into the confidence of the distillers. Now, the only way you'll get to taste pastis is in a bar on the tree-lined place de *La Promenade*. Each year a team from Bessan flies to China and all points east to select star anise and more to bring back for extraction ere the elixir is bottled ready to be savoured by the boulodromes of Provence: The aniseedy aroma nature's ideal accompaniment to the click-click-smack of a game of *pétanque* .

To see artisanal Pastis production, visit **Marty** in **Saint Thibery** – page 229

# Special Brew: the beers of the Etang de Thau

**Brasserie Croix du Sud**
2 quai de Toulon [2] **B2**
06 25 24 59 40 www.brasseriecroixdusud.com
Behind the vats and *cuves* of the cave co-operative and beyond the walls where the barrels of *Noilly Prat* take the sun, on the very banks of the Etang de Thau, a fine profanation is taking place. Here in the land of the grape and the garrigue, the **Croix du Sud** brasserie brews a brace of *blondes*, a *bière blanche* and an *ambrée*. Alas, in the early days, it still lacks a bottling line, for home purchasing. So, unless you are in the market for a 30 litre cask, best to look out for the Occitan cross logo in cafes and restaurants or head for the bar when you attend a festival or concert. Picpoul purists need not scoff. This is no Jean-come-lately concept: Before the War, Hérault had dozens of breweries. Think of it as a revival. And, like all good revivals, it is born of a passion. American artist Eric Lansdown turned his back on a career making bespoke dolls houses for A-Listers for the simple life in Languedoc. And he quickly sussed that nothing quenches like a well-nurtured artisanal beer and so began to develop a hobby into a business, gaining a name for a quality brew of choice for fêtes and summer concerts. Taking a leaf from the modern wine-makers bible, he looked to the New World, and young Australian Sam Gardiner joined the team as brewmaster. With local nousse provided by Marco Baudet from Beziers, the trio quietly assure that long hot summers of Languedoc may be assuaged with the incomparable delight of an ice cold beer reflecting the *terroir de Thau*. Call for a private tour of the brewery and get to know the range.

**Brasserie d'Oc**
RN 113, Zone Industrielle, 34140 Mèze [5] **C2**
04 67 24 85 15 www.brasseriedoc.com
Closed am and Sun
Just across the vineyards, beyond the fields of the route de Mèze and over the roundabout On the industrial estate by the roundabout at the crossroads of Marseillan, Mèze and Montagnac, the first modern micro-brewery on the lagoon produces a range of bottled beer bearing labels celebrating local tradition: images of jousting, the lagoon, oysterbeds and even roman winemaking. Yet, even in the land of grapes, these bottles still owe their existance to barley and hops. A pair of *blanches* (white beers) prove perfect cloudy and refreshing companions to local seafood, and popular blondes, some ambrées and a pilsner style lager cater for all tastes. The brewery visit includes a guided tour and a video history of 8000 years of beer and is rounded off with the essential tasting session. Modest admission fee.

# The Joy of Heresy

THIS WAS TO BE an evening of happy heresies: *hirondelles* playing second fiddle to invader conqueror colonising *goeland* gulls, gliding and diving on the robust winds of a long drawn out sunset; that gust tonight itself not our domestic *Tramontane* nor *Marin*, but a tiresome *Mistral*, first panting, then sighing, nudging unwanted night clouds past Montpellier towards the Rhône to present a sheer blue canopy to the evening waters as first summer nightlights began to garland the headland of Saint Clair. Harmonising with music of the elements, the crooning voice from the CD player was that of Jean Sablon, rather than the étang's ubiquitous George Brassens; neither had the lagoon furnished our table: not an oyster to be found on our menu, nor seabass, bream nor sole, instead tuna from open seas beyond the dunes now immersed in its marinade before valedictory grilling. Even that final gastronomic hurrah, was not to be toasted by the village: our master of ceremonies, of wine and of revels had granted honours to Burgundy.

But what Burgundies: *Grand crus* and *premier crus* on the *buffet* each attending the correct course for reverence. For some, it had been a long wait. The *Chambolle Mussigny* had known the cool shade of cellar and shelf since 1985 for her moment in the moonlight; her younger sister, a mere 17 chaste years ere flattery and praise in the glow of summer candles.

Tavernier Bruno had enjoyed pleasant agonies of selection. He did not snub lightly the *cépages* of home. His shop proudly boasts 500 labels hailing from garrigue and littoral, slopes sheltered by the Mediterranean's joyous pine and sad cypress from prevailing Occitan winds. He knows alchemies of tradition and expedience, of sage and brush, thyme and rosemary-scented soil, almond, olive and cherry fragranced breezes that, with the heartache and joy of generations make up the *terroir* of his region's most cherished product. He can flourish a *Faugères* to lighten a lazy lunch or conjure a *Corbières* to bedevil a dinner into an occasion. He may judge a diner's commitment to the grape and present a *Pic St Loup* for dalliance or *Terre Megère* to tease. He knows which will please on first acquaintance and which require mutual commitment to reap reward.

But on this Monday, my innocent reflection that my father prefers a red had sparked a challenge in the mind of our vintner. Closing the catalogue of his nearest and dearest, he ventured further afield: *Côtes du Rhône*, tad aggressive for steak that was yet a fish; *Bordeaux*, far too solemn. He mused: Of course the *Loire* has its sirens, but then again, *La Bourgogne*. Grandiose without taking itself too seriously, well-mannered yet fun. Certainly potential. More than potential. More than possibilities. Burgundy would be the perfect match. So a 1998 *Chambertin* and that 1985 *Chambolle Mussigny* made their way to the little house in Port Tabarka.

A rather special single malt whisky came through the door in time to be offered to Armand, who had laden his trusty Rover with several head of vine stock, in response to an innocent request for *sarments* – vineyard twigs. Too huge to lug through the house, the cargo was driven to the terrace, negotiating the ring of rocks designed to keep the infernal combustion engine away from the port wasteland. Heaved and hauled over walls and piled next to the barbecue, gnarled and twisted trunks made the very coals in the pan blush to their embers. Our octogenarian benefactor positioned the first log and the air was scented with exotic charm of winewood in generous surrender. Armand called us to the fire, raised his first tumbler of liquid amber to friendship and our evening began.

Neighbour, Henri, watching from his own table across the fence, warned us of the dangers of cooking over vinestock. Pesticides will be released, said the soothsayer, be vigilant. He raised his glass to his eyes, then his lips and nodded sagely "*bon apetit!*". Bruno arrived bearing more sarments, a tray of apricots from his mother's garden and wild almonds from the *arrière pays*. Nodding complicity to Stéphane, the first of the Burgundies was uncorked.

Stéphane sniffed the cork of the more venerable vintage and glanced across at his fellow *oenophile*, Bruno stretched out his hand for a tasting glass and the two of them, squinted, swirled, stared and sniffed, but neither sipped. Nor did either say much at this time. Eventually, once eyes and nose had told two thirds of the story, lips graced glasses for *dénouement*.

Bruno's eyes became eloquent.

"Is it bad?" we asked.

More reflection, glass held aloft once more, beige tinged plum colour flowing against whitening powder blue of a diluting sky, and Bruno spoke.

"No, a wine does not go bad. It has a life and it should be treated differently at different stages in its life. You should know when and how to drink it. A young wine is ... one thing. But there is also a special time in its life to be celebrated, and a time to behave more gently, and act with a little more respect. You do not make love with a twenty year old in the same way you appreciate her at 30 or 40 or 60. This wine is still a good wine. It is perhaps, a little more fragile now at this stage in its life. But maybe not for the tuna. This will be elegant with the dessert. How is the *Chambertin*?" This last question directed at Stéphane, who had excalibured the cork from the second bottle and whose grin from the sparkle in his eyes to the stem of his glass told its own story.

"OK" said Bruno and swung back on the quad. "I will find another Burgundy and bring back a rosé for the apéro."

# Bars & Cafes

W HEN PEOPLE ASK ME the difference between a bar and a café, there is never a definitive answer. Generally one does a lot more standing around in the former, and sitting down in the latter. Bars generally stay open later than cafés; in a city or a resort, often well after midnight until nightclubs take over for the late shift. However, since you may enjoy a coffee in a bar and quaff a beer in a café, your choice really depends on where you feel most at home. In the village of Marseillan, this is very much a matter of taste.

Whilst the words café and bar may lack sharp definition, two signs outside bars show their specific identity. The red cigar symbol indicates a *tabac* (you'll sometimes see this outside newsagents and stationers as well). Here you'll be able to buy cigarettes, stamps, phone-cards, mobile and dongle top-ups, sometimes even bus tickets. The green white and red **PMU** logo marks out establishments licensed to take bets on horseracing and sporting events.

Sometimes, you may find two sets of prices on display. In most cases, the lower price applies to drinks served to those standing at, or leaning against, the bar, and the higher for waiter service at a table. In hip city establishments, second columns often indicate a 10–20% price hike after 10pm or midnight. In a neighbourhood bar, one orders drinks, enjoys them and pays on leaving. Busier, fashionable hangouts may expect payment at time of ordering. If all this sounds stressful and complicated, don't worry. Settle down, have a drink and forget about it. There is never any pressure to move on once you have ordered your first tipple. A modest espresso could last all afternoon, if you've a mind to settle down on a comfortable terrace, and a glass of beer may be nursed as long as you like as the evening dissolves past the witching hour. Beers come in bottles or on draught (*à la pression*), served usually as a *demi* (25cl) in a tall glass. You may not find the range of beers on the Med as you'd expect in northern Europe. But small local breweries are sprouting up (*see page 132*) and you may be surprised by what's on offer. Some alcohol-free branded beers are available in cafés. A refreshing compromise is a lager shandy, known in France as a *panaché*.

On a café terrace, the tipple of laziness is not beer but wine and, unless you opt to indulge by the glass, it is usually ordered as a jug or *pichet*. A *quart* is the most modest option at 25cl, and pours out a couple of small glasses worth; the *demi-litre* is slightly less than a bottle-full and fine for sharing; and a *litre* choice of friends settling down for some serious conviviality and probably planning a top-up. Don't be too specific when ordering wine by the *pichet*. You don't need to know your grape varieties, colour will suffice. Ask for *rouge*, *blanc* or *rosé*. *Rosé* is a popular choice on a sweltering summer's day. In Marseillan, wines often arrive with a side order of ice cubes. Not sacrilege, simply practical, with temperatures way past 30 degrees, you need to keep the wine in your glass well and truly chilled!

The *Midi* classic refresher *pastis* is a time-honoured cooler, and just a whiff of the aniseedy aroma sends the soundtrack of *Jean de Florette* ringing in the ears. A long slow drink and the ritual of topping up from the pitcher, as timeless an occupation as filling and drawing on a pipe. *Ricard* is bottled up the road in Bessan. Of course, you cannot visit Marseillan without tasting the local *apéro Noilly Prat*. Go for *rouge* (sweeter), *dry* (extra dry and white) or a blend of the two, known as a *Marseillanais*. Rather lovely *ambrée* a delicious alternative to sherry. Another local taste is sweet *muscat* wine from Frontignan, behind Sète, unless from Rivesaltes in Roussillon.

Whilst a *kir* (white wine with *crème de cassis*, or other fruit liqueur) is still popular, the *kir royale* (made with sparkling wine or champagne) is more common, and it is also quite normal to order just a glass (rather than a bottle) of plain champagne. Ask for a *coupe*.

There is more to soft drinks than mere *Perrier* (which is as like to be *S Pelegrino* on the more fashionable terrace). These days, the old favourite *Orangina* tends to be somewhat eclipsed by the ubiquitous *Coca-Light*; ice-tea (pronounced and spelt in the English fashion) is a popular refresher, and some people still order a *diabolo* (mint or grenadine cordial, with lemonade). If you just want the mint syrup with water, ask for a *menthe à l'eau*, that may be topped up and diluted for ages. A *citron pressé* is freshly squeezed lemon juice served with a jug of iced water and loads of sugar, an echo of home-made lemonade from someone else's childhood. When it comes to coffee, don't bring your metropolitan and airport lounge baggage with you. Tall skinny *lattes* don't feature on the radar down here, and as for *frappamochalifestyloccinos*, forget it. France does not do gimmicks. France does proper coffee. A *café* means *espresso*, at any time of day. A decent white coffee is a *café crème* (perfect at breakfast time) or *café au lait*. If you want a dash of milk in your espresso, some places will offer you a *noisette*. And the only Italian sounding option is a *cappuccino*, which in most cases will turn out to be what you expect, but has been known, in some corners of France, to be a white coffee with the addition of a squirt or two of aerosol cream kept behind the bar for emergency banana splits on chef's afternoon off. If in doubt, stick to a standard *café au lait* unless you can see a *Gaggia* machine in working order. Plain old-fashioned filter coffee is *café americain*. Decafinated coffee is a *déca*.

Tea is probably *Liptons* orange label or a small sachet of Earl Grey served with a pot of hot water. Ask for milk or lemon. Fruit and herbal teas (*infusions*) are inevitably camomile or verbena (*verveine*). Hot chocolate (*chocolat*) is usually absolutely scrumptious, redolent of bedtime and birthdays, yet a perfectly acceptable option for grown ups at any time of day or year.

## Bars in Marseillan

One of my favourite treats on an idle afternoon is playing "spot the invisible bar". For, once upon a time, Marseillan boasted as many bars and cafes as were hours for drinking. True neighbourhood rendezvous, more akin to the *estaminet* counters of northern France or the *Auvergnat zinc* bars of old Paris, where locals chewed the fat, and fishermen or winegrowers would knock back a glass or few, as womenfolk pumped water from the well and climbed calf-taunting stairs to prepare the evening meal. Old photos in every family album shared with strangers on September's heritage and ancestry days invariably show groups of friends, colleagues and team mates ranged outside some long-forgotten bar. The clues are in the architecture. A private house along avenue Gambetta reveals the street's former life as the main road to a railway station, a *Café de la Gare* if ever I saw one. Other corner houses in the village hint at a convivial past. There remain less than a handful of traditional bars in the village. Reminiscing on the eve of his retirement, a village shopkeeper gestured towards a bland office window. That was once a bar, he told me. When he was young, there were bars for communists, for the Spanish, others for workers, he recalled. But then, he had stopped visiting bars once he got married. That's what happens, he said. You spend evenings in a bar until you marry. And then a thought struck him: And again, twenty-five years after you marry, he added. Once you start to get on your wife's nerves!

Bar culture has evolved since his day. Yet, the camaraderie of an elbow on the bar, and shared shouting at the TV during the match, handshakes of arrival and departure, these remain essential part of French community life. A barman's leaning across the counter, dishcloth thrown on the shoulder to free a right hand for the grip of greeting, the nod toward a table when you arrive deep in conversation with a significant other, and the promise to bring the your drink over: these conventions are as timeless as the jerk of the head from a waiter standing by your table to acknowledge your imminent request for a *café,*\*pastis* or *demi-pression*.

### Café du Boulevard
32 boulevard Lamartine [1] **B3**
04 67 77 22 03
Not the hotel and restaurant of the same name next door, this is where the locals gather on market morning, and town centre and town hall workers pause for café before their shift and the overspill for putting the world to rights by the *grille* opposite. The pool table in the main bar is a rival gathering point for the village menfolk. The ladies have their sporting venue too, thanks to the egg-timer-style light-switch in their toilet that ticks down the seconds before the loo is plunged into pitch darkness. Nought to knickers-up in 60 seconds, the current land speed record.

### Buvette Le National
5 avenue Chassefière [1] **B3**
04 67 77 23 51
A new PMU bar for sporting tips, tabs and rumours, housed in one-time wine shop of the *Domaine de Laux*. A venue change from the original **Koala** bar behind the theatre and post office, where once players would retire from the *boulodrome* by the car park to continue disputing points of their game of *pétanque*. Closer now to tournaments on Allées Roques, and traditional bar heartland of place de la République, the *Mairie* and *Grille*.

### Le Marine Bar
04 67 77 63 78 [1] **B3**
The evening starts here. The image of the notorious nautical mural outside is reflected in framed pictures within. Sport ever on the telly, local fixtures posted on the wall. Daytimes, the terrace is popular with visitors wanting a

138

coffee in the heart of the village, and catching up with emails thanks to free wifi under the smart new awning; evenings, locals gather by the bar for a quick *demi* that can overspill into night. Handshakes all round.

**Le Relax**
39 boulevard Lamartine [1] **B3**
04 67 77 23 51
Council workers, tradesmen and all who need a good square meal in the middle of the working day. One of the last small neighbourhood bars. Not so long ago, Marseillan boasted many such *comptoirs*.

**La Marseillanerie** *(see page 252)*
Marseillan's *Croix du Sud* beer *(page 132)* and oysters served by the church.

## Cafes & Terrasses

For all the town's pride in *égalité*, and women having the right to drink at café bars in the 19th century, the truth was that few unaccompanied women would have frequented the bars. And certainly most husbands would have frowned at their wives drawing on a *Gauloise* over coffee at a working man's bar. Women had their own *cafés d'un sou*, counters in groceries and food shops where they'd take a coffee with shopkeepers and neighbours to catch up on gossip whilst doing the chores. Nowadays, a bar for the lads may be as much a café for the girls, as market day outside the Marine Bar proves every Tuesday. Now ladies who brunch or plonk designer handbags on an adjacent chair whilst catching up with the goss *entre-amis*, have **Chocolatée** *Salon de Thé* by the theatre roundabout as an alternative daytime rendezvous (*see page 269*).

As well as the surviving bars of the village and the **Manne d'Or** bakery, with its tables on the cobbles outside for enjoying a coffee and croissant in the mornings, the port is very much the place for sitting and sipping and turning the pace of life down a notch of two. The restaurants of the port (*see pages 255-266*) often take on the mantle of *café-bars* between meals. There is still a bar at the brasserie **O' Soleil** with comfy seating indoors, away from the dining terrace and in the mornings and afternoons the restaurants **Entre Ciel et Mer** and **Côté Sud** have long been favourite spots for watching the port move at a sail's pace. Further along, the **Maison Camille**, with its comfy new patio furniture, will welcome a request for a glass or cup of something long and lingering just as cheerfully as an order for *crêpes* and ice-creams. The **Taverne du Port** has its wine bar in the *boutique*, for enjoying a verre across the barrel tops (and now offers wifi access as well). Across the water, the **Château du Port** has always kept a cluster of smaller tables in front of the neighbouring wine *cave* for café-bar purposes. And these are sought after during the summer sports days for settling down to enjoy the *Capelet* or jousts over the rim of a chilled wine glass. Remember, however, that these places are first and foremost restaurants, whose primary business comes from serving meals at lunchtime and in the evenings. So if tables are laid for a meal, and you fancy just a couple of euros worth of coffee, then it is only good manners to consider stopping elsewhere. Several restaurants have a few smaller tables free from napkins and cutlery for the *café* contingent.

## Bars in Marseillan Plage

Bars and cafes around the market place in the resort are for traditional sipping and gathering in the French fashion. Along the main drag of restaurants, takeaways and emporia of inflatable impedimenta *des sables*, find lively convivial holiday-mood bars, for poster-coloured *glaces*, pitchers of beer, *sangria* and cocktails. Some offer karaoke, others host live bands, and you'll even find a **PMU** bar on avenue de la Méditerranée for a flutter.

**Brooklyn**
398 avenue Campings
04 67 21 82 87

**La Case à Rhum**
705 avenue Campings
04 67 01 62 55
Cocktail bar at the
**Paillotte** caribbean restaurant.

**La Bodéga**
7 avenue de la Méditerranée

**Le Charlemagne**
447 avenue des Campings
04 67 76 94 64

**Le Mooréa**
75 avenue des Campings
04 67 21 84 64

**Le Neptune**
6 avenue de la Méditerranée
04 67 21 50 06
Corner site, resounding to the sounds of live music on balmy summer nights, PMU sports bar

**Le New Orleans**
17 avenue de la Méditerranée
04 99 43 09 76

**Le Pescadou**
place du Marché 04 67 21 97 06

**Le Pub du Marché**
place du Marché
04 67 76 08 99

**Sonny et Jojo**
Chemin de l'Airette
04 67 00 16 49

# How to be very very lazy ... away from Marseillan

The sandy spits, the shore-lock'd lakes,
Melt into open, moonlit sea;
The soft Mediterranean breaks
At my feet, free.

Dotting the fields of corn and vine
Like ghosts, the huge, gnarl'd olives stand;
Behind, that lovely mountain-line!
While by the strand

Cette, with its glistening houses white,
Curves with the curving beach away
To where the lighthouse beacons bright
Far in the bay.

Ah, such a night, so soft, so lone,
So moonlit, saw me once of yore
Wander unquiet, and my own
Vext heart deplore!

- Matthew Arnold (1822-1888)

THE ORTHODOX VIEW IS THAT A TRAVELLER in possession of a spare hour must be in want of a renaissance altarpiece in a 13th century Romanesque church, some tableaux of 19th century village working practices featuring an authentic rusty rake, half a plough and a salvaged typewriter or the opportunity to visit the birthplace of a little known pioneer of clock-making. So the travel guidebook industry has long intimidated its loyal readers that these are the very spurs that drive the voyager from his homeland and on to unexplored pastures.

In actual truth, albeit universally denied, what leads the honestly lazy traveller to venture from the adopted heartland of bed, beach, bottle and bar, is lunch. The rest is but a slice of kiwi-fruit or single coriander leaf to the lamb, the veal or the trout. Other towns and villages are discovered in casual delight by the hungry as a prelude to the restaurant, or by the replete as backdrop to the post-prandial saunter. Greatest surprise and most treasured nugget of wisdom gifted to us by the aging process is the realisation that life is not a test; there are no written questions to answer later; facts are merely raw material for convoluted memory and eventual anecdote; and dates do not matter.

The beautiful village church is there to be admired and appreciated for the moment. Brief sentences engraved on the plaque should tease a genuine tear of complicity with better and braver men of the past. The story of a people and its town is told not in a dry catalogue of dates and decrees, but in the faces that you see outside the Café des Sports on the square or down by the waterfront, pottering with their nets and with knives. Neither do the clearest views of the past come from pushing buttons on an audio guide, but through improbable fables of carnival and harvest-tide.

The value of any little local museum is not the sum of its parts, but in the passion and pride of its collection, the light in the eye of the curator. Just as the *terroir* of the wine is richer than the minerals in its soil, the *patrimoine* of each town and village is the alchemy of life itself.

As for those of us who have come to learn that life begins with lunch; we know also that the lazy journey brings the most memorable views. Lunches and other meals may be planned a little later in this book. Life outside Marseillan begins on the next page.

# Agde [5] C2

To beach party pleasure seekers, the naked man on the roundabout by the hypermarket might be the only clue that Agde existed before the age of pink concrete. Not because of the nudity. Bare cheeks are the public face (or *fesses*) of Agde in the eyes of the wider world, since the naturist "city"

at Le Cap has long provided tabloid fare for the planet's red topped press and cable TV channels. It is the fact that the bronzed buttocks in question are modelled on those that first arrived in Agde some 2000 years ago, when the classical colonists of ancient Greece established Marseillan's big sister settlement along the estuary of the river Hérault.

Today's Agde is at least four destinations: the historic city itself, purpose built resorts of **Le Cap**, the old fishing village **Le Grau d'Agde** and **La Taramissière** across the estuary. **Le Cité**, the original settlement, is to be found a little way up the river, spilling into suburban trading estates and separated from the newer destinations by the D612 Sète to Béziers dual carriageway.

**Tourist Office**
**Cap d'Agde** rond-point du Bon Acceuil; 34305 Le Cap d'Agde
04 67 01 04 04 www.capdagde.com
Jul, Aug: 09-20 (Sat 09-05). Jun: 09-19. Oct-Mar: Mon-Fri 09-12, 14-18; Sat Sun 10-12, 14-17. Apr, May, Sep: 09-12.30, 14-19
The main tourist office at the central roundabout is a one stop advice shop and has a ticket desk for all events (usually closing earlier than the main information counter. One of the few remaining bureaux de changes in the area, now that most banks no longer change currencies in cash. The free street map is essential to negotiate the complex resort.

**Old Town** Maison du Coeur de Ville, rue Jean Roger 34300 Agde.
04 67 62 91 99 Tue – Sat 09-12, 14-18
**Port** quai du Beaupré, Centre Port, 34300 Le Cap d'Agde 04 67 01 51 57
Daily in summer

# Agde: Le Cité

France's own Cape of Good Hope: Ionian Phoceans settling here more than 2,500 years ago, named their colony *Agathe Tyche* (good fortune). A trading post midway between the Rhône at Marseille and new markets in Spain, Agde swiftly grew beyond mere safe haven and dock. By the 5th century, a wealthy town had risen along the Hérault with ramparts and grid-planned streets; its river port, safe from vagaries of the cape winds, and protected by Mont Saint Loup's look-out vantage point, last in the chain of volcanoes linking Auvergne to the sea. Mediterranean colonists, Iberian and Ligurian, Celt, Roman and true Greek, all contributed to civilising a chunk of lava into a basalt city hewn by each generation to create ever more elaborate and sophisticated buildings. Eventually, no less a frequent traveller than Marco Polo declared Agde "The black pearl of the Mediterranean"

Modern Agde is a lively and charming spot, the historic centre still flanked by ramparts and river and now bisected by the Canal du Midi: mute monument to one of the town's rare moments of oops. By refusing to chip in with funding for Riquet's Canal, which otherwise would have flowed naturally to the sea at Le Grau, to unite Old World and New, Agde lost out on the biggest money spinner of the 17th century, and the canal merely crossed the river, doubling back to the étang, assuring the fortunes of Marseillan and allowing Sète to challenge Marseille as Daddy of the Med. Of course, Agde was never really a loser. The 1697 civic arms feature three blue bands: sea, river and canal too. The seigniorial Bishops of Agde virtually owned Marseillan, politically, spiritually and commercially, right up until the Revolution, so were still keen to share in the spoils of trade. The church's dominance as lord of the county is reflected in the uncompromising angular silhouette of St Etienne's cathedral dominating ramparts, river and skyline. The region's litany of power battles between Franks and Moors is the thread of Agde's heritage. But here the tale has more fireworks. Whilst Marseillan had a discreet Revolution; in Agde, mobs took to the streets and the city supported and supplied the French armies along the Mediterranean coast. The bishop, Monseigneur de Saint-Simon, fled to Paris, seeking sanctuary, but nonetheless succumbed to the eventual and irrevocable justice of Madame la Guillotine.

Ever a magnet for refugees, the *Retirada* influx of half a million Spaniards fleeing Franco's regime in the 1930s led to the building of an internment camp. The site was called back into service on the eve of WWII, when Czech exiles used the base to form an ex-pat army to fight Germany. In a bitter twist of fate, the camp's role as refuge for Jews escaping persecution across Europe, was reversed, when Nazis seized control in 1942, their prey ready rounded up for shipping to the notorious Drancy transit camp, outside Paris. Adversity nurtures heroes. Just before Belgian refugees Hélène and Symcha Popowski, were deported to Drancy and Auschwitz, Sabine Zlatin, working as a Red Cross nurse, smuggled their baby daughter Diane to safety. Sabine gave the little Diane a sugar cube to suck on and distract her from crying as she hid the baby under her clothes, walking past the guards without being caught. In town, she tracked down Diane's grandmother, then hid the old lady and baby in nearby woods. By 1943, Sabine had founded an orphanage for the children she saved. The camp is no more, but images and personal memories remain at *Yad Vashem* holocaust memorial in Israel.

A lively and bustling city, the old town never rests on its historic laurels. Summer's entertainment rivals the resort: with riverside grandstands for *son et lumière* and jousting sessions; a floating stage on the Hérault to host free concerts by veteran singers. Ashore, jazz quartets perform on place de la Marine. Sometimes a hurdy-gurdy turns where the seductively named rue de l'Amour meets rue Montesquieu and place Gambetta, beguiling tourists as housewives with wicker baskets scurry past in search of fresh fish, salad and herbs. This is the place to shop – colourful art and pottery in the narrow side streets, and provender at **Les Halles** covered market; well signposted from all parts of town. Thursday's street-market day stalls wrap around the building and spill into nearby streets all the way to the ramparts.

Mostly mediaeval walls enfold the old town, but look closer on the river side to see traces of earlier fortifications from 4$^{th}$ century BC. Ramparts provide backdrop to daily life: one afternoon a *brocante* flea market, next morning racks of t-shirts for Cap escapees; otherwise a car park canopied with leafy trees; this is the Promenade, lined with cafes and bistros and a sauntered easing into the historic centre. Rue Jean Roger, by the Marianne fountain, links promenade to riverside and rues Louis Bages and Honoré Muratet encircle a quarter of tiny boutiques and craft shops, unexpected murals and 15$^{th}$, 16$^{th}$ and 17$^{th}$ century mansions. This is the oldest part of town. Along the Promenade, place de la Glacière has an ice house which gives its name to the quarter (*see page 148*) and is home to Agde's Catalan Roma community. Should you be in town during a gypsy wedding, pause to relish flamenco music and dancing. More Hispanic nuptial influences across the quarter, at the tourist office in the arcaded renaissance-style **Maison Consulaire,** rue Jean Roger. Built of volcanic rock in 1651 this was once the town hall and a magnificent staircase leads to the Salle des Marriages, decorated in 1939 by refugee Spanish artists.

Discover grand statues: At the roundabout as you arrive from Marseillan, the **Belle Agathoise** fountain. Auguste Baussan's allegorical symbol in carera and African marble is Agatha, spirit of Agde, protected by three lions. Her national sister, **Marianne** (*see page 36*) rises in Delacroix defiance from a twin fountain at the top of the Promenade. Not the original statue from 1909, since the Vichy regime melted down all bronzes, but a 1995 copy. Close by, a cross of Lorraine honours the *Résistance*

Midway between the monumental fountains, another Baussan bust shows dashing *corsaire* **Claude Terrisse** in Dumas hero style. Whilst *La Scribotte* is part of Marseillan lore, so the story of the "Good Pirate" is fondly retold in Agde. Terrisse was a privateer, a corsair who seized ships and cargo in the names of Louis XIII and Louis XIV, much as Drake and Frobisher had looted the high seas for Good Queen Bess. Respectability will follow wealth and he became Agde's consul, but won the people's hearts when he left his entire fortune to the poor. The tale often features in summer entertainment.

*Marianne of the Promenade*

Step down to the river bank for **Amphitrite**, aka Mrs Poseidon. The goddess of the sea balances atop a huge globe on **place de la Marine**, home since she left Paris' Trocadero in 1936. This is the quarter of *pêcheurs*, nets, boats and narrow cottages all around, and tourist waterfront restaurants augmented by traditional fishermen's bistros. Keep an eye open for votive statues and carvings of virgins and saints on street corners and in hidden nooks; prayers and thanks for safe return of mariners a way of life here for centuries. Continue along the waterfront to join locals queuing for fresh fish from the boats in the morning. By the way, the name of the city, often mispronounced as Adge (as in Madge), should be articulated to rhyme with dragged, sagged, lagged and bagged; past participle of the verb *to ag*.

**Cathedral Saint-Etienne**
In 1173, seigneur bishop Guillaume converted a 9th century Romanesque church into an impregnable castle cathedral, part of the actual ramparts with toy-castle crenulations. Walls up to three meters thick and the main keep some 35m high. Great concert venue, the German Baroque style organ is of more recent vintage (1990). The building segues into town walls, an hotel and even a distinctly secular nightclub at crypt level on the quayside where posters for swingers' parties are more in the spirit of the Cap than the Cité.

**Château Laurens**
Across the river, hosting July's all-night jazz marathon and many a country market, this park began life as a farm, became an island when the Hérault was spliced by the **Canal du Midi** and its *Canalet* below the weir. Château Laurens stands in the **Belle Isle** park; trophy mansion of a 19th century explorer and traveller. Emanuel Laurens travelled widely in search of art and inspiration and built his villa between 1898 and 1901 to house his collection. Architecturally inspired by contemporary European and eastern art movements, the château is a confection of classical colonnades and balustrades with *art nouveau* stained glass and ironwork.

**Ecluse Ronde**
With three exits, a 29m diameter ring of local basalt stone is the only round lock on the **Canal du Midi**. Big enough for boats to turn a full circle and enter the main canal to Béziers and beyond, the final spur towards the Etang de Thau and Marseillan or take to the Hérault and its estuary. *See page 343.*

**Eglise Saint-André**
Close to the market place, this was the site of one of Agde's first two churches. The building dates back to 1525 with 19th century neo-gothic main door and interior décor. An archeological dig in the late 1980s revealed 5th and 6th century graves.

**Eglise Saint-Sever**

The fishermen's church by the place de la Marine is dedicated to a 5th century Syrian prince who founded a monastery in Agde. Dating from 1499, it is home to a dazzling wooden sculpture of Christ on the Cross, almost certainly as old as the building itself.

**La Glacière**

5 place de la Glacière, 34300 Agde

Not merely the name of a square and quarter in the old town, the ice house itself still exists, providing a teasing glimpse into a forgotten way of life. From the 17th century, this 8 metre deep, 7 metre diameter basalt dungeon beneath the ramparts was the store room for winter ice to be used for keeping fresh fish from the port all year round. Harsh winters led to a new *métier*: ice farming. Ice would be cultivated in the ditches between river bank and ramparts and along the vineyard lanes. Carried to the ice house and insulated with straw and sacking, ice was sold in summer under the arcardes of the **Maison Consulaire**. Not just for refrigeration, but to make the (then) harsh wines more palatable and for medical use: with olive oil and herbs to ease skin complaints, serve as a painkiller, even treat cholera.

**Musée Agathois**

5, rue de la Fraternité, 34300 Agde

04 67 94 82 51

Closed Tue and 21 Dec- 3 Jan

Daily life in Agde, from first classical settlers to the 20th century, is seen in a string of two dozen audio-guided galleries of a renaissance family home. Discover domestic vignettes and glimpses of long-lost trades, crafts and skills. The story of water jousting, wine making and fishing, legends and costumes all presented alongside an interesting art collection featuring French art nouveau and other works brought to Agde from far off lands.

# Agde: Le Cap d'Agde

Not one, but the best part of a dozen purpose-built Mediterranean holiday resorts, midway between Spanish Costas and French Riviera. Casino bling and shiny white yachts, golf greens and technicolor rainbows of ice-cream, make a polychrome backdrop to a seaboard chain of secluded coves, vast sandy beaches and alternating ranks of sunbeds, parasols, pedalos and jet-ski stations. Vacation conurbation where every possible is assured: splashing on waterslides or rambling through nature reserves; where you may set sail on a midnight conger fishing trip or shop for couture in your birthday suit. Officially, France's biggest tourist resort with enough beds for 175,000 people: 50 years ago this was but a wild headland on the rocky coast, the same lava cliffscape that might have greeted Greek or Egyptian sailors in millennia past. Flicking through photo albums, from just two generations ago, Le Cap was a gentle wilderness, a small cluster of homes amid rocks and beaches. Then on the cusp of the '60s and '70s, France's grand plan to create a new holiday concept changed the coastline forever.

The original idea for nurturing *la perle noir* did not come from President Pompidou, but was the pet scheme of an *eminence rouge*. Louis XIII's mentor Cardinal Richelieu planned to create the ultimate Mediterranean harbour by building huge jetties stretching from the banks of the Cap out to the island of **Brescou**. Rubber-stamped by the King's council, work began in 1632. However, Paris enthusiasm waned on the cardinal's death in 1642, and planned subsidies evaporated. Eventually, nearly two decades after the scheme was launched, the grand port of Le Cap d'Agde was quietly shelved and the coast kept from the limelight for another three centuries.

Mosquitos around the wetlands and the success of the Riviera to the east and Biarritz across the Pyrenees had seen Languedoc shunned by tourists during the original 19$^{th}$ century craze for seabathing. So a grandly titled *Mission Interministérielle d'Aménagement Touristique du Littoral Languedoc-Roussillon* was set up to create six tourist resorts in this vast forgotten corner of France. Irritating insects were eradicated and the concept of **Le Cap d'Agde** agreed by the town council in 1963. Six years later, architect Jean Lecouteur began to make his designs a reality:

Fanning out from that original settlement on the coast, now known as Le **Vieux Cap**, would be ten distinct districts; each landscaped with pine groves and beaches and tinted with oleander and bougainvillea to soften the inevitable outbreak of concrete. Inspired by form and shades of traditional Languedoc villages, hues of sand and terracotta, rose pink and sunset ochres and yellows, the concept was to alternate bustle and calm in an arc around a central port. Bridges spanned to four islands in the harbour: **Iles des Marinas, Ile des Pêcheurs, Ile St Martin** and **Ile des Loisirs**. This marina with its **Saint-Martin** port district was first to be developed. During the 1970s, **La Môle, La Roquille**, and the greener, quieter quarter of **La Clape** grew out to the east. The same period saw the evolution of the most famous of the Cap "villages", the naturist quarter with its independent **Port Ambonne**, marina and 2km long beach. Tabloids and the more sensational cable TV documentaries paint the entire resort as a 24/7 orgy; unrestrained shagopolis of lust and depravity, every vista framed by sweat, debauchery and rampant genitalia. The truth is more wholesome, but no less extraordinary. The family naturist "village" is the world's largest "city" for nudists: self-contained community where up to 80,000 summer visitors may travel without risking Ryanair's baggage surcharges. Apart from the beach, holidaymakers may go shopping, visit the bank or the doctor's surgery or launderette (why?) and dine *sans textiles* in restaurants and cafés. Most visitors are pure naturists, on holiday with no sexual agenda, but, as in any modern resort, a more explicit romping scene also thrives. But let's not forget that a conventional *auberge* by a village *en route* to Montpellier has a flashing sign on the roof offering *Soirées Libertine,* and swingers' *echangiste* venues are common in the most respectable towns of France.

Whether wife-swapping in the seventies-snigger manner or gay cruising to the max, a rampant raunchy element exists within dedicated night clubs and venues and certain areas of the beaches and dunes. Two self-contained libertine complexes, named after the gardens of Eden and Babylon (why Eden, where the raunchiest moment involved a reptile and a bramley?), encourage public sexual activity, but these are far from general tourist areas and family *plages naturistes* remain free from unwelcome distraction. I cannot decide whether a local councillor was being naïve or shrewd in 2010 when she declared swingers had turned Le Cap into a "Disneyland of Sex", winning global headlines. In truth, you will not find yourself here by accident and clothed perverts may not descend on beaches to ogle nor salivate, since patrols of discreet stewards ward off "textile" visitors. Voyeurs not admitted and cameras banned. March to October, "frontier" checks with swipe cards are required to enter the village, and an admission fee is payable. Long before the resort was mooted, much of the area was owned by *la famille* Oltra, olive farmers who regularly rented camping pitches on their shore to holidaymakers with a taste for nude bathing. When town planners stepped in, the Oltras lobbied for a naturist quarter. The etiquette of naturism has its own guidebooks, and evenings tend to be semi-nudist, with T-shirts sported sans-dessous, and enough designer accessories to nudity to eclipse egalitarianism. Ironically, the only place on the coast to buy *Chanel* and *Hermes* is within the **Village Naturiste**.

Over the next decade, before the final **Rochelongue** district was born, the resort came of age with a western expansion named for **Richelieu** himself. Leisure was key: international golf course, *Aqualand* waterpark, an *Aquarium* and the *Ile des Loisirs* playground island with funfair, nightclubs, cinema and the casino. Now the Cap could compete with the mainstream.

The stamp of cultural respectability came when Paris' *Louvre* museum returned *l'Ephèbe,* the celebrated statue of youth, to the shores where the 2,300 year old marvel first rose from the deep and to a dedicated museum of underwater archaeology built amongst the pines to house France's prized collection of antique bronzes close to the waters in which they were found.

Myriad holiday apartment blocks in mini-neighbourhoods of restaurants, grocery stores and cycle lanes jostle another residential level of marinas, home to both gin vessels and genuine adventure craft. Glamorous gleaming white fibreglass and smoked glass dock by ever-varnished wood. 3,000 moorings at the main *Port de Plaisance* and another 300 at the *Port Ambonne*. Yacht club and *capitaineries* welcome new visitors and old hands alike. Shuttle boats link all parts of Le Cap and go out as far as Grau d'Agde. Gantry hooks remind passers-by that tuna fishing on the high seas is as much a local sport as the mini-golf between manicured flowerbeds, and fishermen sell fresh catch from tables at the avant port, beneath olive shadows from roof garden duplexes of wealthy landlubbers for whom *la grande large* is a mere lifestyle design component of the perfect view.

Golf club, casino, waterparks, funfairs and beaches determine individual holiday styles. And the inevitable **Petit Train** motorised road train caterpillars around the resort, with a multilingual soundtrack. Four one-hour options available from the pick up point on quai Jean Miquel, Centre Port : eastwards towards the volcanic landscape; westward ho, for ancient history; panoramic view from the hills; shops in the old city. Summer evenings, hop on and off at Richelieu and Rochelongue plages. **www.lepetittrain.fr**

**Aquarium**
11 rue des 2 Frères, 34300 le Cap d'Agde
04 67 26 14 21 www.aquarium-agde.com
Jul-Aug 10-23; Jun, Sep 10-19; Oct-May 14-18
Download a free MP3 audioguide to your phone for a walk through displays of sharks and jellyfish, coral and seahorses.

**Aqualand**
avenue des Iles d'Amérique, 34305 le Cap d'Agde
04 67 26 85 94 www.aqualand.fr   Mid Jun-early-Sep 10-19
Huge waterpark for all the family, with a smaller **Captain Jacko** park for the under-12s. Closes an hour earlier at the beginning and end of the season.

**Capitainerie** rue de la Capitainerie, Bassin 1, 34300 le Cap d'Agde;
04 67 26 00 20; Summer 8-20, off season 8-18
Harbourmaster for information on moorings and facilities for boat owners.

**Balneocap**
88 chemin de Notre Dame à Saint Martin 34300 le Cap d'Agde
04 67 21 20 59 www.balneocap.com daily
10-20; Fri 20-22
Day spa water and volcanic mineral treatments. Alternatively, **Résidence Natureva-Spa** (04 67 32 16 51 http://natureva-spa.com) in the naturist quarter.

**Casino**
Ile des Loisirs, 34300 le Cap d'Agde
04 67 26 82 82
Sep-Jun 10-04; July Aug 10-05
Glam casino package with 180 slot machines available all day. Blackjack, roulette tables and poker room from 21h. Free admission to gaming rooms (with passport). Restaurant and bars and floor shows, from cabaret through glitz and feather floor shows to ladies' nights of abs, bowties and baby oil.

**Club Mickey**
Parking plage Richelieu, 34300 le Cap d'Agde
04 67 26 76 93
Jul-Aug, Mon-Sat 10-18
Supervised children's holiday centre. Playground, trampolines and swimming pool. Boating, diving and riding activities for over 7s; playgroups for toddlers.

**Dinopark**
Ile des Loisirs, 34300 le Cap d'Agde
04 67 26 65 13 www.dinolandpark.com
Family theme park with animated dinosaurs, crazy golf and rides, with boucy castles at Dinoland. Various ticket and pass prices for multiple visits. Serious dinosaur fans should visit Mèze (*see page 191*).

**Musée de l'Ephèbe**
Mas de la Clape, 34300 le Cap d'Agde
04 67 94 69 60
Jul-Aug: Mon-Fri 9-19.15, Sat Sun 12-19; Nov-Feb: Tue-Sat 9-12, 14-17;
Mar-Jun, Sep-Oct: Mon, Wed-Sat 10-12 14-18, Sun 14-18
The eponymous *Ephèbe* itself has become the unofficial symbol of Agde, far more so than the Parthanon-style muse *La Belle Agathoise*, and replicas can be seen across the city – including that roundabout by the hypermarket. The Greek bronze is supposed to be inspired by portraits of Alexander the Great, but as even the shallowest scholar of politics (or rolling news) is aware, world leaders tend not to be drop-dead gorgeous, and I guess this was more PR than an accurate representation. The sculpture was found in the muddy waters of the river back in 1964, and was soon snapped up by Paris where it stood as male totty with the *Venus de Milo* and *Mona Lisa* in the *Louvre* before returning home to Agde. Don't miss two recently discovered roman statues (a cupid and a child), canons from the age of Louis XIII, pottery and household items from the ancient city and trophies from a thousand years of shipwrecks.

**Golf du Cap d'Agde**
4 avenue des Alizés, 34300 Cap d'Agde
04 67 26 54 40 http://golf.ville-agde.fr (*See page 374*)

**Manade Sauvan**
Les Verdisses, 34300 Agde
04 66 53 92 24 www.manade-agde.com
Jul-Aug: Tue, Thu 18; May June: Sun 10.30; May, Jun Sep Thu 18.
The little black bulls of the Camargue are as legendary as the horsemanship of the *guardiens*. No need to travel to **Aigues Mortes**, as here, on the Vias road, expert ranchers show their skills on a farm where *taureaux* are raised.

**Village Naturiste**
rond-point du Bagnas, 34300 le Cap d'Agde  04 67 26 00 26
End Mar-Sep: welcome and entry control point.

## Walks

**Le Mont Saint Loup**
Stunning panoramic views all around: this extinct volcano has dominated the skyline for the best part of the past million years, as largest of the last three volcanic hills of the Auvergne's mountain chain. A protected natural park, no cars allowed, it is perfect for nature rambles, seasoned by scent of pine cones, crunch of acorns and crush of garigue herbs underfoot and heady spring fragrance of almond blossom. Rising above the nature reserve of **Bagnas** (*see page 47*), weekly escorted walks around the volcano booked through the same organisation ADENA (www.adena-bagnas.com). From the 113m summit, look south to the hectic bustle of the cap, westwards to the cliffs and on to the Grau and Tamarissiere lighthouses, then north to the étang and wetlands for an unforgettable palette of muted colours.

At the summit of the Mont Saint-Loup, the **Sémaphore**, built in 1836, was principal beacon of the coast until 1903 when Sète's lighthouse took over. Lantern room and gallery live on as a naval signal station. On the south slope, stand ruins of a basalt Pyramid. No relic of ancient civilisations, but the work of military engineer Mareschal who designed it as part of a string of watchtowers that lined the Languedoc coast - including **Castelas** on the beach road from **Marseillan Plage** and another at **Sète**. A warning flame could be lit atop the 23m tower and as many as three sentries at once would be stationed there. Built in 1750, this **Tour des Anglais** was named not for tourists, but less welcome arrivals, after a 2000 strong Anglo-Dutch fleet attempted to land at Agde during the Spanish war of Succession. The *Petit Train* (*see page 151*) offers a photo opportunity excursion to the volcano district, travelling just as far as the smaller **Mont Saint Martin**, now home to many luxurious private villas. The trio of hills is completed by the **Volcan Petit Pioch** overlooking the golf course

**Underwater trail**

Explore the *Sentier Sous Marin* but forget stout walking boots: this hike requires flippers, goggles, wetsuit and a snorkel. Stroll from **La Plagette** beach to discover hidden beauty of an underwater land and seascape. The trail is a 400-metre circuit in and under shallow waters. Discover flora and fauna of volcanic sea-bed, plateaux and canyons. Unaccompanied trails for independent explorers are marked with buoys and undersea information panels; on organised eco-trips arranged by ADENA, qualified guides escort groups of eight, explaining wildlife, marine and volcanic environment and includes loan of flippers and masks, waterproof guidebooks, even underwater cameras. 06 10 97 04 22 www.adena-bagnas.com

**Winegrowers walk** *(see page 47)*
**Reserve Naturel du Bagnas** *(see page 47)*

## Watersports and boating

Sailboarding, kite-surfing, jet-ski, kayaking, scuba diving and even swimming excursions amongst dozens of organised and supervised activities and classes on the water. Volleyball and other sandsports on shore. With fishing trips or renting a pedalo for an hour or a motorboat for a week at sea, you have the ultimate range of diversions for the sports minded. Passenger boat trips leave the ports of Le Cap, quai Merric at Le Grau and the banks of the Hérault in the Cité. Download the latest list of sports and boating organisations, venues and prices at www.capdagde.com

## Agde: Le Grau d'Agde

Between the trading post of the ancient world, development of a political seat of power behind city walls and hedonism of the modern Cap, Agde's heart has always followed the pulse of a simple Mediterranean fishing community; tucked away at the mouth of the Hérault, where freshwater meets the sea. Le Grau d'Agde, was once a modest cluster of poster-painted fishermen's cottages, growing from hamlet to thriving independent community when an influx of Italian families (already stalwarts of Sète's fleet) set up home at the turn of the 20th century. Between the two world wars, a modest holiday resort sprung up with *résidences secondaires* amid *peupleraie* and *pinède* groves of poplar and pine. Marseillan families too set up summer homes behind the beaches. Pleasing marine and domestic architecture, a nicely-proportioned modern market place, first-rate local shopping and even schools nudged along the roadways as eventually the place become something of an upmarket suburb of Agde: an easy drive, even easier cycle ride, into town.

A bike path tags the river's left bank, part of a 16km network of cycle lanes linking Agde's varied communities. Thursday, boats ferry locals and visitors between the Grau and the market of the *Cité*, and a ferry shuttle links Le Grau with **La Tamarissière** on the opposite bank. Le Grau has two shores: the beachside from St Vincent to the estuary lighthouses, and the riverside quai Commandant Merric, where restaurant terraces are nuzzled by pleasure boats: purpose-built sightseeing craft and old wooden schooners promising moonlight fishing, daytrips to the resorts, and excursions to the island, canal and out to the étang.

Horizoned on a delightfully low-level small scale, a pleasant drive from the old town offers a view more akin to Henley-on-Thames than a traditional Mediterranean scene. Fishing boats skim past at a varsity oarsman's pace, only the squawk of rapacious gulls in their wake, and the echo of the *Criée*, quayside fish auction, belies the mirage. This trade market is a daily highlight, as restaurants reconsider their *plats du jour, selon le marché*.

Away from the water, a hinterland of stables and studs, leafy lanes and high walled villas, promises two intriguingly named diversions. One is the *Université des Temps Libre* (University of Free Time) a concept to thrill the soul, and reality of uplifting, inspiring lectures. The other is a chocolate box quaint string of photogenic chapels around the priory sanctuary of **Notre Dame de Grau**, a pretty diversion for pilgrims on the trail from Saint-Gilles to Saint-Jacques de la Compostelle. As you drive past in the confusion of a one-way diversion back to town, you see a picturesque spot where locals chain their *vélos* and play *boules* in the dust under the shade of old pines, waiting for the hamlet's only restaurant to open.

Many visitors merely snap a photo of the garish 1920 Virgin of the Rock statue and look no further. That is their loss, since the chapel next door celebrates a tsunami miracle, promises and delivers the preserved kneeprints of the Blessed Virgin and was once so popular a place of pilgrimage that it clocked up a record 172 processions in 1612 alone. The original 5th century monastic retreat, founded by Agde's Syrian prince St Sever, has been home to Benedictine and Capuchin orders. Fame came with a later place of worship: when at the end of the 16th century, Henri de Montmorency, head of the French army, commissioned a chapel and church on the site of a local miracle when the community had been saved from tidal wave by divine intercession. The story goes that, as waters engulfed the land between sea and city, one monk refused to leave and stayed to pray in the face of the rising tide. The sea spray cleared, and a vision of the Virgin herself could be seen, kneeling in prayer alongside the holy man. As the apparition vanished, so miraculously did the sea retreat, and the land was saved. The sun evaporated the last traces of flood and on the rock could be seen the imprint of the Virgin's knees. These marks are still the greatest treasures of the church of **Notre Dame de l'Agenouillade** (Our Lady of the Genuflexion) also known as the kneeling chapel (*La Genouillade*).

### Fort de Brescou

Brescou Island is best visited as part of a boat trip from le Grau d'Agde, better yet on a sunset *sardaignade* fish barbecue on the shores (*see page 286*). A classic fortress, this was actually a 17th century upgrade; reconstruction of a weaker earlier 1586 fortification, destroyed in 1632, restored as gateway to Richelieu's aborted Cap d'Agde development. It was rebuilt to Vauban's designs in 1680, as part of the military architect's famed ring of 300 walled defences around the Sun King's realm from Lille to Luxembourg and Perpignan to the Jura. Perched on the only volcanic island in the Golfe du Lion, a mile off-shore, it became a prison at the time of the Revolution and continued as Languedoc's Alcatraz until 1851. Choose a boat for your trip from kiosks along quai Commandant Merric.

## Agde: La Tamarissière

To glimpse what this coast might have been like before a concrete eruption upstaged the volcanos nearly half a century ago, hail a water taxi shuttle from the quayside at Le Grau d'Agde to the opposite bank of the river. Apart from the gentle low level cluster of homes and rather good restaurants, La Tamarissière remains closes to its original identity, a huddle of tamarisk and pine groves, waterfront woodland first planted in the 18th century when work began on preventing the mouth of the river from silting up. Escape from the crowds of the Cap to walk in the woods or fish from the jetties. Until 1905, the forest was closed to the public, but now it is a listed protected site with the reed beds of **Le Clôt** left to wild birds, and the pine trees to squirrels. For 3 months each summer, a camp site allows a limited number of holidaymakers to experience the area. Property developers would love to get their hand on the site, but common sense and a respect for the environment has prevailed, and houses here rarely find their way onto the open market.

# Agde – The Beaches

Eleven distinct *plages* stretch from the **Cap** to the **Tamarissière**. The widest, broadest central stretch offers a good ten miles of unrestricted sunbathing, and smaller rocky coves, sheltered by the cliffs, are a world apart from the bright parasols and coca-cola signs of the main drag. As the coast turns, enjoy superb views north to Sète and, on a clear day, south to the Pyrenees Don't forget the barbecue on the shores of **Brescou Island**, as an alternative to a traditional beach. Since the resort was developed in the age of the motor-car, you'll find ample parking close to all beaches.

**La Grande Conque** Locals favourite black sand beach - a niche sliced through volcanic cliffs. Iconic twin rocks *Les Deux Frères*.

**Plage Naturiste** Strictly controlled access to the broad and spacious naturiste beach *(see page 149)*. Family section is closest to facilities, regular organised sports and games. Further along are the more "adult" cruising areas. From the main entrance, disabled sunseekers may rent *tiralo* beach wheelchairs.

**Le Môle** and **La Roquille** Central beaches with easy pedestrian access from the resort. Organised sports at the eastern end and facilities for the disabled at La Roquille's shell beach. Caters for the family holiday market and its attention spans.

**La Plagette** Prettier and smaller beach by the cliffs. Start of the underwater trail *(see 154)*

**Richelieu** A good and spacious run of family beaches in the newer western section of the resort. Bucket and spade heaven for kids, diving and seaside sports and plenty of places to eat for a mass-market holiday crowd. Beach club bars and organised water sports.

**Rochelongue** Another well landscaped space, this is part of Agde's modern answer to Barcelona's ramblas along the Mail de Rochelongue. Beach volleyball tournaments organised during the school holidays. A beach library offers free loan of over 1000 novels, comics and newspapers.

**Baie de l'Amitié** At the end of the chemin des Dunes , where the resort of Le Cap gives way to the resident community of Le Grau is a sleepy beach, with an excellent restaurant.

**Saint-Vincent** Along the avenue du Littoral and the private villas and low level housing is a mixed sand and pebble beach, where the sea is deep enough for swimming close to shore.

**Le Grau d'Agde** The mini resort plage of Le Grau d'Agde, the other side of the lighthouse to the quays of the Hérault . Facilities for disabled.

**La Tamarissière** Unspoilt beach by the pine woods. *See opposite page.*

# Aigues Mortes [5] D2

"The walled town that a school-boy draws upon his slate. Extraordinarily pictorial, as if it is a very small sister of Carcassonne" so wrote Henry James on his first visit to the capital of the **Petit Camargue**. Famed for its 1,634m ring of stunningly preserved ramparts, walls and fortified towers; unlike Carcassonne, Aigues Mortes still resembles Louis IX's early 13th century creation. Lazy arrivals go straight to a café by the eponymous statue on place St Louis after indulging at the *caves dégustation* or stocking up on local rice and *fleur de sel* at Wednesday and Sunday morning's market on av Mistral. Them, fortified, take a shuttle boat to tourist trap beaches at **Le Grau du Roi**. The more active discover **Camargue** on horseback, by sightseeing barge or bike. From Marseillan, the "other" canal beyond the *étang*, tucked behind Sète, leads to this city of a king dubbed *Le Saint Louis*; perfect mediaeval fortress in a rugged triangle of open country between **Montpellier**, **Nîmes** and **Espiguette** lighthouse and beach (*see page 77*). Somehow, it seems unfair that a king who civilized a malaria-ridden swamp should die of typhoid in a strange land. But history rarely does happy ever after. Aigues Mortes was not founded on altruism nor hygiene. Papal pressure had been put on Louis to lead fresh crusades to the Holy Land, but in 1245 France did not own a single Mediterranean port. Languedoc belonged to the Spanish, and Provence was German, so Louis bribed Psalmody monks with decent fertile faming land by Sommières in return for *les aigues mortes* (dead waters) of a rank and stinking swamp linked to the sea by a branch of the Rhône. Aigues Mortes was the very last (albeit mushy) French soil the king would tread. In 1270, he left on his 8th crusade and shortly thereafter died in Tunisia. The city, completed 15 years later, glory days lasted barely 200 years. In 1481, France finally grabbed Marseille, trumping forever a port in a bog, reliant on silt-prone estuaries.

At the tourist office, by leafets on cycling, jet ski or 4x4 safaris, grab free city maps showing each gate and tower, whether you choose to walk or whistlestop by *petit train*. Ramparts are wheelchair accessible, and audio guides offer livelier soundtracks for youngsters under 12. Most famous site, the imposing drum **Tour de Constance** (originally known as the *Tour du Seigneur du Roi*), notorious as an 18th century prison for non-Catholics; the guides tell tales of heroes such as Abraham Mazels who escaped, and Marie Durand whose 38 year incarceration made her a martyr. 3km from the city, **Tour Carbonnière** gatehouse still provides top views on the original road through the marshes. Within the walls, grey and white penitent chapels are rainy day options, but this is sunshine country for the great outdoors; romantic land and waterscape of wild white horses splashing along the coast and dashing *gardien* cowboys chasing bulls; twitchers come for a vast range of birds, migratory and sedentary. History provides another visit: *Les Salins*, working salt farm that predates the city. 26000 acres of sea water evaporates to crystallised salt, forming the 20m-high, 400m-long white mountain known as **la Camelle**.

**Office de Tourisme d'Aigues-Mortes en Terre de Camargue**
place St Louis, 30220 Aigues-Mortes
04 66 53 73 00  www.ot-aiguesmortes.fr
High: Mon-Fri 9-20, Sat Sun 10-20; Mid: Mon-Fri 9-19, Sat Sun 10-19;
Low: Mon-Fri 9-12.30, 13.30-17.30; Sat Sun 10-12, 14-17.30

## Manade ranches

The iconic image of the **Camargue** is that of the *gardiens*, those black-hatted, tight waistcoated horsemen who ride the wild country and round up the little black bulls destined for the *Cours Camarguaise* bullfights, where the young animal is not killed, instead chased by plucky lads who try to throw ribbons around the horns without being injured. In nearby **Saintes Maries de la Mer**, haunt of Hemmingway and Picasso, where the biblical Marys (Jacobe, Salome and some say Magdalene too) arrived on French soil after the crucifixion, having sailed from Alexandria, accompanied by their Egyptian maid Sarah, Romany folk from all over Europe gather each spring for a season of gypsy weddings and dancing. Sarah is patron saint of the Roma and her statue is carried from the church down to the sea over several days partying and young girls choose a husband from the *gardiens*. See cowboys at work year round at **Manade** ranches. In summer, riders and gypsy musicians offer unforgettable evenings on the farm: sounds of guitars and aromas of cooking: seafood barbecues and local beef dishes, red wine and sangrias.

**Manade Lafon**
chemin de la Vieille Roubine - 30220 Aigues-Mortes
06 03 43 46 85 www.masdelacomtesse.fr
Leave by boat for 90-min ranch show of horsemanship and bull running, with a traditional meal (Jul, Aug: Tue, Thu). Summer Friday evening rancher *aperitif.*

**Manade Saint Louis**
Mas de la Paix, rte des Stes Maries de la Mer, 30600 Vauvert
06 11 42 24 14 www.manade-saint-louis.camargue.fr
Gypsy music, cowboy demonstration and barbecue meal (Jul, Aug: Wed Fri)

**Manade Agnel Frères**
prés de Chaberton, 30220 St Laurent d'Aigouze
06 12 33 57 48
Friday morning breakfast picnic and ranch visit

# Balaruc  |5| C2

Don't forget your socks when you leave Balaruc. You will have taken them off quite early in the day. Officially, Balaruc is two places at once: **Balaruc les Bains** and **Balaruc le Vieux**. In reality, there is a third identity: the *Centre Commercial* by the A9 exit offers a day's chain-shopping to those who never realise that a splash of history, decent swimming, excellent dining and a cure for arthritis exists five minutes beyond the 10 items or less check out. Leave the 4x4 shopping traffic to wend its way back to the fast lane, and instead concentrate on life beyond the loyalty card. As a well-groomed contemporary resort, with plenty of landscaped and palm-shaded gardens and parks for the mornings, afternoons of of lido swimming and pedalos and a nightlife of blackjack, cabaret and restaurants; the strip of contemporary hotel blocks might lead a casual visitor to assume **Balaruc-les-Bains** to be the modern, shallow, callow younger sister of the mediaeval village of **Balaruc-le-Vieux**, perched high on its panoramic vantage point looking out across the waters, the wetlands and the **Gardiole** forest.

In fact, it is the resort that boasts the more classical lineage, a thermal spa dates from what the French love to refer to as *l'Antiquité*. A plaque at 35 av du Port testifies to the town's healing waters being protected by Neptune himself for 2000 years. There is no record of any earlier colonists of the coast claiming Balaruc for Poseidon, but Roman heritage is strong, with 3rd century villa foundations glimpsed amongst more modern construction in the town centre. Balaruc's steady fortunes are owed, fully and outright, to the healing qualities of the water in France's only Mediterranean spa resort. France is ostentatiously irrigated by thermal stations and mineral springs, from Atlantic to Alps, Parisian suburbs to Auvergne volcanos, and Balaruc is rated in the top three *cures*. Until very recently, a free stay at one of the many spa hotels, with regular treatments from underground *thermes*, might have been prescribed by your GP. The sheer number of blue-badge parking bays suggests a smart secular, less optimistic, alternative to Lourdes. In France, water-cures are considered mainstream medicine, and the local *Mercure* and *Ibis* chain hotels, which elsewhere might rely on travelling sales reps or conference trade, focus on *les eaux*.

Balaruc has long managed the almosy impossible trick of being popular with both the sick and the beautiful. Certainly, holidaymakers here tend to a riper vintage than at **Le Cap** and **Marseillan Plage**, and at close inspection, *tattouage* on the *plage* tends to be the work of varicose veins rather than needle-wielding artists. Yet, good shopping in town and chic outfits on parade at better restaurants testify to a continuing relationship with the

160

well-groomed and modish. Twas ever thus: inveterate society letter-writer and wit Madame de Sévigné urged friends and family "*Il voudrait aller aux eaux de Balaruc*" and in 1687 plied an *habitué* of the resort with questions about how to take the waters: "For what disorders are they taken? Are they taken for the gout? Have they ever benefited those who have taken them? At what time are they taken? Are they drank, used as a bath or is the part affected simply immersed in them?" Modern visitors receive a neat little handbook to deal with 21$^{st}$ century version of these FAQs, whether they go to the new **O'balia** complex or visit rival treatment centres. Mud, water and alternative therapies and massages work on aches and pains. The waters have long been hailed for powers over arthritic and rheumatic conditions, and many are the knees, wrists, hips and ankles that have returned from a week or two in Languedoc feeling younger and more sprightly than before.

The town takes the form of a peninsular jutting into the *étang*. The coast facing Mont Saint Clair of neighbouring Sète, lined with restaurants, has slim stretches of beach and boardwalk leading to a designated swimming area, backed by an unbroken run of restaurants: starched linen drapery on glazed terraces. The other side of the *presqu'ile* belongs to hotels and residences, an occasional restaurant and the serious business of the *cure*; enjoying the best view of the Thau: picturesque shot of beautiful Bouzigues neatly framed package of pastel and terracotta twixt the blues of *ciel et mer*. View of views is higher up, behind the holiday town, by the historic walls of the old village that perches above the marshlands of **l'Angle**, as the last corner of Balaruc's penisular is known to the locals; over the unspoilt source of the freshwater that feeds the lagoon: **Balaruc le Vieux** takes a classic *circulade* shape, its slender alleys and traffic-free streets, enclosed by renovated 12$^{th}$ and 13$^{th}$ century ramparts. Arrive early enough to visit the magnificent 14th century church of **St Maurice**, and wander the narrowest passageways in a quarter redolent of feudal past. History revives here each July, when the annual mediaeval festival sees recreations of banqueting and jousting, equestrian flair and some coarse acting. Some villagers dress as crusaders as others, garbed as lepers and beggars, besiege gateways, poignant reminders that not everyone in the good old days wore white robes or tunics of red, blue and cloth of gold. You may encounter great horsemanship year round, as nearby riding schools have a fine reputation.

Needless to say, most visits do not take place at festival time so visitors must make imaginary puissance and merely dream of noble steeds printing proud hooves in the receiving earth of the **Gardiole** woods and *l'Angle*'s wetlands. Occasionally a misty view from the ramparts might reveal a slim procession of real horses treading a strip of land between the ponds, water rippled by the rustle of wading birds. Do not get too comfortable with your imagination when shadows lengthen. Instead, make eventide way around the rampart trail to the **place du Truc**, above the old original port, and look out across the Etang de Thau, for the ultimate sunset over the oyster tables and a vibrant and quite unforgettable silhouette of the lagoon and its lands.

After dark, the resort has its **casino** for blackjack, roulette and slot machines, a varied programme of stage plays and cabaret in season and year-round cinema to while away an evening away from gaming or dining tables. 2000 years of tourism has not yet weaned the town off the local habit of punning. Just as the town knife-maker works under the name *Cou'Thau*, the only cinema in town, reinforces its commercial status in a destination with a long term captive audience with the word writ large above the door: *CinéCure*. I am now seriously considering opening a basement restaurant selling British cuisine: the *Thau Dinner Hole*. Updated programme of diversions for resident *curistes* or itinerant lotus eaters courtesy of the tourist office. More than merely a brochure brokerage with good tips on days out of town (perhaps the Gardiole forest), the office is found, alongside a brace of art galleries in the **Pavillon Sévigné**, original thermal cure building. And this is where you take your socks off. Outside the *Pavillon* is a foot spa, circular pool fed by healing waters that gush from the earth at a constant 37 degrees Celsius. The low wall around the pool is gossip central, as habitués and visitors share *bavardage* and restaurant recommendations, bare feet tingling, trousers rolled up to the knee.

**Office de Tourisme**
Pavillon Sévigné, square Dr Bordes, 34540 Balaruc les Bains
04 67 78 23 02 www.balaruc-les-bains.com

**Casino de Balaruc**
rue du Mont Saint Clair, 34540 Balaruc les Bains
467 48 00 56 Open daily 10-4

**Centre Commercial Carrefour**
route de Sète , 34540 Balaruc le Vieux
The *Centre Commercial Carrefour* is the biggest retail park on the étang, so most people pull off the A9 and stock up with the heavy stuff here at the usual huge hypermarket. There are several other food outlets amongst the electrical and DIY retailers of the car parks. The *Biocoop* is an organic supermarket with opening hours that appear to be calculated on a lunar basis; *Leader Price* budget yet quality everyday own brand food; *Picard* is for the *Waitrose* shopper, decent frozen food more deli-yummy than industrial; and *Grand Frais* ultimate fruit and veg shop: an entire aisle of

different salads, in season countless pineapples from a dozen countries, and fruits from the far flung to the exotic. All constantly sprayed with cooling mist. 5-a-day to nth degree. Find limousine and charolais beef, pasta and dairy too. *Troc de l'Ile depot vente*, is like *eBay*'s *Buy It Now* writ large. Leave second hand furniture here for others to buy (the store takes a cut) or furnish your Languedoc home without branding it as Made in Ikea.

## La Cure Gourmande
place de l'Ancienne Gare, 34540 Balaruc les Bains
04 67 80 01 72 www.la-cure-gourmande.com
9-20 daily
A pretty confection in its own right on a ribbon of industrial buildings and town-plannified roundabouts, is the quaint old railway station tarted up like a granny's biscuit barrel. Appropriate, since this is the famous biscuit and sweet factory, a business conceived, against all first impressions, way back in the nineteen-eighties when retro-wrap fashion was at its height, to bake old-style hand-made biscuits and sweets and revive the art of evocative tins and packaging. The sweet-shop belongs to a perfect world of Willy Wonka as recreated by Norman Rockwell *à la Française* and is already the winner of any number of prestige awards for artisanal produce. Piles of chocolates and candies, the local speciality *Berlandises* (sweets stuffed with real fruit), and proper suckable lollipops fill wooden dressers groaning with colourful biscuit tins from the turn of an earlier century and rustle up waves of nostalgia. Tour the factory if you call in advance. You may appreciate the extended weekend opening hours as a boon for last minute present buying en route to the airport (Balaruc is on the A9). You might even negotiate a franchise in Lowestoft, Luton, Louisianna or La Paz. The station may have long closed down, but the company is intent on going places.

## Spas
A new health centre **Obalia** opened its doors in 2010 with treatments both traditional and fashionable. Alternative private clinics and hotel spas cater to all tastes, budgets and conditions. The best first point of contact would always be the Tourist Office, which produces an annual guide to spas, treatments, and has prices and details of deals and packages.

**Pedalo hire** 06 31 67 78 32 Peak summer months only.

---

**Bus 10** runs year-round services between Balaruc and the mainline railway station at Sète. Each day. **Bus 14** leaves the shopping centre at around quarter past the hour every hour from 6-19 and runs along most key streets of the town and the resort. €1 per ticket or a *carnet* of 10 tickets for €8.

# Bages [5] B3 *(see pages 208, 290 and 368)*

# Banyuls-sur-Mer [5] B4 *(see page 342)*

# Bédarieux [5] B1

The capital of the *Hauts Cantons* keeps the mountains from the coast. A coach trip from *Marseillan Tourist Office* offers a taste of the hills and villages of the *Haute Vallée de l'Orb*. The rest of us arrive, when foraging for food on a rare Monday market. Or perhaps returning from the goat farm at **Mas Roland** (*see page 360*). Plenty of foodfests: May's *Foire au Jambon*, August's wine event, or mushrooms and chestnuts in November. Bédarieux's summer *cafés vignerons* promise dinner with winegrowers. Briefly English (captured in 1364), long-time Protestant (since the Reformation), the town was once a hive of traditional industries: textiles and tanneries; mining, when coal from Bousquet d'Orb travelled over 27 arches of an 1853 rail viaduct. Mines closed in the 1960s; as fresh air and nature trails formed a new industry. Hikers tramp **Causses** limestone hills, munch lunch on dry stone walls and seek out *capitelles* (age-old shelters) should the weather turn. Best view from **Pic de Tantajo** (518m). **Boucle d'Orb** loop has the **Chapelle St Raphaël** by river vines, where pilgrims dip hankies in a cave spring; holy waters to cure eye conditions. For *patrimoine* without abusing shoe leather, stay in town to hear three fine 18th-century church organs at **Eglise St Alexandre** or the Protestant **Temple** where the instrument is a listed heritage monument as is that of **Eglise St Louis**. In August, place du **Jeu de Boules** hosts the national *pétanque* championships.

Nearby, **Pézènes-les-Mines** was the first Languedoc address I knew, when my sister spent a summer *au pair* in the **château** whose mediaeval walls embrace a picturesque village of streets but an intake of breath wide, and virtual staircases between, beside and behind stone houses. In troubadour spirit, local lad Olivier serenaded Hélène from below the ramparts. Who needs paperbacks, when real life offers such Catherine Morland moments? Years later, we returned to the old roman bridge over the river Peyne, heard that a roman wine press had been unearthed at **Mas de Pommier** and returned to the château (a private home) where the *chatelaine* sells charming ceramics from an estate boutique. She is not alone. In each hamlet, puppet workshops or stained glass ateliers, as artists revive forgotten buildings. Treasures at every turn: 13th century Madonna and Child at **Les Montades**; honeys and *pains d'epices* from wayside farms.

**Maison du Tourisme et Maison de Pays**
1 rue de la République, 34600 04 67 95 08 79 www.bedarieux.fr
Summer: Mon-Sat 9-12, 14-18; Winter: Mon-Fri 9-12, 14-18, Sat 9-12
Maps of the hiking trails and gastronomic dining and driving circuits

# Bessan [5] C2

A legendary rosé to sip at one end of the road and heady aroma of *pastis* coming from the *Ricard* distillery across the way; so you may be forgiven for blaming on the booze the vision of dancing donkeys that greets your eyes as you head down to the riverside for an afternoon at a *guinguette*. Yet, even your most sober companion will have seen the same thing: when Bessan throws a party, the show ain't over 'til the dancing donkey has kicked his hooves in public. Languedoc villages love their totemic animals, carnival time sees wooden, canvas, papier mache, sometimes floral incarnations of each commune's symbolic beast, and these mascots regularly join the parades in neighbouring towns (*see page 192*). I'd like to think that Bessan's donkey represents the high octane kick of country wine and spirits, but the mascot predates the hooch. Old timers talk of days past when Bessan hosted donkey fairs; farmers and wine-growers traded mules and asses for working the land. Perhaps they are thinking of the St Laurent celebrations, as founded by King François I in 1533.

The legend of a town enamoured of an ass actually harks back a further 800 years and around 30 miles upstream, to a tale with echoes of a gaggle of roman geese. Are you sitting comfortably? Then I'll begin: In the early hours of the early years of the 8th century, the town of **Gignac**, south of **Saint Guilhem le Desert**, was roused one morning by the braying of a donkey, alerting the townsfolk to the arrival of Saracen invaders. The raiders, furious at the beast's warning, hurled the poor animal into the Hérault's fast flowing waters. The current carried the donkey along until it reached the banks of Bessan where it was welcomed as a hero. Gigean also has a donkey town mascot. The present day donkey costume, garlanded with flowers and worn by four men, evolved from mediaeval festivities, when for one day each year, the *Bessanais* would revolt against the clergy's substantial power, and crown the village idiot as king for a day, Lord of Misrule. The unfortunate fool would be led through the streets astride a donkey, and then the beast having gorged its full on food and wine was unleashed to run amok in the church of **Saint Pierre**. To avoid the annual destruction of stained glass and other treasures, the priests eventually proposed a man-made donkey mascot be paraded instead.

When carnival is not on the agenda, a popular lazy afternoon option is to while away the hours at the *guinguette* by the Hérault for summer dances by the river, a half hour with an ice cream, or an afternoon on the water on a rental boat. They've distilled *pastis* in Bessan long before **Ricard** moved into town (*see page 131*), and rosé has been a speciality from the 19th

century. Oldest taste of the town does not come in a glass. It may be sampled at the bakers or pattissierie. *La Croustade de Bessan* is a chocolate and walnut confection first whipped up in the 16th century. It would be bad manners not to stop off and indulge. Mask gluttony with an excuse to stay a while, and let a keen appreciation of local history justify the hour or two before *croustade* time. The church, from the 10th century, was subject of a legal wrangle between rival monasteries, with a 40 year court case of Jarndyce and Jarndyce proportions during the 12th century to determine whether monks of Saint-Thibéry or those of La Chaise-Dieu could claim rights to **St Pierre** in Bessan. The Tiberians won and the church evolved through architectural and political fashion and fortune until most recent renovations in 2004. The original steeple was demolished in the 1930s after storms rendered it unsafe, but the bell-tower remains, with the oldest bell in the Hérault, cast in 1388, its younger sister dating from 1567. Three other bells removed during the revolution, melted and reborn as cannons.
**Tourist office**: *see page 218*

**Le Rosé de Bessan**
Cave Coopérative de Bessan, chemin de la Coopérative, 34550 Bessan
04 67 77 42 03
Closed Sun
Where better to taste the famous town tipple than at the magnificent co-operative winery built on the eve of World War Two by architect Paul Brès, whose designs for Agde, Florensac and Montblanc co-ops were already as iconic symbols of the region's developing wine business, as Holden's suburban underground stations were to the emerging Metroland of pre-war London. The shop and tasting room is the ideal place to enjoy *rosé* made from Syrah or Cinsault-Grenache. If you can't decide what to wear for your first sip of *Rosé de Bessan*, the co-op has a second shop in the naturist quarter of **Cap d'Agde**. As a refreshing apero, try *Le Bessanais*, twist on a traditional kir: Bessan rosé with blackberry (rather than currant) liqueur.

**Cactus Park**
By the cemetery on the road to Vias. 04 67 77 16 16
Apr-Sept: open daily. Zoo only: Feb, Mar, Oct: Wed, Sat, Sun (and school holidays) pm only. Closed Nov - early-Feb
It may not be Giverney, but what Monet's garden in Normandy boasts in irises, it lacks in yaks and cacti. When you come south to see water lilies, lotus blossom and aquatic plants in the water-garden of Bessan, you get a surprising range of bonus attractions. For starters, the waters are an unexpected treat in themselves, since this is after all a cactus park, home to thousands of cacti, succulents, palm and bamboo. And children will enjoy an animal park with yaks, goats, sheep and exotic birds.

166

# Béziers [5] B2

I have a soft spot for Béziers. It was founded by an Egyptian saint, has had its share of religious wars, has a canny eye for business and, despite a matador's aim for bulls, adopted the camel as its lucky mascot. The town came into its own financially mid-19$^{th}$ century, when it embraced new railways with more gusto than neighbouring Pézenas, so winning trade for a century and beyond. Respectability then assured with a *Galleries Lafayette* department store and several theatres. Another reason for its awareness of public transport and betterment is that the second most famous son created the Canal du Midi in the 17$^{th}$ century, linking the Atlantic with the Med, and bankrupting himself into the bargain.

The greatest of all *Bitterois* (as the good folk of the city are known) was the remarkable *Résistance* leader Jean Moulin (*see page 174*); yet in the immortality stakes, canal pioneer Paul Riquet is a pretty good hero for anyone's money. Unrecognised in his own lifetime, the 19$^{th}$ century saw the townsfolk erecting a statue to the great man in the middle of the eponymous **Allées Riquet** grand promenade that splices the city centre.

*The cathedral city, from a picnic spot on the Canal du Midi*

167

Few retired tax-collectors win that sort of public acclaim. *The Allées*, from the grand theatre down to the **Plateau des Poètes** park spilling down to the railway station (and new shopping mall) are for strolling in the cool breeze of the evening, subsiding into a rattan chair and ordering a *menthe à l'eau* after some serious shopping in the sales: chain stores ring the top of the avenue whilst the narrow back streets towards the **Madeleine** and **Hotel de Ville** have superb boutiques, well worth the browsing. You may sit outside and order a *plat du jour* as tray-swaying waiters nimbly negotiate snail-pace traffic that kerb-crawls along ranks of cafes and restaurants on the ground floor of ornately carved and balconied 19th century buildings whose lintels are signed by architect and mason. Friday's market is a bewitching marriage of caged birds and lavish foliage (*see page 248*). But neither the *Allées* nor the statue are the true Riquet monument. Step down from this hilltop Cathedral city and pass beyond the 11th century Romanesque **Pont Vieux** spanning the river Orb to see the **Canal du Midi** in full bloom. An elegant aqueduct carries the canal over the river and the **Fonserannes** ladder of locks takes the waterway to the summit of an even greater hill than that of the city *(see pages 172 and 347)*.

Always at forefront of transport trends: Just as it recognised the potential of the canal, so Béziers was poised for the original railway revolution and gained control of the 19th century wine trade; at the dawn of the 21st, it lobbed local money at its aerodrome and created an international airport to woo *Ryanair* from Montpellier. Meanwhile, the city began to develop a modern business district by the TGV station whilst national politicians were still arguing about the high speed rail route to Spain. A ready-made crossroads awaits, between London, Paris, Brussels and Barcelona. The new **Polygone** combi shopping mall, dining, bowling and leisure complex is already up and running by the station. Free parking for cinema and a shuttle bus into the centre of town **www.polygone-Béziers.com**

Pioneering spirit is literally in the soil. The commercial wine trade is the *raison d'etre* of many fine restaurants in town, and *vignerons* have vision. Monsieur Pugibet, the creative *vigneron* who developed a low alcohol *vin plume* for business lunchers without compromising on quality, is now experimenting with virtually alcohol free wine. You cannot remove alcohol entirely or you end up with the sugared juice other nations have attempted to slip onto a market. Yet retain the alchemy that a touch of spirit gives the taste buds, whilst keeping below the fraction of a percent permitted by religious temperance and you might open the world of wine to a massive new market, so confided Pugibet, a few months before unveiling the first bottle. Surely the conservative wine trade will ridicule the move, I suggested. "Would you have imagined ten years ago the French would stop smoking in restaurants and bars?" he countered, "Smokers now even step outside at home now. The world changes." *See page 109.*

Awareness of this outside world did not always make friends. Béziers has a particularly bloody history, its churches have been slaughterhouses as much as sanctuary. Once-upon-a-timing here begins with a trip to the local history museum to round up artefacts from the earliest Neolithic and Celt identities. Pride of ancient times was the Roman era. *Baeterrae* wine considered good enough for export back to Rome. Moors ruled for the first half of the 8th century until Martel's notorious purges. A train of Béziers viscounts ran the entire region, the city title oft coupled with Toulouse and Carcassonne. From the 11th century, the Trencavel family held court until Pope Innocent III's Albigensian Crusade. Innocent did not take too kindly to the city's liberal welcome to the Cathar community. Thus in July 1209 came the massacre. Béziers' Catholics, tipped off about the crusaders' planned attack, did not flee but stayed behind to defend their neighbours. Ruthless slaughter followed. The original cathedral burnt to the ground with perhaps a quarter of the population sheltering within. At the Madeleine church, where so many had gathered on the Saint's day, the Papal Legate made his notorious declaration of no mercy. *"Neca eos omnes. Deus suos agnoscet.* Kill the lot of them! The Lord knows His own!" When Simon de Montfort and his knights finally left Béziers, the entire population had been wiped out. This ricochet between welcome and persecution that marked the Cathars is echoed in the stories of other faiths. Jews were granted sanctuary, exiled, offered renewed sanctuary, shot, and eventually granted sanctuary again plus two synagogues and a kosher food co-op. Archaeologists recently found traces of places of worship on the site of a former ghetto.

By the 15th century the city was back on its feet, a restored cathedral, now with castellar cladding, topped the hill. But blood still dripped. Plaques honour many victims of persecution and political revenge. In 1851 Louis Napoleon's troops fired on Republican sympathisers; the winegrowers' revolt of 1907 turned ugly; and of course there are memorials to the *Résistance* and victims of the Nazi occupation. Even Béziers' totemic camel was not spared political execution. Symbol of founding saint, Aphrodisius, who arrived in town on his exotic mount, a model camel from centuries of pageants and fairs was burnt or destroyed during religious wars and at the Revolution. Religion aside, *Bitterois* unite in love of two sports. A proud rugby town, with a fine stadium, the local team's heyday was between the 60s and 80s winning 11 French titles. Some 55 local players swapped red and blue city colours for the national strip of *Les Bleus*.

The other great game is the *Corrida*, and the *Féria de Béziers* is an anuual highlight. Wines are renamed and a huge taurine silhouette heralds the august festival year round from slopes above the canal. The bullring echoes nightly to the roars of the crowds. Horsemanship, dancing, music and feasting fill streets and squares day and night and none shall sleep over the week of August 15 when a million visitors descend on Béziers. Year round, **bullfighting museum** shares the enthusiasm and explains the culture (*see page 171*). A "new" red brick and stone **arena,** built in 1897 with remarkable acoustics, is also an ideal venue for opera and concerts (although never forget the lovely theatre at the end of the *Allées*). Béziers has had an arena, stadium or theatre since the Roman settlement in 36 BC. The first **Roman amphitheatre** was victim to Martel's destructive tour of the region. Gothic mediaeval buildings covered the site in the St Jacques quarter, until archaeologists recovered the terraces in 1992 and restored several Doric columns. Check with the tourist office for possible visits.

Slaughter aside, I tend to visit during the Middle Ages. Fortunately for me, the mediaeval period returns like Groundhog Day early each summer when the town dons period head-dresses, grooms horses for mortal combat and steps back into the past in time for cherry season. Less violent and ruthless than first time round, **Les Caritats** is a three-day weekend festival that combines historical revival with a superb country market. Shops and cafés join in, welcoming troubadours and wenches; even MacDonald's servers dress up. Taste wines and olives, chocolate, fruits, and honeys on the *Allées*, or join an ox roast on place de la Madeleine. A makeshift citadel, with a war camp on place Jean-Jaurés and *les lices*, "lists" of the age of chivalry. No bank holiday fun day *Sealed Knot* re-enactment in NHS specs, but an exciting, dramatic tournament played by professional cinema stunt riders. No holds are barred and jousting knights bear true scars by nightfall. Religious savagery downplayed, knights of old are closer to the heroes of fiction than villains of Béziers' painful past. Jugglers stroll through the streets and children learn skills: baking to archery. Modern questors run a half marathon through vineyards of surrounding villages.

### Tourist Office
**Office de Tourisme Béziers Mediteranée** 29 av Saint-Saëns, 34500
04 67 76 84 00 www.beziers-tourisme.fr
Jul-Aug Mon-Sat: 9-18.30, Sun 10-13, 15-18; Jun, Sep 9-12.30, 13.30-18; Oct-May 9-12, 14-18
Download free English language audioguide to the city from the website. City bus tickets €3 for a carnet of 10 tickets. But the shuttle bus *Le Lien* offers a free hop-on-hop-off service between station and the Allées Riquet. Branches: place Lavabre (Apr-Sep) and *Fonserannes* (Apr-Aug).

## Béziers Aventure

Bois de Bourbaki, route de Bessan, 34500 Béziers
06 25 43 41 37 Feb-Nov hours vary
Ten acrobatic treetop trails and paintball in woods outside town.

## Cathedrale Saint-Nazaire

Seat of powerful bishops since the 5th century, the grand château that appears on the horizon when arriving by road or water is no castle but a cathedral. An earlier building was razed to the ground by de Montfort's crusaders during the 1209 massacre, according to contemporary accounts "exploding like a grenade". The present Mediterranean Gothic cathedral dates from the 14th and 15th centuries. The sun rises behind bible stories in the choir stained glass and sets through an elegant rose window above a main door that is rarely opened, since it is on the path of the most violent of winds. Treasured tableaux of Moses and Christ by the pulpit were rescued from an abandoned convent. Atop the 120m hill, a vaulted nave looms 32m high, dominating the landscape. Nearby **Bishop's Palace** is now the law court, but the **Episcopal Gardens** survive, elegant patterns of *parterre* planting, reachable by some steps from the tranquil cloisters and offering stunning views of the Orb plain to the Med and Pyrenees.

## Cimetière Vieux

Avenue du Cimetière Vieux, 34500 Béziers
Some days, the monument to *Notre Dame du Moucadou* resembles the aftermath of a convention of Shakespearian Desdemonas. Locals leave hankies here, a gesture said to bring good luck. Shady cypresses canopy this high walled graveyard on the slopes of Saint-Nazaire hill. It looks like a castle, but is more an open air museum of statuary: some stunning 19th and 20th century masonry by the likes of Jean Magrou and Jacques Villeneuve and the ubiquitous Injalbert (*see* **Musée Beaux Arts; Plateau des Poètes**).

## Espace Taurin

1 avenue du Président Wilson, 34500 Béziers
04 67 36 71 01
Jul-Aug 10-18; Apr-Jun, Sep-Oct 9-12, 14-18; Nov-Mar 9-12, 14-17
Lovers of the *corrida* quote Hemmingway to justify the romance of the sport; I cite Noël Coward's retort to the suggestion that no one who ever loved horses could enjoy a bullfight: "nor anyone who loved bulls either!" The bullfight museum is for the Hemmingway crowd; sharing passion for the annual *Féria*. Besides stunning posters for the annual festivities, gems include signed pictures of great matadors, several legendary "costumes of light" and an art collection featuring etchings by Goya.

**Fonserannes – Les Neuf Ecluses**
04 67 28 44 19 (waterway info); 04 67 28 13 05 (tourist info)
Nowadays, seven (or seven and a half for the pedantic) locks make up the legendary stairway that allowed Paul Riquet to take his Canal du Midi up and over a "mountain"; but no less spectacular a cascade (*see page 347*). Gongoozle Central on a sunny Sunday, the inevitable **Petit Train** makes its way up here from the town centre (daily Jul Aug; weekends Sep-mid-Oct). Floating restaurants take diners along the canal as far as Agde, sightseeing trips, electric boat and bike hire all available and occasional exhibitions.

**Golf Saint Thomas**
route de Bessan, 34500 Béziers; 04 67 39 03 09 *see page 374*

**Les Halles**
place Pierre Semard, 34500 Béziers
www.halles-Béziers.fr ; Tue-Sun 7-13.30
On the site of a mediaeval paupers' cemetery, the classic glass and steel covered market hall was inspired by Paris' *Baltard* pavilion. Opened in 1897, renovated in the 80s and again in the 21$^{st}$ century, now a fantastic place for foodies. You can even buy your meat, fish and veg from the stalls and have it cooked and served to you in situ. *See page 247 and 294.*

**La Madeleine**
Place de la Madeleine, 34500 Béziers
Dominating a broad plaza of café tables atop an underground car park, a peach stone's throw from *Les Halles*, inscrutable slabs of limestone make up the flat-faced façade of the church. The Romanesque nave and the bellower still echo to a bloody history (*see page 169*). Church to the ruling Trencavel counts, parts date back to the 10$^{th}$ and 11$^{th}$ centuries.

**Musee Régional de l'Art Contemporain** *see* **Serignan** *page 231*

**Musées du Biterrois & d'Histoire Naturelle**
Caserne St Jacques, Rampe du 96ème, 34500 Béziers
04 67 36 71 01
Jul-Aug 10-18; Apr-Jun, Sep-Oct 9-12, 14-18; Nov-Mar 9-12, 14-17
Natural history and local history collections share these former barracks in the historic St Jacques quarter. With the usual three Bs (birds, butterflies and bones) and plenty of rocks for enthusiastic geologists, a natural history wing also has aquaria of indiginous river and sea species. The *Musée du Biterrois* presents prehistoric, roman and mediaeval archaeological finds and tells the often gory history of a great city and its remarkable people.

## Musée des Beaux Arts - Hôtel Fabrégat
Place de la Révolution, 34500 Béziers
04 67 28 38 78
Jul-Aug 10-18; Apr-Jun, Sep-Oct 9-12, 14-18; Nov-Mar 9-12, 14-17
Of two grand private mansions housing the Fine Arts museum of Béziers, Hôtel Fabrégat has unexpected treasure trove. Besides the predictable Degas, Rodin and Corot, the collection lurches back as far as the 15th century to include work by Holbein among others, and has 20th century galleries featuring Utrillo and Dufy. A very special gem is the bequest by Laure Moulin of the sketches by her brother Jean, whose dream, although coerced by his family into a legal and political career had been to be an artist, even though Destiny had another role for him *(see page 174)*.

## Musée Des Beaux Arts - Hôtel Fayet
9, rue du Capus, 34500 Béziers
04 67 28 38 78
Jul-Aug 10-18; Apr-Jun, Sep-Oct 9-12, 14-18; Nov-Mar 9-12, 14-17
This 16th century mansion houses works large and small by the Béziers sculptor Jean-Antoine Injalbert (1845-1933) and several of his contemporaries, alongside a collection of 19th century paintings. A courtyard garden hosts delightful summer evening performances of concerts and plays. Programmes from the tourist office.

## Plateau des Poètes
Jun -20 Aug 07-21; 20 Aug – Sep, Apr-May 07-20; Oct-Mar 07-18
One of those grand 19th century municipal garden projects to fire the imagination. The coming of the railway at the city's lower level meant that the Béziers new front door was physically way below the main promenade of centre ville. The solution was to create a tiered park from the Allées Riquet down to platform level and so continue the perfect esplanade stroll from the theatre down to the train. Eugène Bühler, designer of Lyon's grand *Parc de la Tête d'Or* created a theatrical cascade of greenery and grand open spaces, with banked flower beds and weeping willows fringing a pond, and flamboyant tumbling planting showcasing the art of the city's finest sculptors. Injalbert himself came up trumps with busts and statues at every turn, and trees and plants from across the globe were blended in dramatic backdrops. The principal poet honoured is Maffre Ermengaud, a 13th century monk and troubadour from Béziers, although the park is dotted with images of many great writers, including Victor Hugo atop a column. Statuary not to be missed includes the grand Titanic fountain of Atlas carrying the world on his back, the war memorial and the stunning tribute to Jean Moulin *(see page 174)*. An underpass avoids the main road.

HÉROS DE LA RÉSISTANCE

POSTES

8 F

JEAN MOULIN
1899-1943

RÉPUBLIQUE FRANÇAISE

## Jean Moulin and Liberation

ANY STORY, and every map, of modern France is peppered with references to the great Jean Moulin, remarkable hero of the *Résistance*; the defiant beaurocrat and secret artist who cut his own throat to keep his confidences and died at the hands of Nazi butcher Klaus Barbie.

Visit Béziers' *Hotel de Ville* for a home town memorial in a foyer bedecked with names of so many local heroes, from the fallen of the Great War to peacetime firemen trapped in blazing barracks. Pay private homage at the memorial at the *Plateau des Poètes*. Witness the great man's private life as an artist *au Musée des Beaux Arts*.

On 22 August, Béziers commemorates its liberation, and the city tells the story on the banks of the Orb. One summer, we joined the *Bitterois* by the bridge. Lasers, that we had seen rehearsing their swirls against water, sky and screen, now prepared to re-enact the legend of a modern Moses in this high tech *seder* of struggle and liberation. A Passover of our times.

On the opposite bank to the old walled city sat hundreds of locals in the park, ranged along tables waiting for their celebration dinner to be served; in the park and all along the stone bridge stood the crowds, including our quartet that had staked a pitch an hour or more before, anticipating the event as the sun set over the ramparts high, the arches of *Pont Vieux* making full circles in the glass calm waters of the river beneath.

Few tourists in this crowd; just the good townsfolk; parents with their children, here to pass on their history to a new generation. It was a most private of public spectacles. The clock struck the hour, and a father next to me placed his daughter on the parapet of the bridge, a protective arm anchoring her to the safe harbour of his embrace. His chin resting on her little-girl locks, lips poised to whisper through the events to come.

Ten, fifteen, twenty minutes after the appointed hour, the town went dark, all street and house lights extinguished and the music began. The voice of the river boomed out, and lasers signed the title sequence: *Libération: Jean Moulin*. And history repeated itself. We saw Béziers after its losses in World War One. We met the young Moulin, heard his ideals, knew his family, felt the Latin heat of a city so close to Spain, joined his fight for justice in the Spanish Civil War, heard his wedding vows as the cathedral atop the hill was illuminated with nuptial glow, and fireworks flared and glared above us.

Then the pyrotechnics took a sinister turn, and they became bombs of war. 1940 arrived and an end to ideals. Paris was occupied and the disdain and scorn felt by Moulin, by now a regional Prefect, for the collaborating Vichy Government reverberated as we heard Moulin's own voice all but spit the names of the rulers of that regime. De Gaulle across the land and sea in London called Moulin to head the *Résistance*, and Jean's war was brought closer, horribly closer, to home. His interrogation and fatal torture at the hands of Barbie and his Gestapo in 1943 was horrid to behold, albeit with mere sounds and Munch-like illustrations.

Tears obscured our view of the fireworks that marked the eventual liberation of France. The *Marseillaise* of home melting into the Elgar of the Allies, as we celebrated freedom with the awareness that this modern Moses would likewise never see his promised land.

Chastened, uplifted, fulfilled, we followed and blended with the crowds into the *Faubourg* park, where a band played Latin music of the 'forties, and my nephew Joe watched his grandparents dance, secure in their freedom so bravely given by a few true heroes, before we climbed up into Jean Moulin's city for a final drink and *tapas* and the drive home.

*"Think of this man as you would have reached out your hands to his poor, unrecognisable face on that last day, to those lips that never let fall a word of betrayal: on that day, his was the face of France"*

**André Malraux, 19 December1964**
**as Moulin's ashes were placed in the Pantheon**

# Bouzigues     [5] C2

There is something of St Ives about Bouzigues on the Etang de Thau. When you come to know the three settlements on the northwest shores of the lagoon, you soon learn their individual quirks: Marseillan is the wise one, the responsible one, with classic good looks; Mèze is the practical one, busy and holding down a reliable job; but Bouzigues is the pretty one, enchanting to visit and even lovelier from a modest distance. Artists are drawn to the village, even if the best view of Bouzigues is from a restaurant across the water in Balaruc. The slightest latent talent begins to tingle the fingers and you yearn to set up an easel the moment you slide off the dual carriageway and arrive at the waterfront of a village built on oystershells. As Venice is made for *Agfa* film, Bouzigues is perfect pretty-please for watercolours. Each negligent arc of a mast or sail in the harbour, the stone breakwater, those rocks along the shore where paths give way to nature, the view over oyster tables to Mont Saint Clair: all cry out for the miniature immortality of a sable brush. This is a fishing village, its secret spilled in the same pastel shades that betray fishermen's cottages from the coves of Cornwall to Burano on the Venetian lagoon.

Stop by the **Musée de l'Etang de Thau**, not just for the quick lesson in oyster farming through the years, but to find the spirit of a community that has worked these waters from simple traditional fishing days through to the age of sea-sells and tourism. Long before the oysters came to the lagoon, Bouzigues was grazing land for sheep: as salt marshes around Mont Saint Michel still furnish Normandy's finest lamb, pastures below Mont Saint Clair once played a similar role in the south. Then came the surf and turf years, when shepherds shared the coast with sedentary fishermen, who, rather than putting out to sea in ships, harvested fish that swam into the lagoon from the *grande bleu* beyond. Fishing won out, and shellfish farming began with indigenous mussels from the étang. The oysters that now carry the name of the town throughout the world are *arrivistes*. At the beginning of the $20^{th}$ century, after a failed attempt to raise oysters at **Frontignan**, beyond **Sète**, a group of fishermen decided to try afresh at Bouzigues. Thus the locals became known as the *paysans de la mer*, farmers of the sea, growing their own oysters from the tables (never say "oyster beds" here) within a flat boat's easy chug from home. In the 1920s, farmer Louis Tudesq set up his distinctive frames, suspending strings of oysters to be hauled up for harvest, and came up with the first *Degustation*, tasting room, serving seafood direct to consumers, and his is still the oldest waterfront restaurant-hotel-farm business (*see page 296*).

The name Tudesq literally runs through Bouzigues, along the road that stretches from coastal snack shacks to fashionable decking facing the marina and view. And Bouzigues oysters bear a name so respected that the town is amongst France's *Sites Remarquables du Goût*, providing us all with a seriously upmarket food fair at festival time. Only the nation's officially listed prestigious foods are allowed in the main tent (another accredited Languedoc nibble is **Collioure**'s anchovy), tasting exceedingly scrumptious, with Armagnac and prunes from the west, wines of Alsace and Champagne from Eastern counties and other treats: Puy lentils or beef of Aubrac presented by *départements* in between. Non-accredited farmers sell no less delicious wares in the streets: a *marché du terroir* for hoarding local honeys, onion *confits*, wines and cheeses. Other oyster fairs dot the calendar and the town's alternative gifts and interests also win occasional showcases. I remember looking down on a side street from a friend's roof terrace and seeing an intriguing sign advertising a school of dance and sailing, since when I have scanned the gait of fishermen on the jetties for tell-tale signs of something niftier than a hornpipe; twist of tango, timestep or hint of latent fleckle to prove the success of one particular establishment.

Bouzigues' artistic bent is served with plenty of little art and craft shops and exhibitions displaying the works of local artists and visiting talents, and the town has often hosted festivals of comic book art. But if you are looking to take home a painted or sketched memory of the place, just look out for the easels set up along the waterfront.

### Musée de l'Etang de Thau
quai du Port de Pêche, 34140 Bouzigues
04 67 78 33 57
You know the sea-life centre is going to be that little bit different and so much more French when aquarium exhibits come with serving suggestions. My abiding and most treasured memory of this museum is not the excellent displays of fishing techniques, images of oyster farming through the decades; nor learning when wood from Camaroon was introduced to the oyster tables, why tables are leased for 25 years and when fishing became self policed. No images of boats nor geological revelations of the lagoon basin peppered my thoughts for weeks. I cherish instead vivid recollections of large fish tanks showing native species of the lagoon. Bream, sole and eels coasting behind the glass, beside neatly printed information cards. But where lesser museums offer such timid extras as Latin names, details of habitat and breeding; here the card above the sea-bass advised visitors to add lemon, garlic, parsley and a glass of white wine and to cook for just 45 minutes.   A well designed and managed exhibition, decent English translations and a comprehensive introduction to the area and its culture.

**Ferme Zoo**
450, chemin des Aiguilles, 34140 Bouzigues
04 67 78 30 13 http:// ferme.zoo.free.fr  closed if raining
Jul-Aug: Tue-Sun 14-19; Off-season Wed, Sat, Sun and School hols 13-18
Many centuries since sheep outnumbered oysters in Bouzigues, but this
little hobby-farm-zoo helps tip the balance lamb by lamb. A sweet little
farmyard began with a few fluffy pets, now has geese, goats and pigs,
shetland ponies and the odd llama and emu to add a touch of the exotic. No
rival to the African reserve at **Sigean**, but a friendly unthreatening treat for
tots as good behaviour reward for sitting quietly and playing nicely earlier
when Mummy and Daddy stopped off to taste yet another Chardonnay.

**Musée du Sapeur Pompier**
Caserne, Zone Artisanale de la Gare, 34140 Bouzigues
04 67 78 32 57 Closed mid-Sep – mid-Jun
Two hundred years of fire-fighting heritage celebrated in the barracks of
Bouzigues fire station. Rows of polished brass helmets from the first days
of the voluntary fire service, models of fire engines and boats tell only half
the story. Informative panels explain how the local brigade tackles forest
fires in the back country and deal with more traditional "shouts" today.

# Carcassonne   [5] A2

I visit Carcassonne when there is an anachronism in the month. For me,
festival time, whether rock concert, *son et lumière*, opera or come-back
appearance by a major recording artist of a lost generation, brings the
picture book turrets and ramparts into perfect relief. Historians may draw
breath to fuel a frown, but let's face it, Carcassonne is simply howbusiness:
a grand what-if reinvention of history, designed for romantics. Hollywood
chose Carcassonne to double for Nottingham in the Kevin Costner-Alan
Rickman flick Robin *Hood, Prince of Thieves*. No wonder the annual
festivals here pull in the big stars. In just one recent summer, you could
enjoy the city's mediaeval charms with a soundtrack performed live by Bob
Dylan, Suzanne Vega, Roberto Alagna, Jamiroquai, the Prague
Philharmonic, Motorhead or a Charlie Parker tribute band, had you not
already spent your money on tickets for Bizet's Carmen or Shakespeare's
Twelfth Night. In truth, like *patisserie*, Carcassonne is more appetising on
the outside than within. As you approach, whether by country lane or A61
motorway, the vision of **Le Cité**, perfectly walled old town, rises above the
treeline and over endless vineyards of the *vin du pays d'Aude* to dominate
the countryside and send your heart into Walter Scott mode, seemingly
promising a golden ticket to the age of chivalry.

Overnighters should take a room outside rather than within the *Cité* to appreciate views of what Carcassonne might have been, rather than waking to the commercial reality of a barrage of commercial logos and souvenir stalls clogging a warren of winding lanes. Just across the river Aude from the newer town, the *Cité* stands 485 feet high, marked by 2 miles of double walls fortified with 52 towers. Round and square turrets from the 12th and 13th centuries appear in pristine condition. This is because in the 19th century, commissioned by Prosper Merimée (then government inspector of ancient monuments, but better known to history as author of *Carmen*), architect Eugène Emmanuel Viollet-le-Duc renovated the entire edifice as a lasting reminder of the golden age of fortification. Like most memories, this re-creation is somewhat hazy on details, adding pretty pepper-pot roofs to some towers to please contemporary tastes of a France that felt freshly warm and gooey over rediscovered illustrated Books of Hours and fairy tale castles. Enter through one of two gateways: **Porte d'Aude** by the river or the twin-towered **Porte Narbonnaise**.

In spring or summer, you might take a 20-minute tour by horse-and-trap or the inevitable **Petit Train**; or you may strap on your sturdiest boots to explore on foot at any time. No charge to walk around, day or night, but the château and museums are subject to opening hours and admission fees. The inquisition chambers, where Cathars and fellow politically-defined heretics were subjected to horrendous treatment during interrogations, now form Europe's most comprehensive museum of instruments of torture. Not for the faint hearted. Open daily until 18h (in summer until nightfall). After visiting the possible tomb of Simon de Montfort and some definitely stunning 13th and 14th century stained glass windows at the **Basilique Saint-Nazaire**, climb the ramparts to imbibe vistas of endless vines. These ramparts are actually two rows of stone walls sandwiching **les lices hautes** and **basses** (upper and lower lists), where knights of old practiced jousting. Tournaments make great summer family entertainment, but visit out of season, ideally during the late October wine festivals, when you may join real *Carcassonnais* celebrating their wine harvest within old stone walls; genuine contact with local tradition.

The wine trade financed a thriving town across the river, flourishing in the dcades between the golden age and birth of tourism. The **Ville Basse** may have Napoleon III boulevards in place of Louis VIII towers, but modest wealth accrued from a key position on trade routes financed a decent **Musée des Beaux Arts** (free entry), the gothic **Eglise St.-Vincent** with its unfinished tower, and the lower town's 14th-century **Cathédrale St. Michel**. These best bits are to be found in the quarter known as the **Bastide**

**Saint Louis**, historic centre with an excellent market around the place Carnot fountain. In any other town without a UNESCO-listed **Canal du Midi** on one side and a UNESCO-listed Crusaders' castle next door, this would be lure enough. Lunch here, away from day trippers, or picnic by the canal; perhaps further afield by sunbather's favourite **Lac Cavayere.** Remember, this far inland, you are in *Cassoulet* country: hearty meals served in and around Carcassonne go rather well with a bottle of robust red.

Such country fare and *terroir* put the city in context: the story did not begin with the age of Crusaders and Trencavel lords of Carcassonne. 2700 years ago, an iron-age settlement grew 2km from the town established by Rome in 118 BC. Power struggles that shaped most of the region consolidated in the 11th century when the Trencavels, who ran almost everything from here to Béziers and Agde, had a decent castle near today's *Porte Narbonnaise.*

Only after de Montfort's crusaders booted the family from Béziers and forced resident Cathars from Carcassonne in 1209's campaign of thuggery did the old order begin to change. From 1226 to 1240, Carcassonne, now fully French, received a fortified makeover by castle-builders from Paris, and a world-class citadel was born. The more thrilling version of history is in Kate Mosse's best-selling *Labyrinth,* in a hundred thousand travel bags.

My first encounter with the *Cité* began in the 1980s and '90s crush of product placement and logos of a summer squeeze, rubbing shoulder's with racks of souvenir tee-shirts, I would escape to the **Ville Basse** for lunch, and spend the afternoon a mile away with falconers, birds of prey hovering in the still summer heat, the distant ramparts an unforgettable backdrop. Then back to the *lices* at nightfall for an electric rock and light show. Later trips, using crowd-dodging tricks learned at Mont St Michel, saw me pass through the gates before breakfast, well ahead of the moment the first tour bus beep-reversed into place and unleashed its gush crush of sightseers: just me, the sunrise and a year-round resident population of 120 within a two-mile girdle of stone walls. A narrow window of opportunity, but for one brief shining moment, the era of mass tourism vanishes and, *grâce à* 19th-century architectural whimsy, you may believe in France's own Camelot.

**Tourist Office**
28 rue de Verdun, 11890 Carcassonne
04 68 10 24 30  www.carcassonne-tourisme.com
Jul-Aug: 9-19; Nov-Mar: Mon Sat 9-18, Sun 9-12;
Apr-Jun, Sep, Oct: Mon Sat 9-18, Sun 9-13
Main tourist office by the lower town station. Maps (downloadable in advance) and transport tips, book river or canal trips and festival tickets. Bus 4 from Chenier stop gets you to the **Cité** Tourist office can arrange shuttle buses for

wheelchair users. Branch office by the entrance to of the old town, 9-17, winter; 9-18 spring; 9-19 summer.

**Château & Ramparts** (04 68 11 70 70)
Apr-Sep 9.30-18.30, Oct-Mar 9.30-17. Closed hols. Last entry 45 mins earlier The castle is a paid-for extra (albeit free to EU citizens under 26). Architectural relic museum, film show, guided tour of the ramparts included. One of 8 national monuments with dedicated welcome for disabled visitors. To enjoy Carcassonne without the crowds, you may even rent the Château and ramparts for private parties, gala dinners, or extravagant *soirées* of nibbles and drinkies. At a price: call 04 68 11 70 72.

# Castelnau de Guers [5] C2

The only problem with Castelnau de Guers is that we remember too late how beautiful is the mediaeval stronghold when we pass en route to Pézenas. For Castelnau is the hilltop village you pass having left Marseillan by the water tower, crossed Pomérols and driven a good ten minutes through vine-land. As roads wind higher to a defensive perched townlet, named for feudal Barons de Guers, panoramas become impressive and streets about as *provençal* as it gets this side of the Rhône . In a single moment, the landscape changes from familiar **garrigue** hues of the home-stretch of Languedoc into something pure Cézanne. Suddenly we could be in the shadow of the Mont Ventoux, the hinterland of Marseille and Aix, a subliminal flash of Luberon in the heart of Hérault.A textbook, brochure or even yoghurt commercial picture of the *Midi*, all worn doorsteps, honey stone walls catching every nuance of the sun's dance; shutters, cafes and shop signs weathered to charm and disarm, and we are in the car, with a lunch table or theatre seat booked for Pézenas , just across the old bridge of the Hérault and under the new path of the A75, five minutes and a hunt for a parking space away. Promise to return and treat as a destination in its own right.

No packed programme of nightlife and entertainment, just a steady trickle of history perfectly lit by the present. With culture boxes to tick, head for the austere **château** by ramparts with views across the Hérault plain. Town walls are still strong, protecting the mediaeval heart of Castelnau. The church of **St Sulpice** is also on the checklist, but explore surrounding countryside to spot vestiges of watermills by the river and glimpse the **Ermitage St Antoine** chapel ruins poised for sympathetic renovation. Close by is the **Rocher des Fées**, fairy rock, where natural erosion creates a lunar landscape, a meteorite's throw from olive groves and *garrigue*.

181

At the **Mairie** is a replica of the **Piquetalen** sarcophagus (for heritage tickers), collect paperwork for a 10km mountain bike or hiking trail beyond the town (04 67 98 13 61) on dirt tracks and barely visible roads as well as more orthodox pathways between vines, river and shady pines. The circuit begins at the **cave co-operative**. There are eight independent wineries in town, so canny timing could set a tasting of wines in the heart of *pays de Picpoul* as the goal whilst you work up a worthwhile thirst, with a weather eye on the walls of Castelnau de Guers, ever on your horizon.

**Tourist office**: *see page 218*

# Céret [5] B4

According to the season, fragrances of mimosa and almond blossom or baskets of freshly picked cherries will welcome you to the Montmartre of the Midi and Montparnasse of the Pyrenees. In the first half of the 20<sup>th</sup> century, Céret, nestling in the orchards of hiking country, was home to Picasso, Braque and the Paris art set. The result is a superb **Modern Art Museum**. Excellent diversion on a trip to **Collioure, Perpignan, Banyuls** or **Port Vendres**. *See page 339.*

# Clermont l'Hérault [5] C1

Clermont l'Hérault's Wednesday market is something of a county fair. Fan off the nice new A75. Then follow signs for *Gare SNCF*, where the station ticket office remains open, although the last train left decades ago. It is a deliciously French joy that the mere fact of a railway line being axed and its tracks tarmaced over should never stand in the way of a nationalised transport system's proud tradition of public service. The SNCF guichet will sell you a ticket to wherever you want to go, just don't expect to board a train where you bought the ticket. Buses line up outside where usual *cafés de la gare* and support services are much in evidence. On a vast swathe of rough ground, where platforms and track are no more, park the car and saunter into town following the sound of a Barbary organ, flash of colour from crafts stalls and scent of Clermont's famous olives. A good market, one of the best, and in season begins a fountain spray from the station: craft sellers line the **allées Salengro** ghetto of restaurants and bars by the theatre before you cross the road and climb a steep high street hill where vendors block each doorway, tables laden with hand-fired glazed *tajines* and trays of *Laguiole* knives. Go straight ahead at the top of the hill and veer left, past the **Eglise Saint Paul**, fortified in the 14th century against the English. It must have worked. English voices now talk figures, converting market prices into sterling, rather than planning a raid on the vestry. By the church, clothes, shoes and bags aplenty might liberate your euros. Turn right at the church and swing towards food, fabulous food, there for the tasting. Men from mountains hand round firm *Cantal* or ladle dramatic gestures of piping hot *aligot* into misted plastic punnets. A baker's boy from a village an hour into the *arrière pays* rips chunks of *fougasse* or chocolate breads to tempt a saint from a Lenten pledge. Farmers' wives flaunt *terrines* and *pélardons*, rose-pink garlic bulbs, plump and buxom, fuzzy-soft summer fruits ripe for a squeeze; walnuts from the hills, fish from the streams and garden veg green as envy. Best of all are the oils and the olives: olives of every shape, shade and hue. For Clermont l'Hérault is city of olives and excuse for so many drives on the long road north. But the aficionado need not wait for Wednesday, mecca lies along another street, (*see page 184*).

500 years after the mediaeval **Château des Guilhem** began to crumble, it was finally declared unsafe and closed to visitors since 2009. Guarding the valley and *hauts cantons* road from atop the **Puech Castel** (castle hill), a stronghold of 11$^{th}$ and 12$^{th}$ century Guilhem feudal lords. Remnants of vaulted halls and a **Tour Guilhem** still loom over the ramparts. Generously, Clermont never pushes itself forward as an attraction, merely settles back secure in its setting, gateway to **St Guilhem, Salagou, Moureze, Villeneuvette** and superb wine lands of the hills beyond. The tourist office promotes the wider country. Should gods of the olive grove smile, your first visit will be as mine on an April afternoon that Clermont l'Hérault celebrated olive-making expertise with its **Oliviades** spring fair.

We stumbled upon the festivities after a typical auberge-reliable €16 lunch, arriving in the late, late afternoon sunshine. Garish earthenware did not tempt me to make free with my wallet; nor did I cast a rod and catch three trout for €5. I resisted olive oil, even olive chocolates. But the sharp fruits themselves beat my resolve. I succumbed to pert and piquant *picholines* and *luques* and some ultra ripe deep dark Dylan Thomas bible black varieties that almost melted in acquiescent surrender. Then followed honey soap and some practically oaken farmhouse cheeses from Aveyron, and we chatted long and lively with the cheese-makers. Eventually, a Dixieland jazz band informed us that not only were the saints marching in, Dolly was nicely back where she belonged, Bill Bailey was wanted at home and it was just one of those things. The sax player and his chums stomped, my foot tapped and, creeping like snails unwillingly to school, we trudged our way back to the car, parked where the trains never come.

**Office de Tourisme du Clermontais**
pl Jean Jaurès, 34800 Clermont l'Hérault    04 67 96 23 86

**Oli d'Oc**
13 avenue du Président Wilson, 34800 Clermont l'Hérault
04 67 96 10 36  www.olidoc.com
Shoppers paradise. More than just olives and olive oils at the olive growers cooperative of the *Moulin d'Augustin*. A variety of local produce: honeys and   preserves, sweets and chocolates, soaps and fragrances, wines and aperitifs from artisans, co-operatives and family kitchens. Newly explanded, but still with a personalised gift basket service. Opposite, **La Maison de l'Olivier** museum, where every visit is followed by a tasting.

# Collioure   [5] B4   *(see page 339)*

# Florensac   [5] C2   323

Tittle-tattled history, as told from father to son, whispered over wine, is the most romantic version of the past. Lined with legend and dressed in wishes, every retelling provides more colour than ever adorned original facts; a gentle and loving blurring that might be described as nature's own Wikkipedia. Thus, a pinch of salt may be required when savouring some local history. Amid roman roads and the Hérault's course, Florensac nestles between better known neighbours. If fame and fashion have passed it by, wine has ever furnished modest fortunes. Perchance history may have seen other crops grown by the river banks, pretty blooms maybe; since there are those who insist the town's name comes from the phrase *Fleur en Sac*, but with the *ac* suffix to so many Occitan settlements, that may be mere whimsy. If, as I more-than-half suspect, the legend was designed to appeal to gullible foreigners, it would be more likely to be flour *en sac*, since the settlement was home to  the $13^{th}$ century **Moulin du Duc d'Uzès** – the picturesque ruins make a lovely photo opportunity – which once ground wheat for *boulangeries*. In the early $20^{th}$ century, the mill was adapted to provide electricity for the village, a local engineer living in the old building kept an eye on the machinery. Actually, the name Florensac is recorded a thousand years earlier, before the legend of the mill, when various roman roads swarmed with pilgrims who would pause at the nearby abbey at **St Thibéry** on the way to the shrine at Santiago di Copostella.

Another legend comes from the story of Thybérius, son of a wealthy 4th century pagan from Agde, who was led towards Christianity by his teacher Modeste. Fleeing the wrath of his father, Thybérius escaped Agde by boat and set up home with Modeste in the Cordat woods. This Christian example encouraged others to build houses nearby and the community inspired a girl named Florence to convert to Christianity, another provenance of the name Florensac. Ponder the theories as you wander around town, checking out the **Church of St John the Baptist** (home to relics not only of the eponymous Thybérius, but also Saint Florence), and admire the early 20th century market hall and leafy promenade – then toast your own choice of founder, be it Florence or Thybérius, millers or even flower farmers, as you raise a glass of wine at **Vinipolis**.

**Tourist office**: *see page 218*

**Vinipolis**
5 avenue des Vendanges, 34510 Florensac
04 67 77 00 20
Open every day; bistro closes Mon and eves (except Sat)
Several years ago, visiting one of the more venerable wine cellars in Eastern France, I followed, suitably awestruck, as my host, Monsieur Hugel, led me down dimly lit passages to view rows of old wine bottles; glass coated by an even film of dust. As we stood beneath cobwebbed vaults, the august winemaker gently eased a bottle from the rack; label obscured by the *poussières* of decades, and asked me if I knew why his shelves were untouched by the feather duster. To protect the glass from light, I hazarded, to aid maturation in the bottle? The father of Alsace wine raised an eyebrow, half-smiled and slid the *gewürztraminer* back in position, then replied: "*Non, Monsieur*. It is simply because the people, they like to look at the dusty bottles when they visit the French wine cellar!"

Many a true word, and a philosophy that has become virtually a given around the country, and so, when the *Cave Co-operative des Vignerons de Florensac* decided it needed to upgrade the village winery, dusty bottles perched on aged wine racks were first casualties of a bold and daring venture to makeover the image of wine-buying in the sticks. From being just another warehouse on a *picpoul* and *Merlot* circuit between the étang and cities of Pézenas and Béziers, Florensac evolved into a wine-lovers destination in its own right, a family-friendly high tech showcase designed to attract modern consumers. *Vinipolis* appeals as much to casual passers by who might be intimated by the rituals of the conventional tasting or being obliged to venture opinions and reveal bald patches in their knowledge when going through the handshake, tasting, debating and selection process with the farmer, as to the keen amateur seeking more information about wine, winemaking and flavours. The shop is self-service, so those happier buying wines from a supermarket rather than a vintner need only pick, mix, chip and pin, but tutored and informative tasting sessions with for those who want to get that bit closer to *terroir*, tradition and tipple.

The key is in the design: glass floors to look down on barrels, interactive computer terminals for multi-lingual self-guided tours of wines and vines and vinification. New self-styled *oeno-thematic* "educational" high-tech wine selection process stand on hip café-style tables with plumbed spittoons for mulling and swilling. Virtual visits and audio visual tours of the region are part of the second wave of diversions, but the master stroke (*see page 303*) is bringing in a *Michelin*-pedigreed restaurant team to run an in-house bistro, where wines may be tasted as they were meant to be enjoyed, with good quality food. This redefinition of the concept of nipping down to the co-op for a bottle of white or a case of the local red is brilliant, has already proved a great success. It barely misses a trick but for one glaring omission. After more than a year in business, with the restaurant regularly sold out sometimes weeks in advance, the technologically pioneering *Vinipolis* had still not sorted out a website to let more people know of its existence.

## Lamalou-les-Bains  [5] B2

Some come for the waters, hot and cold, relief from nervous disorders, sciatica and rheumatic pain; others for the period calm of a thermal resort. As for me, I like the even more dated delights of operetta: matinees with a *Merry Widow* and evenings in the Underworld with Orpheus. Nothing like a good dose of Lehar and a healthy dash of Offenbach for a tonic. About as far removed from the appeal of a beach holiday as it gets. A bus ride from **Béziers** and **Bédarieux**, in the **Cevennes'** chestnut rich foothills, a quaint Massif Central spa town, like Vichy and Volvic. Once, three *thermes* thrived, now just one remains: the others now respected medical rehabilitation and physiotherapy centres. Although listed as a *cure* since Louis XV's time, the A-list heyday was the 1880s when you might share a bath with the Sultan of Morocco, André Gide, Alphonse Daudet or Alexandre Dumas. Nowaday's Dumas presence is no more than a revival of *La Traviata* at the dainty little theatre of the *belle époque* **Casino**, heart of the operetta feast, with other events in venues and cinemas and halls around the resort. A charming Victorian bandstand may be found, surrounded by imposing cedar trees, in the **Usclade** woodland park. Formal gardens lead to a pine forest. The least 19th century building still standing is the 11th century Romanesque church of **Saint-Pierre de Rhèdes**, on the site of an original 4th century chapel. The wider visitor franchise includes the town of **Hérépian**, with several more churches to explore, but especially its **Fonderie de Cloches** where the secrets of 400 years of manufacturing church bells are revealed. Drive on to discover ramparts at Villemagne-l'Argentière and the *paysage* around **Pradal** and **Les Aires**.

186

**Office Communautaire de Tourisme**
1 avenue Capus, 34240 Lamalou-les-Bains
04 67 95 70 91 www.ot-lamaloulesbains.fr
Jun-Sep Mon-Fri 9-12, 13.30-18.30, Sat 9.15-12, 14-17; Sun 10-12; Feb-Jun, Sep-Nov: Mon-Fri 9-12, 14-18; Sat 9.15-12; Dec-Jan Mon-Fri 9.-12, 14-17; Sat 9.15-12

## Limoux  |5| A3

This little town is a delightful detour from the road to **Carcassonne**, and our regular lunch break whenever we turn off the main road and make for the high plateaux of the *Pyrennées Audoises*. Pull away from the wider roads and drive up through Cathar-castled **Quillan** and *da Vinci Cod*ed Rennes-le-Chateaau to high cattle country of **Belcaire** with Alpine chalets, and an unspoilt, unknown, ski resort, **Camurac**: Limoux is the last main town before narrow mountain roads and single track railways heading for manageable summer termperatures, autumn colours to rival New England and thick winter snows without the bustle of tourism. Of course the town merits more than a lunchtime glance, and the Friday market is good fun.

Off season, Limoux comes into its own with a winter festival, erroneously dubbed the *Carnaval de Limoux* in French. In Occitan, *Fecas* means dance and, whilst other towns take to the streets in sultry heat of summer, the townsfolk of Limoux party, parade and dance every weekend January to March, warming the winter until the last hurrah of *Mardi Gras*. Considering the proximity to Carcassonne and Toulouse airports, this is remarkably free of tourist traps. Lazy visitors choose to feed around the arcades of the place de la République, walking off the meal admiring timber-framed houses, colourful window boxes and elegant houses on the banks of the Aude; perhaps taking in the **Musée du Piano** (more than 100 beautiful instruments housed in the former **Eglise St Jacques**) or **Musée Petiet**, 19th-century artist's studio with works by local impressionists and *pointilliste* Achille Laugé. Closed Sun-Tue off-season and Sun-Mon in summer. Enjoy a tour of wineries producing *Blanquette* and *Crémant de Limoux*, sparkling wines said to predate Champagne (*see page 112*). On a summer Tuesday, sightseeing is prelude to an evening wander through a late night market. Worthier types than I use lunch to recharge themselves for a robust hike through stunning countryside of the hinterland.

## Lodève  |5| B1

Up in the hills, where the Résistance  plotted against the Nazis and where townfolk make carpets for presidents and kings, far from the big cities; where else might you meet the first lady of the Impressionists, greatest of

187

all Italian painters and pioneers of 20<sup>th</sup> century art? Lodève is an unlikely cultural detour, but 30 minutes south of the world's tallest bridge, on your way to the Med, find one of France's more important regional galleries. In a season of festivals in town and the wider Larzac, the temporary summer exhibition programme at **Musée de Lodève** is one many capitals would envy. In ten years we've seen seasons devoted to Impressionist Berthe Morisot (bringing nearly 65,000 visitors in 2006), Titian, Canaletto, Bonnard and Gaugin. Check out the programme. **Manufacture de la Savonnerie** is a former royal carpet manufacturer: visits via tourist office.

**Office de Tourisme** 7 place de la République 34700 Lodève 04 67 88 86 44 www.lodeve.com
Jul-Aug Mon-Fri 9-12.30, 14-18.30 Sat 9-12.30, 15.30-18, Sun10.30-12.30, 15.30-18; Jun, Sep Mon-Fri 9.30-12.30, 14-18 Sat 9.30-12.30, 15.30-18, Sun10.30-12.30; Jan-Mar,Nov-Dec Mon-Fri 9.30-12.30, 14-18 Sat 9.30-12.30

**Musée de Lodève** sq G. Auric, 34700 Lodève 04 67 88 86 10 Tue-Sun 9.30-18

# Loupian [5] C2

Like most small towns and villages beyond the main road, Loupian remains merely a familiar name on signposts until you are lured from a regular run by Lorelei promises of a country fair or a last-minute museum. So, the day we slipped off the rat run, we discovered another happy distraction, just behind Mèze. We had vouchsafed Loupian's **Roman Villa** for our first rainy day with guests to amuse, but good weather in early years delayed us a while: eventually a springtime *marché du terroir* (*see page 191*) proved perfect introduction to diverting streets of a fascinating detour. A well-considered walking route, counselled by informative panels, means casual visitors need not miss a trick. Bonus in a town that mapmakers categorise as roman are decently maintained souvenirs of other periods. **Saint Hippolyte** chapel has a listed 7<sup>th</sup>-century façade of earlier fortifications, and a nearby **château** (now **Hotel de Ville**) is a proper toy fort, much reinvented with satisfactory towers and turrets to stir imagination. The 14<sup>th</sup> century **Porte de Caylis** and clock tower by a 17<sup>th</sup> century arched **Porte de l'Etang** on the walls keep the treats coming at every turn. Secular and religious buildings a plenty, with neoclassical and renaissance features, and the rather austere and sober looking gothic church of **Sainte Cecile** stands just outside the town. Nearby archaeological gardens reveal first romano-christian buildings from the 5<sup>th</sup> century. The major architectural magnet is however not the church but the amazing **Roman Villa**, and you should not, like many, wait for a day to dawn dull and grey, the temperature to plummet to shiver nor rains to spatter the terrace before taking time to drive 10-15 minutes from Marseillan and discovering this true treasure trove for yourself.

**Villa Gallo-Romain,**
34140 Loupian
04 67 18 68 18  http://villaloupian.free.fr
13.30-18 (last admission 17h). Also Sat, Sun 11.Closed Tues (Sep-Jun), Jan
You'll hear the tale of the local farmer who, digging between the grapevines heard the crack of iron on mosaic and so discovered Roman remains under his vineyard. But not until you get here do you appreciate what a fabulous find was uncovered beneath a thousand years or more of soil and rootstock. Stunning. Unlike many historic sites where visitors must piece out imperfections with their thoughts; the floors of the villa, home to a roman winemaker or merchant, is amazingly well preserved, with the most complex and beautiful mosaics in 13 fabulous rooms. Intelligent preservation over aesthetic meant a modern warehouse style roof was erected above the floors so rooms may be viewed *in situ*. Walk around 400 square metres of tiles styled from across an empire: European romance of leaves and flowers, Arabic geometric patterns from north Africa. Walkways above allow you to look down on each individual space, yet get a sense of the scale of the entire house. Be struck by the contemporary style of the designs. Besides a few portraits (very renaissance but still a good millennium before that period), patterns of leaves, geometric shapes and wildlife, vivid today as when they were created 2000 years ago, could be Morris or Mackintosh. The visit begins with an explanation of the site at the purpose-built museum of everyday life in Roman Gaul. Look out for some charmingly Barbia and Kennus Romanicus style dolls. Wheelchair accessible. Choose to take one of the guided tours that begin on the hour (ask for times of tours in English) or simply to wander at your own pace.


# Mèze  [5] C2

To mere midweek commuters, the name presages a traffic jam on the Montpellier route home. However, for lazy Marseillanais, Mèze is a Sunday discovery. Before relaxation of hypermarket shopping hours, market day in the next port was only best way to stock up the fridge after arriving in Marseillan on a Saturday evening. A civilised Sunday crocodile of rental cars snake through double parked streets *à la recherche du parking perdu*. Eventually, Renaults safely stored behind the 17th century **Château Girard** – never actually a castle, but built as a *métairie* farming estate then family home from the Revolution until 1995 when taken over by the town as tourist office and exhibition hall. Basket in hand, it is a short walk through the grounds to a Sunday and Thursday market square along rue Sadi Carnot where many stall holders are familiar from Marseillan Tuesdays. Greater emphasis on fresh food: street stalls lead the way to the 1908 covered market hall, where cheese, meat, fish and seafood are sold from chilled counters daily, except Monday. May cherries, nectarines in high summer, melons in abundances, all stacked on trestles and packed in paniers along the pavements around **Les Halles**, whilst saucissons and olive oils add fragrantcolour to the bustling scene. Street confections are complemented by savoury aromas from doorways, as butchers and *superettes*, *boulangeries* and grocers open for business to catch a market crowd. On the **Mairie** steps of place Aristide Briand, a *peña* band may root and toot sounds of celebration, **St Hilaire**'s church bell on the breeze providing counterpoint as the massed and communed spill out to join the chattering bartering throng. When the same bell chimes noon, marketing merrymaking dissolves to sabatical sobriety on the stroke of lunch. The multitide disperses, back to shiny red Citroens and dusty white Peugeots, up narrow side streets to cool of a *maison du village*, or suntrap of a holiday flat, carrying bags of cheese, wine, bread and paté for lazy lunch on the terrace.

The rest of us walk down to the port, an expanded, photoshopped, and more commercial version of Marseillan, thrice as wide and twice as busy. Bright awnings jostle for attention, pavement tables nudge the roadway and cars trundle between menu-boards and moored bobbing pleasure boats, nosing and nudging the boardwalk. Once *kirs* have been sipped, *plats des jours* sampled and the last droplet of *viognier* stroked from the rim of the bottle, walk off Sunday lunch on the *plagette* - a dinky little beach, pocket handkerchief, bite-sized Deauvillette, curved into a niche of waterfront with palm trees on the sands, a café at each end and a brace of retro-striped wooden huts for modest transformation from shopper to sun-worshipper. The waters of the étang are warmer than those of the Med, and, if the weather plays ball, it is sometimes slightly less windy. Back in the main port, jousting is the big summer watersport. Boats have long meant business, politics and power as well as pleasure.

Beyond the *plagette*, above the little *port des Nacelles*, ramparts from earlier uncertain times loom high, and where now stands the **Chapelle des Penitants**, known as the mariner's lighthouse (visits via the *Mairie*, exhibitions in summer), Greeks once had a temple to the goddess of the waters. The town was sacked by Saracens in the 8th century, brought back into France in the 13th and by the 14th fully re-fortified. Bronze age, Celtic, Greek and Roman citizens of *Mesua* took turns working land and water, with a heritage of fishing, farming and wine making. During the *Pax Romana* golden days of Emperor Claudius, land was parcelled into villas and vineyards. With a natural talent for trade, wines were made to suit fashionable Italian tastes. This knack for tailoring to markets remained; centuries later, Mèze developed a dessert wine, *Passerille,* for the sweet toothed nobles of the French court. By the 19th century, the town reinvented itself anew as heartland of cooperage, barrels wrought here sold to winemakers across the region and to Marseillan's thriving export business along the lakeside. Today, a dozen or so private wineries, most on the D51 to Marseillan, and a busy cave co-operative in town, thrive in a 21st century industry mixing food and tourism. Besides wine farm shops selling olive oils and *tapenades,* main roads are lined with oyster counters, honey-makers and excellent *patisseries* for topping up the weekly shop. A clutch of educational and cultural and eco-aware experiences prove the same instinct for change that has steered the centuries is as astute as ever. Inland, follow signs for the **Parc du Sesquier,** a well-maintained 34 hectare park with cycle and jogging trails around a series of lakes and ponds.

**Tourist Office** Château de Girard, 34140 Mèze 04 67 43 93 08

**Musée Parc Dinosaures**
Tel: 04 67 43 02 80 www.musee-parc-dinosaures.com
Sep –Jun pm only, Jul Aug all day
Of course, despite lorries chundering along the main road, Mèze has other inland charms. The main thrill for your average well-informed seven-year-old comes thanks to the discovery by Alain Cabot in 1996 of a cache of dinosaur eggs. A vast stretch of land between the lagoon and **Montagnac** where, as the cinema trailers used to say, dinosaurs once roamed the earth. A dinosaur park and museum allows the family experts on the **brachiosaurus** to top up the inner fact-sheet with life-size models of many prehistoric beasts and offers a view of the original excavation site. In the same park, a twin circuit, perhaps appealing more to adults than the younger visitors, reveals the origins and evolution of man with skulls, bones, carvings, and to keep the kids happy, some early weaponry as well. Budget conscious families may picnic in the park.

**Ecosite du Pays de Thau**
Route des Salins, 34140 Mèze
04 67 46 64 94 Phone in advance
Not far from Loupian's roman villa, this is a third "educational" excursion to justify travelling with kids in term-time. The Etang de Thau's water purification centre is responsible, at the *zone lagunage,* for maintaining the environmental balance of the lagoon. Visitor centre, with guided tours introduces local flora and fauna, has fish farms and a plankton production tank, to provide intriguing insights into hands-on environmentalism and a campaign to preserve the unique ecosystem of the étang.

191

# Spring Fair in Loupian

In spring, a middle-aged man's fancy lightly turns to the larder, but the cupboard was bare and so we decided to to visit a country fair in the neighbouring village of Loupian. A casual ramble through the vines might have been the picturesque route, but anno domini and a knowledge of my own calves suggested the car might be more practical. This was true for 99% of the journey. However, as a sign by the bus stop explains, history has been happening in Loupian for 25 centuries, and streets were planned sometime before the advent of our second-hand Honda. Whilst Renaults with local plates had been abandoned with proprietorial negligence in front of front doors and garages, we sucked in our chassis and inched along narrow roads, following inkjetted signs taped to railings promising parking for 500 cars. Straight on past the wheelie bin; right at the basking policeman, passively enforcing a temporary *route barrée* sign: follow printed pointing fingers past the church out of the village and beyond the old roman villa, to vineyards where we were signalled to swing the car left into a field designated *"parking 500 places"*. The scouts and guides of Loupian welcomed us with broad grins and definite idea of where to leave a well-travelled estate car on the first afternoon of spring.

A woman in 19th century Sunday best was checking her husband's equally vintage garb as they paced the gentle incline towards centre ville. We followed them through a mediaeval archway by the Hotel de Ville, where crowds were already gathering for a view of the afternoon's procession. Oblivious to the treat in store, we wandered left to the first of many many food stalls from across Languedoc and France beyond. We stopped, we tasted, we debated; we passed time with a lady from the Gard selling all things ginger-syrup too sweet, tea smelling delicious, but who wanted hot drinks on a sunny day? Haunches of ham caught the eye of the costumed couple, generous slices presented across a well-worked knife for sampling; other spiced treats, pimented and curried and spooned into pots for us to take away, and unrefined sea salt gathered by a stall-holder's son from a faraway Atlantic coast, as foreign to us New Mediterraneans as is distant Araby. We bought a garland of dried fruits and leaves, entwined around coarse rope at a foolishly low price and took a bright ceramic salad bowl for garlic vinaigrettes and summer leaves. The man who wrapped them so very carefully said we could find him any Thursday in the heart of Narbonne – outside MacDonalds, he said! A cherry-wood honey spoon from a neighbouring stall caught our eye and there was much handicraft to admire.

We had forfeited lunch to come to the fair, straight from the flea-market at Marseillan Plage, where we had bartered for a battered wine barrel which even now filled the boot of the car. The barrel would be centrepiece of a planned garden surrounded by pearl white stone, and eventually host an olive tree, once sander and paintbrush had worked their rejuvenation skills on wood and metal bands of cooperage.

Supressed appetites now roused by scooped *aligot*, plates of tripe, *nutella*-filled *crêpes* and other treats served in village cafes, alongside platters of Bouzigues oysters. We espied a likely table and wooden benches outside the *Café du Commerce*, from where sounds of country bands could be heard, so grabbed a pair of *fougasse*-esque loaves baked with olives and cheese, and a couple of other savouries from a baker's stall (he too would be in Narbonne any given Thursday) and signalled to a waiter for glasses of chilled beer. As jugglers, tumblers and stilt-walkers entertained, happy families inhaled sunshine and artisans topped up their stalls, we mused that, but for fashions and fabrics, this might have been any festive Spring morning since the Renaissance. Then we heard the pipes a-calling. Bagpipes emerged from the café, drums began to beat and kilts to swirl; all eyes bashfully peered to seek clues from the sporran insignia. So many Celts find their way to the unlikeliest corners of France, one may never be certain of anything. I spied a thistle on the regalia so stepped over to greet the Scots. They had come from Clydebank to accompany country dancers invited to join the parade. A parade? First we had heard of it, so we downed the rest of the demi and hurried off to surf the tide of the crowd.

On the way we found honey, ah such honey, with lemon and orange and walnuts and too many sins for Lent. Bought plenty and an aniseed-suffused *pain d'epices* honey cake too. We reflected walnuts soaked in honey might be perfect with *chevre*, so our next digression was for goat cheeses from the *Causses* of *Lozère*. One cheese almost bitter and hard, another creamy and succulent. We claimed five for our sturdy basket. Oh, and *patés* and *foie gras* for friends. Pockets packed with scribbled addresses from each producer so we might buy in future direct from farms and country stores.

Finally, outside the Mairie and Post Office, we reached the head of the processions. Every community has its totem lucky animal, pagan village symbol. First out, a snapping Captain-Hook crocodile style wolf: the size of a covered wagon, a monster supported by a virtual rugby team of virility sweltering inside the costume. Rising and writhing through the crowd, snapping its jaw, this is the wolf (or *Loup*) that gives Loupian its name. Other civic mascots from other towns followed with donkeys, wild boar and snails mingling with marching bands and teams of country dancers, a rain dance with genteel looping and twirling of umbrellas to music so Arabian in origin one recalled the region's Moorish past. Then the Scots pipes and drums with a generic Celtic dragon, followed by teams of mature ladies in Edwardian finery raising parasols to fin *du siècle* gentlemen in smart hats.

We waited until we saw the most magnificent of the totemic beasts the legendary Poulain of Pézenas (*see page 218*), topped with bridal mannequins. To have stayed longer was a great temptation, but we had bags of food and other spoils, a barrel to unload and a drive back to Marseillan under the spring high moon of a summer blue sky.

# Montagnac [5] C2

Don't tell anyone, but despite architectural treasures all around, the lures that get me swooping and looping off the direct routes to and from Marseillan and heading away instead to Montagnac are tomato and cucumber. Market gardeners set up stalls in town on non-market days in summer, selling produce from the *potager*. Home-grown salad takes some beating. Others visit with nobler aims of self-improvement, since the town offers a nicely compact history lesson: a dozen info panels placed at strategic points furnish the brain with just enough dates and names to justify an hour's constitutional. So after the initial neck-stretching ooh-ah moment gazing at the octagonal church tower you may digest the information that the construction coincided with the visit of *Dauphin Louis* in 1437. Of course, if you are already familiar with the architectural riches of Pézenas, this town is something of a baby cousin, with its own historic quarter along the ramparts by the church jam-packed with stunning doorways, lovely courtyards and staircases well worth the peeking at. The serpentine stretch of rues Lafayette and Malirat provide the lion's share of Kodak moments; look up at the junction with the rue Jean Moulin to see a superb 15th century oil lamp. Hands-on and hard-core property junkies visit *Domaine de Lavagnac*, stately home, wine estate and gardens dubbed Versailles of the Languedoc. Soon to be 4* hotel, golf club spa and homes, with residents having shares in the wine business. Less avaricious tours of the countryside are offered via motoring and hiking trails around the local vineyards.

**Abbaye de Valmagne**
34560 Villeveyrac
04 67 78 06 09 (abbey); 04 67 78 13 64 (auberge); www.valmagne.com
Closed Dec 25, January and mornings in autumn, winter and spring
How rare to find a religious building so devoted to the finer aspects of hedonism. Between Montagnac and Mèze, and just outside Villeveyrac, the Abbey of Sainte Marie de Valmagne serves the superior pleasures of life. Known locally as the cathedral of the wines, this is one of very few monastic estates to have retained all its lands. As a vineyard (*see page 106*) it treasures its reputation and some wines are well worth the detour. Music lovers will hear more than vespers and chants in the beautiful cloister. I rounded off a long hot summer with an evening of the coolest jazz one year, and an annual concert programme is as stimulating to the anticipatory juices of the *mélomane* as the wine list to those who smack their lips for pleasure. Diversions aside, the abbey is a charming treat. Cloisters are always perfect balm to counter the effects of modern life, and those of Valmagne are rather

special: a vine-entwined fountain is a natural spring where once monks would wash before prayers. As the waters cleansed the abbey through the years, wine has guaranteed its salvation. Originally a Benedictine sanctuary in 1139, within 20 years it had joined the movement led by St Bernard of Clairvaux and remained a Cistercian abbey, despite ravages and attacks of the Hundred Years and the Religious Wars. A large wine estate, tended by the monks themselves, had been the life's work of 16th century cellar master Frère Nonenque. The order maintained the abbey, its lands and vineyards until the Revolution in 1789, when the last five monks fled days before the mob ransacked buildings and burnt manuscripts and books. Not all were vandals: a raiding party from Marseillan "liberated" the altar (*see page 28*) When sold by the state two years later, the winerery was expanded by new owner Monsieur Granier-Joyeuse, filling religious buildings with vats and barrels, so saving the Abbey from the fate of other monasteries, reduced to virtual quarries. Fortune smiled on the abbey 50 years on, when the estate returned to the market, and Count Henri-Amédée-Mercure de Turenne became wine-maker and abbey custodian. Valmagne remains in the family, and a new generation was widely acclaimed for sympathetic restoration of buildings. With much of the 12th-14th century estate so well preserved, the abbey and gardens and vineyards are open to visitors. The gothic inspired church itself is reminiscent of the grand cathedrals of Picardy, and the exquisite cloister now a charming rose garden, with Cistercian blooms developed by the monks in Burgundy. Outside, a monastic herb garden and a separate vine garden of choice *cépages* as grown and harvested in neighbouring vineyards each have their charms. A new *ferme-auberge* serves lunch and early-evening pre-concert snacks using home grown produce from the abbey's farm and kitchen garden, with wines from the estate. One set menu, inspired by monastic tradition offers a full meal for vegetarians. The restaurant is fully accessible to disabled visitors. Concerts of jazz or classical music every Thursday evening mid-Jun – mid-Sep.

**La Forêt d'Acrobates**
Base Départementale de bassilles, 34560 Montagnac
04 89 84 89 87 www.loisirs-foret.com
Jun-Aug 9-19; Feb-May, Sep-Oct, Wed, Sat, Sun, Hols 14-18
Tree-top trails, assault courses and woodland challenges for sporty families.

# Minerve   [5] A2

Named for a goddess of poetry, crafts and wisdom, and officially one of France's prettiest villages, this inland clifftop cluster of age-old houses clinging to a rockface, surrounded by calming waters and abundant vines will forever be remembered for a massacre. High above a valley between

Béziers and Carcassonne, where twin rivers entwine byways of the *Causses*, stands a lone village, a sheer drop to **Aigues Vives** beneath. The capital of the *Minervois* wine region is gravestone of the Cathars, a memorial on the horizon to victims of Simon de Montfort's crusading armies. Béziers had already fallen when Cathars sought sanctuary in this fortified hilltop settlement faith behind double rows of ramparts. In 1210, de Montfort's knights laid seige. A quartet of catapults bombarded Minerve; the largest, *Malevoisine,* destroyed the **Saint Rustique** well, only source of water. The village surrendered, leaving Cathars to their fate. 140 *parfaits* refused to recant their faith and were burnt at the stake on 22 July, a bloody massacre that continued for 34 years until the fall of **Montségur**.

The village of Rome's virgin goddess of peace and creativity has inspired countless novels and remains a potent symbol of faith. Today, this is listed among *Les Plus Beaux Villages*; picturesque alleyways and blushed stone walls drinking the sunset in a panorama of limestone rocks canyons and gulleys. A martyrs' **memorial** stands by the chapel and the last vestige of the fortress is the **Candela**, single octagonal tower. Perfect walking country, never far from flowing water: little streams tumble through landscape of natural bridges spanning deep gorges of **Cesse** and **Briant**. Alongside the village, the **Cessière** dissappears in tunnels and caves. Take local advice, explore natural caverns where the river passes into the hills. Follow cool crystal clear chill waters for miles around: so many tranquil turns in the rivers for a private plunge. The Cesse is at its best at the nearby picture perfect village of **Bize-Minervois**. Take a dip by the pebble beach (supervised in summer) and buy olive oil from an old mill. The touristy bathing resort is **Lac de Jouarres** Visit pretty streets of **Aigne,** a spiralled mediaeval village with but one gateway from the outside world. Discuss wine in the business capital **Olanzac**. When the sun is high, leafy banks of the **Canal du Midi** provide picnic shade. On high ground, standing stones, dolmens, are nature's temple between horizons of distant coast and hills.

**Office de Tourisme Le Minervois**, 9 rue des Martyrs, 34210 Minerve
04 68 91 81 43 www.minerve-tourisme.fr
Downloadable maps for hikers. For arts, wines, gastronomy etc in the wider country
(including **Homps** on the Canal du Midi) see also **www.leminervois.com**)

### Musée Hurepel
5 rue des Martyrs, 34210 Minerve
High Season 10-13, 14-19; Low season 10.30-12.30, 14-18. Closed Oct-Mar
A pair of winegrowers created this charming museum of the Cathars, the crusades and Minerve, as posed by **santon** figurines in historic tableaux. Information in 10 languages

# Montpellier  [5] C2

With Antigone, city of tomorrows, a sleek and chic tramway dressed by fashion designers, headline-making cuisine, hard-core shopping, world class arts festivals, not to mention a string of Mediterranean beaches for the Paris party set; a lesser city might forget about the past. But Montpellier, fast emerging as a major player on the continental weekend break scene, has a back story that more than holds its own.

This is a city of minds, of a hunger for greatness, a celebration of the possible through every generation. Europe's oldest medical school was founded through a talent for surmounting prejudice and tribal warfare, as Islamic and Jewish scholars united to transcribe and interpret teachings of lost civilisations, transcend superstition and create science. The medical faculty here initially as a cluster of classes in private homes. An honours board celebrates pioneers of medicine from a time when the rest of Europe would take its waters to the wise woman before burning her as a witch.

The arts flourished: Many private collections burgeoned into the city's great museums (especially **Musée Fabre**). Music has mattered from the age of troubadours to the 19$^{th}$ century opulence of Jacques-Philippe Maréchal's **Comédie** opera house, commissioned by governor Duc de Richelieu, and the 21$^{st}$ century's massive **Arena** venue built to host the second coming of Johnny Hallyday in 2011. A tradition that embraces world-class celebration of street music and classics. International dance, film and *Radio France* music festivals are global events and an autumn guitar season saw Joan Baez leading the entire city in the park in sweet-voiced chorale of hope.

Montpellier owes name and fortune to the Monte Pestalario estate presented to 10$^{th}$ century Guilhem counts of Toulouse. An estate on a river by the sea meant trade, and trade equalled fortune, so a fortified *commune cloture* rose up by the banks of the Lez. The **Tours des Pins** and **Babotte** are the last turrets standing. Moats gave way to boulevards as fortunes and populations expanded, and the *Vielle Ville*, where it all started remains, within the original boundaries. Canny marriages to noble and regal families meant that by 1204, the Lords of Montpellier belonged to the Aragon dynasty and when Philippe VI de Valois, King of France, bought the estate in 1349, Montpellier was technically part of Majorca. Business boomed, with spice and silk trading vessels sailing in, whilst exports grew thanks to green oaks on the hillsides attracting beetles prime for crushing into cochineal dye. The medical faculty joined in the 16th century by a legal quarter and religious clout as the Maguelone see was transferred to the city. Tolerant to Jews,

Muslims, even Cathars; this was a Huguenot protestant stronghold, defying a pugnacious French Catholic crown until finally succumbing to the strong will of Louis XVIII whose royal house held firm until the Revolution.

A penchant for strong leaders re-emerged in the later 20th century with controversial outspoken Mayor Georges Frêche, whose almost Napoleonic vision led to the **Antigone** district, trams and the revitalising of the city through *grands projets* of Mitterand proportion. Ejected from his socialist party in 2007, even in handing over city reins after 27 years in office to successor Hélène Mandroux, he nonetheless managed to ascend imperial heights as president of the Languedoc region, which in a *folie de grandeur* he renamed overnight as *Septimanie*; bewildering a world that had only recently learned to appreciate wines and tourism of Languedoc and who thought the new name referred to a medical condition. Thankfully, this Septimania subsided, but grand gestures continued, with a fabulous final scandal in 2010: Millions spent on a series of statues of $20^{th}$ century heroes to stand on the place du XXe Siecle: Churchill, Ghandi and Mandela raised few eyebrows, but a furore raged over paying €250,000 for a new statue of Lenin, when so many freshly toppled Eastern European versions could be had for peanuts on *eBay*. Even a new statue of domestic hero Jean Jaurès courted budgetary controversy since a Jaurès bronze was already centre piece of an eponymous city square. Five weeks after the unveiling, Frêche died, working late at his desk in an office overlooking the metropolis he loved. Post-Lenin; no prizes for guessing Montpellier's man of the $20^{th}$ century for the next round of monuments.

Discovery of the past, politics of church and state: all may be found on an escorted or self guided walking tour. With a future so well signposted and past so lovingly preserved, the present is nonetheless a true siren. The heart of Montpellier is **place de la Comédie**, known to locals as *l'Oeuf*. Theatre steps segue into yet another café, tables and parasols framing the egg shaped piazza. Brasseries, bars and restaurants provide peripatetic audience for a disciplined rota of buskers strumming the theme to *The Deer Hunter* and tapping African beats by the iconic statue of the **Three Graces**. Behind tables are cinemas and banks, their facades held proud by buxom caryatids. The Comédie hosts festivals, markets, a Christmas fayre and big screens for major sporting events. This is the city rendezvous, for coffee or an air-kiss, last lunch before the train home or the launch of a special evening. Each corner leads to new adventure: Beside the theatre walk down to the **Tour Babote**; take rue de Maguelone down to the station, palm-lined route spaced with glass chairs; each engraved with the distance in metres to Kathmandu, Paris, Luxor or Venice, in the confidence that wherever in the world you might otherwise have been, you made the right choice. At the bottom of the hill, by tram and rail stations, a tiny park on **square Planchon** has a moss smothered fountain trickling water into cooling vapours, perfect pause for pondering possibilities of the coming hours.

Back at the *Three Graces*, rue de la Loge, has the width and potential of a Bond Street. Garlanded with Christmas lights in season, it leads to Grand Rue Jean Moulin, place Jean Jaurès and on to the old winding shopping spree of the mediaeval rue de l'Aiguillerie: a souk of lead-soldier and music-box toyshops, ethnic jewellery, fine dining and art galleries. At the far end of the Comédie, where a white **Petit Train** awaits passengers, the Tourist Office stands at the foot of the **Esplanade**: a grand tree-lined walk of fountains, statues gardens and markets and pathway to the **Corum** conference and concert hall. An early *Pathé* cinema frontage to the left, then the entrance to **Musée Fabre** – the city's great art collection.

Bear right at the tourist office for shopping centres. The **Polygone** and **Triangle** malls are an Alice looking glass. Enter from old Montpellier and pass out the other side in the heart of **Antigone** (city of the future), perhaps stopping for a swim in an Olympic pool, saunter through new streets and squares, or maybe hop on a tram or bus, past **Port Marianne** and the grassy banks of the Lez to the **Odysseum** shop-and-playground, final shake of euros from your pocket before the beaches or the airport.

Trams bisect the Comédie by a vintage carrousel to lure you further. Rather than be tempted away too quickly, wander through back streets of the *Ecusson* historic centre, streets too capricious and canny for tramlines, and discover old boutiques, smaller unexpected museums, and the dramatic façade of the cathedral.

Further on, find the **Promenade de Peyrou** regal gardens, raised and laid-out to set off a grand equestrian statue of Louis XIV. An 18th century **Arc du Triomphe** honours the king in an echo, on the site of past ramparts, of the Paris gates Porte St Denis and St Martin: here reinvented by the Mansart-trained architect François d'Orbay, in ochre and yellow tints to *bas relief* and summit and an uncompromisingly regal crest of shining blue. On the official guided tour, you may climb 88 steps to enjoy glorious views. Across the promenade, what appears to be a Corinthian temple is in fact an ornate 18th century **Château d'Eau** water tower, fed by a classically arcaded aqueduct resembling an extension of the roman **Pont du Gard**: actually, a 17th century confection bringing water 14km from St Clement Spring to feed the city's fountains. Under a double row of arches is the *Arceaux* quarter, where locals play *pétanque* and ping pong in the shade, and haggle over organic veg at Tuesday and Saturday morning markets.

Another 18th century tradition thrives in the Sainte Anne quarter. Montpellier has been the Cremona of France since an Italian violin maker set up a workshop in 1768. Within 100 years, 25 *ateliers* and music shops had followed suit. Fashion for private concerts and the advent of the Comédie kept the profession healthy until 20th century wars all but closed down the trade. In recent years, the *luthiers* have returned; today nine professionals craft instruments, inspired by legendary performers lecturing at the International Music Academy. Worth taking the escorted workshop tour, since it finishes with an intimate recital in a private mansion.

Many concert halls and studios around town, half a dozen theatres, several cafe-theatres and fringe venues offer year-round alternatives to grander venues (*see page 206*). Check programmes on-line, at the tourist office or in today's *Midi Libre*. Whilst Kindles may glint in summer sunlight on the Comédie, this remains a city of real books. Summer's international book fair brings over 400 authors and 120,000 bibliophiles to three days of free events in streets and squares, and second hand books change hands at the Plan Cabanes street market every Wednesday. *Sauramps* bookshop, second largest in the land, has branches in the old town, Odysseum and Musée Fabre. Find chain store bookstores, *Virgin* and *Fnac*, and English booksellers (*see page 253*), antiquarian specialists and grand libraries. The future of the American Library, one of continental Europe's largest collections of books in English, currently hovers in the balance.

The principal art form of our age is *cuisine*. Visitors lured by cookery courses under great chefs in prestigious kitchens or a simple mint tea and falafel break in an arab quarter. Find bistros by *trompe l'oeil* murals in unexpected corners, old buildings reinvented for lunch (such as the public bathhouse behind the theatre) and new palaces of gastronomy invented (a glass fronted tapas bar in a wine shop in port Marianne). Once a city was defined by its artists; in other times, by generals, politicians or churchmen. Today's civic icons are a culinary Romulus and Remus, twinkling with *Michelin* stars and garlanded with logos: twin chefs Jacques and Laurent Pourcel, whose love of food was nurtured in Agde and Marseillan.

**Tourist Office**                                                 **Comédie**
30, allée Jean de Lattre de Tassigny, 34000 Montpellier
04 67 60 60 60 www.ot-montpellier.fr
Jul-Sep: Mon-Wed, Fri 9-19.30, Thu 10-19.30, Sat Sun hols 9.30-18.
Oct-Jun:Jul-Sep Mon-Wed, Fri 9-18.30, Thu 10-18.30, Sat Sun hols 10-17
On the Esplanade by the Comédie, excellent info centre for maps and advice. Book tours or rent audio guides daily except Christmas and Jan 1.

## Antigone

Montpellier is a city spun by time and where time still spins, turns, whips and tricks a palpable energy; find it in young faces and minds invigorating the oldest quarters or in the classical proportions of the most modern metropolis in the *Midi*. Many French "Heritage" towns wear their past as a gown of dignity; some as a yoke of responsibility. Montpellier's history is sported as a cape to be flourished and flaunted with Latin passion. The secret, as in Lille, another university city, is a trust in youth. Montpellier preserves its past through faith in tomorrow. So the **Antigone** quarter, commissioned by Georges Frêche and designed by Catalan architect Ricardo Boffil is neither apologetic concrete annexe to the past, nor obligatory bolt-on to catch the overspill of a city too small to breathe fresh air.

A grand neoclassical sweep of utopian idealism is a triumphant post-modern romantic wielding of a baton of honour; taste and style carried forward, heritage borne and worn with pride. This new district blends council housing with big business, university campus with street market; bearing the city on the hill down to the river banks. A proportioned parade of arcades and crescents, squares and circles, archways, *parterres* and pathways, is paced with fountains, classical statuary and well-mannered vistas: the epitome of civilisation. Ozymandias-thighed pillars and ironic Icarus-winged pediments defy the inevitable intellectual snobs of the *avant-garde*. From a vast arc of shaven lawn and those grassy river banks of the Lez, where students sprawl between books and lovers, to the glass edifice of the Emile Zola library, cathedral of the Word, marbled muses, philosophers and goddesses watch over each new generation, just as Three Graces and caryatid sentinels of the Comédie and rue de la Loge maintain the civilisation and wisdom of the past in the old city. It works.

Yet Bofill's vision of a tomorrow will never be the last page in Montpellier's story. The newest arch was merely gateway to fresher inspiration. Jean Nouvel's glazed **Hotel de Ville** rises above the treeline in the latest district **Port Marianne**, an **Odysseum** temple of commerce and leisure reflects 21st century priorities as Montpellier marches on.

TRAMS, BUSES & BIKES: Getting around Montpellier - *see page 389*

## Cathedrale Saint Pierre

**Albert 1er**

6 Bis Rue Abbé Marcel Montels, 34000 Montpellier
04 67 66 04 12

As stark a frontage as the palace of Avignon Pope Urbain V who commissioned the church as a monastery chapel in 1364, a two-dimensional façade is relieved, upstaged, by an extravagant porch of two circular pillars with turrets to wake a Sleeping Beauty or rival Carcassonne. This is mainly for show, as the regular entrance is a small door round the corner in rue du Cardinal Cabrières, with walls still pockmarked from post-revolutionary gunfire. Restored 19th century windows and some good art lure secular visitors. Upgraded to cathedral status in 1536, when Montpellier's bishops and archbishops moved here from Maguelone. Memorial to Bishop Anatole de Cabrières, who distinguished himself during the 1907 winegrowers revolt (*see page 96*), offering sanctuary to protestors. Intellectual and friend of Frederic Mistral, he was made cardinal in 19111. Post-Revolution, the **Faculty of Medicine** moved from its 15th century home in what is now the rue Ecole de Pharmacie (*see page 204*) to the St Benoît and St Germain monasteries next door. Faculty visits via tourist office.

## Centre Régional d'Histoire de la Résistance et de la Déportation

**Charles de Gaulle**

1 place de la Liberté, 34170 Castelnau le Lez
04 67 14 27 45  www.memoire-resistance-lr.fr
Mon, Tue 9-12, 13-17; Wed 9-13, 144-18; Thu 9-12, 13-18; Fri 9-12, 14-16
Housed above a police station in a former mairie, is an important collection documenting Languedoc's Résistance  groups, the fate of those deported to concentration camps, and Vichy propaganda. No mere memorial, but candid exposition of true guerrilla warfare; weapons and explosives, parachuted in by allies for blasting railway lines, hoarded in the Cevennes by Maquis freedom fighters. Visit with a curator; or use audioguides.

## Mare Nostrum

**Place du France**

allée Ulysse, Odysseum, 34960 Montpellier
04 67 13 05 50  www.aquariummarenostrum.fr
Jul Aug daily 10-22; Sep-Jun, Sun-Thu 10-19; Fri, Sat 10-20 Closed Jan
All marine life is here. Imaginative and well presented sea-world aquarium experience, focusing, as the name suggests, on the Med. Naturally, there are sharks and vast tanks of colourful fish; of course, there's a simulated stormy trawler voyage; and delightfully, there are penguins. Cleverly designed and stimulating tour through many aspects of man's relationship with and responsibility to the deep. The team behind the excellent *Nausicaa* in Boulogne created this entertaining and educational experience.

## Mikve

1 rue Barralerie, 34000 Montpellier

A remarkable 13<sup>th</sup> century Jewish ritual bath is the oldest vestige of a community that helped make Montpellier one of Europe's key cities of enlightenment. Closed to the public, but featured in selected guided tours. Superb vaulted ceilings and a fine balustraded staircase, testament to the prosperity of the ghetto's golden age. Visits suspended during excavations of recently discovered synagogue on the site. The building houses an organisation following the teachings of Maimonides, the Rabbi who united Jewish and Moslem wisdom in 12<sup>th</sup> century Cordova.

## Musée Atger                                            Albert 1er

2 rue Ecole de Médecine, Faculté de Médecine, 34000 Montpellier

04 67 41 76 40

Mon, Wed, Fri 13.30-17.45 Closed late-Jul-Aug

An unexpected trove of works by Fragonard, Van Dyke and Rubens amongst around 500 bequeathed to the University's medical faculty in 1833 by Xavier Atger, who collected Flemish, French and Dutch masters. This eclectic and very personal donation includes drawings, landscapes and historical images as well as sketches and caricatures.

## Musée Fabre                                            Comédie/Corum

39 bd Bonne Nouvelle, 34000 Montpellier, 34000 Montpellier

04 67 14 83 00  www.museefabre.fr

Tue, Thu, Fri, Sun: 10-18, Wed 13-21, Sat 11-18

A fine arts museum for of a great European Capital was two centuries in curating, and four years in renovation. And how well worth the dark years is this remarkable collection, finally showcased in a *palais des beaux arts* of our time. As a former curator mused: it should be "a living entity, not a necropolis". Fully accessible, with special short-cut itineraries for visitors with mobility issues, the museum spans the architectural history of the city: 17<sup>th</sup> century Jesuit college, 18<sup>th</sup> century town hall, 19<sup>th</sup> century galleries and 21st century courtyard. The illustrated story begins even earlier, since the chronological circuit starts with works from the 16<sup>th</sup> century. Best to choose an itinerary to suit your passion, since there is far too much to appreciate in one day: 16<sup>th</sup> - 18<sup>th</sup> century French, Italian and Spanish schools; perhaps Flemish artists of the 17<sup>th</sup>; modernist and abstract 20<sup>th</sup> century *oeuvres*; maybe the controversial contemporary expanses of black by living artist Pierre Soulages; 20 uncompromising works housed in a bespoke modern glass wing. Traditional galleries house the principal 1825 legacy by François-Xavier Fabre and many subsequent bequests. If you seek big names, you won't find the impressionist mob that hallmarks most civic museums, even if Morrisot, Monet, Manet and Renoir are represented here. Nonetheless, brushwork of greats, Rubens and David to Delacroix, illuminates galleries designed to be enjoyed gently; with space to sit, recline and reflect on beauty. The collection is digitalised; computer terminals offer vicarious safari. The restoration of a lost classic, Poussin's *Venus and Adonis*, is a must-see: after all, the original was cut in half 200 years ago and a third of the painting now resides in New York. Courbet's local land and seascapes are inspirational and his *Bonjour Monsieur. Courbet* is a delight. Enter from the Esplanade through a contemporary space created by Daniel Buren. Even the museum café has a link to the great masters, run as it is by Montpellier's *Michelin* starred Pourcel twins (*see page 313*).

### Musée de l'Histoire de Montpellier

Comédie

place Jean Jaurès, 34000 Montpellier
04 67 54 33 16
Tue-Sat: 10-12.30, 13.30-18
The invisible church in one of the busiest squares in the city was known as *Notre Dame des Tables*. You may attribute the monicker to restaurant terraces facing twin glass panels - only sign that the long demolished *Eglise Sainte Marie* twice stood here. But you'd be wrong. When the original Romanesque church was rebuilt in the 12th century, money lenders set up their stalls along the walls: thus the nickname. *Notre Dame des Tables* was hub of mediaeval commercial, political and religious life, but destroyed in the Revolution. All that remains is a 10th century crypt, home to an imaginative audiovisual tour through city history told through shadow puppets and clever lighting. One ticket gives admission to *Miséricorde* chapel and pharmacy and *Vieux Montpellier* museums as well.

### Musée de la Pharmacie

Boutonnet

15, av. Charles Flahault, Faculté de Pharmacie, 34000 Montpellier
04 67 54 80 62   Tue, Fri 10-12
Besides ornate jars, vintage surgical instruments in the medical school's pharmaceutical department, find re-creations of 19th and early 20th century pharmacies. See also **Pharmacie de la Miséricorde**.

### Musée du Vieux Montpellier

Corum

Hôtel de Varennes, 2, Place Pétrarque, 34000 Montpellier
04 67 66 02 94
Tue-Sat: 10-12.30, 13.30-18
In a private mansion: a collection of domestic, secular and religious items laid out in salons and old kitchens. On the same three-site ticket as the **Miséricorde** chapel and pharmacy and the **Musée de l'Histoire de Montpellier** in the crypt of *Notre Dame des Tables*.

## Odysseum

04 99 64 23 40

With a Disneyesque logo and addresses inspired by both classical tales of Ulysses and the sci-fi flick *2001 A Space Odyssey*, the leisure and shopping district at the end of the tram line finally links the edge-of-town parking and *Gaumont* multiplex with *Ikea* at exit 29 of the A9. Now with an aquarium, planetarium, *Végapolis* skating rink, bowling and karting, games arcades, *Altissimo* climbing wall and a gym, 16 restaurant and bars, and *Acrochats* kids centre in the entertainment sector around **Place de France** station. **Odysseum** terminus serves a split level outdoor mall between *Géant* hypermarket and the ubiquitous Swedish identiflatpackerie. Tue-Sat, a free **Petit Train** shuttles complex to parking. With chain hotels, many carparks, from park & ride, to subsidised shopper zones, and a *Velomagg* bike depot the area is popular with out-of-towners shopping and playing before hitting the city as well as urban types out for an evening's car-free fun. Among the attractions, is **Planétarium Galilée** (04 67 13 26 26 www.planetarium-galilee.com) with dramatised presentations, including a look back at the space featuring the voice of Yuri Gagarin.

## Pharmacie et Chapelle de la Miséricorde
**Comédie/Corum**

1 rue de la Monnaie, 34000 Montpellier

04 67 67 93 32

Tue-Sat: 10-12.30, 13.30-18

Since the last sisters of mercy of Saint Vincent de Paul left their chapel and convent at the turn of the millennium, their chapel and the last surviving apothecary shop in Montpellier is now curated by the city as perfect partner to other local history museums. Pots and jars of early pharmacists are fascinating as is chapel artwork. The house became home to the Daughters of Charity when the Dames de la Miséricorde settled here in 1622.

## La Serre Amazonienne

Parc Zoologique de Montpellier, 50, avenue Agropolis, 34090 Montpellier

04 67 54 45 23

Tue-Sun: Easter-Oct 10-18.30; Nov-Easter 9-17

Not many cities boast a mangrove swamp, but this Amazon is an extraordinary greenhouse of exotic ferns and vast trees. Neither trees nor plants were taken from the wild, the collection sourced from nurseries in South America, Thailand and the US. And this is no mere plant collection. Living in this virtually natural habitat are ocelot and piranha, ibis and anaconda – remember, this greenhouse is in the city zoo, so caimans and tarantulas and screeching, squawking birds provide set a very authentic scene. Some late night visits to a natural soundtrack of nocturnal predators.

# Montpellier's Music Venues

### Agora: Cité Internationale de la Danse
Louis Blanc
18 rue Sainte Ursule, 34961 Montpellier
04 67 60 83 60 www.montpellierdanse.com
Former 17th century Ursuline convent, with year-round facilities for the National Choreographic Centre, is home to Montpellier Dance Festival. Performances in studios by the cloisters and a **Rotonde** amphitheatre. **La Panacée**, European artists' city, has studios, gardens, galleries in nearby rue de l'Ecole de Pharmacie.

### L'Arena
rue de la Foire, 34470 Pérols,
04 67 17 69 69 www.arena-montpellier.com
14,000 seat concert arena and sport stadium opened 2010 at the Exhibition centre.

### Château d'O
Château d'O
rond-Point du Château d'O, 34090 Montpellier
08 00 20 01 65 www.domaine-do-34.eu
Château and park summer seasons of concerts, films and shows.

### JAM
St Cléophas
100 rue Ferdinand de Lesseps 34070 Montpellier
04 67 58 30 30 www.lejam.com
The Conservatoire of jazz is a great place to find new talent, hear ol- timers show how it is done or take pot luck on world music in an intimate room. From 20.45.

### Opera Berlioz
Corum
Le Corum, esplanade Charles de Gaulle, 34000 Montpellier
04 67 61 67 61 www.opera-montpellier.com
2000 seat home to National Orchestra and Second Home to the opera company.

### Opéra Comédie
Comédie
11 bd Victor Hugo, 34000 Montpellier
04 67 60 19 80 www.opera-montpellier.com
*See page 197*. Classic 1888 opera house on the square. Undergoing renovation.

### RockStore
Gare St Roch
20 rue Verdun, 34000 Montpellier
04 67 06 80 00 www.rockstore.fr
A Cadillac crashed into the wall marks out this former church in a side street between the Comédie and the station as funkier than the norm for such eclectic bills as ska band Steve O'Steen with an Occitan rap duo. Showcases rising artists before they reach the mainstream: Radiohead, Lenny Kravitz and Pulp have played the 800 capacity venue. Post -concert discos and *Etage* VIP room. *Café Rock* bar opens 18h.

### Zenith Sud
10 Rue Joffre, 34000 Montpellier
04 67 64 50 00
First Zenith mega-venue outside Paris. 6300 seat concert venue hosts France's X-Factor auditions, but also Aznavour, Sardou and touring rock shows.

# Narbonne [5] B2

The Hollywood-like sign on the Corbières hillside above the A9 motorway announces "Narbonne: Crossroads of the South". Crossroads as an historic, political and geographical label is unnerving: the title grabbed by every civic percussionist in France. With silk and spice routes, religious trails and centuries of mini-empires, the *Carrefour de l'Europe* has been pinned on every byway and dirt track from Burgundy to Le Touquet. Mind you, even as a 3-way crossroads by the coast, the Province of Narbonne has more right than most to the claim since Rome's first colony in Gaul in 120 BC was based just 4km outside today's city. Let the lady with the umbrella and the voice that carries fill you in on the dates of Roman, Visigoth, Gallic, Saracan and Spanish occupation. Marseillan's history flags up the city's influence on the wider region. Narbonne is studded with references to 2000 years of intrigue and insurrection. From the **Hotel de Ville** plaque to 1907 vigneron martyrs (*see page 96*) to the renaissance **Maison des Trois Nourrices** where erstwhile pretty boy Henri Coiffier de Ruzé, Marquis de Cinq Mars, confidante (and rumoured lover) of Louis XIII, was arrested for conspiring against Cardinal Richelieu; thus inspiring an opera by Gounod.

Explore gently by renting dinky electric boats on a neatly manicured stretch of the canal de la Robine, spur of the canal du Midi serving the river Aude. The waterway glides underneath shops of the old quarter. Otherwise, take a deep breath, find a parking space and mooch from the excellent produce stalls of **Les Halles** to place Hotel de Ville, with its exposed section of the **Via Dometia** (*see page 220)* at the core of a pedestrianised square of café tables and 13<sup>th</sup> century **Ancien Palais des Archevêques**. The palace houses a town hall, **Musée d'Art et d'Histoire's** famed collection of porcelain, and the **Musée Archéologique's** roman frescos and sarcophogi. Classical glories of Narbonne also celebrated at the **Musée Lapidaire** on place Lamourguier, with finds retrieved after Napoléon III's dismantling of the ramparts staged in musical *son-et-lumière*, in a dramatic glimpse of the past. The real thing is **Horreum Romain** under rue Rouget de Lisle, basement galleries of a warehouse from the 1<sup>st</sup> century BC. Times, prices, tickets and 3-day passes for all museums from the tourist office. Roman Narbonne does not reach the skyline. From afar, ramparts of the palace and its conjoined-twin **Cathédrale Saint-Just-et-Saint-Pasteur** provide a forbidding defensive silhouette. Work began in 1272, but stopped abruptly 60 years later when funding ran out when just the choir had been built – albeit the highest in all France. Use Narbonne as a modern day crossroads: a great base for exploring the **Corbières** winescape and a rugged romantic

207

étanged coast and countryside, where a walk in one direction has you treading on crunched thyme and lavender, and in the other finding wild orchids under vine leaves. Head for the beach: but don't try to walk there. It is unusual to find a seaport 10 miles from the sea. Centuries of silting mean that, whilst the étangs of **Bages** and **Sigean** are within a turret's shadow of the city, **Narbonne Plage** now a spectacular drive away through undulating country of vines and inland cliffs of **La Clappe**. Like Marseillan Plage, it has the air of a ghost town in winter, but is a lively summer resort. So visit **Bages:** the climb through breath-catching steep and narrow alleys to heart-stoppingly perfect square is as good as France gets. The perfect cinematic proportions of the shoebox Mairie, scaled down bistro, epicierie and fountain, upstages even the best hillside view this side of the Italian border.

## Tourist Office

31 rue Jean Jaurès, 11100 Narbonne
04 68 65 15 60  www.mairie-narbonne.fr
Housed in a 16<sup>th</sup> century watermill, with excellent info desk and guided tour options. Visitors may claim 30 minutes free wifi each week. A touch-screen outside offers 24/7 access to tourist information when the office is closed.

### La Maison Natale de Charles Trenet

13 av Charles Trenet, 11100 Narbonne
04 68 90 30 65
Nov-Mar: Wed-Mon 14-17; Apr- 14 Jul: 10-12, 14-17; 15 Jul-Oct: 10-13, 14.30-18
Before Bobby Darrin serenaded *The Sea*, Charles Trenet wrote and warbled *La Mer*. Said to have been inspired by the coastal train ride any Marseillanais would recognise from the view along Sète's *Lido* to the shimmering Med, this song of the sea is a French national treasure. As was Trenet himself: poet and *Fou Chantant*: the singing fool, as his bill matter had it. Trenet died in 2001, four months after a final concert with Charles Azanour at the age of 87. His birthplace (May 1913) is now a museum. Trenet insisted it be no mausoleum, but an escorted musical walk through his mother's home, with the crooner's songs echoing through every room.

*A mural of Trenet watches out over the quarter where the singer grew up.*

Unsuitable for wheelchairs, late-comers not admitted until the start of the next tour. Aznavour appeared at the 2010 Trenet music festival.

### L'Abbaye de Fontfroide
route départementale 613, 11100 Narbonne
04 68 45 11 08 www.fontfroide.com
Daily: 10-12, 14-16. Tours: 10, 11, 12, 14, 15, 16. Gardens closed Dec-April.
Come for the architecture, stay for lunch and leave with a case of wine. *L'Abbaye Sainte-Marie de Fontfroide* is around 15km away. Founded in 1093, the monastery flourished from 1144 when it joined the Cistercian movement. Involved in Cathar witch-hunts, Fontfroide monks were themselves expelled when the Revolution came. A few bonus decades of religious life granted when monks from Sénanque abbey settled here in 1858. Architecturally restored as a gallery in 1908 by artist Gustave Fayet, it remains in private hands. Vaulting, colonnaded cloisters and gardens are charming (especially the 30,000 rosebushes in season), Guided tours and visits include a gallery devoted to Fayet. Only the dormitory is inaccessible to disabled visitors. *La Table de Fontfroide* restaurant in the old *bergerie* has always attracted top chefs and bears a *Gault Millau toque*. The abbey vineyard produces *Corbières* wines to taste and buy.

## Nezignan l'Eveque [5] C2 *see page 121*

## Nîmes [5] D1

Although its greatest gifts to the world are the blue jeans made from the textile that bears its name (*serge de Nîmes* = *denim*), Nîmes is ancient Rome in Languedoc. For 500 years, gladiators fought to the death in the **Arènes**, probably the finest surviving amphitheatre in the Empire. The preservation is more remarkable since later generations built houses inside the arena. Fortunately, the 133m diameter stadium was restored in the 19th century. Though gladiators are no more, they have been succeeded by matadors. The region's lust for bullfighting (*See* **Béziers**) never had a finer setting. I recall one festive evening walking deserted streets outside the bullring, brasserie tables deserted, stillness broken by cheers rising from behind the curved 21m walls of the roman circle, followed by chunks of brassy music from the band. The air ripe with the smell of horses, my mind echoed to the last act of the opera *Carmen*. Romance, choruses, marches and arias danced through my imagination and I saw some kids peering through cracks in the wooden doors of the 20,000 seat coliseum, jostling for a glimpse of the action. Then I noticed the rivulet of blood finding its course between paving stones under the gates, and the reality of a summer sport silenced my private *séance*. Seasonal bullfights (*ferias*) take place during February's Carnival, Easter, Pentecost and September's harvest; proof that history does not belong behind polished glass. In these parts, the past informs the present and life is never a museum piece.

The pedestrian friendly historic centre has charming cafés and little shops. But, despite such diversions, you will come to Nîmes, where Languedoc nudges Provence, nor for coffee, but in search of Rome and its glory. Two original gates from 15 BC with arches and colonnades still stand on the *Via Dometia*: **Porte Auguste** (or *Porte d'Arles*) and **Porte de France** (or *Porte d'Espagne)*. The other entrance is no roadway, but an even rarer treasure. Remains of the only surviving **Castellum** of its type (besides that of Pompeii) mark the spot where water arrived in town to feed fountains and baths. This cistern was gateway for the **Pont de Gard** aqueduct, 27km away (*see page 212*). Perhaps the best preserved temple in the Roman world is the **Maison Carrée**: with neat first-centuryCorinthian columns, built to honour Caius and Lucius Caesar, adopted sons of Emperor Augustus. Opposite is the **Carré d'Art,** a 20th-century "reinterpretation" by architect Norman Foster and home to the city's contemporary art museum. From modern cube to an early octagonal tower: the three-storey **Tour Magne** once dominated plains and garrigue, Two levels remain but the view from the 32m summit presents Mount Ventoux and the Alpilles. Pore over an on-site map of Roman Nîmes.

Remnants of a temple to Diana, the huntress stand by the **Jardins de la Fontaine**, France's first public park. Rediscovered in the 18th century and sympathetically landscaped, it has preserved the shrine of the original spring that founded the city. Ancient Celts, *Volcae Arecomici*, settled here in the 6th century BC, declaring the spring a deity and worshipping the waters. Since a neighbouring spa is still revered today as **Perrier** (*see page 129)*, that showed remarkable prescience. The Volcae ceded the land to Roman legions in 120 BC. Rome defined the region and Nîmes' imperial mint created a commemorative victory coin celebrating Octavius' victory over Cleopatra's Egyptian fleet in 31 BC; the coin's image of a Nile crocodile chained to a palm tree is now the city's coat of arms. Glory years of art and architecture lasted until 5th century when Visigoths ran both colony and economy into the ground.

For much of the Middle Ages, Roman remains were plundered for building materials, but when vines, olives and sheep brought trade once more in the 11th century, the city recovered its mojo, built new walls and a cathedral

(**Notre-Dame et St.-Castor**) and survived the 16<sup>th</sup> century wars of religion. Protestants chose a simpler life, trading textiles rather than preaching. From domestic wool to the silk route, centuries of bandwagon jumping peaked in the 1870s when Levi Strauss imported indigo-blue-dyed denim to America, where the soft but rugged material was worn by miners and workmen. By the way, though the fabric is *Nîmois*, the word "Jeans" comes from *Gênes* (French for Genoa in Italy) where the first trousers were stitched. Cash from exports led entrepreneurs to set up vineyards and build mansions near the new railway station.

**Office de Tourisme**
6 rue Auguste, 33000 Nîmes
04 66 58 38 00   www.ot-nimes.fr
Jul-Aug: Mon-Fri 8.30-20, Sat 9-19, Sun 10-18; Apr-Jun, Sep: Mon-Fr 8.30-19, Sat 9-19, Sun 10-18; Oct-Mar: Mon-Fri 8.30-18.30, Sat 9-18, Sun 10-17;
Pick up excellent maps and find suggested walking itineraries

**Musée des Beaux Arts**
rue Cité Foulc, 30033 Nîmes
04 66 67 38 21
Tue-Sun 10-18
Antidote to the **Maison Carrée** is the traditional fine arts museum (second regional collection after Montpellier) with usual Flemish masters, Italian works from 16<sup>th</sup>-18<sup>th</sup> centuries and a strong 19<sup>th</sup> century French presence. The ground floor atrium features a full roman mosaic.

**Carré d'Art**
place de la Maison Carrée, 30000 Nîmes
04 66 76 35 70
Tue-Sun 10-18
Within the **Maison Carrée**, find 400 contemporary *oeuvres* from the 1960s onwards. Leaning towards movements from the south of France, such names as Takis, Martial Raysse and Philippe Starck feature prominently in an unorthodox collection of galleries. Many world-class temporary shows.

**Musée des Cultures Taurines**
6, rue Alexandre Ducros, 30000 Nîmes
04 66 36 83 77
Jun-Oct Tue-Sat 10-18
Close by the **Arènes**, a museum of bullfighting displays folklore and glamour, the gore and the glory: classic fighting and the gentler camarguaise sport, as well as the tradition of Camargue bull farming. See **Aigues Mortes** (*page 158*) for more on the Manade ranch culture, or if time is short, visit the local ranch in Agde (*see page 153*).

*Roman icon and a UNESCO listed treasure. Now with a visitor centre, museum, film show and food outlets. Admission to the Pont du Gard includes access to supervised beach under the arches.*

**Musée du Vieux Nîmes**
Place aux Herbes, 30000 Nîmes
04 66 76 73 70    Tue-Sat 10-18
Several local themes, but the interesting exhibition about the story of blue jeans charts the progress of local denim from French military uniforms to global youth culture. Discover the life of local indigo dyers (see their quarter when mooching around the *Ilot Littré* in the centre of town).

**Perrier** Tour of the spring, factory and gardens *see page 129*

**Pont du Gard**
30210 Vers Pont du Gard
04 66 37 50 99 www.pontdugard.fr
(museum/shops) winter 09.30-17.30; summer 09-19
A delightful detour (bus 168 from Nîmes or exit 23 of the A9, then follow signs via Uzès). Imposing three-tiered aqueduct spanning the **Gardon Gorge**, a magnificent triumph of Roman engineering. Bringing fresh water from the spring at **Uzès**, the bridge was part of a 50km man-made waterway constructed at the end of the first century BC. Hailed as a wonder of the ancient world, the World Heritage site has been refurbished to stunning effect, though you may no longer climb onto the bridge itself. The triple row of arches complements the landscape and soars 49m above bathers and picnickers on the river banks below. Its top level spans a remarkable 275m. Massive stone blocks, weighting up to 6 tons each, were assembled without the use of mortar. Its gentle, yet precisely engineered, incline of just 24cm per kilometre continued to supply water until the 9th century, when lime deposits and lack of maintenance finally impeded the flow.

# Perpignan    [5] B3

For a man who lived in a world where watches melt in the the sun and moustaches defy gravity, the declaration that Perpignan is the "Centre of the Universe" was inspired by a refreshingly normal and prosaic fact of life: stroppy civil servants. Salvador Dali made his notorious statement after becoming frustrated with bureaucracy at Figueres, his local Spanish railway station, so decided to despatch canvases from across the French border. The change of depot was accompanied by an epiphany: Dali vowed he had a vision at **Gare de Perpignan** on 19 September 1963. "Suddenly, all appeared crystal-clear to me, I was in front of the centre of the world" And so he painted his celebrated impression of the station: an image to grace a Dr Who or L Ron Hubbard paperback. The artist's praise writ large over the platforms, Dali himself inspired the décor of the station roof and paving.

With history and geography the stuff of paradox, such surrealist endorsement is fitting: The last city in France before the border, is also known as *Perpinya*, after Barcelona, the second city of Catalonia. The Catalonian nation within a nation concept may be a curiosity; but that is nothing compared to the rest of the story. France's oldest palace was once home to the king of an island lying 350 kilometres off Europe's mainland. Welcome to Perpignan, France, the town that for less than a century was dynastic capital of the island of Majorca. Visit the **Palais des Rois de Majorque** to find out more. This anachronistic dynasty lasted only 68 years; created in 1276 by James I of Aragon (who also flirted with **Montpellier** along the coast) as a treat for his youngest son. The palace, now within a citadel, still has its chapel, great hall and royal apartments.

The city between the snowy peaks of the Pyrenees and the Med's rugged shores and coves became French in 1659. The centre is rich in ecclesiastical *patrimoine*. A gothic **Cathédrale St-Jean** boasts a 15th-century bell housed in an 18th-century cage. **Campo Santo**, next door, is France's only cloistered cemetery, with four marbled galleries. **L'Eglise St.-Jacques**, built in two parts in the 14th and 18th centuries, stands in charming gardens. The 13th century **Notre Dame des Anges** on rue Foch, once a Franciscan convent, became a military hospital chapel. Beautiful gilded vaulting. The **Eglise des Dominicains**, rue Rabelais, created by the Aragon kings for a leper colony, also adopted by the military, remains army property. Public may visit exhibition spaces here and at the neighbouring 16th century **Minimes** convent, on the site of a Jewish ghetto.

Plenty of gasps from secular buildings too. The 14th-15th century **Castillet** is the rose brick gatehouse of the original fortifications that wrapped the

213

city until around 1900. It dominates place Verdun, and has excellent views from the roof terrace. A museum of Catalan history and culture reopens here soon. Who needs a museum? Under the boat-shaped weather vane of the Loge de Mer 14$^{th}$ century maritime court, place de la Loge is where the traditional *Sardana* is danced in front of Aristide Maillol's curvaceous statue of Venus. French northern Catalonia is less heavily politicised here than its sister movement in Barcelona. Other Spanish influence from Republican refugees fleeing Civil War in the 1930s; and African style followed the fresh wave of immigration after Algerian independence a quarter of a century later. **Musée De l'Algérie Française** tells colonial war stories in a second floor apartment on rue Foch (04 68 35 51 09)

Before Dali, other artists took the train south to discover the Roussillon light. Perpignan makes an excellent base for an art heritage trail in the steps of Matisse, Picasso, Chagall, even Charles Rennie Mackintosh, through **Céret** in the back country and the ports of **Banyuls, Port Vendres** and **Collioure** (*see page 339*). Maillol's bronze women garnish city streets and fellow Catalan Gaudi inspires interiors of trendy bars and clubs. Pick up work by new talent at the art market held on the first Saturday of the month alongside the weekly fleamarket of the Allées Maillol. Excellent shopping, from *Galeries Lafayette* and big names on wider squares to Hispanic pottery on rue Sant-Vicens and some great little foodie shops rue Paratilla. Organic food market day is Saturday at Place Rigaud. Price conscious shoppers cross the border (*see page 386*) for Spanish bargains on booze, fags and scents, but there is so much to discover in the region around town. Drive to wine estates in **Maury, Banyuls**, and **Rivesaltes** and don't forget the perfect **Collioure** anchovies.

### Office de Tourisme
place Armand Lanoux, 66002 Perpignan
04 68 66 30 30 www.perpignantourisme.com
Jun-Sep: Mon-Sat 9-19, Sun 10-16; Sep-Jun: Mon-Sat 9-18, Sun 10-13
Good guided tours, included adapted circuits for disabled, and info in Braille and MP3 format for blind visitors.

### Musée de l'Aviation
Mas Palegry, 66100 Perpignan
04 68 54 08 79 www.musee-aviation.com
Unusual aviation museum dedicated to pilots who never returned to base. In the family farm of French airforce pilot Charles Noetinger (1934-1995), whose family escorts vistors around the collection offering a very personal account of their father's passion for flying.

**Musee Des Beaux Arts Hyacinthe Rigaud**
16 rue de l'Ange, 66000 Perpignan
04 68 35 43 40
Tue-Sun 10.30-18
Named for Rigaud, Perpignan-born court painter to Louis XIV and one-time resident of the **Castillet**, this 18th century mansion houses 800 years of Catalan art and sculpture. Nonetheless, some 200 contemporary works are the wider attraction: Maillol, Dufy, Picasso and Miro are the crowd-pullers.

**Musee Bella**
Espace Primavera, 6 avenue du Languedoc, 66000 Perpignan
04 68 22 97 11 (visit free by appointment only)
Long before Barbie became prototype for surgical ambition, and Cindy put swinging London on the *dansette*, little French girls had their own wholesome doll. From 1946 until the 1980s, *Bella* was not defined by waistline, but gamine *regard*. 500 dolls and much memorabilia on show.

# Pézenas [5] C2

"Jean-Baptiste Poquelin was born in Paris in 1622, but it was in 1650 in Pézenas that Molière was born". Wise words of Marcel Pagnol on a city's most famous adopted son; France's most celebrated playwright was not born, he was invented, a jobbing actor in the right place at the right time. Stratford-upon-Avon thrives on Shakespeare: *Merry Wives* tearooms and *Romeo & Juliet* romantic weekend breaks (don't marketing people ever read the end of a story before printing leaflets?). Pézenas has echoes of the life and works of France's favourite playright. *Les Femmes Savantes* offer pizza, Scapin's savoury snacks and wines are named for le Prince de Conti; though *antiquaires* avoid references to Misers and Misanthropists.

Only 15 minutes cross-country from Marseillan to the former regional capital, and its hidden Renaissance courtyards, art galleries and charming summer theatre. Share an after show *verre* with the players to feel the buzz of Southern culture or walk old streets, past antique and junk shops, to discover cellar bars for late night jazz or poetry recitals and forget that you are just a step from a rolling landscape of vineyards and olive groves, the country of farmers and fishermen that is *Les Pays de Pézenas*. Antique shops, *brocantes* and bric-a-braceries epitomise the charm of Pézenas. If some capitals are designed for *flânerie* promenading and others created for eavesdropping at café table amphitheatres; Pézenas is made for poking around, peering into dimly lit passageways and taking the unfamiliar turn.

Dozens of places to pick up true treasure or well-polished tat, burnished and buffed to apparent value; scores of *ateliers* and studios where glass is blown, iron wrought, leather tanned and jewellery designed before your eyes. Cobbles lead to galleries showcasing emerging talent. Hunting for 1920s armchairs, 19th century armoires or ornate Empire clocks, the antiquing snail trail follows avenues Verdun, Briand and Montagne. Arts and crafts tucked in alleys between the **Collegiale** and the **Ghetto**. Visit www.antiquites-Pézenas -france.com

In a market town, where traders from afar met thrice yearly at warranted mediaeval county fairs, seek the oldest streets: Ground floor *échoppes*, essentially French compromise between an actual shop and a market stall, with wide low slabs outside as counters for fish, tripe or cheese. Street names, *Triperie Vieille* and *Orfèvres*, echooriginal wares where today's watercolours, designer bath taps or original wedding gowns are sold. Many still display food: *berlingot* boiled sweets for which Pézenas is famed, jams and patés, and everywhere *Les Petits Pâtés de Pézenas*, tiny *toque*-shaped meat pies, blending mutton, fruit and spices, introduced to the town in 1768 by Lord Clive of India. Saturday's excellent market fills wide avenues, linked to old quarters by rue Conti's browseable side streets of tea rooms and bookshops for immediate diversion, and restaurant menus for anticipating evenings when squares are lit with an eye for romance. Strong ex-pat community, so English books sold alongside French lace and couture. *See page 254*

The old town is guaranteed serendipity: Rue Emile Zola has the house of **Nostradamus** (number 10) and **Jacques Coeur** (number 7; a begargoyled must see), and leads to the start of the former Jewish **Ghetto** at rue de de la Juiverie *(see page 350)* and to cours Jean-Jaurès where you should pause by the **Hôtel des Landes de Saint-Palais** and **Hôtel de Latudes**. Rue de la Foire is best walked with head turned upwards and jaw dropped; the better to appreciate renaissance windows of **Hôtel de Wicque** at number 7, sculpted child musicians above the door of number 22 and a gorgeous round staircase at number 10, **Hôtel Carrion-Nizas**. Nudge open doors of 15th and 16th century *hôtels particuliers* to discover ornate courtyards of *langue de chat* paving, exquisite vaulted ceilings, galleried balustrades and staircases to put Florence to shame. Since many of these are listed buildings, the public have the right to gawp. Ask the tourist office for a list of addresses where a polite peek is permitted. Certain buildings such as the **Hôtel des Ribes** are well signposted with red plaques by the doorway. When you park for free on promenade Pré St Jean (or for pay at place 14 Juillet), pause by the **Molière Monument** by Béziers sculptor Jean-Antoine Injalbert *(see pages 171-173)*.

Step behind a curve of restaurants and cafes to immerse yourself in the old town, **Hôtel Lacoste** is the first stunning old house worth peering into. Vaulted galleries hosted the *Etats Généraux* of Languedoc in 1613 and 1614 welcomed the Sun King himself in 1660. During the 19th century it was a literary salon, but today is home to a bank. These meetings of the Languedoc General Estates redefined a town whose original Latin name (think of the modern French *piscine* for swimming pool) meant fishpond. Like neighbouring **Montagnac**, Pézenas muddled through, growing from farm community to market town. When political turmoil endangered cities such as Narbonne, these *Etats* tax gathering junkets moved to Pézenas; influential nobles and high flyers answering directly to the king settled in town. Suddenly Pézenas found itself back on the Southern European trade route. County fairs returned in the 17th century, bringing wealth from beyond France. For a century or so, the town even became regional capital. A later slump in fortune, when the city lost the first railway route (and thus trade) to Béziers, actually saved the town from redevelopment. When trains eventually arrived, half a century too late, its feeble branch line failed the test of time. The abandoned **Gare du Nord** is now an arts centre.

The *Etats Généraux* of 1650 proved more than a political pow-wow; it was a quiet cultural revolution. For three years, a troupe of performers, run by failed actor Jean-Baptiste Poquelin, had toured plays round Languedoc's smaller towns under the name *l'Illustre Théâtre*. Invited to entertain visiting bigwigs (just as Eurovision spawned *Riverdance)*, *l'Illustre Théâtre* became the essential treat whenever the Estates sat in Pézenas. Poquelin's hastily assumed new identity as Molière, Lord of the Laughs, proved a smash hit. The 1653 sessions were the turning point: Armand de Bourbon, Prince of Conti, settled at the Grange des Prés in Pézenas. An unrepentant playboy with an eye for southern totty, he appreciated good lively stage romps featuring a well proportioned actress. He became Molière's patron until an influential confessor turned the prince's head towards sudden Puritanism.

Molière and his crew headed north to Paris and found an even more important benefactor in Louis XIV himself. Court composer Lully knocked out incidental music to please an upmarket audience. Time in Pézenas had not been wasted. Conti's lifestyle inspired the play *Dom Juan* and the religious mystic who had put an end to the prince's libertine ways certainly shaded Molière's greatest hit *Tartuffe*. Pézenas is justifiably proud of its role in nurturing France's most enduring comic talent and, in the 19th century, reinvented itself as Molière's rebirthplace. Unlike Stratford, which is packed with Shakespeare heritage from the playwright's era, Pézenas has had to work harder. You may spot **Maison Gély** on place Gambetta, home to a barbershop where Molière spent most mornings drawing on his fellow patrons for characters, or stay the night at **Hôtel Alphonce** where he performed his plays. Arts festivals abound and in 1804 the town's theatre was converted from the *Eglise des Pénitents Noirs*. The strolling player tradition thrives in an old wine warehouse. Reviving the **Illustre Théâtre**, a talented rep company stages bills of Molière classics mixed with contemporary boulevard comedies and experimental new drama in summer seasons: a different play each night, and drinks with the cast in the garden after the show. *Cafés philos,* poetry, jazz dives, classy buskers are for locals, just as street entertainers and costumed historical guides strut their stuff for summer tourists. Visit during off-season festivals when the totemic *poulain* dances in the streets, a humungous foal borne by nine men in homage to 1226 when Louis VIII's favourite mare gave birth in the town.

**Office de Tourisme de Pézenas Val d'Hérault**
Place des Etats du Languedoc, 34120 Pézenas
04 67 98 36 40  www.Pézenas -tourisme.fr
Sep-Jun: Mon-Sat 9-12, 14-18, Sun 10-12, 14-18; Jul-Aug: Sat-Tue, Thu 9-19, Fri 9-20, Sun 10-19.
Pézenas' information centre is also tourist office for 15 surrounding inland towns and villages: **Adissan, Aumes, Bessan, Castelanu de Guers, Caux, Cazouls d'Hérault, Florensac, Lézignan la Cèbe, Montagnac, Nézignan l'Evêque, Nizas, Pézenas** and **Pinet.** The office is now housed in the renovated Hôtel Peyrat, home to *Scénovsion Molière.* Architecture on the ground floor; free exhibitions upstairs.

**Collégiale Saint-Jean de Pézenas**
plan Jean-François Lépine, rue Chevaliers St Jean 34120 Pézenas
*(Treasury)* Jul-Sep, Tue-Sat 15-18.30, Wed, Fri 21-23; Oct-Jun, Tue-Sat 14-18
The church, once base of knights Templar and of Malta, rebuilt after the bell-tower crashed through the roof. Famous for its organ, but the real gem is hidden amongst gold and silver displays in the chapter house treasury museum: a rare smiling black Madonna, damaged in the Revolution yet saved from total destruction by a Madame Vidal who asked looting vandals for the "old bit of woodworm" as toy for her grandchildren. A copy is venerated at Friday mass at **Eglise Sainte Ursule**, rue Reboul.

**Hôtel Alphonce**
32, rue Conti, 34120 Pézenas
04 67 98 10 38
Jul-Aug, Mon-Sat 10-12, 14.30-18.30
Best preserved of the *Hôtels Particuliers*; the house where Molière acted. Modest admission fee to view galleries and courtyards. Unique, amongst the Molière sites, you may stay the night in spacious *chambres d'hôtes.*

**Musée Boby Lapointe**
1 place Gambetta, 34120 Pézenas
04 67 21 02 87  www.bobylapointe.com
Jun-Sep 10-12, 16.30-20; Oct-May, Tue Sun 12-12, 13.30-19
If genetic engineering blent DNA of Tom Lehrer and Jacques Brel,
scientists may create a second Boby Lapointe. A comic genius for lyric
writing is wit that transcends cult. Dazzling wordplay and an ear for the
absurd made his punning patter songs cult hits with students, intellectuals
and off-beats alike throughout the 1960s. Born in Pézenas in 1922, he died
aged 50, but his songs and humour live on. Fan club *Eh! Dis Boby* runs this
museum celebrating his life and work and stages an annual festival in April.

**Musée de la Porte et de la Ferronnerie**
5-7 rue Montmorency, 34120 Pézenas
04 67 98 35 05
Mon-Fri: Nov, Dec, Feb 14.30-17.15; Mar-Jun, Sep, Oct 10.30-12.30, 15-
18.30; Jul-Aug 10-30-12.30, 15.30-19.30 (+Sat 15.30-19.30)
When I visited the door museum in Brussels, it was closed. But this one is
at least ajar. Domestic front doors in the region are works of art and fine
craftsmanship. A stroll through Marseillan's historic quarter reveals many
antique marvels restored and recreated by today's master carpenters from
Pézenas, a town renowned for fine wooden doors and ornamental ironwork
knockers and hinges. The museum is well worth a visit, and is a great point
of contact for finding an artisan to work on your own restoration project.

**Musée du Jouet**
2b Rue Montmorency, 34120 Pézenas
04 67 35 92 88  http://museedujouetPézenas .jimdo.com
Jul-Sep 10-20; Oct-Jun 14-19. Closed Jan, 15-31 Mar, Mon (Oct-Jun ex holidays)
Toy museum with a vast collection of vintage cars, and spinning tops, dolls
houses, tin vehicles and, in *Molièreville*, tuppence-coloured paper theatres.

**Scénovision Molière**
Office de Tourisme (*see page 218*)
04 67 98 35 39 www.scenovisionmoliere.com
Sep-Dec, Feb-Jun, Mon-Sat 9-12, 14-19, Sun 10-12, 14-19; Jul-Aug Sat-Tue, Thu
9-13, 15-19, Wed, Fri 9-13, 15-20 Sun 9-13, 15-20. Last entry: 75min earlier.
An entertaining diversion: 55-minute audiovisual tour of the life and times
of the playwright, played through 3D projections and animations screened
in each room as you walk through the 17th century mansion **Hôtel de
Peyrat**, home to the tourist office. Scenes switch between Pézenas and
Paris. Sometimes Molière and his patrons and players come to life in the
fireplace of an elegant salon; in other rooms a stage is set behind a curtain.

You've read the bottle, you've sipped the wine, now meet the village that turns a grape into an *appellation*. It may have been mere fruit that got the village onto the wine map in the 1940s when *Picpoul de Pinet* was first recognised with a VDQS (*Vin Délimité de Qualité Supérieure*) stamp on its labels and raised the status even further when it became an AOC in 1985. However, the village has played its part in history since 118BC when the Romans decided to build their main road from Rome to the furthest flung Iberan colonies. More specifically Gnaeus Domitius Ahenobarbus, Consul of Rome and grandfather of the more famous Enobarbus that you first thought of: the one in the Shakespeare play. Ahenobarbus decided to create a military and trading route through the Alps to the Pyrenees, setting up staging posts, and eventually towns and cities along the route. This led to the establishment of such key roman towns as **Narbonne** and **Nîmes** and thus the **Via Dometia** ran through Languedoc and some 6km of the road may still be walked from Pinet.

On a modern map, the route is still pretty much the best way to get to Spain, since the modern A9 motorway takes a similar course, several vineyards further out of sight and earshot, and there's talk of the new TGV line to Barcelona following a parallel path. But if *grande vitesse* is not your priority, the old Roman road between the vines, remains an enjoyable ramble on a spring afternoon. Follow signs to the car park at the **bois de Vallongue.**, By an attractive mosaic marking the spot, take in a splendid view across the Etang de Thau and admire a cross section of Roman road to see the original construction. Informative panels offer a potted history lesson and suggest a good walking circuit. Return the sat nav to the glove compartment, lock the car and walk in the footsteps of legions past to work up an appetite for an obligatory tasting of *Picpoul de Pinet à Pinet*.

The Roman period was certainly the road's heyday. Conquering armies set up the winemaking tradition, and by the 16th century, the *Piquepoul* grape was generally reckoned to be something of a class act. But eventually, waterways, railways, even motorways, bypassed the *Via Dometia* and nothing much happened until 2004, when Pinet got its first traffic light and the infernal combustion engine finally trumped the chariot. Should you get lost, you could do worse than scan the horizon and follow the advice of a precocious seven year old marching his family along the *Via Dometia*: "Pinet's the village with the really pointy church." The pointy church spire is that of the 19th century **Eglise St Siméon**, home to a year round nativity scene featuring some 300 characters acting out scenes from Pinet village life. History buffs will clamour to see vestiges of two minor roman roads at the **Croix de Ménard**. Other than historical paths and *provençal santons* of balancers and farmers, the true lure is wine. When in 1860, politician Duc de Morny, half brother of Napoleon III was served wine from Pinet at the wedding of Empress Eugenie's personal physician at the Paris Tuilleries, he claimed "This wine finally reconciles me with the Hérault Republicans".

Whether or not you need to bridge a political rift, you'll find half a dozen *caveaux* for tasting Picpoul in Pinet, and besides the eponymous *cépages*, a wide range of other varieties may be experienced. After your cellar visit, a walk is recommended, and if you do not fancy returning to the roman road, a pretty diversion on a sunny afternoon is to wander the streets of the old quarter hunting for virgins. That is, seeking statues that architects and wealthy home owners carved into the frontages of village houses. Some are colourful dramatic divas, arms outstretched, blessing the streets below; others simple and modest, but the game is a great child-pleaser. By the way, if you think you have spotted a Loire Valley or Bordeaux château emerging from the tree-lined horizon, don't blame the the *Merlot*: the fairy tale palace is a private home, built, in the *anglais* fashion of a gentleman's folly for pleasures out of time and place, by *bordelais* architect Garros in 1903.

**Tourist office**: see page 218

**Domaine Ormarine**
13 avenue de Picpoul, 34850 Pinet
04 67 77 03 10 Closed Sunday
Recognize the barrels from the co-op, as they have been stamped by a red hot branding iron, a tradition dating back to the final years of the Monarchy, when Louis XVI's minister Turgot issued a decree giving permission for the people of the Community of Pinet, in the Diocese of Agde, to brand every barrel *Vin de Pinet*. By 1835, Picpoul de Pinet was being exported to England. The eau-de-vie *Mistelle de l'Ormarine* once filled the award winning chocolates of **Guy Bouzigues** (*see page 223*)

# Pomérols [5] C2 323

As you drive from Marseillan past the oyster-shell-coated water tower, and your car's suspension pays homage to the Roman chariots that would recognise both view and bumps from the days of the *Via Dometia*, the next community heralded by vines is Pomérols. Roadside panels announce your imminent arrival at the grandly named cellars of Beauvignac. This is the

221

cooperative winery of Pomérols, now merged with those of **Mèze** and **Castelnau de Guers**. And these *picpoul de pinet* wines, regularly cited in the *Gault et Millau* guides, are served at restaurant tables from Oxford to Osaka, New York to Beijing. Now the co-op has opened its brand new purpose-built sales and tasting centre on the road into Mèze (by its own unadorned *château d'eau*), most wine-buying passing trade bypasses the town of Pomérols altogether. A pity, because of course, for years the second great lure of Pomérols was chocolate, but even sugar-free rovers found that the old centre alleys provided a pleasant leg-stretching moment or two, whilst wandering from the co-op to a €13 lunch at the **Olé** café on the square, a treat not likely to be matched on the lorry route of the D613.

Most houses in the oldest quarter date from 14th-16th centuries. The centre is dominated by the bell-tower, with its steel cage. The building at the base of the tower was once the insurgents' headquarters during the French Revolution. The actual **Eglise Saint Cyr et Sainte Julitte** was dedicated to 4th century martyrs and founded in the 9th century, well before anyone, apart from a handful of holy men with an agricultural flair, came to live here, and it certainly pre-dates the village itself. The present church building, founded by monks of the **Abbaye Saint Sever** in Agde, is from the 13th century; choir and two lateral chapels listed historic monuments. The moment of awe for visitors is in appreciating the stunning 17th century altarpiece: a gilded triptych, framed with vine draped columns. This frame is work of the Agde based sculptor Cannet, with gold leaf applied by Balthazar Tirgit of Pézenas. Flanked by statues of Saint Peter and Saint Paul, a painting, possibly by a Béziers artist, depicts a trial of mother and son patron saints at the court of tyrannical Roman emperor Diocletian.

If Pomérols had ever wanted to appoint a secular saint, the village need look no further than the bakery on rue Quille for a story of humble beginnings touched by greatness, inspiring so many contemporary pilgrims. Though the *boulanger* decided to hang up his apron for health reasons whilst at the peak of his career in 2011, his tale is worth the telling.

What becomes a legend most, but chance, fate, fortune and anecdote? France's finest have always enjoyed draping origins with fable. Whether the tale of Dom Perignon and fizzy wine (a saga long refuted in **Limoux**) or the chestnut about the shepherd boy whose bread and cheese lunch got wedged between a rock and a wet place when he left lunch to rescue a drowning sheep: that story goes that months later, when he remembered, he was one sandwich short of a legend, as the stream had dissolved the mouldy bread into veins in the cheese. That very Roquefort plays a minor role in another story: that of how the village baker from Pomérols became chocolate maker to princes and presidents. Locals will tell you that that once upon a time, distracted by a visitor to the shop, Guy Bouzigues returned to his baking but confused the fillings for his savoury and sweet baking, and thus a cheesy mix for a Roquefort *quiche* ended up wrapped in fine cocoa. So goes the yarn and the rest is history. No one would consciously have married blue cheese from the hills with perfect dark chocolate, yet when it happened, the alchemist had created tastebud gold. It may sound dreadful, but reality is heaven, and soon the smartest hostesses on the diplomatic circuit would serve a tray of Monsieur Bouzigues' culinary consequences as perfect accompaniment to aperitifs. For, once enrobed in chocolate and hidden from view, cheese does not taste as you might expect it to, but adds a savoury wow-factor to the bonbon. I once attended a very smart blind tasting of wine and chocolate in St James' and the joy of watching London's most pampered and nurtured palates dicing with adjectives over the perfect marriage of anticipated AOC with an unexpected guest. Sage and other herbs ellicited scents of the *garrigue* to flatter a robust *Coteaux de Languedoc*, and *Picpoul de Pinet* itself featured in more than one filling (*Picpoul* and saffron a heady combo). As for goat's cheese and fig, Roquefort and banana, even sea-salt and caramel, not to mention olives! So *Maître Chocolatier* Guy Bouzigues became France's most celebrated confectioner, his chocolates feted and served across hemispheres and timezones. But in Pomérols, where cocoa-coated creations are but a memory, his address remains simply the *boulangeie* that closes on Wednesday. *Chocomanes* should visit M. Servant in Marseillan (page 251).

**Tourist office**: *see page 218*

# Port Vendres  |5| B4  *(see page 339)*

# Portiragnes  |5| C2

Rather sweet little baby sister to the livelier Vias, on the Canal du Midi between Béziers and Agde, Portiragnes is most likely to be on your agenda if renting a boat for a week on the waterways. The port, a basin between locks, is self-sufficient starting point for many a holiday afloat, with its own parking, restaurant and bar (*see page 343*), midway between old Portiragnes and Portiragnes Plage. The canal is the nicest way to travel from the resort and the mediaeval village, ideally by bike. The original community is a couple of miles from the coast, a typical little Languedoc settlement with the required age-old house fronts, a brooding 12th century church and a co-operative winery. Down by the sea, the charming little resort (*see page 79*) is neat and tidy, with well-manicured gardens, nicely-maintained campsites and a Tuesday midnight seafront market. The beach is long, sandy and easily accessible from restaurants and hotels. Very much the unassuming family holiday destination that you remember from long-ago childhood or French films of the 1960s and 70s: self-contained with cafes, street markets, small shops and cheery folk selling fruit, seafood and ice-creams by the beach. And, of course, there is the serendipity of an unassuming hotel with its fabulous restaurant for that holiday meal you still talk about years later. Triangle of open country, delineated by village, shore and canal, is home to wildlife, from herons in the reed-beds to black bulls and *Camarguaises* horses that you pass when cycling the tow paths. These creatures are poised for celebrity, as the area hosts a summer season of bullfights, not usually the bloody Hispanic events, but *Cours Camarguaises*, better associated with **Aigues Mortes**, where the Matador is at risk rather than the bulls, and instead of going after the animals with spears, the sportsmen try to loop rosettes and ribbons over the creature's horns. No bull is harmed and the sport is playful rather than bloody.

**Tourist Office:** place du Bicentenaire 04 67 90 92 51 www.ot-portiragnes.fr

# Roquebrun  [5] B2

Not to be confused with the more famous Riviera town Roquebrune; yet orange trees and mimosa groves are the lure here too. Come to February's Mimosa carnival to inhale the rich citrus fragrance and enjoy colourful floats and infectious music. Roquebrun has it all: Gorgeous gardens (www.jardin-Méditerranéen.fr), quaint streets, and a beach on the Orb, where canoeists take on the fast-flowing waters of the weir by the bridge. If you arrive with neither kayak nor flip flops, find a café terrasse table and toast the splashing below with a glass of Saint-Chinian Roquebrun AOC.

It is easy to become blasé with so many of France's *Plus Beaux Villages* to choose from. But this one has a cracking legend. The **Château de Roquebrun** was built by bold bad Baron d'Openac, who regular stole livestock and produce from local farmers. The baron had a profitable sideline offering hospitality to pilgrims en route to **Abbaye de Fontcaude**, then robbing and stripping his guests, before turning them out in their underwear. He met his match when Poncian, a young monk, settled nearby, planting three trees; orange, lemon and mimosa. Each day, Poncian sat on a rock by the nearby village of **Ceps** to pray for his plants. The jealous baron summoned the devil and offered his soul in return for a powerful storm to destroy the smallholding. Power of prayer proved stronger than Satan's harshest storm and the little orchard survived and thrived. The baron was livid and refused to hand over his soul, so the devil sent a thunderbolt to destoy the castle and the baron with it. Today, just one tower remains and Poncian's land continues to thrive and a chapel at **Ceps** offers thanks for this fertile oasis. Close by is the old city of **Cessenon-sur-Orb;** with churches and chapels and a roman sarcophagus for serious visitors; good food and riverside attractions of the Orb for the rest of us. **Chaos de Réals** is a virtual white water asault course for hard core canoeists, climbing and acrobranching for drier daredevils. **Coumiac** quarry provided the White House's marble facade in Washington. Another transtlantic connection is **Lugné**, between Roquebrun and Cessenon: bring a camera, since you won't often find the **Statue of Liberty** in a village of 15 houses. The sea captain who transported Bartholdi's famous statue from Paris to New York retired to live in Lugné, bringing a replica of his celebrated cargo.

**Tourist Office**: avenue des Orangers, 34460 Roquebrun  04 67 89 79 97

# Saint-Guilhem-le-Desert  [5] C1

With so many jaw-drop distractions whenever you turn off the main road, the Hérault is not exactly camera shy. Front runner in the picturesque stakes is Saint Guilhem-le-Desert, nestling in the ravine they call **Le Bout du Monde**, high up above the **Gorges de l'Hérault**. Ideally, you should discover Saint Guilhem just out of season, since a village founded by a hermit becomes a swarm of humanity in summer. Visitors clutching vibrant pottery and carved wooden toys throng the Romanesque church; in the main square, they gawp at a tree so old and vast the trunk has swallowed its original bench, and gasp at improbable fairy tale cottages and gardens as they flush along stone paths behind the monastery.

How different to the once-upon-a-time. Those same sharp and slender canyons had long provided shelter to hermits and philosophers, hiding from a cruel world when personal religious reflection was considered a political threat. In the year 809, one such recluse was Guilhem, Count of Toulouse. Like so many French nobles, he had a nickname. Sobriquets for rulers are not always flattering (William the Bastard had to conquer England to upgrade his handle; fellow dukes and kings have rejoiced in such titles as the Bald, the Short, the Lazy and the the Stammerer). Guilhem was known as *Court-Nez* (Short Nose). Fortunately canonisation was his due and so his sanctuary was never called Court-Nez-le-Désert. Guilhem, whose early life as grandson of the warrior Charles Martel had been somewhat battle-scarred, founded the monastery of **Gellone** and this peaceful settlement carved high in the cliffs bears his name. Around town you will find the sea-shell symbol of *Saint Jacques*, marking the famous *Santiago de Compostela*

225

pilgrimage route: this is the halfway point from Arles to Toulouse on the path that cross the Pyrenees and runs the top line of Spain. The abbey reliquary houses what Guilhem's grandfather declared to be a piece of the True Cross. Innevitably, today's pilgrims are as likely to be followers of the *Da Vinci Code* as the *chemin Saint Jacques.*

Arguably the most stunning of local UNESCO sites, the vision of the magnificent church roof emerging like a Romanesque carrousel from a shower of weeping willows on the rock-face is simply unforgettable. This is officially one of the *Plus Beaux Villages de France*. On cliffs above town, shadows of a ruined Visigoth **Château du Géant** catch the sunlight, and inspire tour guides to conjure yarns of Saracens and troubadours, ogres and heroes. In the **Abbey**, the famous relic is still a lure. On a perfect day, the magnificent organ will be playing as you step into the cool spartan interior.

Remains of the cloisters retain their tranquillity; albeit a stripped-down, mocked-up affair since the original was shipped to New York 100 years ago to become part of the ecclesiastical architectural combo of The Cloisters museum. Nonetheless, this is a good place to pause before returning to the bustle of the **place de la Liberté**. Artists sell exquisite ceramics and pottery, from their summer shops here; even guttering and drainpipes may be works of art. Their real studios and workshops are down the hill at **St Jean de Fos**, however, where you may buy their wares in the more moderately priced off-season. Taps and spouts in dry stone walls gush with pure spring water, so bring a stock of plastic bottles. Behind the church, honeywarm stone cottages and rustic gardens, where black chickens and white ducks scratch and peck by the fast running *Verdus* stream: a scene so quaintly French you'd swear it was a backlot in Burbank.

From the square, take rue du Bout-du-Monde to the hillside path known as **Les Fenestrettes**, a donkey trail through rocks and wild country (the official hiking route GR74) which tacks back and forth up steep inclines beneath the Château du Géant Allow a good hour or more before returning to the village for a coffee or pricy *crêpe*. White-water sports to be enjoyed on the gorges, a lovely curved beach down the road below the **Pont du Diable**, and the **Clamouse** caves to complete the family day out. Not many guests realise this, but your parking ticket may be exchanged in the church for a free audioguide in English or French. Saint Guilhem is now part of one of France's listed Grand Sites, encompassing five communities, all linked by the Pont du Diable: the other villages are **Aniane**, home to the monastic settlement of *l'Abbaye Saint-Sauveur*, the fortifications of **Montpeyroux** (also known for its wines *see page 110*), **Saint-Jean-de-Fos** and the mediaeval *circulade* village of **Puéchabon**.

**La Maison du Grand Site**
Pont du Diable, 34150 Aniane
04 99 61 73 01 (Apr-Oct); 04 67 57 58 83 www.saintguilhem-valleeherault .fr
Jul-Aug 10-19.30; Apr-Jun, Sep-Oct 10.30-18
Until this visitor centre opened, the road along the Gorges snaked with air-conditioned Renaults and Peugeots with rental-car licence plates and there was a sluggish queue up the hill for a parking place. Now, in summer, we can avoid the traffic and park by the *Maison du Grand Site*. More than a tourist office for the five villages of the site, here you may buy local crafts and taste food and wine, even dine at the brasserie. A one-stop shop for booking adrenelin sports, advice on fishing, swimming and hiking, as well as artistic and wine-buying trails. A free shuttle bus links the centre with Saint Guilhem and Clamousse, daily in peak season, and at weekends in May June and September. Languedoc locals who visit regularly may buy an annual parking pass for just €9.

**Argileum: Maison de la Poterie**
6 rue du Monument, Saint-Jean-de-Fos
04 99 62 58 76
Jul-Aug: 10-19; Feb, Apr-Jun, Sept Tue-Sun: 10-12.30, 14-17
For 600 years Saint-Jean-de-Fos was the region's pottery capital until the early 20$^{th}$ century when the last ceramic workshop closed its doors. Then in the 1980s a small artist colony settled here, reviving the traditional crafts and climbing the hill in season to sell their beautiful glazed pottery to visitors to Saint Guilhem. Eventually, the reputation of Saint Jean spread wide and soon art pilgrims began knocking on *atelier* doors. Now a museum and information centre opens 8 months each year to welcome those too timid to march into a working studio. Ideal introduction to local talent.

**Grotte de Clamouse**
34150 Saint-Jean-de-Fos
04 67 57 71 05 www.clamouse.com
Jul-Aug 10.30-18.20; Jun, Sep 10.30-17.20; Feb-May, Oct 10.30-16.20
The *Cathédrale du Temps* is a unique *son et lumière* experience. Not simply because of the combination of classical music and illumination of stunning caves deep in the rocks beneath St Guilhem; but because it is the only grotto in Europe to be lit entirely by energy saving LED lights. The subterranean walk passes incredible mineral formations, stalactites and natural glistening peal white sculptures created by a fast flowing underground river, ever chased and paced by rainwater and melting snows from the mountain peaks, eventually gushing out through the hillside in 15 cascades and springs.

# Saint Thibéry [5] C2

We came to St Thibéry for August's jazz festival and found ourselves in deserted streets: not a dog walker in sight, nor the Saturday night blare of television from an open window. We walked in silence towards the lights of the centre, and as we turned into the main square, were greeted with sounds of contented anticipation. Every possible space was filled with long trestles, chairs and benches, and it was a challenge to find three places at a table. We stared through 360 degrees of pleasant bewilderment, as the man with the nod struck up the band. In Saint Thibéry, the music is free, you pay only for paper plates of cold meats and cheeses and liberally flowing local white and red wine. This was our first taste of *Côtes du Thongue* by the *côtes* of the river **Thongue** itself. Blame the music, the geniality of marching players winding their way through tables between musical sets or the nocturnal buzz of bright lights and chatter after the heat of a summer day; but *vin du pays* has never been more refreshing.

The Thongue runs through Saint Thibéry to spill into the faster flowing Hérault, whose current provides the race for veteran water mills. The 13$^{th}$ century **Moulin à Bled**, (or *blé*, as we would now spell wheat) once had four wheels turning and plying the current to grind grain to be stored in the Romanesque tower of a **Benedictine Abbey** on the St Jacques pilgrimage route. Paths of history cross where waters still churn through the mill: after school on Wednesday, local lads perch on rocks and remnants of a **roman bridge**, whose nine spans were the longest water crossing on the *Via Dometia* (renamed today as Grande Rue). Time and fortune kinder to the **mediaeval bridge** over the Thongue, but the Hérault **suspension bridge** remains strictly Indianna Jones territory. The abbey church is home to two fine paintings *The Last Supper* and *The Meal at Simon* after the style of Nicolas Poussin. Art lovers will find ever changing exhibitions in town, as a thriving community of painters has settled here. Nature remains the most talented artist. Volcanic rock of the earliest Celtic citadel **Cessero** (whose name lives on in wines) forms strangely exotic columns in the shape of organ pipes. Free tours on summer evenings, otherwise follow arrow signs, **Tourist office**: *see page 218*

**Parfums Marty**
route de Montblanc, 34630 Saint Thibéry
04 67 77 75 94 www.parfums-marty.com 9-12, 14-18
*Ricard* may no longer offer tours of their distillery in **Bessan**, but this small family business offers to share the secrets of distilling pastis, liqueurs and fine perfumes. In 1977 aromatherapist and oenologist Bernard Marty began creating his own fragrances, and the distillery now encompasses perfumery

and drinks, with artisanal alternatives to absinthe and liqueurs from sands of Hérault shores and plants of the plateaux of Larzac. Escorted by Rodrigue, Alexandre, Quentin or Bernard himself, see alchemy in action and discover poppy, lychee, chestnut and rose syrups to invigorate a soft drink, vinegars for dressings, men's and women's fragrances and a range of heady spirits.

# Salagou     [5] B1

Sometimes Mother Nature needs the nudge of an accountant to realise her potential. Every few hundred years, the landscape changes forever as the whim of a visionary is indulged by bureaucrats: Rome funded Aeonobarbus' dream of a *Via Dometia*, to take his middle name and open the Languedoc hinterland to a continent of visitors. Paul Riquet persuaded Colbert to release royal purse-strings and bring the Atlantic to the Mediterranean by way of an iconic tree lined-avenue of water. And in 1958, the *Conseil Général de l'Hérault* agreed to build a dam across the modest Salagou River and turn a valley into a lake. More than a lake: the **Lac du Salagou** is a magnificent other world, just 4 km from the solid stolid city of **Clermont l'Hérault**, and as a dramatic alternative to the customary vines and olive groves offering a Martian shoreline of rich red *ruffes* rocks and soil, backed by a mountain ring. Desert plants and succulents line kaleidoscopic waters reflecting ever changing skies. Nowhere better to halloo your name to the reverberate hills and let the babbling gossip of the air cry out to birds who patrol between the elements of earth and sky. Owls offer contrapuntal approval to nightingales once the sun has set, and dawn is greeted by waders on the shores and chevron squadrons of ducks in flight. Cormorants settle on spindly twig branches of trees topping handbreadth islets of hills kissing the surface. You might take the plunge and swim anywhere along the 28km shore, though there are proper beaches: Near a campsite at the northern tip of the lake closest to **Cartels**, hire canoes, sailing boats and pedalos; closer to Clermont, follow signs to a sailing club and try your hand and knees at windsurfing; less formal swimming from the bank, just beyond the ruins of **Celles**. The water may be 28 degrees in summer. Flip flops recommended on shell and stone *plagettes*: you may be at the water's edge but you are actually hill walking at 140 meters above sea level. Don't let murky water put you off, it just the iron of the soil. Wait until you reach the 357m **Barrage de Salagou** itself to tread conventional tarmac.

Once Salagou was but a river, affluent of the Lergue which rises in the Causse du Larzac and tumbles into the Hérault itself. Then, in the post-war agricultural depression, winegrowers lobbied to turn vineyards into orchards. Since that required irrigation, in 1958, the council approved a barrage across the river to flood the valley and create Languedoc's largest lake, at 750 hecatres and up to 45m deep in places - where they say a forgotten village lies below.

We drove up to the lake one bracing sunny October day. Unlike **Lamalou les Bains**, a "proper" lake destination, Salagou does not have a formal resort. Postcodes and addresses are vague and directions open to misinterpretation. Driving higher and higher in search of an *auberge* we'd heard about, the lunch hour almost slipped away since there was no-one to offer directions. Twice we passed the same countryman with his donkey; in vain we looked at notice-boards and non-committal street signs; eventually a kindly local pointed us in the direction of the inn. Lunch was a treat, views worthy of the food, and promising an afternoon of fresh air and exercise as yang to the yin of sauce and calorie.

That is when we discovered the abandoned village of **Celles**. The houses remain, a church and schoolhouse, streets wind between homes and barns, but this is a town without people. Yet, unlike other deserted settlements here is no sadness. The dereliction of a vanished, vanquished community destroyed by war or famine chills the soul. But Celles is different. For five years, the then 80 residents bartered and negotiated with authorities to sell their homes and be relocated in comfort. They left, rewarded, the dam was built and in 1969, three days of storms filled half the basin in one downpour. The lake never quite submerged Celles, and an opportunist DIY brigade descended like locusts to strip tiles, bricks and beams. This was the 1970s, so for three years Celles became a hippy community. Now, abandoned anew to elements, wire fencing encasing unsteadier *bâtiments*, there is talk of repopulating the village: not with weekenders, but a real community. But on that afternoon, just we four post-prandial moochers and a pooch wandered the empty streets; a couple of anglers sat out the afternoon by the water, attending promise of *sandre* and *brochet;* and sailboards were steadied in the carpark by a cluster of sporty types in microfibre. For us: time and place for linking arms and rummaging for cameras, for sitting on rocks and letting Holly the dog run off her lead. Clare and Stéphane stepped through a wall to explore the remains of the churchyard, Nathalie, shaded her eyes from reflected glare and made friends with a cat sunning on a step, and I secretly renamed the village *Ile de Kernach* (French for Kirrin island) as I regressed to vicarious childhood adventure, and Holly presented me with yet another stick, beachcombed from the shore. Celles may be a town without townsfolk, but it is still French, and in France, they have four loves: *la patrie* and *le patrimoine*, country and heritage; *la gastronomie* , the food and the wine of *terroir*, but

230

above all they love bureaucracy, After all, the civil service built the road, the canal and this very lake. So, whilst Celles no longer has a population, it has a fully functioning **Mairie**. The one building restored with electricity and all services is the town hall, home to the civil service and above all, a democratically elected mayor: its sole resident. Two years after everyone left the village, Henri Goudal was elected in 1971, a post he held until 1994, when succeeded by daughter Joelle. Perhaps the most French gesture of all, on Henri's retirement, the population of Celles decided to rename the main square in his honour. *Vive la France.*

**Tourist Office** *see page 184*

### Cirque du Mourèze

The village of Mourèze, just a few kilometres from the lake is famed for its *Cirque* of standing stones, carved by the elements and millennia into fantastic sculptures of beasts and monsters. Best views of this natural circus from the *Parc des Courtinals*; lazier travellers prefer an Auberge terrace table to admire a perfect vista of dolomites between mouthfuls of finely presented seafood.

# Serignan [5] B2

Yet another 3 miles of sandy beach on the Béziers stretch, beyond Agde (*see page 79*). Coastline is protected from vulgar development, and the listed *Orpellières* zone of beach, dunes and marshlands is threaded with footpaths. Summer concerts are held at *La Promenade*, market square of the old village, where a 12th century church known as *La Collégiale* is undergoing a major renovation programme until 2014. Unusually, the shape of the church mirrors the form of Christ rather than the cross, with the choir tilted from the aisle slightly to the right along the line of the Saviour's head *inclino capite*. The nave is studded with shells for the *Chemin St Jacques* pilgrim route. Just as Perpignan's modern art collection is to be found at Ceret, Serignan is unexpectedly graced with open-air works at various points in and around the town, created by the celebrated Daniel Buren (whose Paris Louvre *Palais Royale* courtyard is internationally known). He designed the striking façade of the Regional Contemporary Art Museum.

### Musee Régional de l'Art Contemporain

146 avenue de la Plage 34410 Sérignan
04 67 32 33 05 www.ville-serignan.fr Tue – Sun 10-18
The contemporary art house has works from '60s to the present day. Three or four temporary exhibitions each year. Fully accessible. Free parking.

# Servian [5] C2 (*see page 122*)

# Sète     |5| C2  323, 9

From Marseillan, it is the curve that shapes our horizon and defines our day. When mist on the étang hugs the waters to infinity, it is a day to put away childish things and turn away from dreams; but should the hump-backed silhouette of the **Mont Saint Clair** emerge with the sunrise in the distant crook of the lagoon's embrace, the air will be clear, the sailing good and Marseillan will be on fine form. To Greek and Roman sailors in the age of adventure, the near island rising out of the sea looked like a vast beached whale. So they dubbed the headland *Cetea* (sea monster). And, as *Cetea* became *Cetus*, the constellation of the whale in the southern heavens; so the Mediterranean town became known as *Cette*, a name it kept in maps, arts and literature until 1928 when civic pride decreed the spelling be changed to *Sète*. For the word *Cette* that once meant monster had become a mere pronoun. Little honour for sports fans whose heroes were known merely as "*That* team". Six years after the name change, Sète FC became the first club to win both the League and *Coupe de France* in one season.

The city port has had other names too. For poet Paul Valéry (*see page 368*), his home town was ever *l'isle singulaire,* that strange virtual island, the Mont Saint Clair rising out of the water, wrapped on two sides by the sea, and a third by the étang, its tenuous hold on the mainland by promontory and isthmus. And the network of inland waterways linking the ports and seas provided another inevitable *soubriquet*: The lazy travel writer reaches for one trusty phrase the minute he sets his eyes towards any town with a canal and a brace of towpaths. I can think of more than a dozen cities, from Gdansk to Bruges to Manchester, subbed and dubbed *Venice of the North*. Interesting that no-one has yet christened Venice: *Birmingham of the Adriatic*. How very frustrating for the prefab-travelogue industry that Sète cannot be called the Venice of the Mediterranean. After all, those muted pastel colours of some of the houses along the Canal Royale have an Italianate charm and the waterways hewn by genuinely Neapolitan hands.

Happily, Sète defies cliché: charms and traditions, diversions and talents are ever at an oblique angle to the obvious in a place whose very name has been twisted out of kilter. Not tourist-trap pretty, so the expansion of the cruise ship terminal will not lead to hordes of Nebraskans swamping quays and churches. Sète is real; exactly what it was and has always been: a working port. Plenty for visitors: strings of holiday eateries, and ubiquitous **petit train** (from quai Durand 04 67 46 00 10) slithering through stalled traffic. Essentially, quays, squares, shops, markets and entertainment are there to help genuine locals work, rest and play.

Visit in summer and the appeal is obvious: Conviviality spills like pools of lamplight onto the quays. A song rises from a waterfront bar, a party tumbles from squares in the higher streets, lights from the *Théâtre de la Mer* and the *AmeriKa Club* splash on rocky shores below. Out of season visitors should come twice. The first trip; daunting hopeless quest for parking and bewildering dither over where to go for lunch. Next visit; planned with a purpose, takes in a gallery opening, concert or dinner; an after-hours jazz jam on the beach, or a hilltop drive to a view over sea or lagoon: if Sète never quite has you at hello, it certainly wins you over well before *au revoir*. Quirkiness stems from its very inception in the 17th century as a modern port. Up until then it had been a contented backdrop to other stories – look for the magnificent mural of the Etang on the side of a house in old Marseillan (*see page 24*). But when the Canal du Midi shrugged past Agde and ended up at Marseillan, docks were required, and so France's second Mediterranean seaport was born; a rarity, in that it is a port without a river. Instead, the King commissioned Sète as principal harbour to étang and canal. Since then Sète has never looked back.

233

Navvies from Naples arrived to dig canals, establishing a tradition of Italian immigration and dictating the colours and style of the new port-city. Even today, Italian and French communities divide fishing honours between them, sea from étang, and Italians provided Sète 's signature dish, *Tielle* seafood pie with rose-tinted soft pastry infused with tomato. The opening of the port proper in 1666 and the first stones lain for the building of the **Môle St-Louis** jetty celebrated with jousting and celebrations – a talent for partying that has never left. *Fiesta Sète* and world class jazz week in summer pack the city and resorts with visitors and *Fête de la Musique* in June sees *Setoises* themselves packing every public space and square from the Môle to the mount with live bands and soloists; even waterfront bars become a ripple of chanteuses belting out torch songs to the night sky.

Biggest crowds in August when the Saint Louis is cup-final of jousting. For much of summer, the air is rent by cheers that reverberate from smack of lance upon shield, rearing toot of hautbois and tattoo of tambour. Yet, any day Sète's soundtrack is unmistakable: an unlikely fugue of city and sea: flush of breaking waves on low rocks rent by visceral fog horn blasts of trawlers, crank of a winch and wet smack of catch being unloaded and tossed across the market to banter of porters and fishwives and the avaricious hysteria of *les goëlands*. As you climb the hill; gulls give way to cicada in protected groves. Walk along the promenade Leclerc to the **Corniche** and onto summer's **Lido** and the sea's rhythm is smothered by squeals of a crowded public beach returning to underscore the paced silence of private beaches, where only the clink of ice in an ever-replenished tall glass upstages the slap of *ambré solaire* and rustle of a turned page. Some declare the most *setois* sound is the cheer that runs like a Mexican wave along the quais on the day that hundreds of bream race from the étang to the sea and the waterfront is thronged with hundreds of fishermen rods to catch the swarm of daurade.

Yet ask anyone for the defining sound of Sète and they will whistle the tune that echoes through so many pages of this book. *Les Copains d'Abord* is the *Setois'* Auld Lang Syne to round off any evening of conviviality: family get-together or waterfront festival. Final song of the night to clear the dance floor as lights go up when the barman of the canalside **Bodega** prepares to clear the last glasses and walk home. And of course it is anthem of Georges Brassens. And Brassens is to Sète what Piaf is to Paris. Discover the man and his music in a walk through his life at the **Espace Brassens**. Or do the touristy thing through an evening at a cabaret to feel the affection in which he is held. Singers yet ungotten and unborn when his was the voice of gallic vinyl, take to a small stage and give voice to the songs every Frenchman knows by heart.

The unexpected trading port proved more than a gateway to canals and export of Marseillan's wine and sardines. Other Languedoc industries also benefited. State-run *Manufacture* at **Villeneuvette** exported cloth to Syria and Egypt. The canal network grew with the centuries, new basins, bridges and waterways to meet the needs of a growing town. Some local place names echo a history of a cultural melting pot. For many, the trail from the Môle to rue Jean Vilar will always be the *rampe des Arabes* or *montée des Bédouins*. Vaubanesque fortifications, **Citadelle Richelieu** and forts **Saint-Pierre** and **Butte-Ronde** defended this crucial commercial gateway after the British invaded at dawn on 25 July 1710 until repelled by the Duc de Noailles later that day. Who knew Sète had been British Empire timeshare?

Churches consecrated from grand St Louis to smaller parish and votive chapels. Sète adopted and adapted to railways in 1839, shadowing Riquet's canal in a fraction of the time. Even now on the TGV links to European capitals. For 30 years, trams served an expanding town, now buses run narrow streets, up **Mont Saint Clair** and out to the beaches: **La Corniche** with its casino and the newest **Villeroy** district on a 21$^{st}$ century esplanade of boardwalks and chic beach bars on the Lido strip to Marseillan. Take the bus or wear strong shoes beyond the canals where huge seagoing trawlers moor between touristic glass-bottomed boats outside the restaurants.

Discover less obvious districts: up the hill, **Le Petit Naples** is an Italian quarter of jousters and fishermen, now home to artists' studios; views out to sea from the legendary **Cimitière Marin.** Climb higher to gaze down on the city and its waterways by the frescoed chapel **Notre Dame de la Salette** from the eastern belvedere, or cross the crest, look south-west along a ribbon of sands and vines separating sea from étang from a viewing platform in the **Pierres Blancs** forest of over 700 species of plants on the Thau side, and on a clear day, see the Pyrenees. Allow yourself a healthy hour's trudge under pines and blossoming almond trees through heather and gorse scrubland, wild thyme and countless orchids. Beyond cantilevered bridges *Carnot* and *Foch*, where boats leave the *étang* to work passage to open seas, you may discover Sète's true fishing village and secret soul: the picturesque and bewitching **Pointe Courte** of rickety wooden jetties, darned nets and patchwork shacks and huddled cottages. Street names evoke a lazier timeless small-scale France, of rowing out to lay a line and rolling *pétanque* in long evening shadows.

There are four museums and over 30 art galleries to visit. On the first Sunday of every month, artists open their studios and workshops to visitors. For addresses and details call 04 67 78 56 24. Sète is rich in theatres: **Théâtre Molière** is the grand luxurious *belle époque* National

Theatre; fringe and cabaret venues across town have packed programmes all year. An essential address is the open air **Théâtre de la Mer**, carved from the Fort St Pierre with a Med-wide backdrop to the stage. At the foot of the ramparts, check out the ports. Ferry boats go to Morocco from the **Bassin Orsetti** and cruise ships glide in to dwarf tallest houses and belfries, lofty suite decks across city rooftops. The pathway to the **Criée** fish auction in the **Vieux Port** is lined with tiny workshops and chandlers where you may buy hammocks and lamps and craftwork. Escorted fish-market visits: 15.30 weekdays, Feb-Oct. Not to be confused with daily retail fish and produce market **Les Halles**. Walk the **Môle Saint Louis**, where a plaque recalls the legendary departure of the *Exodus* in 1947, defying Britain's naval blockade, the *Sètoises* helping 4,530 Jewish refugees flee to a new life. Continue to the lighthouse, lantern beam that wraps around the mount, sweeping the waters through the hours of darkness. You will see the beacon tonight, before you go to sleep; from the port of Marseillan, a steady nightlight across the bay.

**Office de Tourisme**
60 Grand rue Mario Roustan, 34200 Sète
04 67 74 71 71 www.tourisme-Sète .com
Jul-Aug 9.30-19.30; Apr-Jun, Sep-Oct 9.30-18; Feb-Mar Mon-Fri 8.30-18, Sat, Sun 9.30-12.30, 14-17.30; Nov-Jan Mon-Fri 8.30-18, Sat 9.30-12.30, 14-17.30, Sun 9-13 Information, *bureau de change*, festival tour and show tickets. Rent audioguides. *CityPass* for cutprice attractions, free museum entry and audio tour.

**Casino de Sète**
place Edouard Herriot, avenue du Tennis, 34200 Sète
04 67 46 65 65  http://Sète .groupetranchant.com
Sep-Jun, Sun Thu 10-03, Fri, Sat, eve of Hols 10-04; Jul-Aug daily 10-04
Hub of the *Corniche* district where the *Lido* beach road swings up to meet the Mont Saint-Clair, a typical resort casino, with a restaurant, a hall of slot machines, where breakfast is served to the tinkle of tumbling *sous* at 10, and patisseries for afternoon crowd. blackjack, roulette and poker rooms from 21. Old-style tea dance every other Monday afternoon, Saturday night dance floor and shows from feathery cabaret to solo artists. Off-season programmes heavy on tribute acts to legendary French *chanteurs*.

**Centre Balnéaire Raoul Fonquerne**
avenue Jean Monnet, 34200 Sète
04 99 04 76 50
Mon, Wed, Thu 12-18.45; Tue, Fri 12-19.45; Sat-Sun 10-18.45
More than a municipal baths and not quite a water park; with a water toboggan slide, wave pool, jacuzzi and spa. Hosts the national synchronised swimming and water polo championships. *(Phone for term time hours)*.

**Centre Régional d'Art Contemporain Languedoc Roussillon**
26 quai Aspirant Herber, 34200 Sète
04 67 74 94 37 http://crac.languedocroussillon.fr
Along the quayside from private galleries and not to be confused with the *Musee Régional de l'Art Contemporain* at **Serignan** (*see page 231*). Meeting place and melting pot for local, national and international artists, with a versatile exhibition space and ever changing programme of shows.

**Cimitière Marin**
chemin du Cimetière, 34200 Sète
The view from the fishermen's cemetery, high on the hill, immortalised by poet Paul Valery in 1920, *Cimitière Marin,* recalls sea beyond stone memorials and swaying pines; sails skimming water as doves on a rooftop. The "rich man's graveyard" *Cimetière Saint-Charles*, renamed for the poem. Valéry buried here in 1945, and filmmakerJean Vilar in 1971. Brassens lies on the étang side of town at paupers' **Cimitière Le Py**, opposite his own museum!

**Espace Brassens**
67, boulevard Camille Blanc -34200 Sète
04 67 53 32 77 www.ville-Sète .fr/brassens
Jul-Aug daily 10-18; Jun, Sep daily 10-12, 14-18; Oct-May Tue-Sun 10-12, 14-18
Perfect introduction to newcomers, and a welcome home for fans; meet Georges Brassens: songwriter-poet of the 20<sup>th</sup> century (*see page 234*). Headphones audio-guide you through a well-planned tour of places and people that influenced the man behind the songs. Midway, a glass wall opens to Brassens' last resting place (*see above*). A poignant moment, as the tour continues through words and music of a life well-lived. A little concert room screens rare performances of the man himself in cabaret and on stage. Excellent archive and programme of events in season.

**Musée International des Arts Modestes (MIAM)**
23, quai du M. de Lattre de Tassigny, 34200 Sète
04 99 04 76 44 www.miam.org
Apr –Sep daily 9.30-19; Oct-Mar Tue-Sun 10-12, 14-18
I mourned when Sète lost its truly eccentric museum of the Sardine, which included an interactive moment of canning from the perspective of a fish. Time is a great healer and its place in my heart has been won by this not-quite-dotty collection of things men do in sheds, boys hoard in bedrooms and women save for the evenings: collecting, arranging and creating on an unquestionably domestic scale. Thus, seemingly random glass cases have almost frenzied OCHD order in their arrangements of cheese labels, empty food packaging, Barbie dolls or tin planes. A celebration of the intimate

importance of ephemera in packing our memories and preserving our secret lives is extraordinarily life-affirming. Turning what most people keep in drawers or attics into bewitching artistic tableaux is the genius of a gallery, founded in 2000 when artist Hervé Di Rosa teamed up with self-dubbed artist-collector Bernard Belluc, for whom collecting is an art form between poetry and nostalgia. They persuaded city and state to provide a 3-storey museum and courtyard on a prime canalside site and Belluc personally welcomes visitors at 15h first Saturday of each month. Special exhibitions are worth a look. A recent needlework show featured subversive revolutionary images in cross-stitch, a dainty tea table with swastika embroidery and hard-core porno tapestries amid stuffed toys and samplers.

**Musée Paul Valéry**
rue François Desnoyer, 34200 Sète
04 67 46 20 98 www.museepaulvalery-Sète .fr
Wed-Mon from 10 to 12 am and from 2 to 6 pm (daily Jul- Aug). Free 1$^{st}$ Sun
As the Brassens space has its sudden glimpse of the étang, so a window in a gallery dedicated to poet Paul Valéry, whose lines on the *Cimetière Marin* dwell in the national soul, opens on the famous graveyard (*see page 237*). Canvases in permanent galleries highlight distinguished domestic talent, and a maritime theme is carried through the building. More than an art collection and venue for some serious exhibitions (Raoul Dufy in 2010), this recently renovated museum tells the story of Sète and its port. Replacing a dedicated museum, one room tells of canal jousts (*see page 85*) inaugurated here in 1666. Shields, honour boards, superb paintings Fête 300 years of sporting heroes. Gardens host poetry recitals and *cafés literaires*.

**Sète Croisières**
Pont de la Savonnerie, quai de la Résistance, 34200 Sète
04 67 46 00 46 www.Sète -croisieres.com
Glass bottomed and conventional boat trips on canal, sea and étang.

# Sigean [5] B3

Beyond **Narbonne** and the happy distractions of **Bages** and **Peyriac**, lies the town that names the next étang. But most people drive past Sigean. The A9, A61 and A75 motorways keep most excursions within 30 minutes. Luckily sunkissed vines lure us to departmental roads with invitations to stop, taste and buy wines of *Corbières, Fitou* and *Saint Chinian*. These old roads, free from tolls are positively plastered with posters advertising the **Réserve Africaine**, safari park with lions, giraffes and bears wandering in *"semi-liberté"*. The promise of a visit, with conditional best-behaviour clauses, guarantees angelic tranquillity whilst grown ups smack their lips, suck in their cheeks and hold glasses up to the light in the time-honoured fashion. Stéphane's young niece Chloe rode paragon some years ago, when we stopped *chez* our favourite vigneron to stock up on the good stuff before lunch. A new vintage had just been bottled but not yet labelled, so we sipped *sur place*. Then, true to avuncular contract and conscience, it was off to Languedoc's African plains.

Untold acres of scrubland populated with around 3,000 wild animals and birds. Enough freedom to forget zoo status - at least if the marital or extra marital behaviour of a lion and his lioness, right in front of our car, was anything to go by: more than a casual feline knee trembler, since new cubs are regular attractions. By such dangerous animals, you remain in the car. The majority of the safari is undertaken on foot. Our hearts were stolen by Akili, a young elephant then two years old. We had first met her, aged just 4 weeks, in 2001. This time, the "terrible twos" were in full flow when her parents beckoned her away from the crowd to join them in shadier pasture, she threw a temper trantrum. Akili stamped and sulked and trumpeted and hid behind a rock; she shook her head and refused all entreaties. When, eventually, her keeper turned up, she waggled a substantial defiant *derrière* at him and skipped out of reach. Finally, her parents took her by tail and trunk, *Barbar et Celeste* style, and marched her away, nudging the infant towards the elder of the herd, 200 yards or so away. Any hope of mature counsel foiled again, as the little one shook off the wrinklies and ran joyously, trumpeting loudly, back towards her human admirers.

We like monkeys teasing snooty peacocks and a raucous gathering of flamingos, storks and pelicans and other seabirds along the lakeshore. Less warmth towards ostriches that reckon blue Renaults resemble lunch. Nor the optimistic vultures assuming Tibetan bears aslumber might be on their last legs and thus also on the menu! With brilliant sunshine and powerful winds, you might stay outdoors for ever. In practical terms, budget at least 4 hours and ideally a day.

If safaris surpass finances, try **Port-la-Nouvelle**, not-so-new resort beyond the étang. In 1820, it was Narbonne's trading post at the end of the Canal de la Robine, now thriving tourist beaches and usual diversions, with the closest train station to Sigean. Another bargaining chip for winetasting with kids in tow is the promise of a vast skeleton at nearby **Domaine de Jugnes**. Winemaker Jean-Louis Fabre discovered a beached whale on **Rouet Plage** in 1989. With help from neighbours, a Citroen 2CV, a tractor and the cutlery drawer, M Fabre preserved the 20 metre skeleton in his barn, as centrepiece of an amateur **Musée de la Baleine** on his wine estate. Sigean itself has few large mammals outside the park, but Akili's forebears might have had a passing interest in the **Musée des Corbières**, since local lore claims Hannibal seized the town for Rome in 218 BC. Local history and archaeology displays show Greek and Etruscan pots and vessels, with earlier buckles, bangles and blades from **Pech Maho** Iron Age settlement (site tours from museum 9am Sat). Another worthy distraction is **Terra Vinea** (*see page 116*). Summer jazz and concerts always worth catching.

**Office de Tourisme de Sigean & des Corbières Maritimes**
place de la Libération,11130 Sigean
04 68 48 14 81  www.tourisme-sigean.fr

**Réserve Africaine de Sigean**
Route Departementale 6009, 11130 Sigean
04 68 48 20 20  www.reserveafricainesigean.fr
Apr-Aug 9-18.30; Sep 9-18; Nov-Feb 9-16; Mar, Oct 9 – 17
Safari in your own car for around 7km, the rest of the park on foot. Picnic or use park cafeteria. Prices and hours online. *See page 238.*

# Vias [5] C2 210

Once upon a time, the fortunes of a small town depended on the patronage of the church and feudal lords; today the *seigneur* of success for many a town or resort is Mr Michael O'Leary, big cheese of Ryanair. The daily influx of tourists and second home owners on low-cost hops to "Béziers" airport at Vias keep the local economy buoyant. Back in the late Middle Ages, the Bishops of Agde held sway, as landowners and dispensers of patronage. The summer seat of power for the church, the **Demeure des Eveques d'Agde** is the oldest house in Vias, distinctive 12th and 16th century architecture features mullioned windows and volcanic rock and sculpted stone façade on the rue de la République. To see fireplaces and preserved features inside the bishops' summer house, stop for lunch at the **Vieux Logis** restaurant. Other houses sport grand 17th century Italianate doorways. On Wednesday or Saturday morning, discover more architectural heritage at the **Maison du Patrimoine**, in a former blacksmiths on the place 11 Novembre.

Traces of civilisation date back 2000 years BC, but the glory days began with the fortification of the town in the 12th century, the original castrum guarded by ramparts with access through four drawbridges. Just the **Porte St Thibéry** remains today. Otherwise, history by osmosis is best delivered via a stroll around town, noting gothic gargoyles at the **Eglise St Jean Baptiste** and above all soaking up the atmosphere of the market square, place 14 Juillet. Here curved arches of a 19$^{th}$ century covered market hall offer cool shade. But many prefer to nurse *pastis* or wine at a café table in summer sunshine by the waters of the **Grifol** fountain, a three-metre high obelisk topped by the cockerel symbol of the republic. The picturesque square is capped by a square belfry tower of the former **Mairie** and is home to an evening craft market on Tuesdays. Food market stalls spread out from the church each Saturday, and on spring and summer Wednesdays. For local produce, turn away from the old town on summer Monday mornings when a *marché paysan* is held by the beach at **Vias Plage** (*see page 79*).

The resort is the culmination of post-war expansion, which saw Vias bursting through its fortifications in an expanse of new build to serve a new wine-marketing economy, spilling over from **Béziers**, and eventually joining in the development of tourism along the coast in the wake of **Cap d'Agde** and **Marseillan Plage**. The long strip of sandy shore, backed by dunes, is a popular alternative to some better known neighbouring resorts. Not shy at spotting a trend, the beach is backed up by a full range of allied attractions, besides obligatory watersport and pedalo hire, most notably the famous **Europark** fairground. This *Parc des Loisirs* quarter also hosts karting trails and equestrian activities. There is even a choice of mini-golf courses including an 18-hole Californian style park with more than an acre of landscaped greens with waterfalls and lakes, and open after midnight in summer.

An airport may have put modern Vias on the map, but it has been on other itineraries for years, since it is part of the last stretch of the **Canal du Midi** between the theatrics of the **Neuf Ecluses** at Béziers and the final outpouring into the étang at Marseillan. Tree lined banks where the canal meets the waters of the Libron river are popular with cyclists and walkers, and a summer attraction is the engineering ingenuity of the "mobile aqueduct" carrying the river above the canal to avoid flooding. Vias began planting vines and creating wine estates in the 19th century, and the tourist office can suggest visits. Weekend breakers should consider an early September wine harvest festival, with cycle trips, breakfast picnics and music or the July Jazz festival in the older streets of town.

**Tourist Office**
Av de la Méditerranée, 34450 Vias Plage 04 67 21 76 25 www.ot-vias.com

## Aéroclub de Béziers Cap d'Agde
Aéroport de Béziers Cap d'Agde, RD612, 34420 Portiragnes
04 67 90 99 30  www.aeroBéziers.com
Before the international airlines moved in, the local airport was something of a den for the local flying club. The Association has a lively calendar of events including open days with free demonstrations and trips in light aircraft. Apart from freebies, you may book lessons and private trips.

## Europark
Parc des Loisirs, 34450 Vias Plage
04 67 21 55 01  www.europarkvias.com
mid-Jun - mid-Sep 20-02
France's biggest permanent fairground has the country's largest rollercoaster ride, 780-metre long, 32-metre high *EuroLoop* and scores more attractions and rides, many of which are adapted for disabled funsters. A new 4D sensation cinema attraction, interactive wild west show  and celebrated skyrider and adrenalin pumping rides (some reach speeds of over 80mph). There are gentler rides and attractions for younger or more timid adventurers. Listen to local radio, or check with tourist offices for promotional discount or half-price evenings. Rides cost 2-5 *ecus*, the park's own currency. Change your euros for *ecus* at ATMs and kiosks around the park. Be warned, the park *ecus* cannot be used to buy food and drink. Restaurants open from 7pm. Dogs welcome (on lead), but remember to leave pets at home during the fireworks show at 9.30pm every Friday.

## Ranch Fumat
Parc des Loisirs, 34450 Vias Plage
06 89 68 28 85
Pony and horse rides on the sands or by the canal, for adults and children.

## Theatrical and Musical Cruises
Apr-Sep: Selected Fri 18.30
Comic sailors and rollicking accordionists make lively fellow passengers. With actors from the *Scènes d'Oc* and musicians of the *Meute Rieuse*, this Friday evening cruise on the *Bateaux du Soleil* offers entertainment, music and drama, with wine tasting. Details from the tourist office.

## Vias Evasion
04 67 11 91 76 www.viasevasion.fr
Closed Nov-Mar
Hire boats by the hour or the day to explore the canal and work the lock gates from Marseillan to Béziers. No licence required. Next to **Europark**. €400 deposit is required.

# Villeneuvette [5] C1

You might have stepped onto the set of a Gérard Depardieu costume drama. Crystal water trickles over cobbles and leaves dapple monochrome slate and stone. Find artists in shady studios and lunch well at a *Logis* restaurant garden by a toytown *Mairie* on city walls. We would drive out to marvel at **Navacelles** or **Mourèze**, stop to buy olives in **Clermont l'Hérault**, but always pass by the sign for Villeneuvette. Then, one Christmas afternoon when the need to walk off a particularly good lunch persuaded us to park up and explore, we finally discovered a tiny city, smaller than a hamlet. Walled and picturesque, with but 85 inhabitants, this ruritanian settlement boasts city status as Louis XIV's military drapers. For the fresh waters that glisten *les pavés* once nurtured a woollen cloth industry to keep the army warm and supply an export trade from Sète to the Levant from 1667 until the advent of electricity made old methods redundant in 1954.

The main road from Clermont to Bedarieux once ran through the city, until a bridge diverted it across the **Dourbie** waterway. 800 workers were employed within the walls, an equal number of sheep grazed outside to provide wool for the factory. Since the mid-19th century, the city has hailed a single hero: explorer and colonist Casimir Maistre, who had a settlement named after him in Chad and led expeditions to the Niger and Congo in the 1890s, before taking over the factory. In a craft shop (*ateliers* and the restaurant are the last remaining commercial ventures, besides a stables caring for traumatised ponies), we encountered an elderly lady selling delightful native jewellery to raise funds for African orphans; stunning ebony and silver lent a glow of altruism to avarice. Another woman, an artist, created amazing furniture from recycled cardboard boxes. To those who asked, she offered a day's course, sharing her techniques and serving lunch on the main square to her students *du jour*.

In the cemetery is a memorial to Yombo, an escaped Congalese slave, who, as a 12 year old boy, returned with Maistre to Villeneuvette and lived here for 31 years. Visit the slender *Pont d'Amour*, discover çourtyards (remembering always to respect the privacy of private homes) and pause to explore the factory church, which in 2010 joined the fountain and monumental archway as a listed historic monument. The gateway itself, rendezvous for 3-hour guided hiking tours of the area on the first Saturday of the month, provides the single involuntary shudder of the visit: inscribed above the entrance is a 19th century motto *Honneur Au Travail*, evoking memories of a crueller 20th century institution.

**Tourist office** *see page 183* www.les-amis-de-villeneuvette.fr

# Market days

## In Marseillan:

Street market (Tue 8-13) pl Carnot, pl 14 Juillet, bd Lamartine [1] **B2/3** *page 246*
**Les Halles**, market hall (Tue-Sun, 7-13: biggest choice of stalls: Tue, Sat) [1] **B3**
**Marseillan Plage** (15 Jun-15 Sep, Tue 8-13) pl du Marché and allées Filliol;
daily summer food stalls in the market place (8-13) [4] **A2** *see page 246*
**Marché Artisanal Nocturne** sq 8 May 1945, by port tourist office chalet. Arts
and crafts (19-24) [2] **A2**
**Brocante**: Flea market, Marseillan Plage (Sat-Sun). Best on Sunday [4] **A2**

## Away from Marseillan

### Monday

| | | |
|---|---|---|
| Bedarieux *page 249* | Montblanc | Valras Plage |
| Le Cap d'Agde | Pomérols | *(food only)* |
| *(Rochelongue)* | Sète *(Ile de Thau)* | |

### Tuesday

| | | |
|---|---|---|
| Balaruc les Bains | Lamalou-les-Bains | St-Thibery |
| Bessan | Marseillan | Servian |
| Le Cap d'Agde | Marseillan Plage | *(food only)* |
| *(Avant Port)* | *(summer)* | |
| Florensac | Pinet *(food only)* | |

### Wednesday

| | | |
|---|---|---|
| Le Cap d'Agde | Loupian | Tourbes |
| *(Barbecue)* | Montblanc | Vias |
| Clermont l'Hérault | Sète | |
| Gabian | Tamarissiere *(food)* | |

### Thursday

| | | |
|---|---|---|
| Agde *(old town)* p *247* | Le Grau d'Agde | St Chinian |
| | Mèze | |
| Frontignan | Pomérols *(food only)* | |

### Friday

| | | |
|---|---|---|
| Balaruc-les-Bains | Gabian | Sète *(Gare)* |
| Béziers *page 248* | Montagnac | Valras Plage |
| Le Cap d'Agde *(Mole)* | Nezignan l'Eveque | |

### Saturday

| | | |
|---|---|---|
| Le Cap d'Agde | Frontignan | Vias |
| *(Barbecue /* | Marseillan Plage | |
| *Gevaudan)* | *(summer)* | |
| Florensac | Pézenas | |

### Sunday

| | | |
|---|---|---|
| Agde | Capestang | Marseillan Plage |
| Bessan | Olargues | *(fleamarket)* |
| Le Cap d'Agde *(Môle)* | La Salvetat-sur-Agout | Mèze |

# This p'tit cochon
# went to market

THE TRULY LAZY TRAVELLER would choose just one market and be done with it. But when you have but a week in France, it is a long wait from Tuesday morning's social round in the heart of Marseillan until the weekend's rummage at the *brocante* flea market by the Plage. And so, like many before and many to follow, I plunged.

There is no such thing as a typical market. Though we see the same stallholders in different towns each event has a personality of its own. Fleamarkets are a gentle way into bartering culture. Marseillan Plage once boasted two rival *machés aux puces* each Sunday, one each side of the old Sète road. Now just one *brocante* remains, the biggie around the wine co-op and summer fun fair. The other, behind the tourist office, sold its last rickety barrel in the early weeks of 2011.

There money in tat, as my mother discovered as she stepped out of *Lagarrigue's* boulangerie by the church early one Sunday morning, heading home with baguette and croissants. She saw a middle-aged woman sitting on the kerb outside the *Marine Bar*, huddled amid a pile of black refuse bags. My tender hearted *Maman* could not simply walk by. *"Pour vous"* she said simply, and handed over her bag of croissants. The radiance of a kindly deed made up for our simpler than usual weekend *petit déjeuner* and it was with a gentle glow of virtue that we made our way down to to the fleamarket later that morning. At the first stall, my mother cowered behind me, whispering an imperative "Cross the road. Go to the other market".

Vintage jewellery and classic lalique glass decanted from her plastic sacks, the stall holder who had ranged her wares on tables around a top-end Renault saloon, was the recipient of the morning's pavement largesse. Stay, I urged my mother. You bought breakfast, maybe she'll pay for lunch.

Fleamarkets are fun. Nephew Joe, rather than pay £40 in baggage charges, bartered for a battered old guitar in the market at less than half what he would have paid *Ryanair* to carry his own instrument, and thus the rocks of the Port Tabarka echoed to his bargain strumming for many an evening.

*Les Puces* in Marseilan Plage are one thing. Fashionable *bric-a-brac* quite another. My initial faith in the tradition of honest deals was admittedly somewhat shaken the afternoon the rather nice ornament that I saw at the back of the bric-a-brac stall along the road to Pézenas town centre had a price label of nearly eight thousand euros. It may have been negotiable, but, since I had lost the power of speech and rational thought, the very concept of haggling over a *sou* or a grand was academic!

Tuesday is Market Day in Marseillan. Officially held between two central squares, and in practice trailing along boulevard Lamartine, to the roundabout by the theatre, this is a weekly rendezvous, Languedoc's answer to speed dial. If you have not seen your friends and neighbours for a few days, mooch around the market for an hour or so and you'll bump into everyone you know. Clothes, pots and pans and numberless hats and wallets and belts on the outlying stalls; in the heart of the market, have a waxed tablecloth cut to size or look for excellent dried herbs (secret blends for cooking fish and making spiced salad dressings are fabulous and superb value). The stall holder is a mine of country lore: Red vine leaf infusion for easing weary joints. 72% savon de Marseille soap in the bed relieves cramps, but get that from the soap man by the traffic lights. Living herbs, vines and all you need for your own market garden from the shelves outside the marine bar. But why farm, why grow, when the street is a buffet itself.

Buy *rôtisserie* rotating basted corn-fed chickens, their juices dripping on punnets of roast potatoes. Eggs are thirteen to the dozen, and you must taste scrumptious olives, tapenades and confit garlic or maybe dried and lightly sugared ginger. Treat yourself to Daniel and Nathalie's imcomparable Vietnamese dishes prepared fresh to take home for lunch; in *Les Halles,* the every-day market hall, find fresh fish, fruit and veg, meats and cheeses and always ask for what is local, what is best and which tomatos are for cooking and which for crunching. The market twists round past the church, past English books and the chance to pick up this months *Blablablah* magazine, and the needlecraft stall for patternbooks and yarns, to the original covered market on place Carnot where shiny new watches cost five euros, including the battery, and where the newest chopping or cooking gadget is demonstrated outside the pharmacy. At this end of the market, stop for coffee at the Boulevard, or loop round once more for a pause between laps if you can find a seat outside the Marine Bar.

Two days later and the doorbell rings. Friends are off to Agde for the market, would I like to come? Of course! It was a public holiday, so the world had come to town it seemed and parking took on inner city dimensions. Eventually we parked far away and worked the streets. Rather nice galleries and posh frock places have opened up in the quieter backwaters: the word *Hermes* etched on more than one glass door. But it was the market we were after, so pausing to admire *trompe l'oeuil* murals that make a tiny square that seems like a wonderful Mediterranean village in its own right, we followed traders' cries to the streets around a small church we might never have otherwise noticed (*see page 147*). Inside the church, dogs wagged their own and sniffed each others tails, old ladies knelt by paintings of Christ and the saints, and the old crypt was being excavated, revealing ancient stone sarcophagi. "*Mais non, Cherie*, the bones are not for you!" one doting mistress told her poodle.

Outside, in the bright sunshine, stall holders displayed rank after rank of green and white asparagus, in the first week of the season. Creamed scents only overwhelmed by those of strawberries grown under wild sage and thyme in the scrub beyond the Béziers road, here piled in punnets for morning masses. Other traders vied with each other to top the temptation. Our own Tuesday dried herb man was doing a roaring Thursday trade here in Agde. Farm veg on each corner all but wilted under aroma of cooked food from every other stall. France's answer to *gefilte* fish, *acras de morue* (cod fritters) sold by the box gave me a *haimishe* fragrance for the rest of the day. We were hailed by a trader, who had the food-love of a chef, as he itemised his wares, lingering over the recipes of the traditional dishes in vast embrace wide pans. Try the paella he said, or how about the couscous, fresh mutton, not just lamb, and spicy sausage as well, perhaps you would like the mussels, parsley, breadcrumbs and herbs from the garrigue. Go on taste, taste, he urged. Then, with holidaying humanity as our tide, we rode the crowd through sidestreet and alley and upwards to the main market place that stretches almost the length of the former ramparts.

Shoes and clothes, hunting knives with special leather safety pouches for nudists, binoculars (no link to the aforementioned naked hunter-gatherers), kitchenware, iffy perfumes and dodgy plastic kitchen utensils. All ingredients for a happy hour in the noonday sun, and thus our bank holiday was spent amongst the people of Agde, and I returned home with my cod, four succulent new potatoes and a carrot. That should be enough market for anyone's money, but Friday means Béziers. My friend Ruth wanted foam rubber to make cushions, and I needed no other excuse to tag along. We arrived in town at the allées Paul Riquet a grand tree lined promenade through the middle of the city. My favourite spot, a 3 minute walk from the bus station when I make my own way on the school bus from Marseillan. Lined with tables belonging to cafes, brasseries and pizzerias across the road, here waiters dodge traffic to bring hot food and chilled wine across to lazy lunchers and flirty evening drinkers eyeing up the talent parading the length of the alley. Friday – and this was a Friday – sees the promenade filled with flower stalls in long, long flower and plant market.

Fruit trees, olive trees, rose bushes and yukkas all dwarfed by centuries-old plane trees, and cascades of jasmine, gushes of iris, willowy lilies and billowing baskets of trailing plants: all share floorspace with African handbag sellers. Cages of exotic birds, crates of ducklings and trays of baby rabbits provide distractions for the pigeons confused at the concept of incarceration, and intrigued at these temporary low level alternative perches to their usual lamp posts and wrought iron balconies. A happy stroll through the flower market, a nod at the far end, where traders sell cartons of melon, courgette and lettuce plants, and a promise to ourselves to return here for lunch before the visit is quite through, we asked a street cleaner where the Champs de Mars market might be, since we could not find it on the any town plan.

Directions received, we made our way though back streets to a huge central area covered with hundreds of stalls selling household goods. It is not marked on the map. The name does not even appear in an index. Like Brigadoon, it only exists for the locals. As luck would have I,t the foam rubber seller was at the closest corner of the sprawl so we ordered the cushioning and agreed to collect it from the lady on Sunday at Bedarieux's special spring fair market (yet another excursion in waiting). Scores of clothes stalls, dozens of hardware vendors, lots of haberdashers, with tablecloth material by the metre, and a supplier of pet accessories, a dealer in ghastly lampshades, a woman knocking out cheap *Clairol* and *l'Oréal* products and men selling earthenware pots by the kerbside. We dived out early and soon found a food market on place David d'Angers with live guinea-fowl, pullets and rabbits unaware of their destinies, a baker from the next country who created wonderful cakes and made breads from orange blossom and hazelnuts. All this is far too much to discover in one visit. Another time, we promised ourselves, and that other time introduced me to the delights of the covered food market, an excursion in its own right, where you may buy fresh food and have it cooked for you right there and then (*see page 294*).

But foam rubber was the reason we happened to find ourselves at a sprawling spring fair at Bedarieux. Stalls filled Monday's market square on a Sunday, then hugged the river Orb, its banks and bridge. On our way through we found Christophe, who sold amazing sea salt infused with wild herbs and spices, fine Muscat wines and delicious jams and chutneys sold in Fauchon (Paris' answer to Harrods and Fortnum & Mason). I heard a call of recognition from another stallholder. It was the jam maker from Pézenas who had once sold me home made onion-confit and tapenades at a Christmas Fair in Bouzigues. She welcomed us with a cheery greeting and pressed samples upon us. We tried onions with ginger and cinnamon (delicious with yoghurt, would you believe) and a chutney with onion fig and walnut. We had her preserved peppers and a scrummy tapenade, and promised to look out for her at Béziers market next time we passed.

Oh we walked and we wandered and we finally found our foam rubber lady. She had just sat down to lunch. French market traders will not settle for a sausage in a roll. No. They have table, chairs, and the full sit-down lunch and good luck to 'em. She was mortified when she saw us. "I cut the foam to size last night, *M'sieurDame* and put them on the kitchen table. But I left home without them." Her contrition was total, our reassurance genuine and we went to hunt food stalls in search of sustenance for our lunch and a chicken for neighbours, due home that evening. *Hélas*, no joy.

So, we had passed dinner hour and after a fruitless forage for any of the four major Sunday afternoon food groups (Gastronomy, Chocolate, Pizza or Sandwich – real restaurants close 'til Monday night), we hit Pézenas on the solar plexus of the Spring Antiques fair. 18th century clocks, ornate dining tables, useful metal giraffes and a tailor's dummy reincarnated as a lampstand amongst distractions on all sides. None of the above ideal for hunger pangs. A clown with a Karaoke machine sang torch songs from the 1930s, an amateur band gave us jazz in strict 3:4 waltz-time. A *bouquiniste* trusted me to take away a French Harry Potter and pay another day (neither he nor I had change), but no sign of a sandwich, until a cheery, decently upholstered waitress with hair colour adopted rather than inherited, saucy tee-shirt and a generous grin, took pity on us and rummaged in her kitchen to find something to eat, long after the curfew when food spills off menu.

The long-anticipated and well-appreciated *comté et beurre* baguette and a week's haul of strawberries, spring rolls and beignets, crisp salad, rosemary, black olives with garlic, bread and cheese certainly flavoured some aromatic memories. But, whilst I recollect each mouthful and crunch, and certainly paid back the bookseller his euro, I really cannot recall if we ever picked up that foam rubber.

## Our daily Bread

The *Carrefour Market* has an in-house bakery, but nothing beats the scent of fresh air, buttery croissants and virtue that comes from a pre-breakfast trip to the *boulangère* for crusty bread and piping hot *bavardage*. *Au Pain Viennois* on the roundabout is good for traditional *banette* loaves rather than *baguettes*: a second branch in the front room of a house in the oldest quarter. The *centre historique* has three other excellent bakeries. *Lagarrigue,* by the church, for scrumptious *baguettes* a morning *rendezvous*. At *La Manne Dorée*, where they sell and slice multigrain loaves, you may sit outside with coffee and croissant. *Les Saveurs d'Eugène* behind place Carnot, is best known for speciality breads, long queues on the day they bake *pain pétrisane*. By the *gare routière*, the *Point Soleil* promises warm *pains au chocolat* when you take the early morning bus to Agde or Sète. Bakeries open around 6-12.15; 16.15-9.15 and closing days stagger, so somewhere always open mornings and afternoons. Other bakers and *depots pains* in residential quarters and several summer counters at Marseillan Plage. Most bakeries sell cakes and tarts, but there is also a specialist *patissier* in rue Emile Zola.

**Le Croustillant de l'Etang** 1 chemin de la Belle Bouche
**Lagarrigue** place du 14 juillet 04 67 77 29 88 **[1] B3**
**La Manne Dorée** 9 place Carnot 06 76 17 38 51 **[1] B2**
**Au Pain Viennois** boulevard Lamartine 04 67 01 72 56 **[1] C3**
**Au Pain Viennois** 11 rue du Commandant Rivière 04 67 77 33 14
**Point Soleil** 10 avenue Chassefière 04 67 01 70 45 **[1] B3**
**Notre Pain** chemin de l'Imprimerie, route d'Agde 04 67 01 77 51 **[3] A4**
**Les Saveurs d'Eugène**, 21 rue Claude Goudet 04 67 35 96 28 **[1] B2**
**Les Airettes** 185 chemin de l'Airette 04 67 21 86 21 **[4] A2**
**Chez Pierrot** 9 rue Georges Brassens **[4] B1**
**Les Deux Délices** 3 place du Marché 04 67 21 96 98 **[4] A2**
**Holidays Bread** 396 avenue des Campings 04 99 43 02 06 **[4] A3**
**Le Phocéa Point Chaud** avenue la Méditerranée 06 24 49 89 70 **[4] A3**

# Shopping in Marseillan

Shopping hours generally around 9.30-12, 15-19; sometimes longer. Some food/flower shops open Sunday morning. Many shops close on Mondays. Off-season, hours vary. For Marseillan Plage addresses, see page 74

## Cakes and Chocolate

**La Bonbonnière** 9 rue Emile Zola 04 67 77 25 39 **[1] B2**
Gateaux and patisserie, for desserts, occasions or indulgence.
**Douceurs d'Oc** 11bis rue des Artisans 04 67 26 06 41 **[3] A3**
Emanuel Servant is a talented young *chocolatier*, passionate about his art and a *Flavours of Marseillan* pioneer (*see page 51*). Sniff out his atelier behind Carrefour. Fine delicious treats, including *Le Marseillanais* (*Noilly Prat ganache*), pick and mix *ballotins* of fine milk, white and dark *pralines* and truffles with choc from Madgascar to Venezuela. Once memorably dressed oysters in cocoa to be served with whisky at the Taverne. Edible art and sculptures, and private commissions undertaken from a sugar-free treat for a diabetic to a grand dinner table centrepiece. www.chocolaterie-douceursdoc.com

## Fish & Seafood

**La Rascasse** 6 pl du Marché 04 67 21 97 03 **[4] A2**
Oysters may be bought farm fresh along the *chemin des Parcs* and *la Bézarde* in the **Port Les Mazets** (*see page 60*) Otherwise find counters in the village, the Plage resort and fishermen's homes in residential quarters:

**L'Aégagropile** lieu-dit Prés Soupié 04 67 77 64 49
**Daniel Azaïs** (*see page 267*)
**Annie Castaldo** Domaine la Fadèze 04 67 77 20 64
**Alain Constans** 3 rue Fbg St-Pierre 04 67 77 22 66 **[1] A1**
**Distrimers** chemin des Parcs 04 67 43 16 56
**L'Ecailler** 3 avenue Gabriel Péri 04 67 77 24 42 **[1] C1**
**Emma** boulevard Pauline Bouisson 04 67 77 24 89 **[1] C1**
**Gaec Coquimar** ch Tabarka, Les Mazets 04 67 77 32 82 **[1]A1**
**Gaec Negrou** chemin des Parcs 04 67 77 65 36
**Gaec Voisin** Montpenèdre 04 67 77 36 12
**Gaston Parc** la Bézarde 04 67 77 20 55 04 67 01 73 90
**La Grande Bleue** (*see page 268*)
**Michel Thieule** chemin des Parcs 04 67 01 46 73
**Moreno** rue de l'Airette 04 67 77 35 31 **[4] A2**
**Nathalie Congras** la Bézarde 04 67 77 22 06
**Occi Marée** route des Parcs à Huitres 04 67 01 09 10
**Philippe Ortin** 4 allée Pervenches 04 67 01 72 13
**Guy Pujol** la Bézarde 04 67 77 29 87

**Ricard** 9 boulevard Pasteur  04 67 77 62 47  **[1] C3**
**La Rouquette** rue Abbé Grégoire  04 67 77 21 57 **[1] B3**
**La Rousette** rue de l'Airette  04 67 21 97 63 **[4] A2**
**La Stroumpfette** 12 ter chemin de la Belle Bouche  04 67 77 37 92
**Henri Rouquette** la Bézarde
**Christian Vila** Mas 16, chemin des Parcs 04 67 77 69 17

## Fruit and Vegetables

Don't forget the summer fruit & produce
stall on av Chassefiere beach road, and the
off-season Sunday morning food market by
the Marseillan Plage fleamarket

**Les Jardins de Thau** 3 av Victor
Hugo 04 67 01 73 69 **[1] B3**
**Le Fruitier Marseillanais** 6 rue
Emile Zola  04 67 77 30 89 **[1] B2**

## Groceries

Marseillan is self sufficient, but larger
hypermarkets found on city outskirts.
*Hyper-U* and *Intermarché* at Agde;
*Carrefour* at Balaruc (*page 160*).
Supermarkets no longer provide free bags. Re-usable bags for life: 50-70c.

**Carrefour Market** route de Bessan 04 67 77 29 10 **[3] A3**
Mon-Sat 9-20; Sun (Jul-Aug) 9.30-11
Previously known on the Pradet as *Champion*; now twice the size and new edge-of-town location. Clothes to microwaves, garden chairs to PCs and full grocery section. Optician, phoneshop, newsagent, fuel station, car wash on site.

**Spar** 3 place Carnot  04 67 77 22 21 **[1] B2**
The only general grocery store/mini supermarket in the heart of the village, ideal for most everyday items. A decently stocked minimart open on Sunday mornings year round. Original centuries-old wine cellar has a surprisingly varied selection.

**La Marseillanerie** 4 place Général Guillaut 04 99 43 51 27 **[1] B3**
Food souvenirs: best-of Marseillan produce shop and outdoor oyster bar.

**Le Divin Temps du Vin** 1 bd Bertouy 04 67 00 28 91 **[2] B2**
Truffles, potted gastronomic treats, vintage wines from the **Taverne** next door and *pastis* gift sets, olive oil soaps and marine themed souvenirs, decor and trinkets.

**Philippe Epicier** 8 boulevard Bertouy 04 67 11 93 07 **[2] B2**
Sep-Jun: Fri-Sun 10-12 15-20 ; Jul-Aug daily 10-12 15-20
Not the period shop façade, but plate-glass cornershop next door. Philippe & Co originally launched the eponymous restaurant opposite, after Parisian success at *Pile ou Face*. Now they run an up-market deli in a quayside *triangle d'or* of restos and wine shop. Home made pasta, luxury sauces and *tapenades*, teas and tableware.

**Late night: Epicerie Mont Joly** 13 av 8 Mai 1945, 34300 Agde 04 67 26 51 84
Corner shop grocer on road from Marseillan to Agde: open late afternoon til 1am.

## Meat
**Valette et Fils** 8 place du Général Guillaut 04 67 77 20 60 [1] B3

## Books
**Maison de la Presse** *(see Newspapers)* [1] B3
**Carrefour** *(see Groceries)*
**La Marseillanerie** *(see Groceries)*

## Chandlers *(see page 61)*

### English books
**Market** (Tue) 04 67 96 68 87 *(see page 244 also Bédarieux Clermont l'Hérault )*
**Book Exchange** 11 bd Lamartine 04 67 77 38 64 Sat Sun Tue Wed 10-12, Sat 14.30-16[1] B3

### English books - further afield
**Le Bookshop** 8 Rue Bras de Fer, Montpellier 04 67 66 22 90 www.lebookshop.com
**The Globe** 2 rue Carbonnerie. Montpellier 04 67 58 59 29 www.SouthOfFranceBooks.com
**English Bookshop** between Post Office and Church, Pézenas (Tue-Sat 9-18)
**Café de la Bourse** pl 14 Juillet, Pézenas *(English book swap* 3rd Sun 10-12)
**Café l'Escale** 8 avenue de Roujan, Gabian (English book swap, last Sun 10-12)

## Clothes
*(also chemin de l'Airette, rue des Commerces, av des Campings, av de la Méditerranée in Marseillan Plage)*
**Atelier de Verena** *(see Gifts & Décor)*
**Aux Anges** 1 place Noilly 04 67 35 09 84 [2] A2
*Original womens and menswear from former costume designer. New lines in stock every 3-4 weeks. Household décor and gifts also on display.*
**Cap Kids** 9 avenue Chassefière 06 76 16 98 05 *(Childrenswear)* [1] B3
**Elegance** 6 place Carnot 04 67 00 21 76 *(Prêt à porter for ladies)* [1] B2
**Le Fil d'Eliane** 8 av Chassefière 04 67 94 12 91 *(dressmaking & repairs)* [1] B3
**Thau Boots** 5 rue Emile Zola 04 67 21 14 61 *(Shoes)* [1] B2

## Computers
**Sud Informatique** 14 rue Emile Zola 04 67 09 03 74 *(repairs)* [1] B2

## Flowers
**A Fleur d'O** 6 rue l'Abbé Grégoire 04 67 11 50 27 www.afleurdo-marseillan.fr[1] B3
**Jocy Fleurs** 7 place Carnot 04 67 21 90 35 [1] B3

## Gifts & Décor
*(See also Groceries:* Divin Temps du Vin, Philippe Epicier *and* La Marseillanerie*)*
**Atelier de Verena** 50 quai Antonin Gros 04 67 21 64 55 [2] A2
Original bespoke jewelery, clothes and *objets d'art* in artist's quaint portside studio
**Aux Anges** *(See clothes)*
**Jean-Claude Chabrol** 4 rue des Droits de l'Homme [1] B3
Talented local painter, captures the spirit of Marseillan
**Chocolatée** *(see page 270)* [1] C3

253

**Duo d'Ateliers** 10 bd Lamartine 06 16 11 79 69 **[1] B3**
Personalised deco, tiling: stylish crafts by Sylvie and linens stitched by Maman.
Try also home made cakes and macaroons. Level access in rue l'Abbé Grégoire.
**L'Etang Déco** 12 rue des Suffren 06 21 52 36 86 **[2] B2**
Brocante, antiques, bric a brac in a rumagable garage. Mornings and evenings.
**Grange aux Muettes** quai de la Résistance **[2] B2**
South of France sunflower yellow dishes, oils, syrups, bonbons and evocative
souvenirs on the quays. Artisanal ice-creams. Open til Midnight in Summer.
**Poterie Antoceram** 19 r Zone Industrielle 04 67 77 69 10 poterie-antoceram.com **[3] A3**
Local ceramics, superb tableware and gifts. On site, on line and at markets.
**Secrets de Chloe** rue Noilly **[2] A2**
**Cédric Torne gallerie** 2 bis boulevard Lamartine  04 67 39 08 58 **[1] C3**
**Trésor du Pirate** 27 quai de la Résistance 04 67 01 53 74 **[2] A2**
The original classy shop on the quay has imaginative furnishings and novel knick-
knacks from local talent. A true Aladin's Cave and a genuine warm welcome.

## Hardware
**La Boîte a Clous** 37 bd Lamartine 04 67 77 24 90 **[1] B3**

## Jewellery *(see also Gifts & Décor))*
**Marinor** 4 rue de Général de Gaulle 04 67 77 21 08 **[1] B3**

## Markets *(see page 244)*

## Newspapers, Stationary, Tobacco
**Le Graffiti** 43 bd Lamartine 04 67 77 20 23**[1] B3**
Tobacco, pipes, pens, stationary and gifts.
**Maison de la Presse** 5 rue Général de Gaulle
04 67 77 21 50 **[1] B2**
The village bookshop, newsagent, stationer and
tobacconist on the market square.
**Presse du Soleil** 21 pl Théâtre 04 67 01 79 26 **[2]A2**
Newspapers and tobacco close to the port.
*See also* **Carrefour Market**

## Opticians & Pharmacies
*(see page 374)*

## Photography
**Cathy** 22 bd Lamartine 04 67 21 26 19 **[1] B3**
Stunning imaginative wedding and portrat
images make her shopfront a true art gallery.
**Photo Art Loisirs** pl Théâtre 04 67 77 69 48**[2] A2**

## Television/Satellite
**Audio-Video Chobot** 26 bis bd Lamartine
04 67 77 24 72 **[1] B3**

# How to eat very very well in Marseillan

| | |
|---|---|
| € | Menus start under 15 euros |
| €€ | Menus start around 20-30 euros |
| €€€ | Menus start over 30 euros |
| | |
| | Lunch deals often much cheaper |
| | See page 5 for key and advice |

## Around the port...

**Le Château du Port**   €€
9 quai de la Résistance **[2] B2**
04 67 77 31 67 (Easter-September)
Marseillan most iconic building (*see page 25*) with distinctive Haussmann style architecture, Mansarded windows to what were once the *chambres des bonnes* and delightful wrought iron balconies, adds a true touch of class to the harbour. A recent incarnation as the celebrated and lamented **Château du Port Hotel** faded and the upper storeys became a private residence. New owners, *noblesse oblige*, restored not only the building itself, arranging for stunning illumination, but took responsibility for bringing the façade of the neighbouring co-operative winery in line to raise the profile of this distinctive stretch of the quayside. Meanwhile, on the ground floor, more moves were afoot for refreshment. This corner of the quai de la Résistance had long been home to a rather special restaurant. Patricia and Charley Chicheportiche had, seemingly forever, been mine convivial and stylish hosts at the Château's eponymous brasserie. Monsieur would sit at the bar setting the world quietly to rights with the regulars, habitués of the port and marina.

# A tasty tour of Marseillan and the region

In Marseillan it is easy: Oysters. Fresh from the étang; taken as nature intended (though not gulped, but savoured, say locals) or lightly grilled gratinée. Mussels too and *palourdes* (clams) with a daily catch of *daurade* (bream), *loup* (sea-bass), sometimes as a treat, sweet little *sole*, like delicate dabs, simply grilled, or panfried, sprinkling of herbs dash of white wine. Around the étang (especially Bouzigues), this is as authentic as it gets. *Bouillabaisse* here is no soup-stew, but poached panoply of fish, like the *Parillade* grilled banquet, but with the soup on the side. Agde has a (mainly) monkfish and garlic *Bourride*. Sète its twin legends: *Tielle*, soft shelled blush-hued tomato and octopus pasty, as defining snack or *entrée* (best from a stall such as Cianni in the market hall, and *Encornets Farcis*, stuffed squid. Local biscuits: *zezettes*.

Step inland to pop a *Petit Pâté* at Pézenas (*see page 216*), probably the original mince pie: a lamb and fruit pastry nugget from the British Raj, size of a retro *vol au vent* canapé. *Bonbon* of choice here is the *Berlingot* boiled sweet, just as Montpellier sucks its *Grisettes*. Every town has its speciality; be it confection (Bessan's fruit and nut *Croustade* cake – *page 166*), or produce: Portiragnes strawberries, Easter cherries in Céret, summer sweet onions from Lézignan-la-Cèbe, Nezignan figs. Aubrac raises beef and lamb reared on mothers' milk whilst Roussillon grows soft fruits. Recipes define a region and spill across borders onto neighbours' menus. Find variants of *Tapenades* everywhere, when olives of the hills meet anchovies of the coast. In the Pyrenean county of Perpignan [5] B3/4, meals begin (especially at Collioure) with remarkable anchovies, and end with a *crème catalane*, a local twist on *crème brulée*. Dessert or apéro, try *Rousquilles du Vallespir* cakes that knock Proust's *madeleines* well into *temps perdus*. The north west of the Aude [5] A2/3 is country of true *Cassoulet de Castelnaudary*, a stickily slow stew of beans, meat and veg, sausages and lashings of duck fat: one of the great iconic dishes of France and a definitive winter warmer; as is the *Aligot* of the Aubrac, up in Lozère, that slow cascade of potato puree reinforced with *tome* cheese and garlic.

Head eastwards to the Gard [5] C/D1 round Nîmes for *terre et mer*. From the sea, *Brandade de Morue*, a creamed revival of salt cod, powerful flavour; from cowboy country comes *Gardiane de Taureau*, like a *Boeuf Bourgignonne* for men who scratch their trousers in public: a herdsman's stew with a litre of strong red wine to each kilo of beef. Ideally served with local rice from the *Carmargue*.

Choose your meal as you choose your wine. *Terroir* goes further than the bottle – just as the oyster is soulmate to the Picpoul, find the red for your *Cassoulet* or *Gardiane* and the very *Muscat* for your *Rousquilles*. You do not need a camera to record your memories. *Confiance à vos papilles:* Trust your tastebuds.

And Madame, raven black hair swept back and an equally jet back dress accentuating elegant *Renoiresque* curves, would glide amongst the tables, in full sail; charming, welcoming and entertaining; the perfect hostess. For those sitting outside on the quay, twice yearly cabaret of *Lou Capelet* (*see page 81*) and, for longer seasons, squalling tumblings of excitable *hirondelles* foraging, feeding and nesting in terracotta tiles above. *Plus ça change*, and as the hotel above went into private retirement, Montpellier's most celebrated chefs, Jacques & Laurent Pourcel supervised a makeover of the grandest building in Marseillan's port. Back in 1988, let us not forget, they had won three *Michelin* stars at their flagship restaurant in Montpellier, the **Jardin des Sens** (*see page 314*). This renovation was not undertaken alone. Their partner, vivacious and gregarious Laetitia Chicheportiche, continued the welcoming tradition of her charismatic parents. And the Pourcel name thrust the Château onto the posh travellers' foodie checklist

Then, in 2011, all change once more as new proprietors took over. Like **Chez Philippe**'s Parisian provenance (*see page 258*) the Pourcel reputation would certainly linger enough to sprinkle fairy dust over future incarnations. As we went to press, *le tout Marseillan* was agog. New owner, Monsieur Blaszak, had only just garnered *Gault Millaut* praise for his **La Raffinerie** on the Canal du Midi at Béziers when doors opened at the **Château**. Three courses from value €19 (daily specials of pesto-punched *salade caprèse* via a *crouton* stack of skate-wing and med-veg to sweet nutty *crème brulée*) to a €28 *carte-menu* (two-course option €22). Opening day's dairy and veggie *millefeuille* followed by grilled bass, zingy springy risotto and sauce *vierge* was plated wisdom and finesse and our guest hummed happiness across hazelnut-infused gossamer *carpaccio* of duck, beef and veal, and a *ventriche de cochon* with its oh-so-subtle suggestion of ginger. Wine list is very reasonably priced (€12.50 for 50cl *Moulin du Lene* rosé). No room for the dessert, but poached pear perched on a nutty crumble with hot chocolate *coulis* and pear sorbet is more than an excuse to return soon. And the early day verdict: the Château's status as a class act is safe and in worthy hands.

**Chez Philippe**  €€
20 rue de Suffren **[2] B2**
04 67 01 70 62
Closed Mon (in season);
Mon, Tue (off-season)
The little legend of
Marseillan: When owners
and staff of a Parisian
*Michelin*-noted restaurant
decided to move south,
lock, stock and *coulis*,
they opened a pastel-
picture-perfect place in
Marseillan. *Le tout*

fashionable society came too and expensive motors testified to chic favour. It even had the ultimate Parisian trait: a selective door policy! Then they sold up. Spiritually and temporally never far from the restaurant, their **Epicierie** is just across the road (*see page 252*). At the restaurant itself, each new proprietor to date has kept the décor and and upgraded the all-embracing welcome. By the *provençal* façade, an awning under the sway of the tall trees shades a terrace screened by huge potted shrubs.

The original set menu philosophy has shed its occitan subtitles and is €28, now with alternative permutations. Shaking off and living up to a reputation is not easy: but each "new" *Philippe* gains favour. Ever friendly; always refreshing. Current team, Christophe and Pascale Michel, formerly of Corbières' *Auberge du Château de Bonnafous,* arrived in 2009; and have settled in nicely. Keen flavours and reliable ingredients are professionally prepared and served with *finesse* and *tendresse*. €19 3-course lunch with coffee (€15 for two courses) offers gorgeous delights: understated cheese-packed peppers perfect; basil sorbet (was that condensed milk?) added bravado, but the piquillos needed no gilding. As for a tartlet of lightly whisked egg and *fin du saison* asparagus: disarming seduction. A *brochette* of *poulet* was virtual *confit*; good juicy thigh strewn with lip-teasing veg. Time has enriched the repertoire and fine fish jostles for attention with rustic rabbit, whatever the main attraction, each plate tickled with savoury sideshows whether pearl barley risotto or *escargot*. The kitchen is flexible to modern diets and chef invents vegetarian dishes on demand.

Worth the supplement is a cheese dilemma of *pelardon* goat cheese or pollen-dusted mascarpone sorbet: mini triumph of the unexpected and highlight of a very happy lunchtime. Facing such a choice, I urge you to do as we did and order one of each and mix and match across the table.

**Coté Sud**  €€
18 quai Antonin Gros **[2] B2**
04 67 01 72 42
A one-time traditional restaurant, when **Coté Sud** had its original revamp, it was the first of the modish, almost metropolitan style contemporary brasseries to challenge the conventional dining rules of Marseillan. A smart room where zinc and fabrics blend to provide a sharply inspired background to a meal of professionally presented Med standards is home to polished and welcoming service. The Guy Falco inspired décor that marks this row of eateries is here well-matched by a judicious and canny *carte*.

The original owners departed some yards eastwards to the **Maison Camille** creperie, and new *regime* **Coté Sud** wisely opted to stick with a winning formula – budget-priced lunch platter still a midday signature. Otherwise it is very much an *à la carte* type of place. Good *tapenade* type *tapas* and, as a guilt-edged treat, a chocoholics dream of an ice cream dessert make for excellent snack moments to be enjoyed whilst sitting by the waterfront and glancing across the gently swaying masts of sailing boats to the quieter side of the port opposite.

From the *apero kir* to a digestif shot of *limoncello*, via local *picpoul* to go with the oysters or the fish, folk linger with no intention of remembering where they left the car keys or even the car. Those with a busier schedule and a responsible conscience, find an imaginative alcohol-free option in the *Bora Bora* house cocktail of freshly squeezed or crushed juices, *à la* smoothie, and rich with flavours that follow the seasons and the market. Reliable main courses feature expertly grilled fish and meat dishes. Daily desserts are imaginative and moreish, usually served in the 21st century's ubiquitous tumbler. The terrace has its long diner-style bench amongst the tables for facing out front and enjoying the fab location, as a well nourished neighbourhood cat purrs and insinuates around your legs or a vociferous duck quacks from the quay to demand bread and a bowl of drinking water.

**Entre Ciel et Mer**  €€
0 quai Antonin Gros **[2] B2**
04 67 09 45 60
The story begins with another lunchtime, another year and another city. *Il etait un fois à Béziers*, once upon the time that two unassuming young restaurateurs took over a modest bistro on place de la Madeleine. Word of mouth in Marseillan gradually led regulars away from our own village and port, to brave pre-prandial traffic jams on roads into Béziers. An hour's shopping for fresh food at the covered market and lunch under parasols on the square by the Madeleine church.

There, chef Sebastien, one-time *protégé* of the toast of Paris fine-dining, rusticated safely away from the spotlight with skill and flair borne from his days and nights under a *Michelin* star. Partner David flourished plates of modest perfection with good humour and charm. And there, we marvelled how such skill and gentle *finesse* could work such magic with the simplest and most under-stated of ingredients. Anyone can make a splash with lobster and game, but,  like alchemist chef David Beve, 500 miles away in Lille, who transforms winter root vegetables into culinary gold at *N'Autre Monde*, so *Le Petit Montmartre* took dishes usually hailed as hearty and turned them into seduction.

When they left Béziers just before summer 2008, *habitués* sighed at losing inexpensive pleasure so close to home. A year later, the duo, who had first worked together under the initial and celebrated manifestation of **Chez Philippe,** prodigally opened the doors of **Entre Ciel et Mer**. Long term and loyal diners from Béziers days delighted to find a formula that performed so well elsewhere transferred almost seamlessly to the port. Half a dozen starters, four or five main courses and a handful of desserts on the main menu, three courses still around €22 euros (supplements for special treats), two courses around €17, day and evening. Old favourites, including drop-dead gorgeous *cabillaud parmentier* with lime, a not-so-humble-potato-and-cod-pie that could make a grown man whimper, appeared on the inaugural menu, and fine meat dishes such as tear-drop shavings of beef, laced with liquorice also made welcome re-appearances. The roll of €7 starters featured lightest hand made cannelloni with summer salad, and a *boudin noir* and apple reinvention of *croque monsieur*. More recent spring *entrées* included asparagus *feuilleté* with curried mussels. Witty vegetable accompaniment to fillet of bream might include spaghetti strands of courgette interwoven with the pasta. Another Béziers legacy (acclaimed by

*Gault & Millau* as worthy of a *toque*): duck with red wine and figs proves an unofficial challenge to discover lipsmacking secret ingredients in a sauce whose provenance and inspiration defied foodie forensics. Another regular treat features lightly grilled oysters, with a confection of leek lining the shells. Tried and trusted formula runs side by side with a "best of" the quayside venue's previous *café-glacier* days. So, tasty, toasty *tapenades* still available for snackier tastes, traditional seafood and salads also on offer, and anytime ice creams on hand for lazy afternoons between meals.

**La Luna**     €€
32 bis quai Antonin Gros **[2] A2**
04 6701 73 59
Breaking what is otherwise a perfect run of oyster and seabass menus, comes a brief taste of another Med. An Italian restaurant offering rich and savoury alternatives to the obvious. The pedigree is still Marseillan, since *La Luna* comes from the same stable as the *Soleil* up the street. In fact it is a return to tradition, since before the site was known as *Le Quai*, it had been a pizzeria. Pizzas (now cooked over real wood smokey fire) and pastas of the set menu share the *carte* with contemporary Italian fare, gnocchi and risotto on the carb list and osso bucco amongst popular meat and fish dishes. In the early days, perhaps, an abundance of flavours was a complex rush for the palate; since then, dishes have gradually been refined and there is always an appreciative crowd behind the glass windbreaks enjoying varied holiday fare lunchtimes and evenings. Very friendly and welcoming staff. Good budget lunch deals.

**La Maison de Camille** €€
12 quai Antonin Gros **[2] B2**
04 67 94 18 51
Elegant *crêperie*, ice cream parlour and *salon du thé* that first brought sheer style to abandoned vermouth warehouse at the end of the port. Bright, light and friendly, there is a civilised quiet air about the place, a step further from the casual lunch brigade's usual haunts. Hosts know and greet regulars, whilst making newcomers feel equally comfortable. They always manage to recruit bright and attentive front of house staff: more than half the secret of a good restaurant. Once, family influence spread along the quayside. Whilst his father ran **Maison de Camille,** Philippe brought a modern cosmopolitan approach to portside dining at **Coté Sud**. Slick décor revamps led to a tapas-style café for all day-snacking. Now, having sold the other venues, Philippe and Stephanie have taken over the *crêperie*, saving successful concepts from their previous addresses. So, a good value lunch platter, usually around €10 is already a firm favourite with lighter noontide

appetites: Perhaps *penne arrabiata* in a wide glass, with Italian ham salad on the side, or a *brochette* with summer soup. A daily *quiche* at the same price. For dining outside usual mealtimes, delicious crepes or light salad. When willpower wilts, choose ice cream sundae, or small carafe of rosé and wallow in three-day-old Sunday papers, nodding to the boat-people as they clamber ashore to walk their dogs at Parc Tabarka around the corner.

Outside, the terrace has been upgraded anew, now huge conservatory style sofas and armchairs sprawl over decking, amid conventional tables and chairs. Inside, a chandelier strung dining room has expanded to absorb space until recently taken by gift shop where once well-heeled American widows, disembarked from hotel barges moored at the jetty, might be heard exclaiming with delight at quaint candlesticks and ornate champagne flutes and cooing with appreciation at linens as they fumbled in purses to pay for a set of delightful demi-tasses that would be just the thing, my dear, quite perfect, for a daughter-in-law back home. Now, when *Athos* or *Anjodi* dock after a week canopied by trees, the ladies, fed and watered to the highest standards aboard from Carcassone to Capestang and Homps through Les Fonserannes, walk up to the roundabout where the original boutique is reborn as **Chocolatée** (*see page 269*). Today's **Camille** is the breakfast rendezvous on the quay, offering coffee or chocolate, croissant or tartine and juice for €5.50

**O' Soleil**      €€
34 Quai Antonin Gros [2] A2
04 67 01 72 42
To some, this place is ever a sunny terrace for a coffee or long cool drink as they watch the world go by. For others, the name is synonymous with an early evening cocktail or refreshing glass of beer by bobbing boats of summertime as they surrender to mellow evening sunshine and plan the rest of the *soirée*. Regulars choose the brasserie for breakfast coffee as port shops and restaurants set up for the day. Holiday season arrivals favour a lovely early-evening pause over a *demi* on summer sports days. Once, brasserie **La Belle Scribote**, named for the legend on page 81, more recently, it was dubbed **Brasserie de Soleil**, true bar-brasserie on the port. Now, redesigned with snug sofas inside and a fashionable look for the terrace, it bears a jauntier monicker **O' Soleil**, complete with trendy *apostrophe*. It remains, of course, perfect vantage point, since most of the port *flânerie* is obliged to pass the terrace. This bank, never mind the Haussmann architecture of the **Château** across the way, is closest the *quartier* will ever get to a *grand boulevard,*. It is here at the *tête du port* that you may engage in Yves Montand's truism *"y'a tant de choses, tant de*

*choses, tant de choses à voir*", whether watching morning hosing down of streets and watering of the hanging baskets by restaurateurs, or locals scurrying past *en route* to *boulangeries*, housewives returning from the market or townies strolling down to book lunch by the water

You may be entertained by a houseboat resident cycling home on his bike, well-trained collie trotting alongside, or a fisherman hailing an old friend for a conflab over a beer. See the **Trésor du Pirate** opening for business on the other bank, and note all manner of intriguing artefacts in the street outside the shop. From Easter 'til autumn, when the wind is in the right direction, birdsong is augmented by the insistant beep-bleep of coaches reversing before disgorging its cargo of visitors at **Noilly Prat**. Indeed, the site has long proved a magnet for tourists looking for a traditional port snack of *moules-frites*. Now, with lunches from as little at €13, locals too come to sniff sturdy staples amongst the mains (rich flavoursome rabbit stew, traditional chunks of lamb done to an old style turn). The popular menu is €19 and food well-presented with some imaginative and refreshing flavours and serving twists (ginger in salmon *tartare)*, glitzy and even tasty garnish, more than merely reliable holiday quayside dining. Trends and tastes, accrued near and far, keep plates up to date. As Tuesday's market closes, tables fill with families and friends, the place hums with shoppers comparing trove, visitors tweeting the view and an occasional estate agent wooing prospective punters as friendly staff sashay the length of the awnings. Between meals, afternoons bring distractions: Neighbouring chefs perch on metal bollards, gossiping over a *cloppe*; a young band sets up kit on a makshift summer festival stage for an evening's quayside concert. Plenty to see on cheery afternoon, nursing a succession of shandies!

**La Pacheline**
28 quai Antonin Gros **[2] B2**
04 67 21 47 31
A facelift and new life for what was once upon a time an occasional table, whose opening times were as unpredictable as the breeze tickles and ripples the still waters of the port. Through varied regimes, **La Pacheline** has been a fine place for *coquillages*. Locals recall a portside seafood bar serving platters of other gems from the étang, plated and flourished by those that plough the lagoon. Since 2011, week by week, month by month, this place has been getting better and better.

A talented and genuinely welcoming young team have worked hard to create something decent on a site that could easily get by with the ice cream hungry Noilly-Prat tour carriage trade. Instead, honest local fish dishes are

263

given a gentle modern feel (daurade served with med-veg and polenta for instance) and fresh dishes of seafood and salads presented with simple style. The kitchen talent has earnt its stripes along the quayside, providing flair in presentation with interesting sauces and stylish takes on fish dishes. Signature seafood remains the main attraction. Whether you fancy lazy lunch, tucking in as you watch "bumper boats" attempt mooring between craft of serious sailors, toast regular mariners tippling on deck once Midi sun passes the yardarm, or simply pull up a chair in the evening to indulge your seafood munchies or have a sundae from myriad flavours on display at the counter, expect service with a smile from lively happy staff.

**Rive Droit**   €€
quai de la Résistance **[2] A2**
04 67 21 36 51
The best cocktail bar and nightspot Marseillan has never had is a splendid building on the "other" side of the port. Prime location with its courtyard for balmy summer soirees. A gated, tropical palm-tree-filled courtyard looks just like the sort of terrace you'd imagine as backdrop for a gentle overspill of what Hollywood used to call "dress extras"; tuxedo sleeves steering Dior-tucked waists towards port lights to the murmer of a slender chanteuse in shimmering beaded cocktail dress huskily mouthing Cole Porter to the percussive slide of champagne bottles into ice buckets. One day, perhaps. Meanwhile find a family-oriented waterfront pizzeria. Meeting demand for alternatives to oyster and *crème bruléed* Full Med Monty, the magical location lends itself to any meal. Dining outside, under parasol shades, especially on a carnival or musical evening in the port brings its own thrill. The courtyard is certainly a privileged location. Inside, sense of space is supreme. Comfortable chairs and tables, luxuriously drawfed by the high ceiling – or lack of ceiling, since the room opens to a traditional warehouse-style pitched roof. Magnificent tree-trunk-girth beams hold up traditional tiles, dangle modern chandeliers. Lunchtimes, all is bathed in natural light, as glass doors north and south let the luminosity flow through the building. Shock-proof pizza menu features customary toppings and home-made holiday dishes for starters, mains and desserts.

**La Taverne du Port**   €€
4 rue Edouard Adam, quai Antonin Gros **[2] B2**
04 67 01 78 78  www.lataverneduport.com
Just 15 years ago, the quaysides would have been unrecognisable to today's visitors. No tabled terraces nor Menu board baracades. Then, Bruno Henri, owner, sommelier and caviste at the Taverne wine shop began serving his grandmother's recipes to showcase an enviable collection. More than 500 labels to choose from, and table prices not much more than shop rates. Best

selection of Languedoc wines for miles, the cellar also features classic Bordeaux, Burgundy and beyond at a fraction of the regular price elsewhere. Every bottle tells a story, so let the wine waiter know your taste and budget and leave the selection to the experts. Canniest summer regulars order simplest offerings from the menu (fresh catch of the day, salad of goat cheese, seafood feuilleté). *La famille Henri* family is 8th generation *Marseillanaise* and (especially in busy summer) best choice is basic fish. The honourable exception to the rule of the sea being the off-season, when autumn *cèpes* and winter truffles inspire special menus and in early spring, when a farmyard bill from the family farm takes over.

I can attest to provenance of the mushrooms. Early one autumn morning, we gathered outside the Taverne and set off in convoy to the hills of the *arrière pays*. Through rare mist and drizzle, we drove. Unaccustomed wipers hauled into reluctant service screech-scraped the windscreen. Secrecy vows redundant as we recognised no landmark through chill downpour. Parked, we knew not where, we followed Bruno into the woods, and tried our best to be of some service. Fortunately, our guide ignored our assistance. But instinct, experience and confidences of older countrymen, led us to hidden fungal trove. Six, perhaps eight, hours later, we decanted the last of our haul into the car boot, a mountain of treasured *cèpes* ready to take back to the restaurant. Our reward: the second best omelette I have ever tasted (the finest was another unplanned Taverne trove from fruits of a

sunnier springtime walk through the *garrigue*; a trudge that yielded the most superb hairsbreadth-fine new season asparagus, whipped up with fresh eggs and *pelardon* cheese from the Mas Roland (*see page 360*) into heaven on a plate). For a few weeks, mushrooms adorn steaks, sidle into fish sauces and take a solo turn in a Madeira cream as vegetarian starter spilling over light puff pastry, savoury tsunami riposte to humble *vol au vent.* Next off-season turn is that of the black diamond truffle. Preened and hauled into the spotlight, rough nuggets of flavour flaunted from table to table whenever *plat du jour* boards bear the chalked legend "*omelette aux truffes*". But the truffle is not merely a one dish pony. It is star of its own kaleidoscopic cabaret. A friend shared a "special" birthday with her entire family here, and truffle shavings even found their way into the *Bollinger*! Budget goes to the winds of Languedoc when guests opt for a full truffle dinner. We know people who only visit Marseillan in January, simply for the joy of striding a seasonal menu. Others dive into several courses. Most memorable dinner was a mycelian litany that began with a *carpaccio de st jacques aux truffes*, the house speciality oysters *gratinée* (here truffled), omelette, followed by a glass of hot bouillon with truffles and foie-gras (for many, highlight of the meal), *tornedos* of beef or fillet of bass with an unbelievable truffle-blown jacket potato, home-made truffle and Madagascan vanilla ice cream and finally a camembert laced with just a dash of the old tuber melanosporum!

Meanwhile, across France in a modest farmyard deep in rural Corrèze, the family pig will have scoffed its last apple and mash. Each year, the *tavernier* oversees the despatch of the provider of much of Marseillan's off-season porcine menu. Fattened up to the realm of 170 kilos, the beast is slaughtered with dignity and due ceremony. Subsequent spring menu brings hams, smoked meats, black puddings and *patés* gala of French country fare.

Regular menus rely on locally sourced produce. Wednesday, goatherd Eric brings a tray of cheese; another morning, Evelyne with a crate or three of oysters (at the Taverne, raw or very lightly *gratinée*); mussels from Marseillan's Negrou clan. Local families land bass and turbot, sweet miniature sole and celebrated bream. Just as Bruno or his father Jean-Paul may name the *vigneron* who nurtured your tipple, or whisper the poignant family reason why a Faugères wine label may bear the appelation of a much-loved child; so ask if today's catch came from Bernard or Raymond, Denis or Claudia. Perhaps, as on my second visit, a full decade ago, when the Taverne was but a slender corner shop with barrels for tables, the fisherman who caught the *loup* might be perched at the next cask and raise a valedictory glass to his catch as it lands on your plate. The restaurant now aborbs the house next door and a new terrace, wrapped around the building by the waterfront, has a seafood bar with illustrated panels by various local artists including Jean-Claude Chabrol. An open-air wine-bar perfect for enjoying a glass of wine, perhaps a small slate plate of seafood, cheeses or Bruno's home-cured *jambon de poisson* (fine shavings of air-dried salted tuna or swordfish), whilst checking on your emails in the wifi zone.

In the expanded dining room, walls are lined with bottles so you may gaze at venerable vintages throughout the meal! Find *armagnac* from the year your grandfather was born, a humble Languedoc wine raised by the cellar-master from a great Bordeaux house. Lunch from €13.50, dinner from €22.

# By the oyster park ...

## La Ferme Marine  €€
Route des Parcs
04 67 21 21 20  www.lafermemarine.com
Closed Tues, Wed (Sep-Jun) out of season; open every day in Summer
A good 15-minute walk from the main port, but this is the oyster fishing district, where France's best seafood is harvested daily. Above one of the oyster sheds, this superb restaurant has the best terrace in or out of town: a vast outdoor dining area overlooking the lagoon and across to Sète . The stunning view is upstaged by the seafood buffet. Fresh oysters, mussels and prawns on beds of ice on one side of the table, hot seafood dishes served on the other. Help yourselves as often as you like for the €22 euro buffet. For five euros more you may enjoy the buffet and then indulge in the fresh fish of the day – perhaps sea bass or bream of *seiche à la plancha. À la carte* selection always a features a non-seafood option for starter and main course. A cool indoor dining room is smart and modern, and this restaurant, where the food is prepared by the families that fish the waters is a very welcome addition to Marseillan's menu. The seafood buffet far outshines the other dishes, and the basic selection is a veritable feast in its own right. Good service, local wines and a professional welcome. On Wednesdays in summer, only the buffet option is available.

## Brasucade Azaïs    €
33 parc à Huitres
04 67 77 68 58
Tue, Thu & Fri in season at 12 noon
Conviviality at its best. The *brasucade* is a Languedoc tradition made for sharing (*see page 336*). If you can't rustle up a full Facebook fifty friends and family at the drop of a seashell, rely on the kindness and company of strangers to augment your group and toddle along the oyster road from the port. The rue 19 Mars links the pleasure port to the *parc à huitres*, by way of the *plagette*. Just long enough a stroll to work up an appetite and a manageable distance for letting wind rustle your hair on the way out and freshen you up once again, on the return a party and a tipple or few later.

From noon on summer lunchtimes, the world *et sa femme* enjoy meridianal alchemy, turning strangers into friends along long wooden tables in the shed behind the oyster farm run by the family of the late Daniel Azaïs. For two hours, lagoon mussels, not the oysters, take centre stage: stars of a 4-course barbecue, with house wine and coffee for under €13. You may order a plate or two of oysters as an extra appetiser (optional extras run the gamut of all seafood ceded by local waters), but most settle for the main event. Paper plates, plastic tumblers and cutlery ready stacked on the table in the covered dining shed, cabaret is thesmoking barbecue pit, wafting aromatic scents of burning vine towards several dozen waiting palates.

First on the frame are shoals of sardines, grilled to a turn. Racks of little fish are brought to trestles, as lunchers launch themselves to the fish; each sardine to be stripped off its bones and slipped down the throat in practiced fashion by regulars and approached with plastic forks and a sense of trepidation by novices. Two courses of mussels follow swiftly on: one, traditional *brasucade* splashed with local white wine and herbs, heady steam hissing in the air. Once more come trays to trestles and plates to tables. By now, holidaymakers and locals, families and strangers are flitting in and out of rival conversations; white wine is flowing and mussel shells piling on the side of each disposable plate. Big black plastic sacks at the end of the table accommodate the detritus. The second mussel dish is spicy and hot. Men poking and tending the barbecue, tossing and turning the seafood, are selectively deaf to requests for the secret ingredients. As embers settle down, slices of *tarte au pomme* are handed round and your hostess does the rounds of the tables with a jug of coffee. By three o'clock most diners have made their way either to the car park or the path back to the village. As she supervised clearing of tables and sacks, I once asked Mme Azaïs why the *brasucade* was a lunchtime only event. Had she considered evening barbecues? She smiled, nodded to the last table not yet decanted into cars, and glanced over at the door of the warehouse where oysters had yet to be graded and sorted ready for customers looking to take home fresh seafood for supper. "We used to do this in the evenings. But some of us have to start work very early in the mornings!"

**La Grande Bleue**
chemin de Fontaurie
06 60 82 20 60; www.conchyliculture.com   *(see guided visits, page 51)*

## In the Village

**Le Boulevard**
2 rue Général de Gaulle [1] B3
04 67 77 21 11
Always packed evenings, all year round, here flock holidaymakers and locals alike for lively conversation with meat and seafood cooked over an open fire. Summer's terrace provides a vantage point for observing the comings and goings of the village. But the heart of this place is its hearth

and inside, Le Boulevard is as far removed from what you would expect a Mediterranean restaurant to be as you could imagine. Despite walls crammed with paintings of the South of France and (bizarrely) Norfolk, the atmosphere by the fireplace is of a traditional rural inn in the deep wooded centre of the country, where coats hanging by the door might have had rabbits' paws and partridge feathers protruding negligently from pockets.

Host Bernard manages to pull off a double coup of whizzing through the restaurant at a G-force speed, yet managing always to appear unhurried and relaxed as he greets and reminisces with each new arrival as an old friend with all the time in the world. Each waitress has the timeless knack of post-house *auberge* hospitality. The legendary Christine, as emblematic and fondly regarded a fixture of the Boulevard as is the Marianne across the way to the Republic itself, welcomes each returning regular with genuine affection, irrestible charm and good humour. The ultimate *multitaskeuse*, she'll take your order with the dexterity of a stenographer, at the same time distributing hugs and admonishments over un-finished plates, whilst urging the more formal *etranger* to adopt familiar *tu-toi* address between friends. Generous grandmotherly-sized portions of honest basics: *entrecôte* steaks turned over flames, scoops of mussels, *tête de veau* and usually one fish offering on a resolutely barnyard bill of fare. You can't go wrong with a starter of grilled gambas, a hunk of entrecote steak cooked over the flames of the big open fireplace in the dining room and buttressed by *frîtes* or veg of the day, followed by a plate of cheese and a home made dessert for comfortably less than 20 euros. Even non-carnivores will not leave unfulfilled. Half a *camembert*, baked with garlic and served with crusty bread and crisp salad, is more than a match for seafood alternatives.

Indoors, enjoy a pichet of rouge, cheery banter and firelight glow of happy eaters; outside condensation on a jug of chilled rose reflects streetlamps as you sink into a pavement chair to watch townsfolk hobnobbing in the bar next door and by the famous railings across the way, and you brush cheeks and shake hands with passers by who dawdle by your table for a catch up. Open every day (closing off-season Saturday lunchtimes only), midday menus begin at around €12 and you may eat heartily for €18-25 plus wine.

**Chocolatée:** *Salon de Thé – Boutique*          €
1 bis bd Lamartine [1] C3
04 67 00 55 16
Those who remember the original **Maison de Camille** on the quay will be delighted to see that the tea room and gift shop has been transplanted, complete with chandelier, to the theatre roundabout. Lunchtime platters of carpaccio, salad, pasta and open sandwiches at under €10.

**Dai Long** €
16 av Chassefiere [1] **B3**
04 67 94 03 99
Just as the quintessential treat for visitors to Britain is a visit to an Indian restaurant, so the cuisine of Vietnam is a delight to be discovered in France. In Marseillan, we have two options. Daniel and Nathalie's market stall fresh from their Béziers kitchen on Tuesday, and every day the Dai Long restaurant for dining out. Food, fresh, flavoursome, woos a loyal clientele.

**Delicatessen** €
4 pl Général Guillaut [1] **B3**
04 67 77 38 93   www.everyoneweb.fr/delicatessen
Closed (off-season) Sat (L), Sun, Mon (E)
Visitors with long memories will recall a cheap and cheerful pizzeria beside the church. Times change and the former **Igloo** is now hot, hip and happening. A huge bilingual panel on the outside wall spells out the bill of fare to passers-by and co-owner Alexandre Nerrière hails arrivals from behind the bar as young colleagues give an equally informal *acceuil* in a trendy retro-styled room: mix and match chairs and tables, menus chalked on big blackboards, winelists painted on bottles and quirky collection of lamps and ashtrays and china piggies absolutely everywhere.

Pigs are homage to the movie *Delicatessen* (A favourite of owners Alexandre and Cédric). *Amélie* director Jean-Pierre Jeunet's style inspired the décor, but cineastes may trust the food's orthodox provenance. Dine outdoors in summer at tables by the church wall, where hang paintings from the nearby atelier of Jean-Claude Chabrol. Pull up a 1950s café chair and work through crisp and tasty salads. Inexpensive undemanding lunch platters feature optimistic attempts to rejuvenate trad standards. Midday menu around €12, evening meals from €15 feature oysters, carpaccio and home made burgers. Options from nibbles to full €29 dinner. Always packed, and a bar-like evening buzz make this popular with anglophone holidaymakers and young locals. Occasional live music for an added pulse.

**Aux Delices d'Oc** €
8 rue Vedel [1] **B2**
04 67 32 29 61 www.auxdelicesdoc.com
Closed Wed
It is usually on Tuesday market day that the uninitiated first spot the menu propped up between the *Maison de la Presse* and the town hall. Now that French domestic food guides, *Le Routard* and *Petit Futé* have found the place, the secret is out. Tucked away, and with a sweet unexpected terrace,

270

this little restaurant is not front line. Boards advertising lunch from €8 are visible lure, and certainly bargain deal of *centre ville*. Tradition and season determine both *à la carte* selection and various set menus, changed and upgraded every month or so. Dish of the day usually a reliable favourite. Off-

season suggestions in winter likely to include comfort standards *choucroute* and barnyard fare from France's heartland. Otherwise, the region has a strong influence: marinated *pelardon* from the hills, and seafood from the *étang*. Selecting from the *carte*, budget perhaps €30 euros before drinks. Set menus are priced from €13 -23 and even less at lunchtimes where a *plat du jour* and glass of wine may cost just €8.

We have found France's classic national treasure, steak and chips, to be among the most reliable options on the menu and salads certainly don't disappoint. Fresh catch of the day and choice cut of meat may be enjoyed on or off the set deals. The terrace in the crook of the rue Vedel, once ramparts of the Hundred Years War, by the rear of the Mairie, is where most people choose to dine lunchtime and summer evenings, but there is a dining room inside, host to a programme of art exhibitions.

### Le Glacier     €€
6 av Victor Hugo [1] A3
04 67 77 22 04 www.restaurant-marseillan.com
Closed Mon, Sun (E)
Where napkins and good table manners still reign supreme and famous for its lobster platters and elegant approach to seafood, a bright, smart room is where Marseillan families have enjoyed traditional birthdays, Mothers' Days and silver weddings for 40 years or more. A place where *Crêpes Suzettes* are still served in the traditional way. Respectable people from nearby towns and villages dress smartly and drive into Marseillan for a taste of elegant dining from the age of well-laundered tablecloths and pert shoulder pads. The restaurant on the main avenue out of town entered a new incarnation in recent years, managing now to integrate contemporary sensibility without shattering the illusion of the *ancien régime*.

271

A strip of kerbside decking is the only clue to a new era. Inside, two distinct dining areas: traditional room with bleached maritime theme, and a modern oyster bar with chandelier of wine glasses. Taking care to rely on quality produce as much as the art of smart linen folding, the main coquillages come from **Azaïs** *(see page 267)* Trademark seafood and fresh lobster continues to dominate the menu, but more modern influences nonetheless nudge their way through. Thus, a *gambas* or *encornet* starter on the basic €29 set menu, might be served *"sur une idée d'une César salade"*. Finer palates may be serenaded by siren call of the vivarium; a seafood platter followed by a lobster of two halves, first dueting with langoustine on a bed of baby spinach leaves, and then tarted up in tarragon and tomato and gratineed with a creamy risotto. This €47 menu also includes dessert. Lobster based *à la carte* dining could nudge your bill towards to €90, but general oyster grazing followed by sole or bream with perhaps a *vacherin* finale might keep free range budget within sight of €40. However, entry level dining comes with a simple *découverte* menu at around €20: unthreatening fare such as a mustarded *faux fillet* or locally vermouthed salmon, following the standard shellfish or cheesy starter, and then rounded off with the expected profiteroles. Midweek lunch deal in the oyster/tapas room features two dishes with drinks for €14.

**Le Jardin de Naris**
24 bd Pasteur **[1] C2**
04 67 77 30 07
Tucked away on the main road into town, surviving competition from long-forgotten fashionable wannabes, is a quaintly old established gem from the Summer of Love, belatedly discovered in 2010 by *Elle* magazine. Eccentric décor both indoors and in the garden encourages the inner child to come out to play; toys in the garden, school books and posters in the dining room and crayons on the table for doddling on the tablecloth between courses. The best artwork finds itself on the "classroom" wall and you feel like you've won a gold star. The out of the way location somehow suits this type of place (more Crouch End than Hampstead) nestling in a backwater of time, where you are as like to be greeted by an ambling rambling cat as your waitress or earth-motherly hostess. Honest food honestly prepared and served. Perhaps brightly coloured salads of beansprouts garnished with thin slices of watermelon, maybe chunky steaks served with blazing dried thyme, or a hearty mushroom and leek *feuilleté*. This latter part of the *Jardin's* USP: a steak restaurant with a healthy respect for vegetarians. As well as the usual bewildering array of set options from €15 upwards (each with a meat-free dish or two), an €18 vegetarian menu boasts loads of quite imaginative choices for all courses. If veggie recipes seem anchored in the

seventies or eighties heyday of the *vol au vent*, then let the nostalgia kick in. After all, in a land where the carniphobe is usually palmed off with an omelette and a glare, who is to complain? A young and enthusiastic kitchen team is matched by a warm and welcoming dining room and garden crew. *Le jardin* is best place to sit, cheek by trowl with other diners, sundry *bric a brac* and fairy lights. A time-warp and a sabbatical from the Med.

**Le Relax     €**
39 boulevard Lamartine **[1] B3**
04 67 77 23 51
You won't hear much English spoken at this bar opposite the Boulevard Hotel and the Mairie: For years, the lunchtime hangout of working men in search of a square meal. Once the culinary cradle of a family business that evolved into the waterside paradise that is the **Guinguette à Fady** at **Balaruc**. Now, one or two owners down the line, an €8 *plat de jour* (perhaps *steak frites*, chicken breast in a cream sauce with heaps of pasta or maybe a vast *paella*) still remains a bargain. Huge portions, with a *carafe* of house red, white or rosé thrown in for free. For €12 we have been known to opt for the full meal, a starter of cold meats perhaps and a dessert as well. Pizza or salad alternatives to the dish of the day.

**Sancho     €**
11 bis avenue Victor Hugo **[1] B3**
04 67 62 98 92
A take-away, with tables serving reliable kebabs, pizza, and panini.

**Panam     €**
11 av Chassefiere **1 [B3]**
09 50 84 26 27
Another take-out/eat-in choice for pizza, sandwich & healthy salads.

**La Table d'Emilie     €€€**
8 place Carnot **[1] B2**
04 67 77 63 59
Closed Sun (E), Mon, Wed
Forget anything that you might have been told by a big red shiny book, this historic house in a corner of the old town (*see page 22*) is the gastronomic high spot of Marseillan Village. . It may not have had the media attention lavished elsewhere but serious foodies hold the place in high respect. And it is the *restaurateurs'* restaurant of choice. A friend, whose day job was as a chef in a *Michelin*-starred *Relais & Château* restaurant, privately sung the praises of the imaginative cuisine hiding behind the market square, and this is where other chefs of Marseillan and beyond choose to go for a special evening out.

Insist on a table in the main brick-vaulted dining room then, from the first breaking of home-baked bread to the last *mignardise,* only prepare to be inspired by the chef's witty and original take on local ingredients, teased and pleased with talents honed on the farthest continents.

Finesse is the watchword; from always original *amuse bouche* appetisers to flamboyant fruity desserts. In the meantime, you may be seduced by a puff pastry balloon of *Saint-Jacques* (something of a signature dish), heady with a herbal whack of *Noilly Prat,* or by wittiest reinvention of cod, bass or mullet. Farmyard fare is treated with the same respect as treasures of the deep. Plates never overcrowded, but taste-buds always work overtime. John Dory *chez Emilie* is presented perched atop marrowbone and *rognons de veau* with *confit* of shallots in Merlot; duck with orange, lemon and ginger; but confections are never thrown together just for the sake of cleverness: when it comes to great beef of *Aubrac,* this will be served in a traditional *jus.* Unlike many gastronomic destinations, fireworks are not reserved only for top-price menus, versions of elite combos just as likely to be found in some guise on even the most budget conscious deals. A weekday €19 three course lunch is accorded the kitchen's full respect, two options for each course, and features a quail and *foie gras* salad amongst the starters. The full range of

menus begins at €28, rising through the thirties and forties to a €50 fanfare created by the chef for your entire party. The showcase menu is a cascade of *"trilogies"*, each course a trio of dishes from the *carte* and beyond. *Entrées* either a selection of seafood or *foie-gras* treats, mains from sea or farm, including inventive approaches to *Saint Pierre* and *Cannette* that I mentioned earlier. And, whilst desserts are always a treat, pace yourself. **La Table d'Emilie** is not a place where cheese is merely an alternative to the sweet course. The table of cheeses here is a legend in its own right, and when wheeled out for the grand presentation of fine blues and hardy mountain classics, ringed by ashen chevres and unctuous creamy delights, this *entr'acte* between main course and dessert can make for the most memorable dilemma of your week. Dress smartish. The food deserves it. And book in advance.

### Le Takeaway Marseillanais

When you've neither time nor inclination for a restaurant, a *Traiteur* will prepare you a restaurant quality meal to take home. Often a classic *paella* or *cassoulet*; other choices could include *gigot d'agneau,* Languedoc fish *bourride* or classic *boeuf Bourgignonne*. Great alternative to the barbecue for garden dining, and useful compromise for picky family groups.

**Chez Pillou** 6 av André Chassefière 04 67 01 67 34 **[1] B3**
**Les Saveurs de Marius** 06 07 23 51 24 www.les-saveurs-de-marius.fr

### Pizza delivery or collection from

**Dédé Pizza** 159 Route de la Plage 06 01 23 79 85
**O'Rigattoni** place du Théâtre 04 67 21 02 68 **[2] A2**
**Bella Pizza** 3 rue Général de Gaulle 04 67 01 61 33 **[1] B2**
**Sancho** and **Panam** (*see page 273*)

And several new eat-in snackeries include **Fleur du Dessert** on rue de la Paix and **La Marseillanerie**'s tables by the church wall (*see page 252*).

# Marseillan Plage

There are literally scores of places to eat at Marseillan Plage, as well as addresses below, find many more pizza, burger, ice-cream and snack venues. Go down to the *plage* to let your hair down, lose your head in the buzz of lively chatter as an antidote to the measured calm of life in the village. I have reviewed several addresses that we have enjoyed over the past few years, and list many that are still under our to-do fridge magnet.

**l'Australian  €€**
43 av de la Méditerranée [4] A2
04 67 77 62 69
*Tres bonzer rapport qualité-prix pour le tucker* when you swap *Bonjour* for *G'day*, and enjoy an Aussie style barbecue lunch or dinner, with a dash of Languedoc seafood and splash of local wine (or Fosters) on the side. Menus from €10 and €16 and kids are €7. There is still a €52 challenging 900g red meat plate, that'd be right. Open year round.

**Brasserie du Marché  €€**
Place du Marché [4] A2
04 67 37 52 65
One of the rare year-round eateries of the resort comes into its own during the holiday season when Marseillan Plage holds its food market. In season, reliable budget menus and *plats du jour* keep a summer terrace buzzing. From late autumn, the few remaining locals top up their spirits on hearty winter warmers and chunky comfort food.

**Le Chalut  €€**
55 avenue de la Méditerranée 34340 [4] A2
04 67 21 88 90
Popular *moules-friterie* on the main road and something of an institution. Grand platters of seafood from humblest mollusc to the plumpest lobster. Even a speciality *Marmite*. Menus €20-30, and lunch deals with a buffet starter, dish of the day and dessert for €13.

**Chez Pierrot – La Guinguette  €**
9 rue Georges Brassens [4] B1
04 67 31 44 15
I rather like this quieter rendezvous in high season, when locals head for *Plage Robinson*, away from the main drag and crowds of both Marseillan Plage proper and the Lido. Beach access is via a path through an apartment complex, but this corner site *dépot pain*, pizzeria and *rôtisserie* is where locals stop for something to take back to the studio and where the rest of us sit, sip and or snack during time off from the beach in the heat of the day. Restaurant menu at terrace tables or just tuck into freshly made pizza to enjoy with beach chums or a good book if on your tod.

**Le Crabe  €€**
Hotel Richmont, 48 allée André Filliol
04 67 21 97 79 www.hotel-marseillan.com
Closed mid-Nov – mid-Feb
When dithering between choices at the resort, a view is usually the deal-maker, so the panoramic dining room at this three-star hotel, practically on

the beach, is ever popular. It is the reliable and flavoursome food that gets visitors coming back. Not the cheapest table at Marseillan Plage, nor the fanciest, but providing precise fare that people seek during a fortnight on the Med. Reliable service, good portions of decent food at each end of the budget-scale. The €15 base menu of *moules marinières* or *soupe de poisson* starters, with fish, meat and seafood standards to follow and a simple dessert. Most popular is a €21 deal, main courses of bream and bass cooked in traditional *muscat* or dill and mustard sauces. Some regulars go for a wider range of dishes on €28 and €39 menus, and may find oysters in champagne amongst starters and grander fish and meat such as a seafood *marmite* or *capuccino de crevettes*. *À la carte* resolutely below €20 for main courses, even turbot and sole. Family friendly, children's menu at €7

**Marina Bay**   €€
Port de Plaisance [4] B2
04 99 43 59 86
The secret weapon in the making over of Marseillan Plage's pleasure port: Just by the hotel *Richmont*, the former *Capitainerie* has been turned into a beach bar and panoramic terrace. Eat on the roof (braving the windiest afternoons) or find a sheltered table on a ground floor deck next to the sands of the Plage d'Honneur. Have a drink at the bar or go for crepes and generous pizzas during the day. Mediterranean brunch and €15 lunch is popular and evening menus at €20 & €25. Kids eat for €8. Food is fresh and flavoursome, service friendly. Open April to November. Popular with locals out of season.

**La Paillotte**
705, avenue des Campings [4] A3
04 67 01 62 55
Gambas flambéed in rum, hammocks to sit in, beach-bar style cocktails, you could only be in the Caribbean, or then again amongst the campsites of Marseillan Plage. Amid palms and bamboo, the clue is in chairs carved from wine barrels. The spirit is that of the distant French territories and the atmosphere is rum o-clock on the isle of Gaudaloupe. So chicken will be caramalised with pineapple, and perhaps coconut milk or ginger may spice up your meat course. Cocktails are holiday favourites, both amongst genuine *vacanciers* from campsites surrounding the restaurant-bar and locals from cities along the Languedoc coast. Pina colada or daiquiri or giant showcase pitchers of exotically hued concoctions might easily be upstaged by the range of rums to choose from. Regulars enjoy *acras* served as starters, not standard salt cod, but a tuna or a prawn version of the fishy favourite. Outside peak season, it opens Friday and Saturday evenings and Sunday lunchtime as early as April. Spend €18-30 per head, plus drinks.

**La Pizzetta  €**
10 rue de Commerce [4] A2
04 67 01 60 76
Family favourite onn a strip of pavement terraces linking two main roads of Marseillan Plage, where hustleteria tout for business. When entertaining the generations, I've never been disappointed dropping in for a bite on a summer Sunday evening at this wittily decorated slice of old Napoli. Decked out like a street scene (the kids particularly enjoy garlands of underwear strung between Italianate balconies above the tables). Cheap and cheerful with genuinely friendly professional service, good banter and safe standards on an illustrated laminated menu that defies language barriers. Pizzas are full of flavour; try a blend of *chevre*, honey and pine nuts. Some come for big bowls of mussels with house sauce, chips and a glass of wine for under €10. Same team runs the new **Moules et Cie** on the main drag.

**Le Scampi  €**
21 avenue de la Méditerranée [4] A2
04 67 01 62 73
Closed: Nov-Mar, Wed (Apr-Jun, Sep-Oct)
Popular with Marseillan Ville types, and acknowledged by French critics from *Le Petit Futé*, a cut above the norm. Meat and seafood handled with skill, panfried scallops done to a precise turn, other seafood offered fresh or as fritters and oysters gratinee gain the townies' approval. Eat outside on the terrasse to watch the post-plage *passegiata* of loud shirts and shorts menu-hopping the length of the avenue. Menus from under €12.

**La Spagheteria**
96 avenue des Campings [4] A3
04 67 93 73 68
Closed Nov-Feb
Famously boasting 64 permutations of pasta and sauces, this is the quickest way to refuel with carbs enough for a permanent playtime lifestyle that begins on the beach and ends on the dancefloor of Marseillan Plage. Since the place does not close between conventional mealtimes, it suits the hedonist, who may breakfast on lasagne at 4 in the afternoon, or inure the system against celebration shots to follow at midnight. Sebastien offers the full gamut of pasta from eponymous spaghetti through penne, fusilli, farfalle conchiglie and macaroni in all their twists, turns and tubes, and your own choice of sauce determines whether you pay a mere €7 for Bolognese or €9 for seafood toppings, by way of cheesy, carbonara and pesto variations. Ravioli and home made lasagne amongst the alternative offerings. Salad and carpaccio style starters, a kids menu for €6.

**La Spezia**
45 avenue de la Méditerrannée [4] A2
04 67 21 81 67
Very much a holiday restaurant. Buffet starter ("as much as you can eat"), *plat du jour*, dessert and wine for €13 keeps family budgets on the straight and narrow at lunchtime, when its too hot to stay on the beach and you don't want to melt the plastic in your wallet. Otherwise, finicky eaters can browse safely on a goodly selection of proper pizzas at €8, steaks around €15 and even a spag bol for the most cautious at under €9, whilst more adventurous souls tuck into a pot of mussels in traditional white wine alongside the obligatory mound of frites. Seafood is fresh and from the lagoon. Three-course menus from all corners of the *carte* €14 or €19.

**Aux Saveurs de la Mer**
Hôtel Dunes *(page 380)* 04 67 21 83 75

**Aux Saveurs Du Sud**
av de la Méditerranée [4] A2
04 67 94 29 19

**Chez Anthony**
3 rue du Commerce [4] A2
04 67 31 60 76

**Le Brasero**
456 av des Campings [4] A3
04 67 01 64 20

**La Camargue**
ch du Payrollet [4] A3
04 67 62 25 09

**Le Charlemagne**
av des Campings [4] A3
04 67 31 45 48

**La Chaumière** 1150 rte de Sète [4] B1

**Le Dar Janna** *(*Kry's Club *page 75)*

**La Jeanne**
25 av de la Méditerranée [4] A2
04 67 21 82 01

**Le Loup de Mer**
rue de Commerce [4] A2
04 67 21 96 23

**Le Marina**
av de la Méditerranée [4] A2
04 67 21 82 93

**Le Mazet de Manon** rte de Sète
04 67 01 26 71

**La Méditerranée**
rue du Commerce [4] A2
04 67 37 68 25

**La Moule Gourmande**
avenue des Campings [4] A3
04 67 00 17 83

**La Petite Marmite**
place du Marché 06 14 57 65 57 [4] A2

**Le Petit Marseillan**
67 av de la Méditerranée [4] A2
04 67 76 95 29

**La Roussette**
37 av de la Méditerranée [4] A2
04 67 21 97 63

**La Salsa**
imp Grau du Rieu 04 67 21 94 67

**Les Saveurs Marines**
av des Campings 04 67 00 09 58 [4] A2

**La Siesta**
10 chemin du Pous [4] A2
04 67 21 94 70

**La Table du Vigneron**
3 rue des Loisirs [4] B1
04 67 21 98 16

**Le Tango**
8 rue du Commerce [4] A2
04 67 01 72 88

**Le Village**
1 rue du Commerce [4] A2
04 67 26 20 44

279

# How to eat very very well
# ... away from Marseillan

## Agde [5] C2

### Le Bistrot d'Hervé €€
47 rue Brescou, 34300 Agde
04 67 62 30 69

Just behind the cinema, a treat in a charming shady courtyard across the road from the school playground. Midweek's €16 lunch menu is worth exploring, and much more affordable than an evening *à la carte*. A sturdy *plat du jour* is topped and tailed by *verrine* glass tumblers of starters and desserts. Desserts are best. You may be virtuous and order just one glass of *pain perdu*, aka *brioche* bread and butter pudding. But, free range and off-menu, we skip starters and instead follow a main with two, three, even four varied potted puds on a slate tile. Warm, honey-moist madeleines, soft fruit confections or reliable *crème brulée*. All classics given a whoosh by chef Hervé Dos Santos, who describes dishes, such as his 7-hour, slow-cooked signature *souris d'agneau,* (with inevitable crumble of vegetables), as *bistronomie*. In 2005, Michelin tipped him as talent to watch, and he won laurels, from native Southwest to Paris, before *Le Bastide Cabezac* at Bize-Minervois secured his reputation. Whilst Hervé tops up kitchen innovation, wife Sabine handless the welcome. In Summer, Hervé's talents move along the coast, as he creates the menu for beach bar *La Voile Rouge* in **Sète.**

### Casa Pepe €€
29 rue Jean Roger, 34300 Agde
04 67 21 17 67

All fishermen have a story about the one that got away. For food lovers, this would be the restaurant they never found. Without a private tip-off, that is. Stuck behind a bar, with no view, and up several steps from a street between promenade and river, it forfeits the panoramas and easy access of a dozen tourist traps in favour of baser pleasure. Here is where fish comes to be loved, adored and worshipped. Turbot or sole that slips off the bone like a negligée from a courtesan's shoulder, simple preparations of plainest seafood, the noblest and the humblest the sea can offer, treated with equal respect. Here, rival chefs and *restaurateurs* relax on their nights off, pampering their own *papilles* and marvelling at the Med's bounty. Here, one chilly night in January, we discovered the restaurant with friends on an extended birthday weekend. We'd already done the rounds of the few winter-opening eateries in Marseillan and now threw ourselves on the wit and resources of local insiders to find a special meal for our guests' final gastronomic memories. Menus at around €15 and €25. But if the catch of the day yields pure gold – disdain the concept of budget and eat *à la carte*.

**Lou Pescadou**     €
18 rue Chassefière, 34300 Agde
04 67 21 17 10
Word of mouth superseded by word of broadcast, since television chef Rick Stein discovered this old favourite address down by the Hérault. Casual visitors might be tempted by more conventional neighbouring waterfront eateries, but sensation seekers avoid the hustlers from rival rooms trawling the tourist tide, and instead keep going they reach **Lou Pescadou,** also known locally as *Chez Bébert*. Convivial seating, often sharing tables with strangers. No one remains a stranger for long, as all tuck into the same set menu: ever fish soup, followed by mussels then main course and dessert. A rare chance for book-led food pilgrims to eat exactly the same meal as the author. The menu has hardly changed in more than forty years, and the feast from the TV show and Stein's accompanying coffee-table/recipe book is still served whatever the season. Thus, that celebrated soup comes with cheese and garlicy *croutons*; *paté* is a huge slab to induce shudders in the shallow and devotion in the wise; hefty helpings of mussels come *piperaded*; and ice-cream with house sauce is designed for either optimists or gluttons, since between all these essential standards is a main course of either lemon sole or steak *flambéed* with cognac. Full five courses for a silly €15 per person. Wine by the litre, all three regular shades €6 a jug.

**Le Plazza** €€
20 rue 4 Septembre, 34300 Agde
04 67 94 16 19 www.restaurant-leplazza.fr
Bar open all day, Restaurant all day Jun-Sep; Oct-May (L)
Just the sort of reliable *brasserie-glacier-bar* to be found on any street corner in Paris. Here, by the *Marianne* and memorial to the *Résistance*, at the head of the promenade, is an ideal place to flop during Thursday's street market and Wednesday's brocante on the town walls. If lunching, no surprises – only hearty standards: *steak tartare* and *entrecôte maître d'hôtel*, not forgetting the obligatory *moules*, from *marinières* to *dijonnaises* via all points of the trencherman's compass. Midday *plats du jour* around €7.50 and set dessert under €3. Portions are hearty and lavish as you'd expect

from mine host Hervé, former rugby player with an sportsman's appetite. Perhaps rugger tradition inspires the bar's range of beers: surprisingly good for the region: *Leffe* on tap and loads of Belgian bottles behind the counter. From first light, when bank staff pause for a *café crème* before work, through idlers *rendezvous* during the mornings and a banana split in the afternoon, a great spot for people watching *en ville*.

**La Table de Stéphane**          €€
2 rue du Moulin a Huile, ZI des 7 Fonts, 34300 Agde
04 67 26 45 22 www.latabledestephane .com
Closed Sat (L), Mon, Sun (Sep-Jun)
This is the least likely location for a good lunch or dinner. In an industrial and trading estate, opposite a cash and carry warehouse, discover the sort of restaurant that gets traditional food critics salivating. Chef Stéphane Lavaux once operated from a trendy address at the Cap, until moving skills and team to an unassuming building, in a business park by builders yards and paint depots. As Monsieur cooks, so Madame and a very young, yet truly ardent, team handle welcome and service with flair and professional passion. When we first drove up to the bland frontage we were not exactly free from doubt, but by the time the non-designated-drivers amongst us tottered back to the parking space, hearts were filled with bonhomie, our post-prandial *embonpoints* lined and boosted by fine dining and our taste-buds resounding with the savoury echo of a tingle to remember.

The setting dissolves from the peripheral vision on first glance at the menu. But for the location, the restaurant would have been garlanded with laurels and filled with beautiful people. A reassuring roll-call of prime meats in subtle reductions, intelligent combinations of flavours and a nice wine list soon settles any unease, and the enthusiasm of the front of house crew set the scene for pleasures to follow. Our waiter on that first visit possessed the fervour of the star pupil of a French hotel school let loose in the world of his dreams. Endearing and engaging, Xavier's passion for fine dining reignited our own zeal for what was to follow. Later he told us that he had encouraged his colleagues to pool their tips in order to organise staff outings to the finest *Michelin*-starred dining rooms. "How else are we to understand what a gourmet diner is looking for?" he explained. Glass cases display a collection of menus and souvenirs from some of the country's most legendary restaurants. And one senses the team's belief that one day their bill of fare might be accorded the same respect. On the €25 *Caprices* menu, discover perhaps the ubiquitous cooked *chèvre* starter, but here presented with *cappuccino* of creamed herbs; a wallow in the €40 menu *Les Humeurs*, serves inaugural *foie gras* in a *bouillon* of pineapple and verbena,

282

then flourishes a quail main course with a *confit* of caramelised and gingered veg. For €59 per person, chef will create a repast especially for your table. Otherwise, prepare to budget around €60, perhaps. But consider a simple working lunch at under €25, complete with a glass of decent wine chosen by the sommelier. The proliferation of suits at lunchtime shows how many local businesses feel the trek out of town to a trading estate well worth the effort. A word to those with special dietary needs: ask for explanations of juices, stocks and marinades, as sometimes a fish dish may may source its sauce from beef or lamb. As I say, it may be a bit of a schlep from the beach or Marseillan, but if you've planned a trip to hypermarkets or DIY stores of Agde's trading estates, then wrap the chores around a lunchtime treat and a duty day will instead become an occasion.

## Agde: Le Cap d'Agde |5| C2

**Les Halles aux Poissons**     €€
45 av des Sergents, 34300 Le Cap Agde
04 67 26 82 93 www.leshallesauxpoissons.com
Open evenings only in season, lunch and dinner Sept-June
Walk past twice before finding the door, since the restaurant is hidden behind a fish shop counter. At times, service borders on brusque, but an off-season lunchtime menu is certainly value for money and, for 10 months of the year, it is packed with business lunchers who recognise a bargain, and estate agents on the pull to offload a seemingly endless supply of holiday studios in the resort. In summer, open evenings only. Fish is fresh, good and handled with care to merit a *Qualité Hérault* listing. Service from slightly harried to professional. Food is consistently fine. Main catch landed and sold at Le Grau d'Agde quayside that very day, and Bouzigues oysters delivered each morning. Good interpretations of regional standards, *rouille à l'Agathois*, and *moules farcies à la Sétoise*, for those looking for classic textbook rather than brochure fare. Menus from €15.

**Le Nautic**     €€
rue de l'Estacade, Avant Port, 34300 Le Cap d'Agde
04 67 26 90 01 www.restaurant-lenautic.com
Closed Wed (L) July-Aug; Tue eve, Wed out of season, mid Dec- Jan
Seafront lunching in a tourist resort is always even more of a gamble than the blackjack table at the casino, yet there are at least two establishments on this parade of decked and stepped terraces facing the yacht club of the *Avant Port* and morning fishermen's market stalls where locals outnumber trippers. This is the place for seafood: always packed, even off-season. One sunny Mother's Day, well before tourist-tide, the wait for a table threatened to last 'til Bastille Day.

Normally, when a successful restaurant changes hands, regulars drift away, leaving plenty of seats for unwary passers by, but latest owners at the **Nautic** have the same gift for preparing hearty meals for the off-duty hungry. New look, contemporary décor replaces seaside standard themes, but same generous portions, good-humoured staff and flair with the catch. Grilled oysters in *Noilly* or mussels in *Picpoul*, and bream with house tapenade is a tastebud tingler. Long-term year-round *Agathoises* a loyal clientele in an area where most tables merely pander to passing trade. Budget around €25.

**Le Pourquoi Pas?**   €€
5 quai de l'Estacade, 34300 Le Cap d'Agde
04 67 26 13 39 www.lepourquoi-pas.fr
Closed Tue (in term time)
When we couldn't get a table at our regular haunt, Le Nautic, we followed the time-honoured tradition of seeking the dining room with least holiday-garb and most working clothes. No contest. The **Pourquoi Pas** posed and answered the question for us and we sat down to a ridiculously inexpensive menu, slap bang opposite the yacht club. The name, by the way, is not a reflection of the casual indecision of grazing vacationers. It is homage, as befits a last meal before leaving shore for the unknown perils of the deep, to a great mariner: Commandant Jean-Baptiste Charcot, grandson-in-law of Victor Hugo and chum of fellow Antartic explorer Captain Scott. Charcot led France's expedition to map the South Pole at the turn of the 20th century in his ship, *Le Pourquoi Pas*. If you are happy with two courses of salad and pizza, you may spend little more on your entire meal than your neighbour at the next table does on his extravagantly brollied and drenched ice cream sundae. The cheaper menu is reliable and as good as you could wish for halfway through a day navette-hopping your way round the various ports of the Cap. Casual moochers drop in for an ice cream or crêpe whilst healthy eaters may lose themselves in a vast *salade niçoise*. If pizza is not your bag, *pourqui pas* splash out on house speciality *La Pierrade* – a choice of turkey, beef or duck *magret* cooked at the table over hot stones.

## Agde: Le Grau d'Agde   [5] C2

**L'Adagio**   €€
3-5 quai Commandant Méric, 34300 Le Grau d'Agde
04 67 21 13 00 www.ladagio.net
Closed Sun (E), Mon, Wed (E)
The serious gastro restaurant along a riverside line up of cheap and cheerful *moules-frites*, pizza and tapas emporia lining the quay at the mouth of the Hérault. Although it is always worth stopping off at the neighbouring

eaturies, especially when the kids are too excited at the prospect of the afternoon's boat trip, save **Adagio** for a special occasion. Not just for the heavy linen tablecloths and starched napkins that are some notches above the neighbours' wipe-clean livery. A fine way with fish and all round sophistication has always come as standard, so when the restaurant changed hands, an intake of breath was held until first reports did the round.

General reaction so far has been a resounding smack of the lips with murmurs of respect for imaginative (yet not too clever) combos: oysters *gratinées* with a Muscat de Frontignan *sabayon*, beetroot teasing of a salmon tartlet and bass (here under its more Atlanticised appellation of *bar* rather than Mediterranean *loup)* with honey, walnut and endive. Fish and seafood the more flamboyant signature dishes, but chef understands meat and his menus feature beef and duck, sweetmeats and *foie-gras*-based essentials to merit a position in establishment guidebooks. Dress smart and pay €30-60, although there is a lunch menu from just €15 and other set options €20-45. The quayside terrace has two steps down.

**Astoria**      €€
8 quai Commandant Méric, 34300 Le Grau d'Agde
04 67 94 13 78
Lively and typical resort restaurant with menus starting at under €14. Good views up the river and out to sea. Fun to watch the seagulls following the fishing boats towards the auction and the pleasure boats out to Brescou.

**La Pergola**   €€
17 quai du Commandant Méric, 34300 Le Grau d'Agde
04 67 94 14 56
How they manage a set menu for under €20 with lobster as a starter, I'll never know, but this is not only the most reliable of the string of holiday eateries along the quay, but also remarkably good value. There is an even cheaper menu and you may pay more if you wish, but three courses of good quality food, prepared simply but well, for the price of a mound of mussels or predictable pizza a few doors away is where smart money goes when the sun shines on the estuary. We first visited at the tail end of a season and were pleasantly surprised by the warmth of the welcome and the standard of cooking. We returned in Spring and the same genuine *acceuil* kickstarted my parents' holiday a treat.

A carpaccio of tuna was succulent and a pleasant, flavoursome alternative to the more predictable offerings elsewhere. Across the table, a friend slipped out of the conversation as the seafood starter featuring half a lobster

**Island barbecue** €€
Fort Brescou, 34300 Agde
By boat from the Quai du commandant Méric. Jul-Aug only
**Le Provence III** (Mon, Tue 19-22.30)
04 67 21 09 88 (July, Aug); 04 67 21 38 72 www.brescoucroisieres.com
**Le Millésime** (Thu, Fri 19-22.30)
04 67 01 71 93 www.agde-croisiere-peche.com

Sunset by the glow of a bonfire on a rocky island, watching stars come out over a sparkling sheet of Mediterranean sea; fresh fish grilling on the beach, a glass of wine in hand and good company. There is life after table manners, and bonhomie without cutlery. Set sail from the quay of le Grau d'Agde on a summer's evening, to a fortress on an island out in the open sea. If this all sounds a little like a grown-up Enid Blyton moment, well, it is. But our castle of Adventure is **Fort Brescou**: of the 17th century ring of citadels, castles and fortifications strung around Louis XIV's kingdom. Brescou perches on a volcanic island off the coast of Le Cap d'Agde (*see page 156*). Several pleasure craft moored outside the restaurants of the Commandant Méric offer a *Sardinade* on the island as an evening alternative to fishing trips and Canal du Midi excursions.

One of the best known is Tuesday night aboard *Provence III*. Captain Claude is a third generation fisherman, who began casting his nets in the Med as a lad of 16. Twenty years ago, he began sharing his beloved waters with visitors and holidayakers, and now, the weekly barbecues on the island are a renowned treat. Board at 19h for the trip to Brescou. Once ashore, captain and crew set to work lighting a fire on a stony beach. When the flames are lit, sardines and sausages are thrown on the grill, and, with bread, cheese and local fruits to follow, and liberal libation of local wine. Guests are encouraged to eat their fill as the sun sets over the fortress walls. Arrive back at the quayside around 10.30pm. The Provence III organises its picnics on Monday and Tuesday. Since 2009, a similar *Sardinade* trip has been organised on Thursday and Friday evenings aboard Eric Bousquet's *le Millésime,* a boat he had especially built in Marseillan, and which caters for disabled passengers and is home to the ship's dog Fanny! Same style menu and welcome. Both skippers charge €19 for the evening, children at €9.

captured his attention. 8/10 his verdict, nothing fancy to mask real flavours; a serious nod of approval that continued to honour the simple steak in a home made shallot sauce for the main course. Seabass was fresh, vegetables delicious and sautéed potatoes served in a trendy glass, as a nod towards the current century. Good chocky desserts, reliable *pichet* of house *rosé* and the fact of more locals than visitors at neighbouring tables proved this place is a stayer. A quayside terrace attracts passing trade (a few steps down) but the restaurant and bar remains the chosen haunt of local fishermen passing the time over a *verre* or bite to eat before setting out to sea or casting a line from the rocks. For the rest of us, it's a fine setting for gazing at the pleasure craft passing along the waters, and for being mesmerised by the ritual comings and goings of the water taxi between our bank and the Tamarissière opposite.

**Les Vagues**   €€
Chemin des Dunes, 34300 Le Grau d'Agde
04 67 01 52 73
To dine on the Mediterranean shore rather than the river bank, follow the Chemin du Littoral away from the centre of Le Grau until the main road veers inland, then walk along the path behind the beach for 500 metres to come to what is certainly not a shack. A beach restaurant on the sands themselves, easily signposted by the double parking of vehicles unable to get a space in the official car parks. This place is very popular with locals out of season, which is why it does not follow the trends of typical beach-bars and close down out of season. We have had to look for an alternative table as early as April. Rocks, palms and loungers on the sands outside, otherwise serious attention to food within, the place is very much a restaurant lounge, with the accent on leisure, and décor and sauces owing more than a nod to the Far East. Thierry Grard specialises in seafood and good meat dishes, prepared and presented and appreciated with a sense of time and place. Expect prime meat and fish served on shiny white plates with pointy bits – even round dishes have corners, the true sign of a chef on trend. From the Saint Jacques starter to the gooey gratification of a memorable fondant au chocolat, flavours rule. Only word of warning, this may be a beach restaurant, but it keeps town hours, so kitchen opens strictly between noon and 2pm,and late stragglers may be disappointed.

## Agde: La Tamarissière   |5| C2

**K'lamar**  €€
33 quai Theople Cornu, La Tamarissière, 34300 Agde
04 67 94 05 06 www.restaurant-klamar.com
Closed Sun (E), Mon, Tue
There was once a restaurateur in Marseillan whose menu was performance art *manqué*. So literate, so poetic the descriptions of each dish, the diner was obliged to wait for a waiter, or even the patroness herself, to recite, nay declaim, the roll call of dishes for each course. This became a tradition akin to foregoing the acceptable, if cursory, HRH when referring to Prince Charles, and instead rattling through the full list of titles from Wales, Cornwall, Chester and Rothesay to Earl of Carrick, Baron of Renfrew, Lord

of the Isles, Prince and Great Steward of Scotland, whilst taking care not to overlook the honours of the Bath, Garter, Thistle and the Saskatchewan Order of Merit. Those in the know would budget hunger pangs accordingly and sit patiently at the table a good half hour before the appetite might kick in, the better to accommodate pre-dinner soliloquy. Not every meal lived up to the diplomatic flattery of the loquacious hymn in its praise, but had points been awarded for verbosity and cabaret, ah well... A glance at the *carte* at this relatively recent arrival across the estuary from Grau d'Agde might kindle memories of gastronomic verbiage *perdu*, but fear not, any over-indulgence of word play begins and ends with the awkward pun in the restaurant title (a local foible that stretches from the **Quai 17** to the **Res'Thau**). Effusive, rambling menu-speak here merely illuminates the individual perspective of an original chef: would you dare to précis *"Brochette en citronnelle de Saint-Jacques juste snackée, jus sirupeux aux fruits exotiques"*? Nor I.

We first heard word that it was once again worth crossing the river– after the passing of the eponymous and much lauded *Tamarissière* of distant memory and *Michelined* esteem – when friends returned to Marseillan after a day's cycling, panting and salivating at the memory of a chocolate dessert. Successive heralds of sweet and savoury delights to be had but a shuttle boat away from the familiar pizzafied quays of the Grau, prompted us to pay the ferryman to ply the water that we might taste for ourselves. We found a laid-back terrace, ideal for gongoozlers upgrading from canal to estuary watching, and a smartly lit, modestly upmarket dining room, with contemporary touches that never masked traditional style.

The menu, whether chalked on big boards outside or flourished over tall wine glasses indoors, is not too wide ranging, concentrating on a small, deftly nurtured repertoire. On the pastural side of the menu, beef is classic *Aubrac*, closest to home of quality breeds. Fishwise, the menu suggests scintillating sensations of local herbs, nuts and funghi in season, at the same time promising that the finished dish will be prepared to the whim of the chef; which, when the fish itself is determined by the haul landed on the quay of the *crée* across the way, is sensible and always appreciated. Even the least exotic catch is handled with care and attention to detail and just enough secret seasoning to push your lips to that elusive Gallic pout that does wonders for your spoken French. Menus range from a top of the list €54 per person celebration of a thousand flavours in ten small dishes, to quote the chef, served to the entire party, through a reasonably priced selection of set meals in the late twenties and early thirties down to the ludicrously low priced lunch deal of main course of the day and sweet for just €12. And as for those desserts that first proclaimed the advent of the

**K'lamar**, I confess to missing out on the *gâteau moelleux au chocolat* with its toffee tendencies in favour of a damned-near-perfect tarte tatin from another age. Food is loved here, where out of season, the chef and self-styled *créateur de saveurs* will happily spend a Saturday morning taking a group of *aficionados* out to the market to choose food for lunch, then present a private cookery course before sharing the spoils over lunch.

## Bages (*see also* **Corbières**) |5| B3

**Le Portanel**   €€
La Placette, passage du Portanel , 11100 Bages
04 68 42 81 66
Closed Tue (E); Wed Sep –Jun; Mon (L), Tue (L) Jul-Aug
An institution and for years the only reason outsiders ever stumbled across this magical village and upmarket time capsule. Climb what seems like a cliff face (in fact, a perfectly manageable path) to the restaurant that seems to jut out of the hill itself. A time-warp for the tastebuds, here traditional and upmarket dining has the seat of honour. Produce of the Etang de Bages reigns supreme, and chief of these are the celebrated eels that have wriggled their way from the Sargasso sea to reach your plate. One menu simply celebrates *les anguilles* in many guises, smoked and marinated, *sautéed* with herbs, prepared as a traditional *bourride* or served with a *brioche* of lagoon seaweeds. The range has long been championed by the serious food guides. *Petits gris escargots* are also amongst the specialities of the house. Regular fish with fins also manage a turn on the vill of fare. First time at the **Portanel**, I threw budget and caution to the winds and ordered freshly landed bass, caked and baked in sea-salt. I have obliterated the price from my memory. Nonetheless, years later, *je ne regrette rien*. Desserts are rich with the flavours of the *garrigue*. Figgy, herby, fruity and spicy. More recent triumphs have included *millefeuille* of *crêpes* with an eye-popping whiff of liquorice, a surprising change from an earlier version which had zinged with zest of orange and the whack of *grand marnier*. Menus from €18 to 40-something, *à la carte* is what bundles of €50 notes were invented for. You may need to book several days in advance.

**La Table du Pêcheur**   €€€
21 rue de l'Ancien Puits, 11100 Bages
04 68 41 15 11
Closed Tue, Wed
Oh the whirligig of time and fame. I remember this as a simple room in a house when Madame served up lunches from the catch of the day. But word

of mouth opened eyes, minds and wallets to this alternative table to the established **Portanel** across the village, so the *cognoscenti* made its way down the rue de l'Ancien Puits to make this too an address of note. Naturally, reinvented for a new market, prices went up, menus changed and days when you might drop in unannounced in peak season, and pay with loose change are but a memory. Today, consider a €40 menu or the *marmite* stew of seven different fish at €25 per *gourmand* (minimum two people). *À la carte* sees most fish main courses, and many starters too, above €20. Of course, nothing is mere housewifely potluck.

Chef has a fine reputation. Serge Canavesi's starters may feature a marriage of stuffed mussels with *foie gras* and even the compulsory *chèvre* salad with pine nuts is *flambéed* with a *marc* sourced from Languedoc *vignerons*; a *magret de canard* main course has essences of Italian *limoncello* and local honey, and in 2010, Chef announced that he was turning to the age of the Knights Templar and Cathars to create unique dishes using traditional mead. Book 48 hours in advance to sample the house speciality fish fondue, *le Caquelon* for €39 per person or perhaps order a special lobster main course. There is an air of exclusivity, the dining room holds but 20 people and the terrace just squeezes in a dozen more. Décor is the province of Madame Canavesi and is perfectly charming, managing to retain the feel of eating in someone's front room, rather than any old restaurant With the superb views over the lagoon, a couple of hours in this recognisably normal terraced cottage prove the perfect alternative to forcing your way through Narbonne's one-way system whilst the Sat-Nav throws a wobbly in the hunt for city centre dining. Just minutes out of town. Ideal.

## Balaruc Les Bains [5] C2

**Les Comptoirs du Sud** €
1 Av Pasteur, Promenade de l'Etang, 34540 Balaruc Les Bains
04 67 18 08 90
Closed Sun (E), Mon (E), Tue (E) Oct-April
Sharp, unfussy, clean and smart, the sort of place that would be packed with business lunchers in a city, here serves the holiday cure crowd at the tail of the promenade. Where some rival caterers woo the trencherman's gluttony, Erick Aranda prefers to pander to more mellow contemporary appetites. Besides the obvious, you may opt for a scallop and bacon crumble or steak tartare from set menus, or merely choose an uncomplicated salad. You could have a *plat du jour* midday meal at under a tenner or select one of 4 menus from €13-26. A recent innovation is the wine bar where you may sip, swirl and savour the *cépages* of Languedoc alongside a simple plate of oysters or a slab of *foie gras* with figgy chutney.

**La Guinguette à Fady**        €
impasse des Calanques, 34540 Balaruc Les Bains
04 67 48 01 37 Closed Mon (L)
In the days before satnav, it took three abortive attempts to find this place
on the "wrong" side of the peninsular outpost. We had blindly followed
signs to the restaurant lined plage coast facing Sète instead of making for
the hotels on the *cure* shore. The trick is to follow signs towards the **Ibis**
hotel and sneak through the car park in order to reach the impasse des
Calanques. You cannot actually see the restaurant from the road, as it is
down a steep slope by the water's edge. The main dining has rich North
African Mediterranean shades and crockery that you want to caress. An
ideal place to eat, but for the rival attraction of an annexed waterfront room
like a *bateau mouche*, seemingly moored on Balaruc's *rives* and offering
the best view of picturesque Bouzigues you'll ever find. This faux floating
space is lapped by the waters of the *étang*, and close by you'll see oysters
clasping exposed rocks, summertime fish jumping somersaults over
driftwood as resting seabirds bob on the water. In the mid-distance, *chaluts*
service oyster tables and winter horizons underscore wisps of smoke as
*vignerons* burn vinestock in fields behind the lagoon port villages. How I
love this place: a resort restaurant that trippers rarely find. The welcome is
lovely. Family business evolved since the days the couple first served
home-cooked *plat de jour* at Marseillan's **Relax Bar**. From the waterfront
**Chez Fady** in Mèze, the welcome now belongs to Balaruc and the
**Guinguette**. Fans drop in to take home speciality seafood dishes.

Imagine delicious s*ardines à l'escabèche* on your own terrace. The simply
scrummy *anchoïade* could be classed as a sin. Weekday lunch menus
ridiculously fine value for money. Even if you go for pricier grand platters
at any time, you'll not be short changed. Choose traditional *moules-frites* at
€10 a kilo or consider a bistro lunch deal, three courses for €13: selection of
seafood starters, brochettes, pasta or steak main course and a dessert. The
next menu (still under €20) has always been my favourite, especially for the
sensational salsa that accompanies a perfectly grilled tuna steak – prepared,
like all the fish here, over a real fire. Non fish eaters with a lighter appetite
may lunch for €8 on salad and chips, but you come to witness the lagoon
finest given an heroic send off. Seafood selections start with the usual
oysters, mussels and allied shellfish, and options rise (literally) to a
towering cascade of the coast's bounty, *boulots* to lobsters in a fountain of
ice, shells and salvers. My nephew Zak was mesmerised when garlands of
clams and claws rise ever higher from the tabletop as the skilled *patron*
prepared a buffet for a group still slurping soupe de poissons. As he said
later, imagine the Christmas tree chez *Fady*.

291

**Le Saint Clair**       €€

2 bis plan du Port, 34540 Balaruc-les-Bains

04 67 48 48 91

Named for a view, famed for the food, this is the more distinguished venue on the strip by the lagoon's bathing pool. *Etang* fare served with a cosmopolitan twist. Where other seafood platters are inevitably presented as salvers of glistening *glaçons* and nacre; here, shellfish have many guises, interpreted in sabayon, creams and *gratinée* as well as Botticellian tide-fresh purity. Should you veer away from the inevitable and look towards lamb and liver, the words *trio* and *mi-cuit* slip trippingly from the tongue of your waiter, and, whilst treating veal and charolais beef with due deference, chef Jean-Louis Martinod has talent for avoiding obvious combinations without losing himself in the confusion of fusion. Hence dill coming into play to enrich a mussel dish, fashionable *carpaccio* is swordfish and even flavours surrounding grand lobster on top-priced menus might feature a touch of pineapple. Dine on proper chairs in the main room or on upright padded recliners outside on a palm-fringed conservatory-styled terrace. *À la carte* woos from your wallet upwards of €80 euros before even a glance at the wine list, with its very comprehensive range from a locally selected €5 glass to pretty impressive *Bordeaux* and *Loires* to pay homage to *homard*, and some Languedoc *grand crus* of fine pedigree. Menus between €30-60, with a weekday lunch option hovering around the €20 level.

**La Vague Sous le Vent**       €€

Villa Saint Clair, 8 avenue de la Gare, 34540 Balaruc Les Bains

04 67 43 49 29

Balaruc-Les-Bains specialises in optimism. At the resort town of the Etang de Thau, albeit with tourism based firmly on hope, thanks to the healing qualities of its waters, trust in chance is tangible. Thus the unwary visitor plays culinary roulette dallying along the beach side of the *presqu'ile* eying menus and coveting damask-draped tables by the water as restaurant terraces evolve into fully glazed dining rooms above the sands. Along this stretch are to be had some good reliable dinners, holiday standard grills and stews and some *consommés* shunned, devoutly to be missed. So, when our seaside score was running at 2-2, we were indebted to *la famille* Diment in Marseillan urging us to walk just a few yards further along the front and check out this unpretentious dining room with its standard French holiday décor, big plate glass windows and just enough chintz to tickle the nostalgia gene without appearing too old-fashioned. Food matches the view, so prepare for platters of oysters, mussels, *encornets* and tentacles. Sunday family meats and soups satisfy France's traditional three-generation family bank-holiday lunchers. But look beyond the obvious and embrace

Languedoc's Catalan heritage with a *zarzuela* from the east, as a riposte to the westward *provençal bouillabaisse* fish stew –latin specialities, including Languedoc's *macaronade,* separate this place from its neighbours.

## Béziers          [5] B2                                210

**L'Ambassade**          €€€
22 Boulevard de Verdun, 34500 Béziers
04 67 76 06 24
Belatedly recognised by the star-givers of *Michelin*, this grand style restaurant opposite the railway station has enjoyed an Indian summer of late. As new, younger restaurateurs in the city were working their way through taller and taller *Gault et Milau* toques, the slumbering giant by the park gates finally awoke to contemporary tastes and its own heritage. Parvenus were hogging the critical limelight, as lighter eating glided into vogue (Fabien Levebre at **Octopus**, the **Petit Montmartre**, in its pre-Marseillanaise **Entre Ciel et Mer** incarnation, **Raffinerie** by the Canal, even the Pourcel twins launch of yet another **Compagnie des Comptoirs** behind the allees Riquet), and then the **Ambassade** emerged triumphant to show the world how a pillar of the establishment might conquer the 21$^{st}$ century. If décor is oddly understated, considering the quality of the food on offer, there is yet a fresh feel to the place; the right floristry, a genuine welcome, menus reflecting the pace of modern business and leisure, with sensibly priced alternatives to old-style marathon blow-outs. An awareness of today's market is impressive: we were pleasantly surprised when booking a table recently and finding chef happy to provide meatless alternatives for one guest. Time was, the word vegetarian would not have passed the lips of a chef keen to stay between the pages of a thick red book.

Chef Patrick Olry's shrewd move to publish videos of his trademark recipes on *YouTube* taps into a generation of media-savvy accessibility (you really should check out the deceptively simple quails eggs served in birds nests of sea urchins – if only to get an idea of why you'll never ever get round to preparing the dish at home). A well-pitched lunch menu scraping in under the €30 threshold brings in people who might otherwise be intimidated.

Entry-level dining may be simple when it comes to price, but does not hold back on the theatricality of menu-speak: Cop a load of a three-course meal that begins with chestnut and *cèpe* fondant, presented *"comme un bras de Venus, quelques sylvestres du moment en pickles, ris d'agneau en brochette grillés, déglacés d'un vinaigre de Xeres"*, and takes in wild duck in a

293

"turban" of quince, and alternatives ranging from sushi-influenced tuna and stuffed rabbit, and you'll realise that lunchtime guests on a budget are not being fobbed off. Even the "discovery" menu at €42 and top line meals at €48-60 are not the highest priced set dinners in town. However, should you choose to go for broke, a nine course banquet with every course invented around the finest truffles to set you back a cool €125.

**La Compagnie des Comptoirs**   €€
15 place Jean Jaurès, 34500 Béziers
04 67 36 33 63 www.lacompagniedescomptoirs.com
Closed Sun, Mon
A spacious sweep of modern brasserieness in the very centre of town, set back from the allées Riquet. Evening tapas option as an alternative to the regular menu. Part of the Pourcel chain. *See review* **Montpellier** *(page 312)*

**La Gargote**   €
Les Halles de Béziers, place Pierre Semard, 34500 Béziers
04 67 49 25 45
Closed Monday
Best of both worlds. For hotel guests, French food markets are exquisite torture. Sure, cheese, *paté* even salad and fruit from the market could furnish a beach picnic or terrace snack, but oh for that fresh fish and those plump perfect Mediterranean vegetables just waiting to be chopped and slipped into an olive-oiled pan. Now you may have your sea-bass and eat it, when you shop at **Les Halles**, the lipsmackingly good covered market, between *Madeleine* and *Mairie*. Browse stalls, choose your meat and fish and veg with practiced air of a local, then take it to **La Gargotte**, market bar and restaurant. There will be plenty of people drinking local wines or eating omelettes and steak from the menu here, but for €2-5, Hélène will cook your shopping *à la plancha* and you may eat your market fresh food right here right now. Pay for drinks and of course you cannot get away without a plate of delicious house *frites*! Market stalls open mornings only.

**Octopus**   €€€
12 rue Boïeldieu, 34500 Béziers
04 67 49 90 00 www.restaurant-octopus.com
Closed Sun, Mon and the last two weeks in August
When this place opened in 2005, it was so cutting edge as to be practically serrated. Dining in Béziers was either a *bourgeois* backstreet bistro affair for expense accountees or tourist traps on the *allées*. The grandest dining room opposite the station (*see page 293)* had yet to be *macaronned* by the *Michelin* man, and the city was ripe for a gastroblast. So the unlocking of this unassuming (from the street) door off the wrong side of the main drag

was a timely ping on the braces of a new generation. Word of mouth did the trick, as classier *vignerons* tipped off their more discerning punters about the better address for sampling their wines *en ville*. It was just such a third-generation whisper that first brought us to the table, where a platter of seven incarnations of tuna, in mini-mouthful portions, alerted us to seemingly infinite talent. Of course the locale is smart: what I tend to think of as "best-behaviour informality". From contemporary, sometimes stark, re-consideration of the concept *bistrot* (with a T) to dining rooms opening to a summer terrace, plates are not to be eclipsed by fluffy personalised décor.

Set menu dining begins at €29 for midday three courses, glass of wine and coffee. You could even ditch either starter or dessert and pay a mere €21. In the evenings, however, things get a little more serious with the €52 or €72 options for 6-8 dishes. And, whilst no plate is ever dauntingly overcrowded, every course conceived by Fabien Levebvre is a twist away from the obvious. So instead of the predictable carpaccios that have crept onto almost every menu within 100 miles of the Med, you could find yourself exploring fine leaves of marinated sea-bass, then experience pigeon with a *Rouennais* twist to the sauce. Discover fine independent flavours, from bergamot to cherry and aniseedy fennel, in dishes where you might never have expected to find them. You might even decide to round off the evening with a pear and liquorice *soufflé*. The wine list is excellent.

**Au Soleil,** *par Accent d'Oc*　€
1 place de la Madeleine, 34500  Béziers
04 67 28 54 26
Tue-Sat 09.30-19.30
Having stocked up on fresh food at the market along the road, this is a nice place for flavour-hounds to pause a while. Part café-tea-room, part *épicerie* and part bookshop. It's the bookshop bit that lures me in. Here you treat yourself to a nice new recipe book then take your purchase to a table on the sunny square and eat light for around €10 as you fantasise on what you will do with those fresh veg and cheeses in your shopping basket. Whilst here, don't forget to stock up on jars of *tapenades*, lemony *confiture d'olive*, and seasoned oils with those distinctive *Accent d'Oc* strip labels.

**La Table Bretonne**　€
21 rue Viennet, 34500 Béziers
04 67 49 00 66 Closed Dec, Jan
A little treat by the cathedral. Cottagey rooms and real Breton cider served in proper bowls to accompany sweet or savoury, but ever authentic, *crêpes*. Perfect light bite when the next meal is to be a gastro-blow-out. Set menus under €10, reliable salads, or drop in for a cider and snack.

# Bouzigues [5] C2

## La Côte Bleue €€

avenue Louis Tudesq, 34140 Bouzigues
04 67 78 30 87
Closed Wed (Oct-Apr)
The modern motel belies the history of the **Côte Bleue**, founded within a generation of the beginning of the oyster farms in the etang. Mason, Monsieur Louis Tudesq is credited with applying that dash of cement to the strings holding the oysters to their beds, and it was he who built the first **Côte Bleue** tasting room by the lagoon in 1925, forerunner to today's popular restaurant. Half a century ago, the Tudesqs sold the restaurant on to the Archimbeau family, who built up the commercial oyster farm and hotel alongside the *"dégustation"* as seafood bars were known. Take grand platters as read, but find home-smoked salmon and an artichoke *fricassée* as well as *escargots de mer* and other anticipated starters, and look out for seabass and turbot, fresh from the fish market at Sète amongst *à la carte* specials. Budget €20-45, but be prepared to shell out more if running amok amongst the nobler fish and more prestigious crustaceans.

## Chez Julie €€

8 Avenue Louis Tudesq, 34140 Bouzigues
04 67 78 47 57
Closed Thu, Sun (E), Wed (E off season)
Consistently reliable and welcoming, a scion of an established family business that had been farming, fishing and servicing the fresh stuff for years before fashionable newspapers and TV chefs discovered Bouzigues. Following in wake of her mother Francine, Julie herself holds court on the waterfront desk and dining room at this key corner site, whilst her menfolk prepare fruits of the sea from a smart shack by the terrace tables. Our first visit saw the couple at the next table working their way through an ocean-sized *parillada* of fresh fish from sardines to sea-monsters, whilst we contented ourselves with dithering between the menus, as a friend decided to concentrate on tapas style snacking. Ubiquitous iced trays of oysters, clams and sundry clawed cousins are core provendor, but stews, linguini, stuffed and baked mussels, *bourrides* and *macaronades* bring a chef's twist to the Bouzigues bounty. Around our table, *soupe des poissons* was pronounced full flavoured and excellent with no salty aftertaste, *boulots* with *aïoli* caused lips to smack and *piquolos* stuffed with *brandade de morue* proved clean and refreshing. Good grilled fish *à la plancha* for main courses. Setting is comfortable, wooden walls hung with contemporary taurine tableaux in the main dining area, a sidestep from more predictable

*planches* of a terrace bathed in year-round silver noonday sunshine. The place is usually busy, but you are not likely to be hustled from the table at the end of the meal. Marrying speedy delivery to unhurried conviviality, service ranges from lovely to genially entertaining – no wonder regulars are so fiercely loyal to the place. You never feel less than a welcome guest.

**La Palourdière**      €€
BP17, 34140 Bouzigues
*(First right turn from the main D613 (N113) Mèze-Montpellier road and keep on driving)*
04 67 43 80 19
Closed Mon
Established classic Bouzigue experience, amongst a fine clutch of similar establishments strung along the *hautes côtes* de Bouzigues, this scores over rivals with a range of alternative options for that inevitable family member with personal reasons of squeamishness, allergy or religious conviction for avoiding the relentless cascade of shellfish. Red mullet, salmon or swordfish entrées, even a *bruschetta* style toast with anchovy and garlic, and standard fish main courses including sole *meunière*. The signature dish is a *civet* of monkfish. But, apart from *that* hallmark view of the lagoon, the *raison d'etre* is the seafood, with a noted wild mushroom flavoured gratin of scallops. The set menu is either unrelenting shellfish, be it *moules marinières*, oysters, stuffed shells or any combination thereof, or those same shells followed by a grilled bass, and rounded off with an *ile flottante*. The place has a true beach bar feel and in fine weather, the rush is for a wicker chairs around a table on the terrace, overlooking the oyster beds. The **Palourdière** has a night-spot, the **Caraibar:** a cocktail rendezvous with parasols, palms and even a hot tub for knocking back tropical cocktails with a chilled musical backtrack. In key summer months, jazz, rock and blues musicians take over the piano bar for theme nights. 04 67 43 80 19

**A La Voile Blanche**    €€
1 avenue Louis Tudesc, 34140 Bouzigues
Tél: 04 67 78 35 77 www.alavoileblanche.com
Smart trendy mod-Med alternative to more traditional bouzigueries, the ground floor of the hotel of the same name, serves an updated take on the local specials. Oysters as standard of course, but gambas are *flambéed* with whisky and there is a ginger *magret de canard* to consider. Noted by all the main French guides and featured in many mags and colour supplements.

Out of season, the tables still bear cold platters, even when Cédric Caltié's kitchen is closed. Just along from **Julie**, with the same drop-dead-gorgeous view of the Etang. Lunches from €15, menus under €20 and *à la carte* double the number you first thought of.

# Carcassonne    [5] A2

## La Barbacane    €€€
Hotel de la Cité, place Auguste-Pierre Pont, 11000 Carcassonne
0 4 68 71 98 71
Closed Tue, Wed, and Nov-Mar
*Michelin*-starred and accordingly priced, the ultimate dining room in the old fortified **Cité** itself serves very fine cuisine and several Languedoc specialities. Menus €65-€115. It has been several years since I dined here, the experience was memorable – but then was staying at the hotel for a full weekend and had time to appreciate the entire experience. When I next get the chance to visit, I'll report back on how the place has stood the test of time. Reviews remain favourable. Other dining rooms in this hotel do not offer the same style menu.

## Château de Cavanac    €€€
11570 Cavanac
04 68 79 61 04
A taste for heady heavy cuisine of the south west (roasts, stews, *patés* and the like) demands a setting worthy of a red wine label. Ticking all boxes for those who head towards *cassoulet* via *terrines* and *escargots* and continue *vers* home-made *patisserie* by way of fine cheeses, this château, five miles south of the city, is an *auberge* with traditional dining room, centred around a vast fireplace for cooking over an open flame. The €42 *cart- menu* features all of the above, topped and tailed by *kir* and *infusions*, with wine from the estate. Those with more contemporary appetites may negotiate the menu and forego the sucking pig, fatted duck and the like in favour of home smoked salmon and a grilled *poisson du jour.*

## Le Donjon    €€
4 rue du Porte d'Aude 11000 Carcassonne
Closed Sun (Nov-Feb)
If you are not in the market for high-end, top-budget gastronomy on what is probably a very touristy day out, and you simply could not face the trek from the mediaeval walled city to the "new" town where real locals like to eat, then make your way to midday sanctuary. Within most budgets and safe from the tourist-grabbing hustlers that emerge in high season; here, the kindly and cheerful waiting staff will recommend a reliable *cassoulet*, steak or white-fish-and-steamed-potato lunch to refuel the day trip with various menus at €15-27.

**Le Languedoc**   €€
2 allée Iéna, 11000 Carcassonne
04 68 25 22 17
Closed Sun (E), Mon
If you like to wallow in a *cassoulet au confit de canard*, then you require a room that looks as old as the recipe. Fortunately, the dining room here has a reassuring antique and brickwork quotient. The rest of the menu is suitably classical, flambéed *crêpes* are retro enough to take you back to the 'sixties and 'seventies in any case. There is a lovely patio for dining outdoors and, should you plan to indulge on heady red wine with your meal, you might consider booking a room at the **Hotel Montségur** across the way, owned and run by the chef and his wife. Menus €17-25. Go rogue on the carte when game is in season and pay much more.

## Clermont l'Hérault   [5] C1

**La Source**
*(see Villeneuvette – page 335)* Just 2 minutes drive out of town,.

**Le Terminus**   €
11 allée Roger Salengro 34800 Clermont l'Hérault
04 67 88 45 00
Sometimes we eat so well down south, with so many new and interesting young chefs flaunting their skill in making perfect little round stacks of interesting foods, be-sprigged and be-drizzled enough to pose for a Conran coffee table book, that we forget the delights of turning up at the local *auberge* in a country town and opting for reliable over sparkle. Go on, admit it: surely you remember when the fish course meant trout with almonds rather than a trio of something deep-sea "in all its states". The €14 basic meal deal at the Terminus has just such a dish on the *formule*, wedged safely between the mussels or *vol au vent* and the ice cream; even if the choice also includes a taco salad. *Menu Terroir* is equally packed with comfort foods, albeit stoutly Languedocien: here, *farandole* of mullet and gambas is coastal homage, whilst the *Gardianne de Taureau* is a true *Camarguaise* taste of a land where bullfighting is still part of the culture.

The hotel is to be found alongside the town's playhouse on tree-lined *allées* between the start of the Wednesday market and the massive parking area still marked on maps as Gare SNCF, although the last train left more than a generation ago. There is a terrace for eating outside and being serenaded by summertime buskers. The dining room inside is usually packed, especially on market day, where good hungry lunchers with a palate to appreciate classic dishes (yup, frogs legs still served here) sit alongside regulars whose lifelong devotion to the grape may well have shot their taste-buds to smithereens. As my mother and I slid dill-infused grilled trout off its frame, and my father bared his sole and the couple at the next table smacked lips after each mouthful of a *magret de canard* with country honey, we looked in numb amazement as a weather-worn old timer carefully emptied an entire salt cellar over his chunk of red meat. First and only time in my life I have seen beef served as a side order to a main course of cruet *à volonté*.

Fortunately, no one else in the restaurant felt obliged to follow his example. Reliable ingredients prepared in the tried and tested manner, served us well enough for comfort lunching.

**Le Tournesol**     €
2 Rue Roger Salengro, 34800 Clermont-l'Hérault
04 67 96 99 22 www.letournesol.fr
Closed Sun (E), Mon Oct-April
Bright and cheerful restaurant opposite a shady promenade. Ever popular with visitors, yet retaining a loyal local mainstay from around the region. Up a flight of steps from street level, a main veranda-style room gets packed on Wednesday lunchtime, and another decked dining area looks out over a swimming pool, pleasant on a balmy summer's evening when winds rustle the palm trees. From outside; garish menus might misdirect passing trade towards assumption of cafeteria standards. But the faithful know better. Grilled fish is popular, but both meat and poultry dishes show certain inventiveness. Lamb in a balsamic and peanut setting has that flash of originality that keeps Tournesol in the filofaxes of the over fifties year after year. Four menu options, neatly spread from €14-29 and *à la carte* works out at €30 or so. Service always friendly and efficient, pulling off the essential double: prompt plates with no hint of hustle. A definite hum in the air, of contented conversation syncopated with the gentle tintinnabulation of cutlery on well cleared plates and clink-tinkle toasting in ice-chill rose.

## Collioure     [5] B4

**Hotel des Templiers**     €€
12 Quai de l'Amirauté, 66190 Collioure
04 68 98 31 10  www.hotel-templiers.com closed Jan, Nov
There are a handful of restaurants in France one visits almost as national monuments – and I don't mean such *gastrophares* as the *Tour d'Argent*: But *Maxims* in Paris is forever *The Merry Widow*; In Auvers sur Oise, *Auberge Ravoux* preserves Van Gogh's bedroom just as you remember it from the photographs; *Mère Poulard* on Mont St Michel serves omelettes

whisked in coppers; So in Collioure, you simply must step across the threshold of the **Hotel des Templiers** (*see page ??*). As a pretty basic hotel, it flourishes to this day, some rooms in annexe buildings past the quayside. But pilgrims come for the art. 2000 or more paintings and drawings smothering walls of restaurant, bar and hotel: testament to a past identity as staff canteen of Matisse and his chums and many generations to follow. The visitors' book has sketches, notes and signatures of everyone from Cocteau to Duffy, all devoted friends of the original husband and wife team of René and Pauline Pous. The restaurant has stayed in the family ever since and Pauline's recipes are still featured on the daily menu, her *bouillabaisse* a particular favourite with Pablo Picasso on his regular visits in the 1950s.

Unlike the other mere shrines to great artists, here the food alone is reason enough to stay for lunch. Inevitable anchovy and red pepper starter (it is an infringement of the Napoleonic code to visit Collioure and spurn the local *anchoises*) lip-smackingly good; fish main courses cooked with worldly wisdom. A Catalan dish of shoulder of lamb with a spiced onion *confit* is almost as legendary as the guest book and, in a town with multicoloured ice-cream parlours every few yards, the house *glace* of fennel and gingerbread with saffron is unforgettable. Seats in the covered terrace by the quay are ideal, Mr Pous *fils* himself held court there on our first visit, but in peak summer it can be pretty noisy when the tourist tide swells past. Inside, all is a little calmer, and do take time to admire the carved bar resembling a wooden sailing boat. Menus from €21

## Corbières  (*see also* **Bages**)  [5] B3

**La Bergerie**  €€
Domaine de Lastours, 11490 Portel des Corbières
04 68 48 64 77
Closed Sun (E), Mon, Tue, Oct-Jun
The restaurant knows its market – and it is not passing trade. Hidden in the middle of the Corbières vineyards, **Domaine de Château Lastours** is more than a winery; it is a dream destination for petrolheads: hosting Paris-Dakkar drivers, and boasting an off-road activity course. No laddishness *à table,* however: Chef Philippe Springer served time in better kitchens of Paris, the UK and South Africa. Though the multi-arched dining room feels like a hospitality suite, tables are set apart enough for whispering, service thoroughly professional and food clean, contemporary and entertaining. The usual suspects turn up in unexpected disguises: perhaps spring rolls packed with frogs' legs given an Andalusian *gazpaccho* twist, or with an edgy citric duck breast. The signature starter is an *escargot*-stuffed tomato! Main

courses of inevitable *loup* and *rouget*, with perhaps a wild lavender *crème brulée* to round off a good meal. Lunches from €25 and dinner €50. Wines are from *Lastours* own cellars. How better to learn the flavours of Corbières, than around one of the region's more celebrated tables.

**Au Vieux Tonneaux**   €€
3 Place de la Mairie, 11440 Peyriac de Mer
04 68 41 49 42
We mourned the passing of the **Café du Centre,** where (beyond the *salines* from **Bages**) a workman's version of the *bourride d'anguilles* or perhaps a *cassoulet* was part of an €11 lunch. Now it's a trendy wine bar; salad and garnish fully balsamic, defying the flavours of garigue. Still, good bar for sampling Corbières, every decent bottle produced in this village on offer here. An ideal option for independent tasting before visiting *caves*. The drive from breathtakingly beautiful Bages, through glorious wetland nature reserve is life affirming, rambles amazing and the village welcome heartwarming. Last time, we sat under plane trees, watching senior citizens waltzing to accordeons between *mairie* and *église*, children on trikes weaving between th nimble feet of their grandparents as *maman* and *papa* broke bread on the terrace. For €6: Roquefort, melon and glass of Banyuls.

## Florac   *(see pages 358-9)*

**Chez les Paysans**   €
2 rue Théophile Roussel, 48400 Florac
04 66 31 22 07
Lunchtime treat, although open evenings too. The **Maison des Paysans** is a co-operative grocery selling jars, bottles and packages from farms across the Cevennes. Delicious fruit juices, true kitchen-table pates, preserved fruits and intriguing condiments. Our shopping basket yielded honeys and a terrine flavoured with juniper berries. Next to the shop is the restaurant, where you may eat much the same food, sourced from farmers the chef will know by name. Eat inside or sit out underneath a fruit-laden vine. The clientele as eclectic as the menu, with market gardeners, housewives, artists and politicians breaking bread together. Easy wheelchair access.

**La Lozèrette**   €€
48400 Cocurès
04 66 45 06 04 www.lalozerette.com
A short drive from Florac, Pierrette Agulhon has put her personal stamp on her family's *Logis* hotel-restaurant, in the fresh finesses one finds in the décor with each new visit. Most of all, her personality shines through in the dining room. An appreciation of good wine is reflected in a delightful list.

Don't be afraid to ask her advice; she tactfully suggested a *Château Puech-Haut* to accompany a main course of veal with *girolles* mushrooms, rather than our original, more cautious, selection; words of wisdom that helped turn an evening into an occasion. A selection of menus from under €20 to nearly €50, and some pretty gastronomic experiences in the 30's. Mark of a good chef is in simplicity, and when I choose *Grand-Mère* Julie's *panade de morue dorée* over more obvious delights of trout, mackerel or an orange and raspberry *magret de canard*; what in less skilled hands would have been little more than a fishcake, proved a positive seduction of flavours and texture in the lightest creamy garlic sauce. Willpower loses its appeal when the cheese board arrives at the next table. That Roquefort, oh gosh, wow. Even the delicious *sablé breton et chiboust citron-fraise* that followed could never erase the memory of a cheese to make your veins quiver.

## Florensac |5| C2 323

**Le Bistrot d'Alex** €€
Vinipolis, 5 avenue des Vendanges, 34510 Florensac
04 67 77 03 05
Open Tue-Sun (L), Sat (E)
I would have loved to have been sitting at the table when someone first came up with the idea: you have a modest village co-operative winery, where most local farmers pool their grapes each September, and you need to find a way to sell more wine to passing visitors. It must have been around the third or fourth bottle of *Côtes du Thau* that the idea of a state-of-the-art visitor centre came up for discussion, and certainly well past the *vendange tardive* when the name of chef Alexandre Fabre was suggested to the farmers and councillors. Fabre used to work his magic in the *Michelin* starred kitchen of now defunct local restaurant **Léonce**, which for many years was the principal reason people drove inland to Florensac and paid €75 euros for a memorable meal. Now, for under €20, the bistro menu brings the Fabre talent to lunchers and wine-lovers as part of an audacious and succesful makeover that turned the *Cave Co-operative des Vignerons de Florensac* into the stylish wine-lovers destination **Vinipolis**.

The classy modern wine tasting room/showroom is the sort of affair you associate with Bordeaux or Champagne, modern terminals and counters, interactive virtual wine tours explaining *cépages* and production, well-run tasting sessions for casual visitors, each day focusing on a specific grower, grape or theme. But, beyond glass floors looking down on oak barrels below your feet, the USP of **Vinipolis** is the **Bistrot**. Instead of sipping, swirling and spitting in a tasting room before settling on a bottle or three of *Picpoul* or *Chardonnay*, here you taste wine in its natural habitat; alongside good local dishes, cooked to perfection. With menus from around €16, wines are sold in the restaurant at trade counter price, so you may very easily get away with paying €5-6 for the bottle with your meal. You might even go for wine by the glass at €2, should you prefer. Once you've victimised your designated driver, there is nothing to stop you ordering a couple of wines with each course for less than the cost of having just one bottle in a "normal" restaurant, tasting the range on offer in the winery: from a lip pinching summer *Sauvignon* to a surprisingly deep and meaningful *Merlot*. The grilled fish *à la plancha* and obligatory oysters, would be the simplest way to discover the qualities of the *terroir*. Yet, some skilful ways with good cuts of impeccably sourced *Aveyron* meat and fowl and the lightest touch with risotto and seasonal veg are equally well worth the drive. Menu is limited, fresh and changes with the market and the tide, and the place gets booked up way in advance, so either turn up in optimism at the crack of noon or be sensible and book a table. Make sure you've room in the back of the car, as you'll want to leave with cases of the local wine. From €3-10 per bottle. Open lunch, occasional evenings.

**La Noria**  €
14 avenue de la Gardie, 34510 Florensac
04 67 77 05 28
If you have ever shared a Sunday with a large extended French family, then you will recognise La Noria. The only outsiders introduced by locals or cousins It took us 10 years to find it; once chums from England had been inducted by their own pals from Pomérols . More a country *salle des fêtes* than a restaurant; a place where grown-up cousins catch up after a confirmation or silver wedding, whilst kids play under shady pines mid-way through five courses. Up a country lane by playing fields to a private *parc*, take a table in the back room open to perfect weather. Djamilia and Thierry's food and welcome unpretentious and resolutely down to earth. Menus of honest old-fashioned meals as pushed by French grandmothers: *soupe de poisson*, *moules* and *encornet farcis*, grilled meat and fish, and a slice of *tarte* after bread and cheese. Four courses at €13 or five for €20. Nowt *nouvelle* about *cuisine*: dinner with friends. Choose bottled wine.

## Mèze  [5] C2

**La Marmitière**  €€
38 rue du port, 34140 Mèze
04 67 43 84 99 www.lamarmitiere.fr
July-Aug: Closed L (ex Sat, Tue) ; Sep-Jun: Closed Sun (E), Mon, Tue (L)
The serious dining room of Mèze is the one without the view. A few yards away from the waterfront, step up to a vaulted 12th century dining room

with stone walls, stained glass and eclectic art. The welcome is professional and genuine, with discretion to set it apart from seaside bonhomie, but never veering towards starchy. Menus reflect the passions of chef Corinne Lefort who manages to imbue a Languedoc *carte* with influences from a lifetime of travels, without falling irrevocably into the over-fashionable trap of fusion for fusion's sake.

My Mèze outings tend to be out of season, so I am more familiar with Mme Lefort's off-peak menu. Winter warmers ranged from *pot au feu* of cod in locally brewed beer to old fashioned, but too often neglected, *sole meunière*. Pan-fried *foie gras* with scallops seduced with a splash or few of Marseillan's unique *Noilly Ambré*, but you may opt for gambas, flambéed with the same exotic cactus liqueur that won Marseillan footballer, rock star and amateur chef Rodolphe Frasson his round of *Un Diner Presque Parfait* (French TV's version of *Come Dine With Me*) though *chez* Rodolphe it was served with ostrich). The hallmark is a flair for the different. Usually pretty successful, although a Christmas Day tropical fish dish on our first visit, some winters back, might have been a side-step too far for me, sitting a net's throw from a perfectly fine local catch.

To be fair, the region has a strong influence on the menu, with honey, beer and cheese sourced within walking distance, as well as *de rigeur* seafood and wines of Languedoc. Set menus between €19.50 and €46.50, although a "surprise" three-course deal is offered for under €20 every weekday Lunchtimes bring the option of fish or meat dish of the day plus glass of wine at around €14, with the option of adding a starter or dessert at just €3.50. There is a small but considered wine list; a nice touch is the alternative to the half-bottle option. Order the full bottle, drink what you will, then take the rest home with you to enjoy with another meal *chez vous*.

**Res'Thau**       €€
28 quai Augustin Descournut, 34140 Mèze
0467512071 www.resthau.com
Closed Mon, Tue and winter school holidays, first week Jul and L Jul-Aug.
French restaurateurs suffer from the same addiction to punning that afflicts British hairdressers, so best pretend you have not noticed the name and concentrate on the menu. At the far end of the port, holiday bistro style, hanging baskets and geranium pots surround tables cloaked in Roussillon summer fruits colours. The menu declares that the establishment, like its neighbours, specialises in fish and seafood. A local couple at the next table might whisper that the place is better known for earthier fare. *Torndedos Rossini* and stuffed guinea fowl have a loyal fan base. Pascal Edewelt established his waterfront dining room after an early career learning classics

of Parisian cuisine: Good traditional sauces, bistro and brasserie sausages and stews studied in kitchens of *Les Grands Boulevards*. Where others serve the *étang's* sweet soles lightly grilled with herbs; here, classic white wine and mushroom sauce will dress the dish, and Madeira may still hold its own against the Languedoc lobbying of *Muscat de Frontignan* or *Banyuls*.Nonetheless, sea still has pride of place, signature seabass flattered by sharp tang of fennel and a *mousseline* of *Noilly Pratted rascasse* a speciality. Leave room for dessert. If you love northern tradition of chicory in sweets, order pear *feuilleté à la crème de chicorée*. Menus €27 and €31.

**Le Sanboulou €**
22 Quai Augustin Descournut, 34140 Mèze
04 67 43 89 20
When you drive to Mèze having forgotten that the **Res'Thau** is closed at summer lunchtimes, you could do a lot worse than settle for a terrace table a few yards away and opt for simple tapas style nibbling instead. Cheery staff, good basic deli-style cold dishes (oysters, grilled peppers, anchovies, tuna *rillettes* etc) and unpretentious hot options (*acras de morue, brandade, calamari* perhaps) to choose from without breaking the bank. We've munched to contentment several times on a simple €13 menu.

**Les Saveurs de Thau €**
quai Baptiste Guitard, 34140 Mèze
04 67 43 53 73  www.lessaveursdethau.com
Closed Mon (L), Thu (L)
Blue and yellow linens on simple garden chairs on a quayside terrace, traditional maritime décor in a freshly cleaned dining room and friendly and efficient service whatever the season. Well presented, sensibly priced and pretty tasty, Philippe offers reliable fish and seafood standards, albeit rather salmony a menu for the Med, with a few house favourites that have won the place a deservedly loyal clientele. The *bourride* of monkfish is a speciality and the gambas and *St Jacques* may be flambéed from either end of the *étang* – be it our own *Noilly* to the south or *Muscat* from the northern reaches. Surprising emphasis towards meat on an otherwise piscatorial port menu. Not merely pork and duck. You are unlikely to find Rossini of kangaroo with home-produced duck *foie gras* in granny's scrapbook of Languedoc recipes. Menus between €12 and €35, but you may lunch here from as little at €8 – 10 on dishes of the day. We've often come here after a Sunday morning mooch around the market, had a happy hour or so around the table with friends, then walked off the meal round the corner at the delightful little beach. Good spot for boat watching, as pleasure craft and working boats pass by the tables, and the yacht club is just along the road.

# Montpellier [5] C2

First stop for most visitors, **Place de la Comédie**, with tables running from the esplanade to the theatre steps. Plenty of cafés and swift-food joints; good to break up the day. However, if you head to the back streets, you will find more interesting restaurants. Halfway up **rue de la Loge** is place **Jean-Jaurès** an almost Parisian square of bistros and snackeries, menus on blackboards perched on chairs and the buzz of a latin quarter. Brunchers and lunchers, serenaded by itinerant accordions and served by hard-working good-natured waiters. Be warned though: amongst the gems are tourist traps: a recent bank holiday brunch on a trendy terrace produced tired and shabby salads, microwaved *aligot* on chipped crockery and truly dreary meats, fish and cheese. Watch where locals sit and spot diners who never glance at a menu but order the "usual"; for that's where you should be. Threshold of **Ecusson** historic quarter, where narrow streets spread from *arc de triomphe* to the *Esplanade* and *Musée Fabre*. Find tiny *restos* with pocket handkerchief patios where locals dine at **rue des Teissiers, place de la Chapelle Neuve** and **place Candolle**. Discover elegant options on wider streets and open spaces. Since **Jardin de Sens** first hit the serious gastronomic map, plenty of young and talented chefs have emerged to be taken seriously; their establishments worth a detour. Try new **Antigone** and **Port Marianne** quarters. Lots of trendy addresses already by the river Lez, and, with the opening of a new city hall by the waterside, good food on the tram route between the centre and **Odysseum** district is sure to be the next big thing. In summer – don't forget **Grand Travers** beaches *(see page 78)*.

**De l'Art ou du Cochon**      €€                          Port Marianne
55 avenue Marie de Montpellier, 34000 Montpellier
04 67 68 51 27
Open lunchtimes Tue- Fri, evenings Thu-Sat only.
I guess this smart modern establishment by the **Port Marianne** district and the new grand *Hotel de Ville* qualifies as a wine bar. The term used by the inner circle is *bistronomie*. Essentially a cluster of tables in the glass fronted mezzanine of a chic and sleek wine shop (*V-Point*), on the tram route midway between the touristy city centre and the new **Odysseum** shopping mall. €32 for the main menu. Wines are offered at the shop price (plus €10 service charge), so a good way to taste a bottle's meal potential before committing to buying a case. Menus are conceived to go well with the rich red wines on offer. No lift to the dining area, so staircase users only. However a charcuterie and nibbles based tapas wine bar menu is served downstairs in the restaurant, with a *plat du jour* option for €13 (or €16 including wine and coffee).

**L'Atelier de Valérie** €€ Comédie / Gare St Roch
8 rue Durand, 34000 Montpellier
04 67 58 15 22 www.atelier-valerie.com
Open selected L Mon-Wed, 12.30 by appointment only
Not strictly a restaurant, but what an experience! For just €22, spend 45 minutes in the kitchen with an experienced chef, have a one-course cookery class and so prepare your own lunch. Aprons, ingredients, chopping board and knives supplied. Valérie Sabatino hails from Sète, where an Italian Mama inspired a lifelong love of cooking. After many years travelling and working as a chef (most recently at **Le Pastis** restaurant in Montpellier), Valérie now runs her cookery school in the heart of the city.

If you can't spare time for a full day or week's course, then this special *Chef Minute* one-dish lunchtime event is ideal. The week's menus are published in advance on-line, so choose a dish you fancy cooking and book your place. Knives out at 12.30, plates ready by 1.15. The sweet toothed may spend €29 on an afternoon hour with Valérie cooking two desserts at 3pm, then tucking in at 4. Saturday afternoons offer a €39 session, preparing two courses to take away and enjoy at home later. Oh, and since the chef understands English, those who may be a little nervous about kitchen linguistics need not fret.

**Les Bains de Montpellier** €€ Comédie
6 Rue Richelieu, 34000 Montpellier
04 67 60 70 87
Closed Sun
Location is everything, and we had just been mourning the passing of an old favourite luncherie in rue de la Loge: a delightful little arcade courtyard conservatory where perfect salads and *plats du jour* were offered up with sheer joy. My parents have never forgotten their first visit, where the young waiter, all bright shining Caravaggio eyes, presented the main courses with the description, "served in a *jus*, wiz cowiandurgh, wosemawie and most of all … wiz lurve" before executing a perfect Playboy bunny dip to sway the plates onto the table then trotting off with the energy of a *corps de ballet* claiming a winning lottery ticket. There is little to match such entertaining upstaging of a pleasant meal, but we had just discovered the *salon du thé (et déjeuner)* was under new management and new identity as a snacktide caff. Where else were we to find such theatre so close to the **Comédie**.

The answer was behind the opera building itself, tucked away between the rue Richelieu and the rue des Estuves. A stunning setting, the gorgeous public bathhouse built in 1770, which had kept the citizens of Montpellier scrubbed, soaped and fragrant until the 1950s, had been rescued from 40 years of oblivion by the talented Guy Falco, designer of much of Marseillan's quayside, as a gastro-venue par excellence: A glorious celebration of the building's original architecture, a buzzing and lively *rendezvous* and a delightful haven just yards from the touristy centre of town.

The building itself is one of those remarkable secular cloisters that France does so well, discreet dining rooms ranged around a central patio, planted with tall palm trees and decked with tables by a refreshing water feature. The *serre*, conservatory, glass that embraces the open space creates the feel of outdoor dining even in midwinter, and witty and studied use of original brick and stone, parquet and tiling, with sympathetic panelling, brass-work and allied deco touches add to a sense of occasion. Intriguing and rather grand doors lead to intimate dining spaces with a modest cluster of tables, imaginative conversions of individual bathrooms. Contemporary furnishings and fabrics serve to highlight more vintage features. An interesting mix of diners, from sueded, lower-middle-aged jazz-club types to sharper business-bods in suits with smartphones on vibrate. Indubitably creative characters from the opera house, well-heeled shoe-shoppers from around the corner and clusters and pairings of old friends keep sound levels at a lively hum without becoming oppressive. Fast moving, experienced and welcoming waiters and bussing staff circulate efficiently, and plates just keep on arriving.

Food is reliably Mediterranean, with the classic know-how to keep fashion at bay, presented well enough to please a design-conscious clientele. Not ground-breaking stuff and certainly nothing to upstage the décor, but satisfying, enjoyable fare justifies the prices. Fish and seafood are of course pretty high profile, but *terre* or *mer,* each is treated well, served generously and flavours never let your tongue feel short-changed. Evening set meal €28, *à la carte* quite a bit more. A truly good value lunch option for €20, so do try to allow yourself enough time to enjoy the meal. I had a meeting scgheduled immediately after our most recent trip and so managed but one course. As other plates made their olfactorily teasing way past my table, I sensed what might have been. Musical events in the wine-champagne bar; jazz on Wednesdays.

Since there are steps from the main entrance, disabled guests should ring the bell at the back door in rue des Estuves – although, as the door is so very close to the kitchen and the bell is not always heard during service, I suggest phoning the restaurant and let them know once you've arrived.

**Brasserie du Corum**  €€    Corum

Esplanade Charles de Gaulle, 34000 Montpellier

04 67 02 03 04

Closed all day Sun and Mon-Thu (E). Open on all concert nights
No canteen; this very modern brasserie at the conference centre cum
concert hall at the far end of the esplanade. Frédéric Husser's good food is
always presented as though in danger of an imminent colour supplement
photo-shoot. Expect very tall and perky portions of the main attraction, a
branch or two from a herb bush at a jaunty angle and little round towers of
veg in disguise. Just far enough from the Comédie to deter casual trade,
most hungry culture seekers will have peeled off into the Pourcel's outlet
by the museum before getting this far. Finding your way in could be a
problem, should the outdoor lift from the top of the gardens down to the
bottom of the tramway steps be out of order; still, you may always make
your way to the brasserie by using the **Corum** building itself and
negotiating a route from inside. You'll be met by sharp service and a
varied, changing menu, and find a table with a view over the cascade of
greenery. Once settled in, prepare for wow-factor fish, classic barnyard too
and some rather good fruity and chocolatey desserts (try the sticky
strawberry macaroon for yumminess). The off-beat option on the menu is
always worth exploring: a saffron-infused risotto given a shakedown with
the sweet and lip-pursing addition of beetroot will not easily be nudged
from the memory bank. You won't find many other conference hall
restaurants that are consistently this busy, even when there is nothing else
happening in the building. Certainly worth booking a table if you've a
concert planned. Pay €30 for three courses, €25 for two, or try the snack
menus at around €15 if you are in a hurry. Oh and you can enjoy a good
selection of wines by the glass

**La Brasserie du Théâtre**  €€    Comédie

22 Boulevard Victor Hugo, 34000 Montpellier

04 67 58 88 80

This remains very much the stage door canteen for the opera-house across
the way. My first proper meal in Montpellier many years ago was reliable
old fashioned brasserie fare of steamed potatoes, fresh and flaky white fish
and dependable steaks, all served with vegetables in that perfect state
between crunch and springiness. It may be a bit of a time warp, but glass
and brass are always polished to the max, the service swift and professional
and the clientele that same mix of *blasé* working lunchers and bewildered
tourists of every French provincial brasserie – only with the extra thrill of
musicians and performers from theatre. Pay €18-27 with menus or budget
around €30 *à la carte*.

**Restaurant Cellier & Morel** €€€ Comédie
Maison de la Lozère, 27 rue de l'Aiguillerie, 34000 Montpellier
04 67 66 46 36 www.celliermorel.com
Closed: Mon (L), Wed (L), Sat (L), Sun, and 2 weeks in Aug
Many years ago, my favourite restaurant in Paris was to be discovered walking distance from Maxims and Lucas Carton, in the unlikely setting of a regional tourist office on the *Grandes Boulevards*. The genius combination of fresh fine ingredients and true local know-how made the *Maison de la Franche-Comté* a special place. Then local politics came into the mix and the restauarant closed down. Happily, there seems no danger of losing Languedoc's most wonderful gastronomic embassy, tucked away amongst ethnic boutiques and quaint toy shops, half way down the rue de l'Aiguillerie. If Languedoc markets itself as "the other South of France", then La Lozère is the "other" Languedoc. No coastline on the Med, oyster-rich lagoons nor endless rows of vines. Instead, the *département* owes more to its other neighbours in Auvergne and Ardèche, with rolling hills, lush forests, the beautiful Gorges du Tarn and good mountain food and spring waters. The simplicity is lure enough, but, alongside brochures for the Robert Louis Stevenson trail and Brigitte Bardot's wild wolf reserve, is one of the finest restaurants in the city.

The professional partnership between Eric Cellier and Pierre Morel in the beautiful vaulted dining room of this stunning private house is as legendary as the marriages between Morel's ingredients: celeriac pureed with vanilla seeds, lobster and Maury wine couscous or the recent dessert of roasted mango with rosemary sorbet and coriander biscuit. Please do not drool on this page, thank you. For twenty years this restaurant has been serving genius on a plate, accompanied by the treasures of one of the city's best wine cellars – 500 wines on the list. The finest Aubrac beef is the stuff of legend, and the fish courses, whether from fresh or salt water, are never short of magnificent. Undisputed highlight of the meal is the theatrical presentation of house *aligot* (here elevated from mere cheesy mash to high art from), an experience that makes the flamboyant *crêpes-suzetterie* of other establishments seem like clumsy adolescent fumblings. The cheeseboard owes much to the mountains, and the desserts are monumental.

This kitchen may not have the global renown of some rival establishments, but for many in the know, this is a highlight of any visit to the region. Whilst you might easily part with well over €100 euros (and not feel in the least bit short changed), set menus at under €50. A €30 lunch option features a main course, that unforgettable *aligot* and a calorific dessert.

**Compagnie des Comptoirs**　€€　　Jeu de Mail des Abbés　
51 rue François Delmas, 34000 Montpellier
04 99 58 39 29
Closed, Sep-June Sat (L) Mon, 3 weeks in August
Presenting a fusion food sub branch of the Pourcel empire, where you may eat without fear of repossession. Now a chain of "accessible" spacious brasseries, here you'll find several starters at under €15 and mains in the 30s and desserts at €11. The menu is split into Mediterranean and Asian inspired dishes, so from the first column you could go for pasta or pastry starters, whilst the exotica of column two offers *tartare* of tuna and bream with lotus chips and the truly fused already *foie gras* with ginger and lychee flavours. Main courses include duck cooked in green tea from the Eastern selection and the Med menu is not exclusively Languedoc, influences from all round the sea from Spain to Italy to north Africa. The idea works and there is a two-course lunch at under €25, However, should you already be paying €36 for three courses of spring rolls, stir-fry beef and tiramisu, without wine, my tip would be to go around the corner and have a three-course midday meal with a glass of wine at the main attraction **Le Jardin de Sens** – only, if you have the willpower to stay on the set-lunch menu!

**L'Entrecôte**　€€　　Comédie　
3 rue de Verdun, 34000 Montpellier
04 67 58 42 56
A blast from the past, the Paris branch featured in my very first guidebook to France two decades ago. No need for a menu since there is just one meal on offer. On a corner site, just yards from the Comédie tram stop and the vintage style carousel, follow the classic formula: salad of walnuts and leaves with refreshing mustardy vinaigrette, followed by the signature dish; the eponymous *faux filet*, finished off at the table, as you stir in the delicious *Café de Paris* sauce. First served by a Monsieur Barbier in Geneva in 1930, and brought to Paris soon afterwards, the recipe is still a strictly guarded secret to make the Coca Cola company seem casual with the corporate notebook. A *Toulousain* winegrower, Paul Gineste de Saurs bought the rights to the recipe when he purchased *Le Relais de Venise,* the Paris restaurant serving the dish, as outlet for his family's wines. Different elements prepared in separate locations and assembled in each restaurant. Part of the fun of the dining experience is analysing the aromatic speciality and guessing at its constituents. The *entrecôte* has always been served with *pommes allumettes* thin fries *à volonté* to mop up the delicious sauce. The first London branch once added a trout option to the main course, and my last visit to the Paris bistro revealed four main course dishes, but here in Montpellier, the restaurant, run by Paul's son, Henri Gineste de Saurs, is

true to its original theme and choice is reserved to wines and desserts. The salad, steak and chips formula costs just €16 and there are more than a dozen desserts (including the original profiteroles) at around €5. An inexpensive evening meal, since a bottle of the house Bordeaux is only €12

**Grand Café Riche**  €€  Comédie
8, Place de la Comédie, 34000 Montpellier
04 67 54 71 44
For over 100 years, essential pavement rdv for people watching. Cooling mist-spray as you sip *pastis* in summer shade, strong heaters as you sup a glass of warming winter grog. Service erratic, but perfect place to restore your head to factory settings the morning after the night before: coffee, chocolate, a *tartine* and gentle hum of life at the pace of metropolitan *Midi*.

**Insensé**  €€  Comédie / Corum
Musée Fabre, 39 bd des Bonnes Nouvelles, 34000 Montpellier
04 67 58 97 78
Closed Sun (E) Mon, Tue (E), Thu (E) mid-Sep-Jun; Sun (E) Mon Jul-mid-Sep
The spirit was willing when we set off for the **Musée Fabre** for a celebrated impressionist exhibition, but knees went weak when we saw the queue to get in. So we decided to try the new museum restaurant instead. From the seemingly unstoppable Pourcel brothers, a new dining room, a new twist on the word *Sens* and the same astute finger on the foodie pulse. The finger belongs to Vincent Valat, young protégé of the twins, who served an apprenticeship across the Pourcel empire. Though you may eat here from as little as €21, we went for the full €28 restaurant menu to celebrate getting a table, and found the meal to be flavoursome and nicely presented. My dining companion was not quite convinced by a *foie gras crème brulée* at the top of the meal, and my own choice did not linger long enough in the memory for me to decipher the handwriting of my notes. Nevertheless, main courses (especially fish and lamb) trumped starters and desserts on that first visit; soundly-sourced produce, skilfully turned out with a weather eye on the trend barometer. All in all, it is a huge improvement on expectations for museum dining. An all-day (10-18) munching option at **Nomad** café, which sells "*Le Snacking*": soups, salads or sandwiches from around €5 or €10 mini-menu of a sandwich, dessert and glass of wine. Perfect location with a smart dining room next to the main entrance of the museum and a decked terrace (with wifi) facing Daniel Buren's garden by the Esplanade. An interesting opportunity to sample the work of a talented relative newcomer. For the full Pourcel experience, you are so close to the flagship *Jardin de Sens*, where the lunch menu is a good entry level excursion into the world of Michelin stars.

**Jardin des Sens**   €€€   Jeu de Mail des Abbés
11 avenue de Lazare, 34000 Montpellier
04 99 58 38 38

When adjectives and emotions collide. There is a menu sitting comfortably below the €50 mark for self-disciplined types on a budget, but when I invited two true gastronauts to experience what had brought Jacques and Laurent Pourcel culinary immortality, chances of restraint were slender, and the meal slid away from its fiscal moorings from the first flourish of the *carte*. Of course, **Le Jardin de Sens** is an occasion – it has to be; the mere association of any other establishment with the region's first three-star dining room is divinity in these parts. So even finding the place has the Homeric air of a classical quest; away from the busy centre in a long residential street, the modern architectural cube set against classic gardens itself a reflection of the talent on offer. Local lads (Marseillan folk still recall the twins as children on the quays of the port, long before any restaurant tables had even been considered on the waterfront) with a true love of terroir, their family produces wine just outside the village, and a genius for harmonising invention and restoration, as much as restauration. They, and business partner Olivier Château, were in their early 20s when they first opened the doors to their garden of the senses.

First step to making mouthwatering memories is a €45 lunch menu, served midweek only; three courses, topped and tailed with the *amuse bouche* and *gourmandise* treats that many starred establishments withhold from mere trippers on the foothills of the food chain. The main course might include John Dory with a swiss chard and parmesan marmalade and lip-teasing suggestions of anchovy and shallot. Fish is what this place excels at and the same menu included a marine *trio* to start with, lining up risotto stuffed calamari, a mackerel dish and a *daurade tartare* with a bready crumble. Consider that this set menu also includes a glass of wine, and it is really not bad at all. Back in the day, it was always quite a leap to the grander pricier meals at the top end of the scale, but now there is a mid-way option, at €80 (including a glass of wine served with each course, and rivalling many less starry establishments for value), dubbed the *Eclat du Terroir en Languedoc*. This features the fireworks one expects from the Pourcel kitchens, with inventiveness tied to celebration of tradition, this the *Vendée* duck could be presented both as a filet with echoes of the classic *à l'orange*, and with mushroom and spinach in a country *parmentier* fashion.

On the day that we forgot the budget, service was not what we might have expected. Friendly but not quite on the ball, but that was in the year the restaurant lost one of its three stars, so we were not the first to notice.

Thankfully, we can report the team is back on track and the whole **Jardin de Sens** experience is now up to the standard of the food. Those same lovers of fine dining still go misty eyed and gooey at the memory of straying into forbidden price strata. Just the word "turbot" leads to effusive reminiscences of textures and flavours, hymns to the green pea soup in which this most noble of fish was presented. Turbot remains on the seven course €125 *Saveurs* menu (depending on the catch, bass may be called upon to understudy) but in newer and even more inventive guise, it follows a first course of lobster cooked three ways and precedes a pigeon given a hero's farewell. The €170 menu with its medleys and celebrations of top notch ingredients is only served if everyone at the table opts for the same experience. For twenty years, the dream team has presented pride in local produce with justified confidence to win to worldwide *reclame*. With a restaurant chain now spanning the continents of Europe, Africa and Asia, this growth spurt was bound to lead to a few wobbles. Now being reigned in, and concentration focused, especially on home ground

**Nomad** €        Comédie / Corum
Musée Fabre, 39 bd des Bonnes Nouvelles, 34000 Montpellier
04 67 58 97 78
*See Insensé (page 313)*

**Piazza Papa** €        Comédie
13 Place de la Comédie, 34090 Montpellier
04 67 70 01 20
A reliable standby for a value hot meal anytime of day, this dovetails nicely with train and flight timetables. Perfect location, tables in the middle of the Comédie for front row views of the buskers. Waiters negotiate the tramlines to nip from the restaurant to the outdoor dining area. Ambiant background noise is a blend of chatter-buzz from the market with inevitable guitar rendition of The Deer Hunter theme and a Judy Garland ding-dong from trams approaching the platform. Off season, go inside for a friendly and bustling pizza joint. Summer casual staff may be a little slow, but a word usually chases the food!

Very inexpensive set menu, good quality pizzas and big salads. Low priced 2 course meal, carpaccios or Roquefort salad, chicken and pizzas for around €14, perfect for mid afternoon arrivals with the munchies. Otherwise budget perhaps a little over €20 for dinner. Find another branch in the Antigone district on the banks of the Lez. Despite logos and laminated menus of a chain, there are just two other branches in France, so you wont face the corporate blandness of larger groups.

**Le Prince de Minorque**  €€  Comédie
1 rue des Teissiers 34000 Montpellier
04 67 66 05 77
Closed Sun (Oct-Mar)
Very friendly, welcoming and lively; you might have wandered into a somewhat kitsch camp private party: a young, arty and very local backstreet buzz. With its changing display of work by Montpellier artists, burlesque drag cabaret on winter Saturdays, even fortune-telling soirées: the place is noisy and fun. Famous for huge, almost arm's length, *brochettes* of beef, gambas, chicken, fish and even ostrich: at €16, you might skip the €18 or €27.50 set menus, since but one of these portions, with house fries and courgettes is enough to satisfy all but the greediest. In fact, most people won't have room for a *tarte tatin* or *fondant au chocolat* at the end of the evening. The full menu might feature such original offerings as shark mousse or monkfish in champagne. Lunch specials at €7 and €14.

**Régis Brasserie**  €  Comédie
3 Place Jean Jaurès, 34000 Montpellier
04 67 60 53 95
From 14$^{th}$ century vaults, a mêlée spills onto the trendy square, place for a reasonably priced seafood lunch or supper. Find a bewildering choice of moules dishes. For those lacking a passion for shells, try the good pasta option - ideal for vegetarians. Menus from €10 to €23 or à la carte €20-25.

**Le Relais Saint Jean**  €€  Saint Jean le Sec
99 avenue de la Condamine, 34430 Saint Jean de Védas
04 67 69 01 11
Closed Sat (L), Sun
This is one to remember when stuck in traffic with the urge to pull off the A9 motorway, 40km and a 2-hour traffic jam from Marseillan or Nîmes . Everything else behind the toll booths at Exit 32 is of the *autoroute* standard *Buffalo Grill* level. But just a short way along from the tram station is the last place you'd expect to find a *Logis de France* hotel. So, in a dining room that looks large enough for business parties, graze on reliable *cuisine de terroir* and regular family style cooking that you'd depend upon at an *étape* halfway through rural France. Menus begin around €16 for two courses and rise upwards towards the late 20s, but the reason I mention it is the midweek lunch special *formule expres* at €8.90: glass of wine and a coffee included. After lunch, ithe traffic situation is still a nightmare, you might simply park up at the tramway car park and escape to central Montpellier in 15 minutes. Return to the frey several hours later, when the traffic jam has cleared

**Le Tire-Bouchon    €**    Comédie
2 place Jean Jaurès, 34000 Montpellier
04 67 66 26 50
If place Jean Jaurès reminds you of a Parisian square in St Germain or Montmartre where, once a kinetic waiter paused enought to show you to a table, you collapsed under the weight of your own shopping and spent an hour refuelling on brasserie standards, then this is the terrace to relive the moment. Reliable food, a lunch *prix-fixe* at under €10, with more expansive options at €14 and €17 to stop you overstretching the reach of a €20 note on the *carte*, and a seat in the middle of a square so packed with tables, you can see, smell and all but taste the food from rival restaurants next door.

**Les Trois Brasseurs    €€**    Place de France
1 place de France, 34000 Montpellier
04 67 20 14 48
Regular readers of my jottings from France will know that I am a long time fan of the original Lille restaurant, founded by the fellow who used to run the famous Pelican brewery in northern France, as a way of regaining the thrill of artisanal brewing that had inspired his forebears. Now a chain of microbreweries, the clones lack the magic of the original, although (*à la TGI Fridays*) they endeavour to recreate the style of the inspiration. The same home-brew selection of *blonde, brune* and *ambrée* beers, and that summer refresher the *blanche*. Served in glasses of varying sizes and best of all, for first-timers, the *dégustation palette* of four small glasses in what looks like a cricket bat with holes in it. Salads, steaks *choucroutes* and the Alsace speciality *flammekeuche* (a cross between a pizza and a *crèpe*, eaten with your fingers and served in savoury and sweet varieties). Quite frankly, the food does not taste the same as up north. However, if you fancy a drink before taking the tram into town, waiting for your film to start at the **Gaumont** or whilst ducking out of a trip to **Ikea**, a cool beer is a pleasant change to the usual *rosé* on a sultry summer's night. And, of the various chain *restos* in the pedestrianised zone between the multiplex, planetarium and the aquarium, it will do for a night in the **Odysseum**.

**Opéra Café    €**    Comédie
Place de la Comédie, 34000 Montpellier
04 67 02 82 65
Originally known as *Welkomedia*, thankfully renamed to reflect what people actually called the place, this is the opera house's café terrace – pretty much an ideal location, with tables and now pergola awnings set up on the steps of the theatre itself. It is a very sensible rendezvous point, especially for first timers, since the building dominates the square. Whilst

many people come here for a drink, new trad wicker chairs give the venue the feel of a proper brasserie and menus reflect the makeover. An €11 *plat du jour* of lamb chops in a creamy garlic sauce with *pommes dauphinoises* is serious stuff. Main courses either side of €14. Open from breakfast til late. Mobility-challenged guests facing the steps in front of the tables should ring a doorbell along rue des Estuves to be escorted to the terrace, via a backstage lift. Most visitors make the most of the view across the square, locals know that the *café-bar* ambience inside has a buzz all its own: there is even a library of books on the performing arts for solo visitors to browse, and a programme of musical themed evenings for conviviality.

## Nîmes [5] D1

**Alexandre**  €€€
2 Rue Xavier Tronc, 30128 Garons
04 66 70 08 99
Closed Sun (E), Mon, Tue Sep-Jun; Sun, Mon Jul-Aug
Arrive early for your flight from Nîmes airport. Early enough for lunch. But I am certainly not recommending the airport restaurant (since, unlike Carcassonne's grill, Nîmes' airport menu is not on my to-re-do list). Instead, turn off on the road to the terminal to find possibly the finest meal the city can offer. The deceptive simplicity of the setting, like any other terracotta-tinged villa in a well-tended garden, plain linens on well-spaced tables, unfussy and free from pretension, allows food to speak for itself. The Languedoc tradition of sourcing simplest ingredients, then spending time and effort to nurture them to the utmost flavour, is well served by the location, perched between two fine regions. Thus the seafood comes from our own Etang de Thau, truffles from the "market" of Carpentras. The salt-cod of the Gard has always created the classic *brandade de morue* – a simple creamy bistro fish dish, as entitled to a place at the *grande table* as any other – and for beef, the little black bulls of the *Petit Camargue* graze within hailing distance of the town.

Michel Kayser arrived at the restaurant some years back, as the original Alexandre hung up his toque for the last time. A deft manner of blending *terroir* with *finesse* soon earned him two *Michelin* stars, the food a veritable seduction of the eyes before it even reaches the palate. His exquisitely-crafted *assiettes* make *Fabergé* seem maoist. If you are counting the final euros of your trip you might stick to the business lunch menu served on weekdays. €46 brings you main course and dessert *du jour*, with a glass of an appropriate wine. Otherwise find a menu of three courses and extras for

€64, or throw yourself on the mercy of your bank and lose count of the number of dishes brought to table on the €134 *dégustation* extravaganza of roast *gigot*, almond and thyme favoured *ris d'agneau*, lobster, a truffled *ile flottante* floating in a *velouté* of *cévenol cèpes*. And more besides. In winter, the house alternative to the traditional *trou Normand* between courses was tea grog.

**L'Ancien Théâtre**     €€
4, rue Racine, 30000 Nîmes
04 66 21 30 75
Closed Sun, Mon, Sat (L)
Plenty of steak places around the roman theatre, and enough mid-range bistros in town to serve an apetite, even in high season,. However, if you were to walk a few streets away from the arena you would find something special. *Steak-frites* may be the French national dish, but Nîmes is famed for *brandade de morue*, and locals reckon few places do a better *brandade* than *chez* Gilles Taliani at the **Ancien Théâtre;** here the dish is recreated without the usual bulking out of potato, but instead using baby spinach leaves and a wild mushroom *jus*.

A reliable and often inspired kitchen, fish is house speciality, including a *choucroute* with its own loyal and passionate following. Interesting pairings such as tuna with *foie gras* in a fruity wine stock, and a legendary 2009 dessert marrying olives and pineapple confounded expectations, but might not be there your next visit, since the ebullient host is not a man to be hidebound by printed menus. The bill of fare is decided on a whim, the welcome all embracing and serving staff persuasive. Four menus €18-28.

# Perpignan     [5] B4
*See also* Collioure *and* Rivesaltes

**L'Assiette Catalane**     €
9 rue de la République, 66000 Perpignan
04 68 34 77 62 www.assiettecatalane.com
Discover a variety of 2-course set lunch menus (with or without win) to fit on either side of a €10 note. But this busy place is more than a bargain for tourists. Locals grab the tables for a midday meal. You'd be hard put to find a brighter touch of colour to break up a day trip to Perpignan. Decor is resolutely regional: rustic bric a brac, echoes of rugby and flamenco and homage to hispanic artists at every turn. If you stray off the value meal deals, choose from *tapas*, *paellas* or sizzling *parrillada* grills.

**Le Figuier**   €€
7 rue du Figuier, place Jaubert de Passa , 66000 Perpignan
04 68 63 14 82
Closed Sun, Mon (L)
Rather than looking across the Pyrenees or up to chic Paris, this self styled *bouchon Catalan* is an authentic back street neighbourhood bistro. The simple terracotta facade, tubbed olive trees and white shutters provide no hint of the buzz that always hums within. This is the sound of habitues sharing badinage with waiters and first timers being taken through the menu with friendly patience. No ping of the microwave, but the sizzle and spark of classic family recipes freshly prepared to order in full view. We tend to choose the dishes and *formules* of the day as chalked up on boards: delicious soups or seasonal starters, roast shoulder of lamb, grilled fish and hope to have room for comfort desserts of choc heavy puds or the legendary lipsmacking sticky *tarte tatin*. Lunch at around €15; but come back later and dine, spending closer to €30.

**Républic' Café**
2 Place de la République, 66000 Perpignan
04 68 51 11 64
Tapas and live music amid the buzz of a lively city. (*see page 339*)


**Peyriac de Mer**   *See* Corbières  **[5] B3**


**Pézenas**   **[5] C2**

**L'Entre Pots**   €€
8 avenue Louis Montagne, 34120 Pézenas
04 67 90 00 00
Closed Sun, Mon
Finally, at long long last, we have a table worthy of the town. As befits a one time capital city, here is quality dining with an eye on something more than feeding passing trade. The conversion of a garage into dining rooms with the keen decorator's eye of the region's interior design guru Guy Falco, who transformed **Les Bains** in Montpellier, might have been be a hard act to follow. Had not the kitchen followed the mantra: take the best that Languedoc can produce and serve it up with a worldly wisdom and skill. So where *sétois* tentacles might normally find their way into a rustic *tielle* pasty, a dish with Italianate origins after all, why not use the filling for a contemporary *calzone*? Even wittier, take the meaty stuffing of Pézenas'

own *petits pâtés*, as introduced to the town by Clive of India, then present it to modern diners in the guise of a samosa. Intelligence is never at the expense of the comforting core produce of home. So your next visit may reveal an array of variations on the theme of the humble Mediterranean sardine on one plate: one bite *en escabèche*, another crunch of a be-basiled spring roll and a third mouthful of a minty coarse paté. Presentation is accorded first class respect, as you might expect when the founding talents of this place came from a well garlanded line of starred and *toqued* restaurateurs. Yet, even the fanciest flourishes cannot upstage the integrity of a *pavé* of *Aubrac* beef with an authentic *aligot* on the side. The sweet-toothed will leave room for rich chocolate or cracking fruity desserts. If your credit card survives the evening, it may yet make a final sortie for an encore, since on your way out, you will pass the restaurant's *épicerie*, where genius is distilled and instilled into gift sized jars and pots. Stick to set menus to keep the budget (without drinks) between €21-30, and at lunchtimes take advantage of a €26 deal. Otherwise throw caution to the winds and indulge yourself. Booking essential.

## L'Entracte      €€
30 rue Conti 34120, Pézenas
04 67 09 33 32
In Pézenas, either chef is a showman or the dining room a show; carefully lit décor, knowingly tasteful, upstaging the food. But there are times, lunchtimes mostly, when I prefer a reality check. Halfway down rue Conti, midway between Molière and the real world, is the aptly named *Entracte*, or interval. The name is sole concession to the stage, as honesty and integrity on a plate trumps *coups du théâtre* any midday of the week. Come for cooking rather than cuisine. Under new convivial management, fresh from grilling in Beziers, simple fare is served well. Mains around €16. But lunch is €13 for large fresh salad of tomato, crunchy raddish and croutons, hefty brace of beef brochettes with generous mound of chunky ratatouille, and coffee. €9-10 buys a crisp, lacy pizza. Spanish starters, including cold meats, begin with bargain €2.50 pan con tomate: DIY virtual cheese-free ploughmans, crusty bread, clutch of garlic cloves, ripe tomato and olive oil.

## Le Molière      €
place du 14-Juillet, 34120 Pézenas
04 67 98 10 00
The largest brasserie on the decent sweep of eateries close to the tourist office and central car park, nonetheless, since locals often outnumber trippers, the Molière is a reliable staging post. Off season, when trendier places close, or whenever the clock upbraids you for loitering in town, stop

here for a coffee, *plat du jour* or quick *prix-fixe* without breaking the bank. Spend as little as €11 or as much as €25 for your meal, a jug of local wine for well under a tenner, and try to identify domestic political celebs in black and white pictures lining the walls. Use the excuse of coffee to make this a rendezvous point when if your party is split between moochers and shoppers on a *brocante* day, you should sit outside on the shady terrace and show off your antique and bric-a-brac bargains at the end of an afternoon.

## Les Palmiers     €€
cour les Palmiers, 10 bis rue Mercière, 34120 Pézenas
04 67 09 42 56
Closed Oct-mid-Apr
No *Marseillanais* may talk about restaurants in Pézenas without mentioning this popular courtyard: open only in summer season. There is a strong family connection to Marseillan's **Delicatessen** by the church, and when the **Palmiers** closes in the winter, the talent has been known to help out in the village. At **Les Palmiers**, diners sit under eponymous fronds, indulging in very Mediterranean dishes, from aubergine in the Greek style to sardines with Serrano ham. Anywhere this smart is legally obliged to throw up gems of invention, so a contemporary twist *du jour* might yield a blend of guinea fowl with liquorice or tuna incognito. Despite influences from other lands, all produce is locally sourced, the wine list worth the browse and location ideal. The courtyard is popular with tourists. Otherwise, the ubiquitous stone walls provide classily illuminated backdrop to modernist metal gantry and sailcloth mezzanine dining space. Budget twixt €15 and €50 per head.

## Le Pré Saint Jean     €€
18 Avenue du Maréchal Leclerc, 34120 Pézenas
04 67 98 15 31
Closed Sun, Mon, Thu (E)
When the partridge met the salmon, their union on the menu at **Pré Saint Jean** was celebrated with red cabbage and blueberries: it was one of those savvy and savoury combos that validate the status of third generation chef Philippe Cagnoli as a *Maître Restaurateur de France*. As a curtain raiser to such a main course, and alternative to the staple *Etang de Thau* oyster starters, early season diners might still order a Jerusalem artichoke *velouté* with white truffle pasta parcels.

Whilst *à la carte*, these two dishes alone will have totalled €35, on the twin-course lunchtime menu you would have parted with a mere €18. Three course menu is available noon and evenings for just €25. Vegetables are cooked to precision and neither mere garnish nor duty. As befits a restaurant of this quality and pedigree, a cheese trolley option at €12 has the usual ashen *chèvres* and fluffy white treats alongside the veiny, the gnarled and the hard stuff. My tip: to go for a very good quality Roquefort at €7, served with a little walnut salad, which brings the clout of a *trou normande* to refresh the palate before dessert. An unpretentious, uncluttered dining room, standard villa style tiles and painted walls, just far enough away from touristy buzz to have to rely on quality food and welcome to keep busy, reputation maintained by good service and a genuinely well-considered menu. There is a terrace in summer, but on a dusty main road alongside a tree-lined car park, you may prefer to dine indoors.

**Au Palas de la Bière**  €
23 rue Conti, 34120 Pézenas
Rue Conti *habitués* are convivial folk; prone to ambling narrow pavements and taking a glass here, a bite there, catching up with news of the quarter, offering a kindly word of encouragement or direction to tourists on arts or brocante trails. The road mixes the smart and the resolutely local. The old *Mir* café, which once hosted jazz and poetry, is boarded up, but a courtyard creperie is ever packed, Molière plaques abound and tentative chords reverberate from shops selling guitar lessons by the hour. For a break from the grape, a couple of doors down from a horse butcher, find scores of international lagers and ales and €8.50 resolutely French *plats du jour*. Lunch outside on the sunny side of the street as locals engage in badinage and *bavardage* with the patron of the bistro opposite. Don't be surprised when, lips and plate wiped clean, bill paid, the guy at the next table finishes his *ambrée* and crossess the road to rinse the meal with a pichet of *rosé*.

# Portiragnes Plage   |5| C2

**Saveurs du Sud**  €€
Hotel Miramar, 4 boulevard de Front de Mer, 34420 Portiragnes
04 67 90 97 67  www.hotel-le-mirador.com
Closed Mon, Tue, and from Nov-Jan
It was towards the Western end of the Piccadilly Line that I discovered this unlikely gastronomic treat by the beach. Shortly after falling in love with Marseillan, I ran into an old friend and travel-writing colleague at a trade show in Earls Court and was delighted to discover that Lynn Storey-Smith was a fellow Marseillanophile. Whilst swapping favourite addresses, Lynn rummaged in her bag and handed me one of the restaurant's trademark paper napkin-rings, each printed with a picture and the properties of a different herb, with the name and address of the restaurant. "Go there" she instructed. And on my return to Languedoc, that's what I did. The **Hotel**

**Miramar** looks like countless other resort block hotels along the French coastline. Smoked glass, pink concrete, curved san serif signage straight out of the late 'seventies – not necessarily the place you'd choose for lunch when there are beach bars, pizza-joints and ice-cream parlours next door. I have a sneaky feeling that the place has looked dated from day one – perhaps as a ploy to keep the fashionable classes at arms length. But step through the doors and prepare to have your taste-buds massaged, tickled, ravaged and invigorated. Take a table by the window, as the beach view is second to none, although you may well forget to look out to sea once the plates start arriving. Chef Michael Labbé has such a deft and sophisticated touch you'll be delightfully distracted as each dish runs away with your spoon. Herbs and spices of the *Midi* tease such honest confessions of flavour from well-sourced raw material on all sides of the menu. It is neither earth-shattering stuff, nor trend-setting. Simply good food cooked well and treated with respect. The grandest option on offer is a seven course extravaganza (at €48 dry or €59 with a different wine selected to match each dish) which starts as it means to go on with panfried foie gras served with an apple caramalised in maple syrup, accompanied by a *Beauvignac picpoul "moulleux"*.

But the more modest menu at less than €20 is excellent value, and lunchtimes bring a two-course option for €15. I could wax lyrical about flavours from the past, but each season brings its new tricks, suffice to say, over several years of return visits, happiness has trumped complacency more often than not. We've come here with friends and with family, as prelude to an afternoon on the sands, curtain raiser to a boat trip on the Canal du Midi or simply to toast the end of another season before the place closes for its annual winter break. And we'll be back again.

## Rivesaltes          [5] B3

### Le Grill de Château de Jau    €€
Château de Jau, 66000 Cases de Pène
04 68 38 91 38 (restaurant); 04 68 38 90 10 (wine domaine) Summer only
This was always going to be a special lunch. As three of us piled into the car to drive westward ho, Armand, our 80 year old neighbour, nipped back into his garage and returned holding aloft a collection of fencing *epées*. To my raised eyebrow, he announced, "we are the musketeers" and so we headed towards the border. We found the old Occitan frontier whilst tramping with Tavernier Bruno through Marc Barriot's organic vineyards at Maury, Occitan cross carved on one side of a rock, and the emblem of the

*Royaume* of France on the other. Inspired by *patrimoine, terroir* and allied gallic virtues, we turned the car back towards Rivesaltes, the 12<sup>th</sup> century wine domaine of the **Château de Jau** and lunch. A real treat, my advice to anyone without a heart hard enough to designate a driver, would find an hotel and take a taxi to and from the wine estate. This lunch merits a snooze and a snore in the shade of an old, old tree at the end of the afternoon.

The winery is hosted by the Dauré family, Catalan proprietors of the equally respected **Clos de Paulilles** at Port-Vendres and the **Viña las Niñas** in Chile (famed for packing its wines in bad-girl shoe boxes). Since arriving here in the 'seventies, they opened a reputed art gallery a castle outbuilding and, whilst the next generation busies itself making good wines, Sabine Dauré runs the gallery and *Le Grill* restaurant. Shaded from the Roussillon sunshine's harsh glare by the gentle filter of a huge and sprawling mulberry tree; 300-year-old branches and fresh new leaves providing almost universal embrace. Tables by the château's stone walls a cool sanctuary for an afternoon of delicious self indulgence. The barbecue is backdrop to the extravagant pleasure of tasting the range of the family's wine production. I may have skipped a course or few, but still felt the glow of satisfaction all the way home.

Lunch begins with the ripping of *fougasse* for the *apéro*, then there is *bruschetta* style tomato bread to go with the ham, before your plate is re-filled with lamb chops and sausages straight from the grill. A hunk of Roquefort precedes orange fruit cake and ice creams before the event is rounded off with *Muscat de Rivesaltes* dessert wine and coffee. All of the above are chosen to complement a range of *Collioure* and *Côtes du Roussillon* white and red wines, and a choice of rosés including *Jaja de Jau*. All this for €31, with a child friendly version of the meal at €19. More recently, the Château launched an evening meal at €39. With light cucumber and *fromage frais tartine* for the whites, chick pea and sausage dish with the rosés, grilled duck breast to show off the reds, and a spicy fruitcake with Roquefort *quenelles* accompanying dessert wines.

If you can still walk a straight line, you'll want to do some shopping. Unsteady diners carry cases of wine to their cars, but the boutique also has some sensational glassware worth checking out and souvenirs of art exhibitions from the gallery next to the restaurant. Luckily the effects of the fine wines and summer air filled with the scent of a fine barbecue led to Armand's duelling swords lying untouched in the car. Fortunate indeed, for the imposing château tower would have been too great a temptation for Dumas re-enactments after the first glass or three of Roussillon's finest.

## Saint Jean du Gard *(see page 359)*

**L'Oronge**   €€
103 Grand rue, Place de la Révolution, 30270 Saint-Jean-du-Gard
04 66 85 30 34 www.loronge.com
An oronge is not a mispelt fruit. It is a mushroom. And no ordinary mushroom at that. It is the emperor of mushrooms, the *amanita caesarea* to give it its appropriate latin name, and often mistaken for a poisonous toadstool, being the edible second cousin to the death cap that did for Claudius and fast-tracked Nero to the top job in Rome. Since the Cevennes positively postulate with funghi, and any country drive in late summer and autumn is punctuated with countrymen and women emerging from woodland with armloads of *girolles, trompettes de la mort, cèpes* and all manner of fodder for a *forestière* aficionado. Jean-Marc Clerc's restaurant, housed within the original 17th century staging post of Saint Jean du Gard, carries a name redolent of empire – thanks to a not-so-humble mushroom that is regularly êon the menu served in the vaulted stone courtyard where once the author Robert Louis Stevenson himself left this "civilised country of stage-coaches." at the end of his celebrated *Travels With a Donkey in the Cevennes*. The land yields more than mushrooms to the hotel kitchen: chestnuts from the trees that blur the boundaries of three counties are pan-fried, then tossed into a *salade au lard* and enrobed with Armagnac cream as a *parfait glace* to top and tail many a meal; game has its seasons and sweet onions make chutneys for a fish course; honey and almonds tease a sweet and savoury sensation from Languedoc's succulent *pelardon* goats cheese, and fresh berries in every season inspire mouth-watering desserts.


## Salagou   [5] B1

**Auberge du Lac Les Crémades**   €€
Le Lac du Salagou, 34700 Le Peuch
04 67 44 45 40     15 Jul-15 Aug closed Mon L; 15 Aug-15 Jul closed Sun E, Mon
We came wth every intention of choosing the recomended *Tournedos de Canard farci au Chèvre et sa sauce au Miel parfumé au Romarin*, but were distracted by the genuine welcome (and our half hour digression from the route, since the restaurant is NOT in the village of le Puech).Tail end of season still produced suggestions relayed from the kitchen and our eventual seduction towards *ris de vau* and simple freshly-caught white fish proved perfection. In fact, so happily diverted were we by unexpected decor (from the outside, you'd expect montagnard tradition, within are bold *fin du 20ème siècle* splashes of colour, and contemporary artwork of androgynous faces on hessian), not only did we forget about the dish that had lured us in

the first place, but we stayed inside instead of enjoying the stunning terrace views, chatted long and happily with the patron, and indulged in a sweetness of deserts (*Nutella* mousse!) and a lingering over coffees and were halfway round the lake before remembering that the idea had been to take notes. Menus €19-28 and theme nights from Caribbean to 70's music.

## Sète [5] C2 323 🚌🚆

**AmeriKclub** €€
Môle Saint Louis, promenade du Maréchal Leclerc, 34200 Sète
04 67 53 02 37 www.amerik.fr
Closed Oct-Mar
I once met a *nouvelle arriviste Marseillanaise* who had invested in the village having read in a Sunday paper that finally "the right kind of people" were moving in. She soon discovered that the St Tropez that the writers had evoked in their eulogies was that of the modest fishing community that had lived in Bardotville-sur-Mer before the A-List took over, rather than the millionaires' playground of today. It was not long before she found out that our corner of Languedoc was neither the new Antibes nor the old Monte Carlo and so went off in search of a region with a more vibrant ex-pat influence on lifestyle. The secret of Sète's success has been that it has always managed to avoid being fashionable. Artistic, certainly (do the Sunday gallery crawl for the true creative heart of the place, then read your Paul Valéry as you listen to your Brassens); international, indeed (influx mainly from Italy and north Africa, not LA and Russia). But despite all this, the very raw authenticity of a community of fishermen and stevedores, poets and mechanics, keeps the place just as bustling and traffic-impossible in mid-December as Bastille weekend. Nonetheless, in one corner of the Sète seafront the nipped, tucked and liposucked, the tanned, toned and designer-phoned may yet be beautiful and expensive in public.

**AmeriK Club** (you have to get used to upper-case puns in restaurant names here: this one is pronounced "Amerikah" with a wince, rather than "Americk" with a furrowed brow) has enjoyed fashionable status since its re-incarnation as an outpost of the Pourcel empire back in 2006. The cliff-face had already been an occasion location since first transformation from military diving school to chic terrace looking out to sea. America does not refer to cuisine, but to the Americas Cup. Headland waters stood in for the imaginary Helvetian coastline and echoed to suspiciously antipodean accents of Swiss sailors trained here to win the Americas Cup in 2003. Open only extended spring into summer season, the restaurant serves Pourcelian seafood classics on terraces resembling decks of grand yachts,

327

menus launching from the mid €30s. As probably principal see and be seen venue and only part of town where international Riviera style encroaches on *sétois* identity, the **Klub** (as it is called) is true *phare* of these rocks. A nightclub under the stars with its dance floor throbbing to the beat of summer DJ's from midnight til 5am and convivial bar around a saltwater pool. (Jun-Sep 11-02); ultimate bar-glacier for sipping cocktails, scooping ice cream or nibbling finger food under awnings watching trawlers, ferries and cruise ships shimmer towards the ports of Sète .

**Les Amis de Georges**          €€
38 rue Maurice Clavel, 34200 Sète
04 67 74 38 13  www.resto-brassens.com
Dates vary – call to check.
Touristy but fun. After all: most memories of France have a soundtrack of raw *chanson*. Whether the breathless pant of a Gainsbourg-Birkin *"Je t'aime"* for those of a certain art-house generation, soaring, searing wail of Piaf's lack of regret for a rose tinted life, a touch of the Maurice Chevalier or Gershwin for vicarious travelling via Hollywood or the jingle tingle of the *Amélie* years. If Paris is Piaf, then Sète is Georges Brassens (*see page 232*), so why not have a holiday meal served with sounds of the city.

One up on conventional rubber chicken of cabarets the world over, menu is decidedly as *Setois* as the music, so *tielles*, sardines and *seiche* enliven regular salmon, duck and steak standards. Be seated by 8pm for slide show and film setting the musical scene for the era of Brassens and his contemporaries. Three courses for €30 (card-carrying students may have two courses for €20) or spend just a tenner and arrive at half nine for the show only. Check programme in advance, since shows vary with musicians chosen from a pool of around a dozen or so singers. Many Brassens tribute acts, but several pay homage to eponymous *Amis de Georges,* other legends of the French charts from Brel to Barbara. Some evenings bring a soloist with guitar, others a duo with accordion and double bass combo. Well worth preparing with a visit to the **Espace Brassens** museum to get yourself in the mood. Reserve your table at the tourist office.

**L'Auberge**     €€
15 rue Pierre Semard, 34200 Sète
04 67 74 32 30 www.laubergeaveyronnaise.com
Closed Wed, Sat (L)
In happy hinterland between quays and road bridges of the canal district is a back-street bistro with a heart in hills beyond the Mont Saint Clair. The name above the door may be simple, **l'Auberge**, but the full title engraved on the heart of the owner is **l'Auberge Aveyronnaise**. Even the least

worldly visitor will know, from stopping off at mouthwateringly tempting motorway services on the A75, that Aveyron means farm produce. Thus a Roquefort salad and plate of *charcuterie* on the starters menu. Main courses are proper country fare, so on our first visit, our dining companions pronounced *tête de veau* and *langue de boeuf*, as verging on matriarchal, as I dallied wimpishly with salad followed by *daurade royale*. With gamey selection from *civet de sanglier, à la carte*, much on the menu is inspired by the *arrière-pays* to the north, although a popular *reisling choucroute*, whilst reflecting a spirit of national *patrimoine*, shows stunning disregard for geography. The GPS *du ventre* is back on track every Tuesday evening however, when €20 platters of *aligot*, sausage and salad is about as *Aveyronnais* as anyone might wish for. Good stuff for the off-season, when nights draw in and memories leave the Med for country inns of deep France. The chef does not simply rely on nostalgia; house specialities reflect seasons and new and original creations. Arnaud Abitbol is particularly proud of duck *tartare* with apple and walnut. Service kindly, if timid. Three-course dinner at €28 is good value, and noon *plat du jour* sees students and workers parting readily with €9. When the place is packed there is a cosy buzz, otherwise, if you are the only diners in the place, a little room may feel quite lonely.

**Les Demoiselles Dupuy**       €€
5 Quai François Maillol, 34200 Sète
04 67 46 16 97
The one that got away from the casual visitor: the main road from the Môle and Théâtre de la Mer, sweeps from the working fishermen's port towards tourist-friendly tables on the quays. But swerve down the slope towards the fish auction, past sheds with colourful nets, by refrigerated containers waiting to take the day's bounty on its overland journey, and wander through the market. Here are bars for trawlermen and traders, tiny narrow counters serving pastis and sardines to those who've worked up an appetite. And restaurants, where *sètoises* outnumber sightseers, have been serving freshly landed, flash-cooked fish for years. Keep walking until you see the faded wooden shutters and signs announcing *Les Demoiselles Dupuy*, its tiny terrace framed by creeping plants and hung with fishermen's lamps.

Within, an intimate cave of a dining room, walls painted with murals and studded with wooden posts from family oyster tables in Bouzigues. Terrace stays open through winter (bar Christmas Eve, Christmas Day and New Year), and snug blankets are folded over chairbacks for protection against winds that whistle around the corner where port meets canal. €20 three course menu, or pay around €30 *à la carte*. Main courses €13-18, most simply fish cooked *à la plancha* (succulent, juicy tuna steaks, sword-fish, mackerel) and smeared with surprisingly subtle and fruity tapenade. Seafood paella is enormous, with giant crayfish, plentiful crabs and, of course, hordes of mussels. Amongst starters, the family's freshly farmed oysters from Bouzigues. Dupuys have raised mussels and oysters for generations, only Gilles Dupuy branching out to find fame and acclaim as an artist and architect before returning to the fold to open this restaurant. The artist's eye understands the true charm of simple authenticity in any design, thus the charm of a seemingly untouched-by-time seafood bar, just retro enough to retain its loyal clientele yet still manage to win new friends.

**Lou Biou**  €€
28 Rue Lazare Carnot, 34200 Sète
04 67 74 82 18  www.webfrance.fr/loubiou
Closed Sun (may close some weeks in peak summer)
You would never imagine you were just two nets throw from one of the biggest fishing ports on the Med. This is carnivore central and no place for the squeamish. Sensitive souls that wince and avert glances from a tank of crabs and lobsters would certainly not appreciate all the fun of the abattoir in a restaurant where guests *en route* to a Saturday night table, run the gauntlet of a glass-fronted refrigerator festooned with carcasses of beasts providing the mammals *du jour*. Just like those brasserie lobsters in other dining rooms, here's proof that beef, pork and lamb is as fresh as can be. Provenance of every piece of meat guaranteed; integrity second to none.

If you seek subtlety or a fine and delicate blend of flavours, then walk on by. As befitting an honest approach to good cuts of meat, grilled to your precise specification over local vine stock and served stacked thick, chunky and tall on the plate, menus lack frills, poetic chi-chi imagery and trendy euphemisms. What you see is what you get. No room for affectation, but a generous helping of bonhomie, good natured banter and plenty of bustle. This place is for people who like the taste of red meat. Period. Neither a showcase for sauces, reductions or fusion concept; that would be the *royaume* of the chef. Remember, **Lou Biou**'s patron Dominique Anciaux was a butcher when he opened this place in the mid 1990s and eating here is the meaty equivalent of sitting on the sea shore sharing freshly grilled mackerel with a fisherman. Décor is standard canteen-caff basic. But as anyone who has ever squeezed a Renault Clio between two rows of double-parked lorries to dine in an unpretentious *Le Routier* establishment in the lay-by of a *route nationale* will know, you don't come to places like this to seek inspiration for the through-lounge makeover. Two rooms in this backstreet linking the canals of Sète get packed with a loyal crowd of regulars, and you may well need to book. The family vegetarian should keep the head down and graze on salad, after checking that no added extras have been thrown on the plate. But the red-meat brigade will tuck in with gusto. We were introduced by a restaurateur who spends six nights a week serving pride of the tide to those who come in search of the cholesterol-light Mediterranean diet. Since this was his night off, it was a case of *à vos forchettes, nos amis* as red meat took over from white fish.Lunchtime menu at €11 is ridiculously cheap for three courses and coffee and in the evenings you'll pay an average of around €20 for a main course with jacket potato, perhaps €6 for a salad starter and the same for dessert.

**Le Nautic**   €€
12 quai Aspirant Herber, 34200 Sète
04 67 74 65 17
Closed much of the winter season
We could see just two bright lights across the water from the bustling main canalside roadway of Sète. Behind us billowed poster-paint hued tableclothes, laminated menus promising standard holiday fare in the wake of a hundred passers-by. A waterway's breadth away, were two lone signs: one flashing the name and hump-backed logo of the "**Orque Bleu Hotel**" to the night sky; the other presenting the simple legend in block letters: "*Brochettes*". Having negotiated the one-way system and bridge to the wrong side of the canal, we discovered that a plastic chair beneath those san serif capitals is the essential place to watch other tourists trapped in garish smart quayside eateries across the water and tuck in to the really good stuff away from the crowd. Just too far along from the bridge to be discovered by accident, yet close enough for a pre-prandial amble from a parking space; come here to eat on a makeshift terrace amid nets and ropes of real trawlers moored a canal's breadth from smarter pleasure craft.

Rather than eat inside under garish fluorescent strip lighting, wait instead for a table in the roadway and read menus chalked on boards. Seafood salad, ubiquitous oysters or perhaps sardines in season followed by pick-your-own choice of those heralded brochettes (bass, bream, monkfish) or surrender to best tuna steak in town. A lovely family welcome, genuine and friendly. Modest prices (budget €16-20). We first came here one fragile Sunday lunch after the Saturday night before, and have returned time and again, when visiting art galleries and museums on this side of the water, as a *fête de la musique* refuge from midsummer night partying of the town and avoiding the chaos of jousting season. In season, live music from bars and restaurants on the *quai* opposite is carried across, filtered by the lapping of the waters, to this quieter side, where wine costs little, the company is good and all is right with the world.

**La Ola**     €€

promenade de Lido, plage de la Corniche, 34200 Sète

04 67 53 07 14

Open April-September, 9-2.

Of course, we Marseillanophiles love to boast that the true charm of **Lido Plage** is its unspoilt and unsophisticated simplicity. However, in summer when the beach is a sprawl of *ambre-solaired* humanity, who could deny a yen for sophisticated superficiality, creature comforts and blessed pampering of space. So it well worth getting into the car and negotiating traffic on the new coast road and heading for the posh end of the beach, by the recently created **Promenade de Lido**. Before the road veers towards Sète proper, pull over into **Parking Villeroy** and make your way up to the boardwalk. When you see the sign on a canvas wall **Ola**, take the path through the sands and discover an almost private VIP lounge on the beach.

This is the beach bar restaurant you expect when booking long haul trips to furthest oceans or far posher parts of the Med. Out on the sand are rows of loungers with thick mattresses, comfy garden suites with armchairs and sofas, parasols, sailcloth shade and potted plants. Under cover, on the deck, find the restaurant, its shady bar and cosy lounge. You may book your place on the beach for a full day, including a light lunch for not much more than you'd pay for a midday snack in town, or you might just drop in for a meal and linger the afternoon away over coffee or a cool drink. Foodwise, this place is not bad; sunlovers won't regret sacrificing quality restaurant time elsewhere. Salads are a speciality, grills pretty good and regional fish dishes are fine. Savoury, flavoursome and original starters on my last visit included a witty rethinking of *gazpacho*, which was perfect for a sweltering summer's afternoon.

Menus from €15-25, or have a lavish *salade Niçoise* for lunch for far less. Since the beach in front of the restaurant is virtually private, the mood is pretty peaceful during the day, and the setting is ideal for mismatched couples, where one partner is a sun-worshipper and the other prefers the cool shade with a drink and a paperback that promises a dozen or more chapters yet to mine. By night, the place takes on a new identity as party central. Live music several nights a week, the house *Mojito* cocktail of rum, lime and fresh mint flows and the dancing spills over onto the sand. An essential date during the July *Jazz Festival* in town, when the programme proper winds up before midnight, and the beach hosts memorable jam sessions with the listed stars and talented locals alike. The music continues well into the small hours. Where better for holding hands? Arriving by boat: call first for the GPS co-ordinates and you can moor by the breakwater. Not the legendary beach bars of Montpellier, but a local treat.

**Pasta Politi**     €
5 quai Charles le Maresquier, 34200 Sète
04 67 78 69 65
Closed Tue
Sète's Italian heritage is not simply down to Venetian canals. Latin fishing and foodie culture is detailed elsewhere in this book, but for me the reference has never been the Grand Canal. The "other" side of the Royale in Sète has always had an Italianate air. But this is more a neapolitan, Agfa-tinted, eye-watering memory inspired by faded pastel shades of peeling plaster façades.

Stimulate other senses at Pasta Politi, where, across the one-way street from a modest doorway on the quayside, a couple of tables amid non-stop traffic designate a "terrace". Frankly, exhaust fumes of impatient Peugeots will never turn 4m of quai Charles le Maresquier into Piazza San Marco, no matter how quaint the fishing boats nor how often you answer your mobile phone with a clipped screech of *"pronto"*.

Be kinder to your lungs and shove your way indoors in vain hope of finding a table at this reliable Italian-styled carb-fest where younger locals refuel on big bowls of very decent hand-made pasta with truly flavoursome sauces. Non-pasta dishes are a franco-italianate alliance. Here, city office and shop workers pile in, as do students and artists working at neighbourhood galleries. Mere first-time tourists wandering in halfway through service will have to wait for a table, and absorb the ambience. Whilst *à la carte* will peel €15-30 from your purse, the real reason you'll need to arrive early is €14 set lunch of *tapenade antipasto,* salad, reliable main course (perhaps duck, beef or fish) and dessert, be it home made fig tart or profiteroles, with glass of wine included, and all rounded off with coffee.

**Le Quai 17**     €€
17 Quai du Maréchal de Lattre de Tassigny, 34200 Sète
04 67 74 71 91  www.legrandhotelsete .com
Ouch, the pun hurts (perhaps almost as much as another local eaterie **Les Temps de Thau**), but don't let that put you off. There is nothing hackneyed to make you flinch about the restaurant of the **Grand Hotel** with arguably one of the best canal views in town. At the confluence of the main waterfares, stunning art-deco tower of the chamber of commerce to one side, more traditional port buildings on the other, a steady flow of optimists seeking a parking space trickle beneath the panorama. Look out, not on looming profiles of sea-going trawlers, nor cruise-liners, but colourful bobbing craft, moored household run-arounds for the appartement-dwellers

of the quarter. Outside, provincial boulevard grandeur of the hotel building could easily suggest a tired trad bourgeois dining room as seen by any old-style railway stations in any time in France. Cross the threshold to encounter a clean and bright space invigorated by a gust of fresh contemporary energy. Huge nautical canvases with retro heyday feel settle between moulded plaster panels of a high ceilinged dining room. Modest, almost gallery-style, tables clustered in intimate huddles, dressed with slim runners rather than draped in damask.

*A la carte*, find Sète's classics, proper *bourride* and *Languedocienne bouillabaisse* (not the soup, the banquet), and there is a pricier *menu dégustation* as you would expect from the dining room of the port's principal hotel. But the hallmark is the light touch of the kitchen, an awareness of – but not obeisance to - modern Mediterranean fashion. A €27 menu (cut-down €19 version for lunch) draws locally sourced ingredients, yet veers away from tradition to tickle a few unexpected treats. Thus, *bouillon* of mussels features ginger and coconut milk and a simple poached egg provides focus for mushrooms and Mediterranean extras to launch a meal in comfort.

Equally welcoming is the service, should *daurade* be announced as dressed in *chorizo*, a request for a non-meat version would be met not with the lip-curl of the snob, but an enthusiastic consideration of alternative accompaniment. Desserts seriously in the *marrons*, chocolate, *nougatine* and macaroon tradition of the South. Untethered to any of the three menus, you could expect to shave a good €50 or more from your plastic before you even glance at the wine list. But you'll not feel hard done by.

**La Voile Rouge €€**
route des Plages, 34200 Sète
04 99 04 09 22
May-Sep
Hervé, from the eponymous **Bistrot** in **Agde** is in charge of the kitchen at this summer only address on the plage des Quilles. A chic beachwear boutique and the usual trimmings of a private beach bar greet you as you hit the deck.

You could simply rent a sunbed and help yourself from the salad counter, or decide to sit at at a proper table, on bold red directors chairs emblazoned with Hollywood A-list names, to enjoy a meal of classic meat and fish dishes. A key music venue in season, with packed concert programme always worth checking out. Consider this the compromise between the cutting edge of **AmeriK** and the laid back chill of **Ola**.

# Villeneuvette [5] C1

**La Source** €€
place Louis XIV, 34800 Villeneuvette
04 67 96 36 95 www.hoteldelasource.com
Closed Tue, Wed
The address is superfluous really. This city is so small that street names seem something of an affectation, and the restaurant is practically on the ramparts. Once, we would drive past Villeneuvette on our way to Christmas Day lunches at an *auberge*, ten minutes away, and it was on the slow return home one year that we first stumbled across a city that is smaller than a hamlet (see page 243). We exclaimed little yelps of surprise at finding that the micro-city has a *Logis de France* hotel and soon we began regular spring trips just beyond Clermont l'Hérault for lunches by the pool on the shady terrace.

There is also a nice vaulted dining room here, but for me **La Source** is sitting in the shade looking at lush greenery and waiting for the "*trio de*" whatever tickles the chef to arrive as a first course, then sneaking covetous glances at the plates of my dining companions. Madame Inge Bernadou is an elegant and welcoming hostess, service is always polite and efficient and we've found the cuisine smart and original without being too clever.

Chicory (that which France calls *endive*) gives a peppery breath to salads or a summer white-fish starter: asparagus is always treated well in April; fresh oysters and country fowl feature liberally on seasonally changing menus, and there is always a little revelation – perhaps that Midi stalwart *brandade de morue* couched on such northern a bed as a waffle, or maybe a creamy fennel and passion fruit dressing-up of a smoked and roasted bream. Over the past few years we have particularly appreciated the lighter two-course lunch option at €19 during the working week, but generally menus will start in the late twenties and rise steadily towards the chef's ultimate surprise menu: five courses invented at the time of your meal, served to everyone at the table at €55 a head. In peak summer only, the restaurant opens on Wednesday which makes for a perfect finale to a morning at Clermont l'Hérault on market day.

# Ici on parle Brasucade

IT STARTED WITH AN INVITATION: To be precise; a demanded invitation. Neighbours, the first wave of transmanche Marseillanophiles, had been buying their house wine from the Domaine Morin-Langaran since they swapped Pembrokeshire for Marseillan. The previous Whit weekend, they had noticed much merrymaking going on behind the trees of the Domaine, farthest of the wine houses on the road out of town and and asked if they could join the party. Invitation only, they were told. Oh well, said Colin, who lacks the bashful gene, can we have an invitation for next year? And make that for eight people!

Thus we went in convoy, a coalition of the nations. Interrnational *arrivistes* with French lotus eaters; pert fresh-breath rental cars of tarmac pedigree and asthmatic dirt-track jalopies. Through the vineyard gates we parked on gravel, and walked to the gap in the hedge. Each of us carrying either a hat, garden umbrella or poodle. The field was scored with long trestles draped in white paper cloths and banked by basic rustic benches. We found a spot for eight, planted our parasols in the earth where the trees shadows failed and settled down to enjoy ourselves. The noonday crowd decanted into the field around 500 today, some 550 had been here the day before.

We watched as estate workers built a pyre of vine root and branch on which they would begin the brasucade: barbecue of mussels. The food was free, bar the option of a plate of a dozen oysters for a handful of euros and there was an inexpensive bar selling estate wines at €5 a bottle. I bought a red and a picpoul and a bottle of mineral water, and several of our party shelled out for trays of oysters as we waited for the barbecue to get going. The hostess at the dancefloor-soundsystem-kareoke led popular chansons, as paper plates and cutlery passed along the benches, then bread and the occasional bowl of marinated olives. Between oyster slurps and smacking of lips, table voices augmented the loudspeakers, and the dancefloor filled when *Volare* segued into the easy strains of *La Valse à Dédé de Montmartre*. Fishermen of riper years waved their shirts in the air at a saucy ditty as the music became more festive; and long-hitched couples sloped off to renew vows in fancy footwork, when the right ballad came along.

Fresh rosé, another Picpoul and mineral water assuaged thirst of summer sunshine and seafood and the mussels arrived, liberally splashed over the embers with white wine, olive oil, garlic, thyme, and rosemary scents to tease the breeze. Bread dipped in olive oil, we inhaled a heady perfume of a meal well appreciated. Bowl after bowl of mussels followed as noon turned to one, and the half hour surrendered willingly to two, even three, o'clock. All the while, easy conversation of good company and no work on the morrow floated across the pleasure-stained tablecloth.

Marcel reminisced on country fares, roast meats in his native Brittany, Monique reflected on a Paris upringing when cosmopolitan pleasures never numbered barbecue. Stéphane danced between tongues in bilingual conversation of our mixed Anglophone-francophone crowd, and Colin married a keen sense of irony with an appreciation of the very wonderful frenchness of it all: his conquest of the native language attaining fresh heights with each turn in the conversation and tilt of the glass.

Soon Stéphane and Ruth were rocking around the clock as the music launched itself into the era of everyone's technicolor-remembered party scene, melting back to Piaf and torch songs so we should all be *à table* for barbecued sausages served with hearty helpings of *haricots blancs*. The Vigneron himself strolled between the tables with his own wine bottle to top up the occasional glass and see that bonhomie was bubbling nicely. Cheers to deserving parties were commissioned from the microphone, before karaoke took over from dance music and selected grandmothers and nephews serenaded the company, before the children's talent contest. As the sun slipped harmlessly behind the tall tree screen, so the sea of parasols subsided, and we no longer wondered how many sunshades printed with names of beers and soft drinks vanish each year from cafés. Then came round cardboard platters of apple pie and we regretfully conceded a meal that had began at noon, to retire gracefully at 5pm.

But where was Colin. The man who professed his French to be basic was not to be daunted by a mere audience of 500. We had had a wonderful time, and a handful of anglophone outsiders had been made to feel so welcome at this essentially local event, where no other foreigners had we spotted. Colin, quite rightly, felt that appreciation had to be noted. So he took the microphone, apologised for what he did not consider schoolroom French because he had not paid attention in class, and said simply.

"*Je n'aime pas Tony Blair. Je n'aime pas George Bush. Je ne suis pas Anglais. Je suis Galois*" (perfect French for this).
"*Merci beaucoup. Vive les vacances et Vive La France!*"

Thus was heard the biggest round of applause of the afternoon.

The toddler at the next table was called Hugo, so his grandmother told us (after Victor Hugo, she said, her daughter's literary hero). And a gamin little Gavroche the lad was to be sure. As I listened to Colin's heartfelt words, in a language that still held for him many depths and shallows yet unswum and uncharted, it occured to me that little Hugo's celebrated namesake could not have put it better himself.

# Languedoc Trails

## Taking time to explore

- Discover 20th-century artists in Roussillon;
- The green waterway of the Canal du Midi;
- Legends of donkeys, monsters and wolves in the Cevennes;
- Jazz loving goats in the Hérault hills;
- Follow the paths of persecution in rugged Cathar & Camisard Country
- Or a Jewish heritage circuit through the centuries of the South

# The art of Roussillon

## Collioure, Banyuls & Port Vendres

S EVERAL HUNDRED MILES from the fashionable salons of Paris, the real French don't put great artists on pedestals. When France's then oldest inhabitant was asked what she remembered most about working as maid to Vincent van Gogh in Arles, she replied simply "He stank."

So when Henri Matisse arrived in the anchovy fishing port of Collioure, the locals judged him not as a mere founder of the Fauvist movement, but for his taste in Banyuls wine as poured by Réné Pouls at the bar of the *Hotel des Templiers*. Likewise, Picasso got the nod of approval for tucking into Madame Pouls' *bouillabaisse* whenever he came to town.

Collioure is one of a thread of open secrets strung like so many pearls along the bays of the Roussillon coast from the Spanish border and through French Catalonia. All just half an hour south of Perpignan; a city that always suggests something extra just around the corner. Perhaps it is the sight of the Pyrenees piercing the metropolitan horizon and upstaging the local architecture; maybe the tang of salt sea air that recalls Mediterranean coves just 20 miles down the road; or it could be the truth that the potent blend combination of French, Spanish and Catalan cultures simply can't be contained by city limits.

No one arrives in Perpignan without being made aware that, in the 'sixties, Salvador Dali hailed the local railway station "the centre of the universe". The city itself is slightly more bashful, revising the quote engraved in situ to "Perpignan: Centre du Monde" This dazzling status should not eclipse another world just beyond Dali's universe, one that seduced many of his fellow 20th century artists. The famous station is after all just one of many options for nipping out of town and heading to the *Cote Vermeille*, the Vermilion Coast, named for the dramatic splash of red on the horizon whenever the sun touches the blue Mediterranean.

Collioure is less than 5 euros and 25 minutes from Perpignan by train or half an hour by bus or hire car. Vauban fortifications, Moorish twists to the spire of Notre Dame des Anges and distinctive boats bobbing by a shingle beach, "Collioure without sails is like an evening without stars" said Raoul Dufy. This port has always been great art waiting to happen.

The only surprise is that, through several centuries of stunning architecture and breathtaking views, it took until 1905 for the art world to recognise the fact. Matisse and André Derain thrilled at the bluest skies and seas and took post-impressionist painting to new heights of audacity by flinging vibrant hues on their canvass and shocking the great Paris exhibition of that year with the birth of Fauvism.

Stop by the Espace Fauve on the quayside and spend 5 euros on *Le Fauvisme à Colioure*, a useful little book guide to the Chemin de Fauvisme, at walking trail with 20 reproductions of Matisses and Derains displayed wherever the masters set up their easels. There is a museum of contemporary art in town with works by Jean Cocteau among others, but the real gallery is the port itself. In high season the salt-scented air is spiced with the fragrances of paints and turps as modern-day creatives jostle for the best views. And at the Templiers hotel and restaurant (*see page 300*), some 2,000 paintings cram the walls: the private collection of mine hosts who welcomed the great talents of the past century. Stay for lunch, the food is still some of the best classic cooking in the Elizabeth David tradition to be had on the Med, then ask to see the visitors book with priceless thank-you sketches by Picasso, Matisse and their contemporaries.

It sometimes seems that every bay, every port has its own native or adopted world class artist. Ten minutes along the coast, you learn that neither sunset shades nor sweeping landscape inspired Banyuls' favourite son. Aristide Maillol immortalised curves of a different kind. Born into a fishing and winegrowing family, this contemporary of Renoir and Rodin sculpted the female form, his nudes inspiring an entire museum in Paris and a superb gallery in Banyuls-sur-Mer. Back in the capital of French Catalonia, meet Maillol's women in Perpignan itself. En route to Place République, walk up rue Louis Blanc from the Castillet fortified gateway, the street Louis XIV feared to drive along in 1660 in case his carriage got stuck, and pass a statue bequeathed by the sculptor. Stop off for a drink at the Républic Café, where music tends towards techno and beer may cost a euro or two more than neighbouring bars on the square, but the décor is pure Gaudi camp, a reminder that Perpignan is just across the border from the most famous Catalan city of all.

If a two-hour drive to Barcelona is an art pilgrimage too far, then nip out of town to Céret, where the **Musée d'Art Moderne** is crammed with work by the greatest talents of the last century: Find Maillol's studies for Céret's war memorial and paintings by Miro and Chagall with Salvador Dali's Noah's Ark (*see page 182*).

Proof that art in Roussillon is no mere cosmopolitan affectation lies in the small print. That Picasso you admired, with its symbols of peace, was paid for by the comrades of Céret's communist party, who know a true lover of Madame Pouls' hearty working class bouillabaisse when they see one.

The people of Ceret are never phased by the darlings of the art world. They are used to mingling with great talent. Once Matisse and the Fauvists had settled in nearby Collioure, so sculptor Manolo, composer Déodat de Séverac and painter Frank Burty Haviland, discovered Céret in 1910. Soon, with the arrival of Picasso, Braque and the early cubists, the town became residence secondaire to the artists of Montmartre and Montparnasse. Max Jacob stayed with Picasso at the **Maison Delcros** and helped turn the **Grand Café** into something of a salon for the Paris set and locals alike.

Britons too have been wooed south to the coast and countryside around Perpignan since long before bargain air travel and lifestyle TV began promoting the joys of Catalonia. In 1924, lured by the light, climate and low cost of living, Glasgow's greatest architect and designer, Charles Rennie Mackintosh became an economic migrant settling with his wife for the simple life in Roussillon for the final few years of his life.

At Port Vendres and the spa town of Amélie-les-Bains, the Mackintoshes reinvented themselves as watercolour artists. Just as "Toshie" was never truly acknowledged in his lifetime as the pioneering father of British art nouveau, so his work as a painter was barely mentioned until the 21st century.

Robin Crichton, who lives in the area, turned detective, tracing locations of 34 landscapes for his book *Monsieur Mackintosh*. At Port Vendres tourist office, pick up a map showing a Mackintosh trail round the harbour and beyond with reproductions of his major works at key sites on easels inspired by his own architectural motifs. Thanks to Crichton's sleuthing, when the Scottish National Gallery of Modern Art opened its Mackintosh exhibition in Edinburgh, only four paintings remained unidentified, but not for long. One VIP at the private view was a French councillor who triumphantly proclaimed 'I think that was my granny's place!'

Back in France, Mr Crichton followed the clue to try to find the inspiration for *A Southern Farm*. "Accosting a farmer pruning his peach trees, I showed him a reproduction. 'Recognise this?' I asked. 'Affirmatif! Affirmatif! It used to belong to my auntie'. It is called *Mas Saunier* and is on the old road from Ille Sur Têt to Boulternère, beside a level crossing. To paint it, Mackintosh must have sat on the edge of the railway line."

Another watercolour identified. Just three more to go. Whilst Matisse's path through Roussillon is now part of the landscape and history of the region; for the Scots connection, the trail is still warm.

**Banyuls-sur-Mer: Tourist Office** av République 66650 Banyuls Sur Mer
04 68 88 31 58 www.banyuls-sur-mer.com
**Musee Maillol** Vallée de la Roume, 66650 Banyuls. 04 68 88 57 11

**Céret: Musée d'Art Moderne de Céret** 8 bd Maréchal Joffre, 66400 Céret.
04 68 87 27 76 www.musee-ceret.com
Jul-mid-Sep 10-19; mid Sep-Jun 10-18. Closed Tue Oct-Apr

**Collioure: Tourist Office** place du 18 juin, 66190 Collioure
04 68 82 15 47 www.collioure.com
**Espace Fauve** quai de l'Amirauté, 66190 Collioure. 04 68 98 07 16

**Perpignan** *see page 213*

**Port Vendres**: Tourist Office 1, Quai François Joly, 66660 Port-Vendres
04 68 82 07 54 www.port-vendres.com

*Monsieur Mackintosh* by Robin Crichton (Luath Press ISBN 9781905222360)

# Canal du Midi

## A week in the slow lane

IN THE 17TH CENTURY, 15,000 people worked to build the Canal du Midi, and the project's founder lost his shirt. In early October, my family decided to cruise the Canal du Midi and the project's matriarch lost her balance. The story of Pierre Paul Riquet and the canal is one of vision, drama, sweat and dogged determination; the story of yours truly and that same waterway is one of chance, lunch, more lunch and a determined doggie.

Just as it has wound its way through this book, meandering through tales of trade and fortune, setting Sète fair for global adventure and granting Marseillan financial independence, the tree-lined Canal du Midi has thread the stories of towns cities and villages, meals and moments the length and breadth of our region and beyond.

In 1663 Pierre Paul Riquet began work on this entwined miracle of nature, mechanics and architecture. Women navigators were among the workforce digging the waterway linking the fast flowing estuary tides of the West to the gentle pools of the South. Fed by the natural waters of the Montagnes Noires, shored up by the clasp of the roots of plane trees and regulated by a network of remarkable locks, this happy confluence of hydraulic engineering and the environment, of Creation and creativity was the dynastic legacy of the marriage between Master Riquet and Mother Earth. The true serendipity of the Canal lies in the unalterable truth that, even at its busiest, the heyday of trade in centuries past or the peak of the summer holiday season in our day, this green and shady thoroughfare is completely without urgency. You may not fax, text, bribe nor cajole water to fill up a lock basin any faster than the laws of physics nor the routine of the lock-keeper have predetermined, nor could you fast track ten miles along the route. You may travel only to the natural timetable of the water, or take it even slower, by mooring at the banks and letting dapple-filtered sunlight play on your eyelids as you listen to the sound of nothing happening.

The blissful irony of the 21st century is that what was once the cutting edge of high-speed transportation is now a slip road from the fast lane of modern life. To take command of your own canal boat for week or two, clocking up 50 miles of travel or less, you may hop on a low-cost jet-plane from Stansted, take the Eurostar-TGV 300kph rail option or motor down on the toll free A75, searing through the lush Auvergne. You might, as do TV chefs such as Rick Stein, hire a lumbering great wooden barge big enough to splice through Suez, you may launch your own little motor boat, or you could, as we did, put yourself in the hands of the experts at what was then *Crown Blue Line* (now **Le Boat** www.leboat.com), whose flotilla of sparkling white craft punctuate the thin green line from the casssoulet country of Castelnaudary to the salt flats of the Camargue, the backdrop to Marseille and the Rhône.

As an adoptive *Marseillanais*, I was no stranger to the Canal du Midi. The lighthouse at Les Onglous, where freshwater finally surrenders itself to the waters of the Med in the oyster rich *étang* has long been a familiar landmark on sunset strolls and starting point for picnic excursions with friends chugging from the Thau to the river Hérault. I have driven past and along the rows of trees reflected in the waters en route to the vineyards from Narbonne to Carcassonne. And I have gazed up at the canal, carried over the river Orb on its mighty aqueduct, whilst watching moonlight *son-et-lumière* at Béziers.

But for one week in October, we were to live on the canal. Our car loaded up with the essentials of a family going back to nature (All calculated to the traditional equation: 5 parts food stock to one part necessity; two parts first-aid to one part food. One never knows), we arrived at Port Cassafières, a practical unpretentious basin near the seaside resort of Portiragnes. Checked in, walked out and trained up by welcoming and professional staff, we were taken aboard the good ship *Salsa*: four double cabins, two ensuite shower rooms and two fridges in the spacious galley. Twin command posts from which to steer the vessel: both on top, where al fresco dining would defy autumnal Tramontane winds; and below, where navigation might be indulged in over breakfast in the main saloon.

The vessel was to have two pilots, my father who, in the livery of the Peninsular and Oriental (coiffure and retail photography division), had played a passive role in negotiating the Panama canal more than a half a century earlier, and my much-loved and now painfully missed collie Shadow, alumnus of Battersea Dogs Home, earning his waterwings at the ripe old age of 13. A first night spent wisely in port, with indulgence at the harbourside restaurant, set us up for our inaugural excursion on the morrow.

As our two-legged pilot prepared to swing the 47-foot craft out towards the open, if narrow, waters of the canal itself, he marvelled at the ease and power of Salsa's bow thrusters which effortlessly negotiated the otherwise daunting first manoeuvre.

"Had we had these in Panama in 1952 we would not have needed the mules!" he declared to the bracing autumn breeze. Automated towpath beasts of burden may now be a thing of the past, but their image lives on in the hee-haw braying of the manual flush-pump system of Salsa's toilets, which rends the night air like the final throes of passion of a pair of arthritic asthmatic donkeys. Flushing duties apart, life on the canal is gentle hedonism punctuated by brief nuggets of responsibility; a long tree-lined stretch of mealtime, unbroken but for the courtesies of lock etiquette and the nod-smile-and-wave acknowledgement of fellow travellers.

No need to plot a course once you have decided whether your journey is upstream or down. Instead, map out the day, with charts provided by the boat hire people and the eating out guide you packed in your luggage. Will it be lunch or dinner aboard today and then which restaurant at which port of call for the other meal? A simple pizzeria or café table at the purpose-built harbour at Colombières where a mere omelette or *steak-frites* reminds you that hearty is even closer to the French soul than chic.

Perhaps the more rustic waterfront **Guinguette** at Agde, where unassuming Sunday lunches segue into convivial afternoon and evening tea-dances. *(Visit from Marseillan: it is just by the Agde railway and canal on the route de Marseillan. 04 67 21 24 11)* Or maybe dining-out city-style in Riquet's home town of Béziers at the **Raffinerie** in the port itself.

Our noses lied to us when we scened new mown grass marinated in Sauvignon at Paraza. Erroneous aroma: the whiff was local melon, which, with ubiquitous fig, seems to inspire half the menu at the **Café du Port**, a bistro hewn from a wine cellar on the banks by canal milestone number 436. Service seductively slow, only haste is the early evening jostling for moorings as pleasure boatmen succumb to a siren signature *magret de canard* on the €24 menu.

*Chief Mate Shadow at the helm*

So many meals we blamed for keeping us from the perennial history-hunter's haunt of Carcassonne, picture-book fortified city, like the Canal itself, listed a world heritage site by the United Nations. The UNESCO badge is worn with greatest pride at Fonserannes, the celebrated "nine" (count 'em, seven actually) locks opposite Béziers, Riquet's ultimate achievement. Ask how to carry a boat up a mountain then look for answers as this ladder of lock gates becomes a fountain of stone basins, a cascade of shrewd displacement and a self-disciplined Niagara, with pleasure craft and working boats alike carried level by level higher and higher above the river Orb in their buoyant and spectacular rise until they look across then down on the imposing cathedral surmounting a hill-top city.

You can spot those at the beginning of their canal holiday as the involuntary gulps from the crews at the foot of the ladder reveal that this is only the third or fourth lock challenge that they have faced since collecting the holiday craft. The first lock from Portiragnes is easy. One family member stationed at each end of the boat, another clambers cautiously ashore to wrap rope around unfamiliar metal or stone protrusions. The captain at the helm to ensure the boat steers clear of other craft in the lock and the gates swinging shut as lock keepers raise the water level to the next stretch of canal. The minor ignominy of a dropped rope leaving hands a trifle clammy and reactions jolted alert for the next challenge. This is nothing to the potential for public humiliation at Fonserannes.

At the foot of an impending torrent, the very hall of the mountain king, daunted is as daunted does and novices follow more confident boatmen leaping and looping in time-honoured fashion to the appreciative calls of scores of sightseers - devotees of ineptitude as spectator sport. By the return visit, skills acquired through dozens more simple locks and the knowledge of having survived the first marathon; one is marked out as an old hand.

My father barked instructions from the bridge, Shadow barked encouragement from the bow, my mother and I attended to our duties fore and aft and, along the steps of the towpath, Stéphane led *Salsa* through its paces from the summit to the base of the hill with the ease, grace and comfortable flair of a proud breeder walking Best in Show at Crufts. Pride in the final navigation of this thrilling network of locks assuages regret that the precious week or weeks out of time come to an end. So many glorious moments: the first glimpse of the spires of Capestang rising from a sea of green fields as you turn a bend in the canal; the delightful picturesque detour of the Canal de la Robine through the heart of Narbonne; the sight of working horses being led along the waterside; the sense of achievement as

*Colombières – tranquil haven on the canal*

hunter gatherers leave the boat each morning to harvest baguettes and croissants from village boulangeries and stalk bottles of Minervois wines from vineyards and estates.

The rough with the smooth: we had slipped our way through the vaulted miracle of the Malpas Tunnel, Riquet's second riposte to the hills of a taunting landscape; when at the prospect of Capestang, my mother, hitherto ever-cautious amidships, suddenly took it into her head to leap like an ambivalent amphibious young gazelle from ship to shore. The leap was impressive. The landing, however, something redolent of unforseen consquence, and thus our family learnt that boats and water must always be treated with the utmost respect. And we appreciated the medical facilities of Colombiers before resigning our naval commissions and motoring to the Emergency room at Sète. Leaps and bounds now relegated to memory alongside thoughts of moonlit towpath strolls, locks well-taken and unregulated lunches in the peripheral vision of anglers and falcons, we pass happy hours ashore counting so many more reasons to return to the water: We have yet to go shopping at Claudine Wytrowa's floating *épicerie* the pretty barge *Le Tamata*, moored at Somail, and stock our galley with crusty bread, fresh fruit and vegetables and wine from the *Minervois* slopes on the horizon.

Perhaps to take the Canal in the other direction next time: to follow its final miles as it crosses the urgent flow of the river Hérault at Agde to pass the Bagnas wildfowl reserve. If the coastguard permits, to take to the maritime waters of the Etang, sharing the lagoon with flamingos and *pêcheurs*. To pause for a boatman's holiday and pretend to be strangers, choosing freshest fish in the quayside restaurants of Marseillan, where summer white wine is our house Picpoul grown on the edge of the lake and the holiday aperitif is the world's finest vermouth *Noilly Prat*, still made to the family recipe, seasoned and sun-ripened within a gull's call of the port itself. To take a day off the boat and watch jousting on the canals of Sète, then calmly to coast towards Aigues Mortes along the Canal Rhône-Sète through the *Camargue* lands of white horses and black bulls. Or to retrace the route of our first odyssette past the time-tinted legacy of an age of chivalry and slaughter that is Carcassonne and the rose-coloured splendour of Toulouse to the mighty River Garonne whose force and will led sailors to the Atlantic for even longer than the Canal du Midi has brought the sea to the ocean.

It took Paul Riquet 15 years and his life savings to complete his vision of the Canal du Midi. More than three hundred years later, for the rest of us, it takes less than a week afloat to realise that the dream is still an inspiration.

**www.canal-du-midi.org**

# When Exodus becomes Genesis

## Jewish heritage in the Languedoc

**M**ONTPELLIER IS TWO HOURS from London, three hours from Paris and, on a cold, crisp and billowy evening in December, just four steps from a handcart. It is often easy to forget, when raging about the inconvenience caused by petulant air traffic controllers or flickering cell phone signals, that our spoon-fed, wipe-clean and cruise-controlled lives, lives that can lightly be upset by the unavailability of this season's fashion in this month's waistline, are for so many, but four short steps from the handcart of their last Diaspora.

That simple handcart that carried entire families from precarious familiarity to the next windswept unknown, from fluent comprehension of the world about us to blinking mute trust in whichever Babel deigned to offer refuge. When the handcart was unloaded in the land where communication became cacophony, the first steady step was in setting up a generation that might stride into the new world in tune with the sounds that so intimidated the arrivals. Every step bathed and clothed each succeeding generation in the mantle of security and success. Until each could walk unaided and un-noted in a world where we each choose the town in which we would spend, not our lives, but an evening, a weekend, a phase; as many hours as we liked from our loved ones, safe in the knowledge that home is always an assured time and distance from our every whim.

And so we learned to sulk at inconvenience and pout at the smallest obstacle and wear life as loosely and freely and comfortably tailored as those people whose lives were always so many more than four steps from any hand-cart. But sometimes, walking through those lands that are the birthright of the many and the privilege of the few, and the beacon of so many more than many unfortunates, we meet other strangers. I first caught the glance of complicit history some years ago as I watched the eccentric local sport Lou Capelet from a café table in Marseillan's port, and my

350

coffee arrived with an ironic aside – in unlikely words of Yiddish a thousand miles out of time and place (*see page 84*).

(*see page 84*)

Over the centuries, countless handcarts have been unburdened in Montpellier. From earliest Roman Gaul, through 13th century ages of study and enlightenment and the exodus from Inquisitors of Spain in the West. The last hundred years brought refugees from pogrom and holocaust to the East and post colonial asylum seekers from Algeria, Morocco and Tunisia across the sea to the South, and finally a fair smattering of lifestyle upgraders from Paris and Britain, a commute a grand vitesse or low-cost from the north. And it was here, at the convergence of seasons greetings that the city's tradition of welcome, acceptance and integration was illuminated so vividly that December evening, when the Jewish festival of Chanukah shared its festive lights with all other faiths.

The Christmas Market was in full swing on the place de la Comédie. Scores of wooden chalets clustered round the Tree. Traders sold jars of foie gras, roasted chestnuts and scooped up ladles of rich reluctant cheesy *aligot* as brass bands serenaded *Silent Night*. Along the Esplanade, a bigger crowd clutched proferred candles, clustering around a bandstand where a vast *Chanukiah* candelabrum swayed unsteadily. Huge candles for a holiday lazily translated as Festival of Lights, but in truth a celebration of liberty and deliverance from oppression. As the crowd drew its breath for a rousing chorus of Hebrew carol *Moatzur*, a distinguished community elder, in black hat and coat and white beard, clambered up a branch of the candlestick to straighten an errant *bougie*. Not just a gathering of the like from one long-dispersed community; It was an embrace of a wider humanity. Christmas songs paused along the way, long enough for several hundred celebrants to sing blessings and prayers; a group of Muslim teenagers broke off from break-dancing for coins on the square and joined the Jewish celebration: cheerful *imshallahs* and *salaam alekeims* could be heard amid the *shalom alechems*, hails and farewells as the crowd dispersed to the *Marché de Noël*.

Montpellier was simply doing what this region has done for centuries. Ignoring labels and religious barriers; accepting peoples as people. Languedoc has a fine tradition of religious independence, only its masters having power to oppress minorities. With state decrees, from revocation of the *Edict of Nantes* to Vichy's *Statut des Juifs*, from jittery kings to knights Templar, ready to run to ground dissenters be they Camisard protestant, Cathar non-conformist, Jew or Muslim, this region has long demonstrated tolerance, wisdom and a talent for trade. When the King eventually expelled Jews from Montpellier in 1394, sanctuary beckoned in provençal Avignon; since Roussillon was not yet shackled to Languedoc, students set up *yeshivas* (schools) in nearby Narbonne and Perpignan, and settled down to Talmudic study as citizens of neighbouring counties grew hoarse with cries of revolt and defiance. Montpellier's ghetto soon re-established by a new wave of immigrants fleeing the Spanish Inquisition. A tradition of shelter echoed vividly from 1940 when *Montpellieriens* hid families fleeing Nazi and Vichy deportation and smuggled them across borders to freedom, even as some opportunist collaborators seized property. Unsung heroes across the region from Résistance  fighters in the Cevennes, to the nurse who smuggled babies from the Nazi camp in Agde.

The Midi Jewish heritage trail stretches from Spain to the Riviera. Under 12th century Catalan rule, studies in arts, philosophy and sciences integrated fluently with mainstream intellectual society. North of the Pyrennees, Bayonne, ironically famous for its ham, credits Jewish settlers for introducing chocolate and coffee to the nation. Jews arrived with the Romans to Agde and Narbonne, in the 5th century, and greatest testimony to integration is the faculty of medicine at Montpellier itself (*see page 196*), courting Hebrew and Islamic students from its founding in 1180 when Guillem VIII granted Jews the right to practice Medicine, a privilege reinforced in 1272 and 1281 by the Majorcan and Aragon kings James I and II. The honours board's roll of Hebrew names testament to the wisdom that in order to found a medical school, you must read and interpret the earliest Aramaic and Arabic texts. Amongst the later alumni, one Michel de Nostradame, whose family had been forced to deny their religious identity by the Spanish Inquisition, later found immortality as the mystic seer Nostradamus.

Despite spats and rapprochement with scholars of Granada and Cordoba, the Maimonodes tradition of the cultures uniting for common good flourished for centuries, academia coupled with a canny knack for trade. Languedoc's ghettoes were originally quarters of tolerance rather than oppression, states within a state, haven from secular law. So successful were Montpellier's ghetto bakers, that a 1364 by-law banned shops from selling to the wider community to stop commercial jealousies bubbling into racism. The main ghetto features on an official tour and was centred around today's rue Barralerie, and eventually, as the community prospered, families built large houses on fashionable squares. Number 1 is home to the beautiful renaissance Mikve (*see page 203*) and a synagogue from the same period, which when restored will be more ornamental heritage site than place of worship. But, as we discovered that chill December night of candles on the Esplanade, a flourishing community has new synagogues, kosher butchers, shops and a bustling community centre as well. Sète, which played a key role in the post-War *Exodus* emigration saga numbers many Marseillanaises amongst its congregation and has a kosher winery.

Historians continue to find traces of past communities. Some old houses in Marseillan have carvings suggesting Jewish silversmiths found sanctuary in the village after fleeing the Spanish inquisition. And the Marseillan port trade began with a nudge from the jewish community of Lunel.

In Pézenas, the 13th century *Quartier Juif* may be explored below the walls. Walk under a low arch into rue de la Juiverie and stroll rue Litanie. The tourist office organises guided visits, and original synagogue stones can be seen in St-Nazaire church. Despite free-trade rules, a ghetto in a litigious city of the Estates General was not immune to prevailing winds of political sensibilities. Portcullis-style gates closed off each end of the L-shaped ghetto between the Portes de Faugères and Biaise, easily dropped down to keep residents quiet when more powerful neighbours started squabbling, but lifted when the markets could open safely!

Across the county line, Nîmes nudges the frontier between the provinces of Languedoc and Provence. A settlement since the seventh century, the first recorded synagogue was founded in the 10th. In the 11th century, Mont Duplan, one of the hills within the city walls, was called Poium Judaicum and was the site of a long-gone Jewish cemetery. The modern synagogue dates from 1793, the dawn of post revolutionary era on the cusp of religious minorities being granted French citizenship, and just before Napoleon integrated Jewish law into French Civil Law with his Assembly of Jewish Notables. The building also has a mikve and a matzo bakery.

From Nîmes; detour to Arles, where, though the mediaeval ghetto along rue du Docteur Fanton is no more, artefacts are preserved at the Musée Arlatan. On to Avignon, Carpentras and Cavaillon, even a detour to St Remy (where Montpelleir old boy Nostradamus wrote his *Siècles* prophesies). Provence always a safe haven: The Vaucluse in particular, under Vatican rule from 1274 until the Revolution, granted unthought of liberties and the community flourished during the era of the Avignon Popes. The area was known as the *Comtat Venaissin*, and Jews here had their own *provencal* dialect, even a distinct local liturgy, and were known as "The Pope's Jews". Three of the four holy towns (*Arba Kehilot*) Avignon, Carpentras and Cavaillon, (the other was l'Isle-sur-la-Sorgue), retain well preserved remains. In Cavaillon, the former synagogue and ghetto bakery is now a well stocked museum.

The 6<sup>th</sup> Avignon pope was a son of Languedoc. Urban V was a passionate believer in education, and dismissed papal trappings in favour of centres of learning. He saved Toulouse's music school, founded a university in Hungary and ensured funding for Montpellier's medical faculty; establishing colleges and libraries across the region, including several in his home county of Lozère, where he commissioned the 14<sup>th</sup> century cathedral in Mende. The same architect said to have built a matching Carmelite Convent and Synagogue: the buildings still stand, but not open to visitors.

Of course religious tolerance is not the most quantifiable of concepts. In 14<sup>th</sup> century Montpellier it might be manifest through a benevolent pope putting young Moishe through med school. In 2010, historians found traces of another hidden synagogue to be restored in the heart of Béziers. The city, once known as la *Petite Jérusalem* (Little Jerusalem), home to several respected scholars, has chapters of oppression woven into its complex tapestry of religious uprising (*see page 167*). The 12<sup>th</sup> century Viscount Raymond Trencaval, who had often appointed Jews to major public office, persuaded bishop Guillaume that a simple tax at Eastertide might be a more appropriate way of celebrating Holy Week than the long-standing local tradition of throwing stones at Jews. Happily, the grateful community was no stranger to Leviticus 24, and when seven years later, in 1167, citizens of Béziers rose up to assassinate Trencaval, Jews refused to take part. And so were saved from the bloody revenge massacre of the city and won another century of freedom to live, work and study in the Béziers.

In our day, the cost of tolerance is so much lighter, but rewards and legacy remain potent. Whether in lively Chanukah party by the Christmas market in Montpellier, swapping the daily baguette trek in the village for a Friday challah and bagel run to the city or in a complicit summer toast by the port; find echoes in memories of those who sheltered victims of the Holocaust or the simple bonhomie of sipping a mint tea with the locals in the modern quarter of north African Arabs acknowledging shared heritage of the sons of Abraham, all finding a safe haven in a welcoming land.

---

**Guided tours in Montpellier, Pézenas and Beziers:** see tourist offices.

**Arles** Musée Arlatan, 29 rue la République 04 90 93 58 11 www.museonarlaten.fr
**Cavaillon** Musée Juif Comtadin, rue Hébraïque, 84300  04 90 76 00 34
**Vaucluse**: 04 90 80 4700; www.provenceguide.com
Avignon, Carpentras and Cavaillon: free booklet *Road to Jewish Heritage*.

# Dare to be different

## Along the paths of Cathars & Camisards

EVEN THOSE WHO ARRIVE in Languedoc without a Dan Brown primer may not escape the legend of the Cathars. The echo of an 800-year-old fundamentalist massacre still shakes stone walls of many a vibrant city, and those drip-fed tales of slaughter and torture in a land whose hallmark is tolerance bring a sudden chill to the hottest days of summer. Most people have just the haziest awareness of era when knights of old rode through France; and those of us raised on a diet of toy soldiers and tales of brave adventure, tend to dismiss this as mere prologue to Crusades proper in the Holy Lands. Pristine re-enactments of chivalry have coloured the history books to obscure what was effectively a papal jihad.

But the tale of Cathars and their extermination is one that threads through the region. And whilst those keen to retrace the full story on lonely hillsides and in ruined castles have a well-documented trail from the coast to the back country, a little background knowledge is invaluable when deciphering the legend of a massacre that spilt its blood mere yards from the welcoming shops and restaurants of tourist cities.

The Cathar cult flourished in 12$^{th}$ century Languedoc, tapping into a non-conformist spirit that still thrives in our secular age. Hippy farmers and itinerant winegrowers in Florac market, communes in the abandoned village of Celles, artists' studios in most unlikely settings today are successors to the Cathars: a breakaway branch of Christianity that rejected culture of power, politics and wealth, lived frugally by the teachings of the Lord's Prayer alone, gave women equal rights and roles as preachers and, crucially, prayed and read the bible in vernacular and not Latin. *Parfaits* (priests) dined as vegans with their flocks. Their legacy survived their fate; as *le Désert* harboured the *Camisards* (*see page 357*).

More than twenty years ago, we stumbled across a country fête high up in the hills of the Pyrénées Audoises, leaves not yet burnt crisp gilt by summer sun, breezes a balm in the late afternoon heat; in a clearing, a beast was roasting over a spit, its juices basting vegetables beneath. Pulled to a bench by villagers and urged to share their feast, we grasped cups of rich red wine and swayed to music from lute and pipe players on a rock above the merriment. When my guest timidly refused the proffered meat, the comely

355

serving maid pointed to a bearded bearlike giant in the minstrels' gallery. *"C'est mon mari"*, she said, her husband. And we cowered at the prospect of vengeful chastisement. Our waitress smiled "We live the simple life, we work the land and we are vegetarian. I have a good vegetable *ragout* at home for his supper tonight. Let me heat some and bring it to you."

The French have never been comfortable with vegetarians. But what might be dismissed as faddish and eccentric in our day, worthy of a mere shrug and a badly-turned omelette, was in another age symptomatic of something far more dangerous. Self-contained, self-sufficient Cathar settlements, with stripped-down philosphies, considered as much a threat at home as Saracen attack from the Middle East: Noblemen liked the simple tenets of the cult, less of a political and financial minefield than the conventional church; peasants were happy with prayers and services they could understand. Pope Innocent III called for the Cathars' destruction and the Knights Templar of Simon de Montfort rode through the region (and many pages of this book) with battle hymns promising to raze to the ground any town that sheltered such heresy, vowing to spare not even a "new born baby". Ironically, in a land that later offered sanctuary from Spain's Inquisition and united Semitic races in the common good, the regimented annihilation of all Cathars in France delivered the promised bloody genocide and slaughter of pacifists. And so Cathars were first in a nation's legendary roll of rebels against the state to be destined for martyrdom. Like Joan of Arc and more recently Jean Moulin (*see page 174*), icons of those who dare say no.

Interest has been reignited by popular fiction: Kate Moss's *Labyrinthe* and Hollywooded conspiracy theories over ruined towers on improbable clifftop outcrops of the Cathar trail. *The da Vinci Code* may be catalyst to lure travellers off main roads and up to the rugged hills of Languedoc, but even regular city-hopping and sightseeing take in key moments of the story. No one may visit **Beziers**, where citizens hid their Cathar neighbours, and be unmoved by the papal legate's chill order to burn down the churches and kill the entire population of the city in revenge (*see page 169*), nor walk the fairy tale ramparts of **Carcassonne** and be unaware of the torture chambers within. In **Minèrve**, wind rustling through rocks and gorges brings no noise but a silence, perhaps an echo of the stoicism of the martyrs. Hikers echoing the simple life, if not the dietary regime, espoused by the Cathars take an official 250km trail of ruined castles from **Port-la-Nouvelle** on the coast near Narbonne winding inland to Foix, with the penultimate stop at **Montségur**, across the border: chilling monument, where 200 men and women were burnt alive strapped to a pyre after a 10-month siege. The path through Corbières and Minervois passes **Espezel**, **Puivert** and **Quillan**.

Maps and itineraries at tourist offices *(see pages 370-1)*. Even with no backpack nor sturdy shoes, such ruins prove a magnet for digression. When turning left at Limoux, by the single track railway and narrow hillside lanes to and from Quillan, en route to mountain resorts of the Aude, **Rennes-le-Château** is where rumour, legend and best-seller would have you believed the 19th century priest Bérenger Saunière discovered the lost treasure of the Cathars, the Holy Grail itself. Almost a century after Saunière's death in 1917 (when his final shrift chilled his confessor), no one knows the truth. Visit daily Mar-Nov (w/e only off-season) to tour Rennes-le-Chateau's sites (admission fee). **Petit Train** up the hill from the station in summer.

The slaughter of the Cathars was not the end of persecution. Whilst, in 1598 Henry IV signed the Edict of Nantes, to end centuries of religious wars, less than a century later, Louis XIV revoked the ruling in 1685, effectively outlawing Protestantism. Temples demolished, children snatched from parents who refused to recant, so non conformists took to the *Désert*, an ironic name for the verdant Cevennes and hills of Languedoc, but a nod to the biblical exodus, as Protestants were forced out of their homes. This untamed topography, where later Résistance   fighters hid from the Nazis, was backdrop to another protestant campaign: the *Camisard* revolt of 1702. Huguenots practiced their religion in secret, holding services in cellars or preaching high on the hillside, with an eye alert for raids from the authorities. The *Camisards* won their name from their *camises*, or *chemises*, white shirts worn at night for easy recognition. At the **Musée du Désert**, at Le Mas Soubeyran in **Mialet**, glimpse the clandestine world of closet protestant, in the home of *Camisard* leader, Pierre Laporte, known to his followers as Roland: evocations of daily life, illicit bibles and a pulpit hidden in a wine barrel. Robert Louis Stevenson continues the tale in his *Travels with a Donkey* at the pretty village of **Le Pont de Montvert,** where rebellion became bloody, and the hunted turned on their tormentors: A fanatical anti-protestant priest slaughtered in his bed.

**Rennes-le-Château** 04 6874 05 84 www.rennes-le-chateau.fr **[5] A3**
**Musée du Désert** 04 66 85 02 72 museedudesert.com Closed Dec-Feb

---

## They who would valiant be ...

More peaceful trails reflect less violent aspects of religion. The **Chemin Saint-Jacques de Compostelle** is the 9th century pilgrim route to the shrine in Galicia, Spain. The *Via Arletanensis* (on hiker route **GR 653**) has UNESCO heritage status: **St Guilhem de Desert, St Thibéry** and **Le Grau d'Agde**, within a comfy drive of Marseillan. An alternative trail runs south of Auvergne via **Gévaudan** in **Lozère** (**GR 65**) Maps from regional tourist offices (*page 370-1*)          **www.chemins-compostelle.com**

# Lozère: a hidden heartland

ALMOST IMPOSSIBLE TO BELIEVE THAT LOZERE is in France, let alone Languedoc. It seems just too big to have been kept secret for so long. The only departement in the region with no coastline, but a bridgespan from Hérault: marked out by the **Cévennes**, granite scored **Margaride** and **Gorges du Tarn**, this territory has left its footprint on history and literature; yet neither subdued nor compromised by tourism. South of Auvergne's volcanos, it is known for the land itself rather than man's 'civilising' imprint. Lozère is my secret detour at the end of a long drive south from Paris and the *Périph*, pacing me into time and place.

I slip into Languedoc by this back door; ignore the clear road ahead and peel off the A75. The motorway has many sirens to keep one from the byways. Park and take photos of the viaducts: the elegant **Millau** crossing and Gustave Eiffel's **Viaduc de Garrabit**, a sweep of ironwork that carries the *train à petite vitesse* to Paris and probably won the engineer the deal for his more famous tower. Much to keep you on the fast track: even motorway rest stops are destinations, locally run shops and restaurants. Roquefort and paté deli at **Aveyron**, dried wild mushrooms from **St Chely d'Apcher** at **Aire de la Lozère** and, just across the viaduct, **Aire de Larzac** has a *Bergerie* restaurant that we discovered on our last drive down. Delicious *aligot* and succulent lamb and mutton from a flock grazing by the car park.

But once in Lozère, we turn off to yet another "Venice of", this time the village **La Canourge**, where I have smacked my lips after many a feast. Then on to **St Enemie**, capital of quaint, and as good a point as any to trot down to **La Malène** and board a boat, to be punted by garrulous bataliers along the fast flowing waters of the Tarn Gorges. The unwritten story of the waters that cleave through the cliffs is evocative stuff: An old stone house perched on high may be where young Jacqueline Bouvier summered long before she ever dreamt of the surnames Kennedy or Onnasis; the rock may rise 50 metres or 500 metres above your head as you lie back, fingers teasing the sheet of pure water that divides the carp from the dragonfly. The facts dance through your mind with as little purpose as truant lads diving and splashing from rocks on the wrong side of the river.

There is a serious city here somewhere, but it is **Mende**, and not on the cosmopolitan party circuit. I prefer **Florac**, the second county town, gateway to the non-conformity of Languedoc here (rarity in France) Protestant temples outnumber Catholic churches, and the tradition of welcoming outsiders is never so vividly illustrated as on Thursday's market day when hippy market gardeners come to town selling honeys, jams, and juices. The knife grinder sports a Mohican crop and the farmer's wife a linen cap; young impoverished *vignerons* beg portions of garden for vines from landowners, paying rent in bottles of wine; here artists' studio doors open to the street. Any day, find farm shops and musicians in shady squares. At Hallowe'en season, travellers warm themselves at the annual soup festival when the purchase of a ladle provides a weekend's sustenance. Florac is gateway to the Cévennes, where grey *lauze* roof tiles, glimpsed through screens of chestnut and oak, gradually concede to Midi terracotta; where parked cars by the roadside are the only sign of hunters and mushroom foragers tramping deep into the woods. Time has been kind to Lozère: **Le Pont de Montvert** (*see page 357*) once famed for religious savagery, today picturesque riverside home to artists and craftsmen.

Robert Louis Stevenson passed through on his famous *Travels With A Donkey*. Today's visitors hire donkeys to carry their kit on a hiking trail, overnighting on farms and in chambres d'hôtes. Like an ardent Titania, I too am enamoured of an ass, so at **Domaine des Boissets**, a tiny hamlet on the **Causse de Sauveterre**, where donkeys chewed my worldy goods, I mooched through barns to see exhibitions of rural life. One of the farm kids rustled up a fabulous lunch to a grandmother's recipe. Several summers on, I still salivate at the memory of amazing aubergine and barnyard fare! If donkeys are too tame, try the werewolf legend of the *Bête de Gevaudan*, a thrilling gothic tale of wild landscapes littered with virginal corpses. In **Gévaudan** and **Marvejols**, we may no longer encounter the creature Stevenson dubbed a lupine Napoleon Bonaparte, but visit a sanctuary, sanctioned by Brigitte Bardot, where wolfpacks still roam. After escaping to and through Lozère, I may loop back to the A75, or maybe meander through **Ales, St Jean de Gard**, the pottery paradise of **Anduze**, where glazed planters are the gardener's Holy Grail, then on down to Nîmes. Perhaps pass a magical afternoon in the Gard at the **Bambouseraie** bamboo park, where wind and water chime the air and still the soul. Stevenson took a similar diversion, through this perfect decompression chamber between real life and the Languedoc coast; he stood on the threshold of Lozère, gazed across the mountains to the distant Mediterranean, and declared this "a view into the hazy air of heaven".

---

**Lozère Tourism**, 04 66 65 66 00 www.Lozère -tourisme.com
**Cevennes Tourism** www.cevennes-Lozère .com
**Gorges du Tarn** www.ot-gorgesdutarn.com
**Les Loups de Gévaudan** 48100 Saint-Léger-de Peyre
04 66 32 09 22 www.loupsdugevaudan.com closed Jan-early Feb
**Steam Train** St Jean du Gard to Anduze www.trainavapeur.com
**Bamboo Park** www.bambouseraie.com

---

# The kids are alright

## Say Cheese in the picturesque back country

We were off to take favourite coals to Newcastle. Our house-guests hailed from the country of *Camembert, Livarot, Pont l'Evèque* and incomparable *Issigny* creams and butter. So where better for a last day in Languedoc, before the long drive back to Normandy, but a trip to a dairy. Having already introduced Albert, Pascaline and Chloe to a two-year-old elephant at Sigean, we set off to share a valedictory breath of Languedoc, up close and personal with day old baby goats.

When the goatherd takes his flock to the hills, farmer's-wifely magic in the dairy makes the finest goats cheese in France (there are so many medals to prove it) which we always order as a salad at the *Taverne*, in lieu of dessert *Chez Philippe* in Marseillan). Pelardon is a Cevenol appellation and a deliciously distinctive cheese that reigns supreme served warm, and equal delightful chilled and fresh in a sandwich. Not powdery, but unctuous and unexpected. So we drove high up through hinterland slopes and crests to find the farm and buy some cheese. The road took us through the protected natural parkland, with its awe-inspiring views.

From Marseillan, we crossed the river Hérault at Agde, took a sharp turn to drive alongside the canal du Midi, and followed the D13 through Bessan, skirting Pézenas and continuing on through Roujan to Gabian. Where a faded advertising mural promises *Du bo, Du bon, Dubonnet,* we turned right and followed the *chemin* Montesqieu/Mas Rolland. Ever a good ten minutes of remote country lanes and magnificent scenery, before self doubt sets in and we fear we have taken the wrong course. Not until the heart sinks, do we see carved caprine-silhouettes announcing our arrival at **Mas Rolland**, and the farm; neat and clean and home to seriously happy and contented animals.

One day, charged with good bread and those wonderful little pelardons from the dairy, we shall wander in the hills, picnic and meet up with Eric, the goatherd, mid-afternoon when he herds his flock back to the milking sheds. This time, we parked in the driveway alongside other five o'clock strangers to await the opening of the dairy counter. Around the same time, the mellow stone walls of Montesquieu echo to a clarion clap of bells and hooves as goats, goatherd and skip-fast, sharp-eyed collies make their way

360

past the old village washhouse and through the gate to the barns. Since, on this sunny spring afternoon, we had arrived at the Mas Rolland a good half an hour before milking, we sneaked round to see the goats. A few tentative chews of our sleeves, the odd nuzzle from a velvety nose and many unblinking amber stares greeted us, as we continued through to the stalls at the rear of the shed, where extra family press-ganged into seasonal service, was organising the afternoon feed. Several nanny goats had given birth in recent days and scores of lively kids leapt around their human nursemaid who deftly, firmly steered the inquisitive youngsters to a row of rubber teats leading from a large vat of milk. Most of the kids seemed more interested in sucking on Chloe's fingers, nibbling toothlessly at my buttons and butting passing elbows than drinking from the tap, but, one by one, the sixty or so youngsters all managed a healthy feed, when not playing king of the castle with an old kitchen chair.

Then, from the milking shed, came the sound of music; grown up music; Miles Davis in his prime. Eric's trad-jazz CDs the signal for mother goats to amble towards and climb the ramp into the milking bays. Patiently allowing themselves to be connected to the pumps, they peered out of the window at visitors, gazing at each new arrival, with the regimented complacency of *les vieilles* at an old-fashioned hairdressers. Some speak of the herbs of the *garrigue*, Eric himself is passionate about organic farming, but I reckon that the chill-out music creates the most contented goats in Christendom and thus the finest cheese on any table.

The business of the tables comes later when queues to taste and buy our cheeses from the tiny counter at the dairy. Since it was the birthing season, regular smooth and delicious pelardons were augmented by some extra creamy day old cheeses, a springtime joy. Transactions are intimate *affaires*, the counter, a confessional, step in and close the door behind you, and be honest as to just when and how you plan to enjoy your cheese: With *pain rustique* tomorrow lunchtime; tonight, toasted on a salad; to share with family at the weekend. For every option, a wise dairywoman will select the right cheese to be in peak condition for its moment of glory. With our clutch of designated cheeses, we picked up some acacia honey made by Eric's neighbours, this for the designated *pelardon* to be drizzled with honey and chopped walnuts, scented with lavender and wrapped in filo pastry for our guests' final taste of Languedoc.

---

**La Ferme du Mas Rolland**
34320 Montesquieu
04 67 24 65 40
Feb-Oct: 16.30-19.00; Closed Nov-Jan

---

# The beat of the Off-Season

Those whose evenings evoke the Yardbird and the Duke tend to drive an old Jag rather than a new BMW and have the dress sense of a material witness or suspect in a 1970s police show. They lead blameless lives, but when night draws in in the autumn, or spring twilight lingers, find themselves at Marseillan's theatre [1] C3 when there is a **Jazzinade** in the month. *Jazzinade* plays three or four gigs in the village, most famously *Fête de la Musique* on the quay, and calls itself a band of *jazzométrie variable*.

So the line-up varies, but always a row of saxmen, young and instinctive to time-tried and trusted veterans; from clarinet's first gulp to last shriek of the tenor sax; a rhythm section of bass and drum to carry you from time to place. Luc on guitar and drummer Pierre, have left, but Guy strums and Matthieu drums in their wake: Benjamin's bohemian fiddling, Bruno at the keyboard and Chantal patting bongos, eyes and mind in another dimension, remain. Ever a soul searing sax solo from Jean-Luc and limelight moments for fellow wind and brass crew Serge, Jean Pierre, Benny, Georges, Francis and Rosalie: *Larry Addleuse*; when Rosalie puts down her trumpet and picks up a harmonica, *vin du pays* becomes *Southern Comfort*.

Simple recipe for an autumn or spring evening of *Jazzinade*: Turn up at the theatre, find a table, and amble to the bar (each evening, another *vigneron* does the honours). With a bottle of something rich, ready, local and ripe, a baguette or handful of peanuts, sit back as local musicians play the first set; *A-Train* to *Caravan*; air heavy with the spirit of Davis and Hancock, and more than an echo of Django and George. Next, the guest artists, professional musicians from another corner of the globe and always a treat, especially if the soloist does for American vowels what Dick Van Dyke did for cockneys, and you realise that tortured pronunciation actually sharpens lyrics. And finally: what France calls *boeuf* and we know as jam. *Jazzinade*, their guests and strangers improvise together. One memorable evening (was it that late night with Bob and Françoise, when we continued playing Chet Baker and Brassens tracks on their terrace til small hours, or another time with other friends and neighbours?) when a young woman, leaving the arm of her mariner escort, walked from the back of the room evoking Gershwin's *Summertime* and Baker's *Autumn Leaves* in a rich mezzo, mesmerising musicians to memorable accompaniment, and transporting Marseillan one step closer to heaven. **jazzinade.musique.com**

## On ecoute la Java ...

**Marseillankordeon** is a new association, celebrating art and music of accordion and organising international concerts. The inaugural event with *Madagascar All Stars* proved world class world music. **www.marseillankordeon.com**

**Massilhan Zinga Zanga** takes to the streets whenever a Brazillian Marching Band is needed. Rehearsing year round, a feature of every fete, their *batacudda* percussion parade in vibrant green and yellow **www.myspace.com/m-zz**

362

# The View from the Rentrée

A MARSEILLAN SUMMER'S LEASE hath all too short a date and once the warm breath of August tires of caressing sun-lazy eyelids, visitors leave for metropolitan diversions, far from such simple pleasures as numbering sails and swallows, whilst losing count of oysters, olives and sips of crisp dry white.

Nonetheless, we are not short of performance here. The *hirondelles* (collective French noun for house-martins, swallows and swifts) are on manoeuvres today. They have been lining up in rows and practicing their swoops and dives with narry the prospect of a midge *tardive*. Most tellingly they are ignoring formation in favour of little independent sorties and excursions within the group. Last afternoon, after the rain, there was some serious checking of wings, tails, feathers and undercarriage. It is all too obvious that Africa beckons and we will be losing the cheery company of the birds until springtime and a new nesting season. It seems so awfully far and distant. I remember last year, on the morning that the telephone wires were *complet, les hirondelles* lined wing by jowel: after half-hour roll call and avian migration check, the flock soared, swooped, circled and disappeared for the last time, destinations climes afar remote. Fifteen minutes later, the last two swallows in Marseillan landed on the wire, looked left and right then turned to upbraid each other in mute reproach for tardiness. Flamingos, remaining on the etang through autumn and beyond, are poor substitutes for chattering dive bombers.

What a difference a few days make. Last week was summer: Restaurants packed with people in unaccustomed shorts and shirts, lobster-bright foreheads and well bitten forearms framing unfamiliar menus, deciphering the

French for all kinds of wonderful fish, cheeses and desserts; night sky underscored with squeals of holiday girlfriends debating whether to succumb to the charms of boys practicing handbrake turns in borrowed cars or revving motorcycle engines; inevitable quarrels between port dogs and interloping pampered pets of holidaymaking *arrivistes* - resulting in the intervention one memorable night of a *chasseur's* shotgun firing warning salvos skyward as two yorkies and a poodle yapped and over-yapped social supremacy against the stardrop. At the first two shots, owners took the squabblers indoors, but a muted campaign of vocal defiance still rent the air. Another shot and one final yelp from a poodle muzzle smothered by an owner's discreet palm.

But that was last week and the weeks before. Final Friday in August, summer migrants began the long return to responsibility; on Saturday even more; and Sunday morning saw the last leave by sunrise. For August 31 is the witching hour, and all good Parisians must be tucked up in their own arrondissements before September arrives bringing a cold shower of reality to those for whom the Mediterranean is but a midsummer fortnight's dream. Those lucky enough to call the sea *mare nostrum*, wake up and marvel at the tranquillity of it all, for this is a special private annexe to summer: September, when oppressive temperatures of August magically melt into refreshing breezes and warming back-rubbing, cheek-blushing sunshine.

Tranquillity annotated by sounds of normality: hammer-clank of workmen returning to their daily work: whether fixing of a tile or jangle of worksite scaffolding: wheezing and rasping of industrial vehicles, called into service a fortnight too early, to deal with unexpected grape *vendange* not anticipated for another fortnight. Another exceptional summer.

With harvest happening as I type, and every casual strike of the village clock bringing another little truck to empty its cargo of grapes into a loading bay, vats must be emptied of last years wine to make way for the new. I recall one year in Maury, two counties closer to the Spanish border, seeing diminutive men in shorts, covered in grape juice, sweeping and scrubbing out underground wine vats like so many munchkins or oompah loompah's from Willy Wonka's chocolate factory. Time is of the essence. So grape-picking machines trundle and intimidate through narrow streets; and one morning, a residential road rendered suddenly inaccessible by the elongated juggernaut that is the area's mobile bottling plant. *Vignerons* have but to supply the wines and the bottles and all is done. A matter of great urgency - yet still at noon, workers take themselves inside the warehouse, open a bottle of wine, and eat a full and grand midday meal.

364

This love of food and of the ritual of dining is something that make life here so wonderful. When we were promised a *son et lumière*, the most memorable moment was in observing technicians, surrounded by scaffolding, wires and huge amplifiers, stopping to dine properly in the hour before the show started. Roadïes and sparks, who elsewhere  might have munched a burger or kebab, swigged a can of cola and drawn on a cigarette whilst clambering up precarious piles of technical equipment, here freeze-framed their working life to indulge in a two course dinner proper.

One sitting on a neighbours wall, using steps as a table; another, shirtless and perspiring, wrapped around a pole, and crouched over a dinner tray; a third inclined against the platform, elbow on plank; and a fourth fellow, perched on a huge speaker, leaning down to his plate. All four men holding their cutlery in the accustomed manner of *habitués* of the starched linen and silver plate circuit, savouring plates of duck and seasonal vegetables: a fork poised in mid air, describing arcs of appreciation as its handler savours subtleties of a sauce; a knife carving through melting potato with the artistic precision of a surgeon and soul of a poet; the measured pace of the main course followed by the scoop and scrape devouring of a dessert, then napkins to lips, cutlery to plates, palms smack-wiped to finality and the men of the Midi were ready to present their *son et lumière*.

So many contrasting evenings and afternoons have coloured countless summers in Marseillan. For three extravagant seasons, Port Tabarka was transformed into 15th century Marseillan and a Kalifa's harem for the epic retilling of the legend of *La Belle Scribote* (*see page 90*). Since Yves Michel became mayor, he has compensated townsfolk for the loss of the annual extravaganza by adding even more locations for late night music in the season. When the Paul Selmer big band sets up stage next to the theatre, the Pradet boulodrome becomes a *buvette* and plastic tumblers are charged late in the night as the professional singers and dancers segue from Beyonce to the Andrews sisters, Jacques Brel to Abba. The last time I had seen the Pradet come to life this way was a long ago *soirée* after a sultry July afternoon when we had found sanctuary from the heat in the cool airy church of Marseillan, as a wonderful flautist, protégée of Yehudi Menuhin, enthralled us with Handel, Bach, Chopin and his own compositions. In the blessed cool of the evening, a family of touring acrobats set up their ropes and stage in the Pradet car park. The last of the strolling players of yore - a circus act without a circus, the last vestige of variety, a dying breed; generations of the same family had doubtless toured with the same act for centuries. The grandfather, who had once been the acrobat, then the ring master, and was now, his youthful hose, well-saved, a world too wide for his shrunk shank, a mere Pagliacci, comic relief, here tested ropes with appreciation and experience taught him by his own grandfather, then mooched around the site as speakers blared out big top band music, and the curious and the rest sat in plastic garden chairs by the ring. A light flickered on in the little refreshment van, parked by the public urinal. In the cart, a tired popcorn machine whirred into action as rubbery leaden corn bounced aimlessly. A girl in spangly leotard stood at the counter selling cups of stale corn at high prices and offered cans of drink and ice creams to the crowds.

Eventually, the show started, brain-numbingly corny audience participation, then circus tricks. Every cliché: trapeze work and an indian rope performed excellently by three girls - daughters and granddaughters of the old clown, his sharp eye and firm grip on ropes tied to lamp posts and trees. His son, middle fifties to be sure, doubtless wondering if the family show would last many more years enough for he himself to take on the mantle, motley and red nose of buffoon, should another generation join the act, gave the spiel. Wheedling coins into hats and buckets the girls passed around, setting up a tombola where pound paper tickets won penny plastic prizes - this being the only source of income for the family act - and acting as straight man for the unfunny clown whose interminable routines served to pad out a fifteen minute acrobatic turn into a 90 minute circus. We glimpsed the continuity of this vaudeville act that had doubtless slipped further down bills and from A-circuit circuses to music hall to side shows to car parks, when the compere's son stepped on stage to do the traditional acrobatic act: those gymnastic balancing poses on specially made wooden chairs and benches.

At one point his father untied his own laces and removed his shoes to join the lad in a pose and a stunt or two. His own body as trained, taut and discipline fit as the more easily muscled kid. The grandfather looked on, baggy clown trousers mocking the passage of time, rubber nose in his pocket, eyes as sharp as ever, remembering other summers, other times, when he had himself been both father and son in that same tableau.

At the end of the show, we, the audience, helped stack chairs that would doubtless be crammed into a van to leave town. Posters that had appeared all over Marseillan would surely be collected and on the morrow be placed at the next stop in the tour of nostalgia, sweat and survival. Grandfather, father, mother, son and three daughters: the family of seven probably took in around €100 that long evening. Subtract the cost of the electricity, fuel and lighting, and that might just have given them a decent supper. I thought acts like this had disappeared after the war. Surely television killed the last desperate acts of variety. But no, somewhere in the south of France, on a town square, or village green, the family will don spangles.

We always miss the *guignol* puppet show in neighbouring Mèze, but find new performers selling songs by the canal in Sète. One summer in Agde, Joe learnt to turn the handle and work the music box of a Barbary organ. The organ grinder so pleased to give his right arm a rest that he let the lad play as he himself sung *Salade de Fruits*. A week later, in Clermont l'Hérault, another organist, this time accompanied by an old-timer plying his bow against a musical saw.

In the unaccustomed still wake of so many departures, I took time to remember the lazy summer days that slipped un-noted past these pages. I might have mentioned the donkey we found tethered in the hilltop square of Bages. The beast had been found eating vines before the harvest, so locals led it to the square where it might nibble on window boxes until claimed; I should have recalled the thrill of the *Tour de France* in the Julys it skirts Marseillan, a ghost port since neighbours and holidaymakers cram bread, cheese and tomato into panniers and pedal to picnic on the lanes of Bessan or Pinet for the ten-second blur of the race and an hour's freebie carnival as the promotional caravan shies keyrings and caps at the crowd; I could remember the midnight disco in our place de l'Eglise with go-go dancers whose costumes went-went; boating days with friends when children swam through oyster tables on the étang and against the Hérault tide, when we missed the last opening of the last canal lock so scrambled up the bank to walk the three miles home past kingfishers and egrets of Bagnas. But that was all part of August, something to do with Summer.

And today we are wallowing in non-Summer, our own private magical time when the sky and the sea are off duty, just calmly being there for the while. Last evening I took some work out to the port wall and sat by the rocks, listening to young ducks finding their voices, and sea-birds yelling their freedom. A lady with yet another poodle came up and we chatted, she is visiting family and escapes from her own paradise in the Alps to share ours whenever she can. She too had settled on an hour by the rocks to look at clouds, breathe the sea air and listen to the sounds of nothing, nothing at all.

We chatted a while then walked back to the street in companionable silence. She mentioned that we should be able to see the planet Mars that night. To see it from the port, like a baby sister moon, at 10.30.

I pondered and mused on walking out to gaze at Mars for the last time in my lifetime, and thought I just might go out to have a look. In the event, with my glass of *cinsault* on the terrace and the gentle strum of a guitar from an open window across the way, I did not bother. Why check out another world when this one suits me just fine.

Je remonte le long de la chaîne de ma vie;
Je la trouve attachée par son premier chaînon
à quelqu'un de ces anneaux de fer
qui sont scellés dans la pierre de nos quais.
L'autre bout est dans mon cœur.


I climb the chain of my life;
I find the first link shackled
to one of the iron rings
embedded in the quay stones of our docks.
The other end is in my heart.


- Paul Valéry (1871-1945)

368

# How to be very very practical in Marseillan

Useful addresses and phone numbers
*For Marseillan Plage, see pages 74*

## Information

### Maison du Tourisme
avenue de la Méditerranée, Marseillan-plage **[4] A2**
04 67 21 82 43 www.marseillan.com
maison.tourisme@marseillan.com
Jul-Aug 9-19; Apr-Jun, Sept 9-12, 14-18;
Oct-Mar Mon-Fr 9-12, 14-17
First stop for all information. Helpful team for advice and brochures. Booking accommodation and tickets for events and tours. Exhibitions and mini museum. Village info desk at the Theatre (*see page 41*) Jul-Aug only:10-13, 15-19 daily. **[1] C3**

### Regional Tourist Office
**Comite Regional du Tourisme Languedoc-Roussillon**
L'Acropole, 954, av Jean Mermoz, 34960 Montpellier
4 67 20 02 20 www.sunfrance.com
For information about Languedoc Roussillon

### Departement of Hérault
**Agence de Développement Touristique de l'Hérault**
Avenue des moulins, 34184 Montpellier
08 25 34 00 34 (premium rate) www.herault -tourisme.com
To find out more about the wider local area of the Hérault.

### Abroad
**Maison de la France** French Tourist Office
**UK & Ireland** Lincoln House, 300 High Holborn, London
WC1V 7JH. 09068 244 123 (premium rate);
**US** 825 3rd Avenue, 29th floor, New NY 10022. (514) 288-1904
9454 Wilshire Bd, Ste 210, 90212, Beverly Hills, CA 310-271-6665
**Canada** 1981 Av McGill College Suite 490, H3A 2WP, Montreal.
(514) 288-2026
**Australia & New Zealand** Level 13, 25 Bligh Street, 2000 NSW,
Sydney 02 9231 5244
www.franceguide.com

The region has its own tourist offices in the US and UK
**Les Maisons de la Région Languedoc-Roussillon**
UK: 6 Cavendish Square London W1G 0PD. 0207 079 33 44
US: 10 East 53rd Street NY 10022. 646 688 7170
www.maisondelaregionlanguedocroussillon.com

## Town Hall
**Mairie**, du Général de Gaulle 04 67 77 97 10 **[1] B3**
www.ville-marseillan.fr Mon-Fri 8.45-12, 13.30-18
**Services techniques** av de la ZI, 04 67 01 08 40
Mon-Fri 7.30 -12, 13.30-16.30
General information from reception, and pick up leaflets on local attractions.

## Library
**Médiathèque La Fabrique** place du 14 juillet 04 67 01 73 14 **[1] B3**
Tue 9.30-12, 15-18.30, Wed 9.30-12, 14-18.30,
Fri 15-118.30, Sat 9.30-12.30, 14-17

## Cultural and Youth Centre (Maison des Jeunes et de la Culture)
**MJC** boulevard Marius Roqueblave 04 67 77 33 35 Mon-Fri 14-19 **[1] B1**

## Police Municipale
boulevard Lamartine 04 67 77 22 90 (*emergency numbers see page 371*) **[1] B3**
Mon-Fri 8.45-12, 13.30-18
Based in the original PTT post office and telegram bureau opposite the Marine Bar, Marseillan's 13 "local" police officers uphold bylaws, check on drink-driving and set speed traps. Foot, bike and car patrols ensure good behaviour and neighbourliness, noise control and security of private property. As bobbies on the beat, they help find an out-of-hours pharmacist, keep an eye on rowdy teens and handle traffic and crowd control during public events. At the front line of paperwork and identity checks. Crime fighting is the job of the National Police and the **Gendarmerie** who should be contacted directly. A new Gendarmarie is planned outside the village (on route d'Agde). Meanwhile, contact a gendarme at:
**Gendarmerie** rue des Goëlands, Marseillan Plage (Jul-Aug) 04 67 21 90 59 **[4] A2**
**Gendarmerie Agde** 04 67 21 10 29

## Banks and ATMs (*see also* La Poste, below)
Caisse d'Épargne 33 boulevard Lamartine **[1] B3**
CIC Bordelaise de Crédit 30 boulevard Lamartine **[1] B3**
Crédit Agricole du Midi 1 place de la République **[1] B3**
Dupuy de Parseval 25, boulevard Lamartine **[1] B3**
*No Bureau de Change in Marseillan. Currency at Agde Tourist Office (page143)*

## Post Office La Poste pl du Théâtre 04 67 01 79 90 **[2] A3**

## Tips and Service
Restaurants and bars include 15% service charge but round-up totals, leaving small change behind. Tip taxi drivers 10–15%, hairdressers 15%. Public-toilet attendants 50c (unless price is displayed). In cinemas / theatres tip the usherette 50c

# Telephones & Communication

Mobile phones with roaming capacity will pick up French networks. If your phone is unlocked, consider buying a French SIM card at post offices or the phone shop at *Carrefour Market*. Phone kiosks: place Pradet, by Noilly Prat, and bd Lamartine.

**Dialling:** When calling France from abroad, use country code (33) omit first 0 of listed number. To call international numbers from France, dial **00** then country code and number (omitting first 0). To call within France, dial ten-digit telephone number. For operator-assisted dialling, key in **00+33+country code.**

### Useful telephone numbers
Operator **12**
Emergency Services in English (Police, Fire, Ambulance) **112**
Ambulance: **15**    Fire: **18**    Police (emergency): **17** (*for local police, see page 370*)
Tourist information anywhere in France **3265**; Weather (France) **08 36 68 02 75**

### Internet
The *Marine Bar* (*page 138*) offers free wifi, as do some restaurants (including *La Taverne du Port*). Hotels and some self-catering homes may also provide wifi. Boats in the port may sign up for internet. All branches of Macdonalds offer free wifi. And the *Tourist Office* (*page 370*) has wifi and public computer terminals.
NOTE: French keyboards do not use the QWERTY layout, so typing is slower!

**Marseillan Historique** (*page 50*) English Internet access bd Lamartine [1] B3
**Internet Kiosk & Hotspot** 960 av des Campings Marseillan Plage www.cyber-t.fr
PCs provided or use wifi. Low weekly rates at *Camping Europ2000*.
*For residents only:* **Médiathèque** La Fabrique (*page 370*) [1] B3
**Point Information Jeunesse** (PIJ) 30 boulevard Voltaire, 04 67 76 75 59 [1] A3

## Pets
*Please clean up after your dog. Round waste bins and free plastic bags in parks and streets*
**Grooming Au Petit Bain** 21 boulevard Lamartine 04 67 21 52 87 [1] B3
Grooming parlour with 'self-service' dog-wash option. Also pet rescue/rehoming
**Au Quat' Pat' de Victoria** 4 rue Emile Zola 04 67 21 50 14 [1] B3
**Kennels** www.lespetitssabotsdanslaprairie.com 06 20 55 50 53 nr Mèze [5] C2
**Vet: La Marseillane** 30 av André Chassefière 04 67 77 62 39 [1] B3

## Worship
**Catholic** Parish church Église Saint Jean Baptiste (*see page 28*) [1] B3
04 67 77 21 87 Sat 18, Sun 9.30 (*services also in Marseillan Plage in season*)
**Anglican** Grace Anglican Episcopal Church, 04 67 00 14 95 Eglise Ste Marie Madeleine, Nézignan l'Eveque or Eglise St Martins, Hameau de Conas, Pézenas www.gracechurchherault.org Anglican/Episcopal service in English (3rd Sun, 10am)
**Protestant** Temple 32 rue Maurice Clavel 34200 Sète. 04 67 74 85 54
**Islam** Mosquée Ibnou Rouchd 300, r Emile Picard, 34080 Montpellier
06 23 81 42 72 http://imam-montpellier.com
**Jewish** 136 ch de l'Anglore, 34200 Sète; 04 67 53 41 40 synasete .free.fr
Association Culturelle Israélite, 19 pl Pierre-Sémard, 34500 Beziers. 04 67 28 75 98
Grande Synagogue Ben Zakai, 7 r Général Lafon, 34000 Montpellier. 04 67 92 92 07

## Hairdressers
**Cap Tifs** 18 bd Lamartine 04 67 77 26 75 **[1] B3**
**Coiffure Chantal** 9 place Général Guillaut 04 67 77 30 65 **[1] B3**
**Haute Coiffure Florent** 14 avenue la Marine 06 23 40 46 48 **[2] A2**
**JM Coiffure** 2 bis bd Lamartine 04 67 76 30 81 **[1] C3**
**LC Diffusion** 3 Place du Théâtre 04 67 77 69 47 **[2] A2**
**Lilou Coiffure** 17 rue de la Liberté 04 67 39 51 91**[1] C3**
**Lis Création** 9 rue de la Plage 04 67 26 15 47 **[1] B3**
**Styl'Coiffure** 6 pl Carnot 04 67 01 70 64 **[1] B2**
**VIP Coiffure** 5 pl de la République 04 67 77 28 60 **[1] B3**
(Barber) **Marcel** 41 bd Lamartine 04 67 77 64 01 **[1] B3**

Beauty Parlours
**Elixir de Beauté** 17 rue de la Liberté 04 67 21 62 27 **[1] C3**
**Harmonie Institut** 6 r de la Plage 04 67 26 95 67 www.harmonie-institut.fr **[1] B3**
**L'Institut** 2 bis boulevard Lamartine **[1] C3**
**Les Ephelides** 3 pl de la République 04 67 77 62 78 **[1] B3**

# Health

French residents *Carte Vitale* subsidises healthcare costs. EU Visitors need a **EHIC** (European Health Insurance) card for reimbursement of emergency medical and pharmaceutical expenses. Travel insurance always recommended.

Hospitals
Montpellier has France's top teaching hospitals. But for emergencies, go to Sète
**Centre Hospitalier Intercommunal du Bassin de Thau** (Sète)
Boulevard Camille Blanc 34200 Sète 04 67 46 57 57 www.ch-bassindethau.fr
From port, turn right at Noilly Prat towards Marseillan Plage. At main roundabout follow signs to Sète. At the end of beach road, veer left towards Montpellier and, at roundabout, left on Boulevard Camille Blanc for 600 metres to hospital.
**Béziers** 2 rue Valentin Hauy 34500 Béziers 04 67 35 70 35 www.ch-beziers.fr

Ambulance **Chicouras** 6 rue de la Plage 04 67 77 68 61
Blood Tests **Laboratoires Galvani** 39 bd Pasteur 04 67 77 65 85 **[1] C2**
Chiropodist **Ingrid Permen** 4 rue de la Plage 04 67 77 66 32 **[1] B3**

Dentists
**Cabinet Dentaire** Chemin de Sainte Germaine 04 67 77 21 88
**Docteur Guieu** 13 rue Emile Zola 04 67 77 32 70 **[1] B3**
(Orthodonist) **Mazaudier, Dumas, Bonhomme** 37 bd Voltaire 04 67 77 62 18 [1] A1

Doctors
**Cabinet Medical** 16 avenue de la Marine 04 67 77 21 32 **[1] C3**
**Cabinet Medical** 27 boulevard Lamartine 04 67 77 25 00 **[1] B3**
**Docteur Christol** 1 place Général Guillaut 04 67 77 33 33 **[1] B3**
**Docteur Parga** 45 boulevard Bertouy 04 67 77 67 16 **[2] A2**
**Docteur Tobena** 22 bis avenue Victor Hugo 04 67 00 25 38 **[3] B3**

Hearing Aids **Renaud Llinas** place du Général Guillaut 04 67 93 32 51 **[1] B3**

## Mobility Aids & Medical Appliances
**Sud Médical Santé** 2 r Charles Reboul 04 67 77 21 59 **[1] B3**
(*Also specialist departments at* **Pharmacies Bastide** and **Terrisse**, *see below*)

## Nurses
**Cabinet d'Infirmiers** 34, rue Émile Zola 04 67 77 65 91 **[1] B2**
**Paulette Drouhet** 33 rue du Moulin Vert 04 67 21 24 09
**Gratiot & Siegel** 4 avenue de Florensac 04 67 21 66 97 **[3] B2**
**Marie Lariche/Julie Moret** 12 avenue Alphonse Daudet 04 67 77 66 24
**Gérard Gaudio** 16 avenue Gambetta 04 67 77 47 69 **[1] B2**
**Béatrice Ravinet** 10 avenue de Fontregeire 04 67 94 06 38
**Sophie, Adolphe & Stanislas Zbawicki** 35 bd Lamartine 04 67 00 26 96 **[1] B3**

## Opticians
**Centroptic** 3 rue Maffre de Baugé 04 67 21 49 53 **[1] B3**
**Marseillan Optique** 29 boulevard Lamartine 04 67 77 66 15 **[1] B3**
**Optique Market** (CC Carrefour Market) route de Bessan 04 67 26 37 61 **[3] A3**

Osteopath **Barkatz** 5 av Chassefière 06 69 40 30 59 www.afo-osteopathe.fr **[1] B3**

## Pharmacies
**Bastide** 6, place Carnot 04 67 77 23 14 **[1] B3**
**Terrisse-Magnabal** place Carnot, 04 67 77 21 73 **[1] B3**

## Physiotherapists
**Bertrand & Dressaire** 35 boulevard Lamartine 04 67 77 31 87 **[1] B3**
**JP & M Servant** 3 rue du Capitaine Bages 04 67 77 21 34 **[1] B3**

Psychologists **Carole & Violette Poulin** 2 rue Ligures 04 67 77 31 41

# Sport in Marseillan

Louis Boudou sports centre and stadium on avenue Florensac **[3] B1**. Outdoor exercise facilities and games courts in **Boudas** and **Tabarka** parks (*see page 46-7*). Public tennis courts by the oyster farms. For all sports, including handball, volleyball, martial arts and gym sessions at the sport centre, contact the Library, Mairie or MJC. Follow (and bet on) sport at **PMU** bars (*page 135*).

### Football **Crabe Sportif Marseillanais**
Stade Marcel Pochon, av de Florensac 04 67 77 29 90 csmarseillan.fr.gd **[3] B2**
Marseillan's soccer team since 1908 is the town's pride and joy. They play in patriotic blue and white strip after ditching original red and black in 1929. *Crabe Sportif* fields a respected first team, reserves, juniors and the all-women *Crabettes*.

### Rugby **Club Rugby Occitan Marseillan** 34 allée Georges Sand 06 03 52 85 32
http://rugbymarseillan.unblog.fr/
Local teams of all ages play the "national" game of the south. Nearest major team Béziers, and Montpellier hosted the world cup. See good college games at Agde.

## Golf

Nearest golf courses to Marseillan are at **Agde** (*see page 152*) and **Beziers** (*page 172*), but **Languedoc Roussillon Golf-Pass** costs around €250 (half price off-season) for five green fees over 21 consecutive days at 14 courses, including **Montpellier, Carcassonne** and the **Cévennes,** and spectacular links further along the coast. (maximum two days at any one club) www.sudfrancegolf.com

## Pétanque & Boules

**Joyeux Pétanqueurs Marseillanais** 06 70 96 20 10
**Crabe Roulant Marseillanais** 04 67 77 35 29
*Pétanque* (whcih gets its name from the *patois* for "feet at an angle") or *boules*, as it is also known, is the quintessential French sport: no rushing, guaranteed shade and never too far from a glass of *pastis*. In Marseillan, casual games played on the **Pradet [2] A2** and the official boulodrome is on **allées Roques [3] B3**. Summer tournaments in village and resort for visitors to take on each other and the locals. Details from tourist office.

**Cycling** Union Cycliste Marseillanaise 04 67 21 57 04
*See also* **MJC's** cycle club (*page 372*) for weekly and monthly social rides around the etang and back country. Occasional rides for hikers *Lous Baroulaïres* (*below*)
**Fishing** Le Loup Marseillanais Port Tabarka 06 78 35 10 68 **[2] B1** *(page 60)*
*See also sea fishing trips from* Le Grau d'Agde *(page 154)*
**Hiking** Lous Baroulaïres 04 67 77 24 03
**Jousts & Capelet** *see pages 81-89*
**Table Tennis** Crabe Pongiste Marseillanais 04 67 77 60 51
marseillantennisdetable.blogspirit.com
**Tennis** Tennis Club de Marseillan chemin des Parcs 04 67 77 34 32 *(page 35)*
**Volleyball** Agde-Marseillan Volleyball 04 67 77 25 32

## Sailing & Watersports *(see pages 57, 61 66)*
*Most watersports based at* **Maison des Sports Nautiques** quai du Toulon **[2] B3**
**Cercle de Voile Marseillan** 3 q de Toulon 06 7 77 65 22 http://cvmarseillan.free.fr
**L'Aviron Marseillanais** 1 q Toulon 04 67 21 95 68 www.avironmarseillanais.com
**Association Atouvents** *(see page 66)*
**Yacht Club** 04 67 21 90 62
**Les Glénans** Port des Onglous 04 67 77 22 73 www.glenans.asso.fr
**Les Voiles Marseillanaises** 34 q Toulon 06 61 88 85 19 http://voilesmarseillan.free.fr
**Diving** Team Poseidon Port Marseillan Plage 04 67 77 67 76 **[4] B2**
**Kitesurfing** Kithau parc Tabarka *(page 47)* 06 87 07 11 93 www.kithau.com
**Waterski** Ski Nautique Club de Marseillan 19 av de Fontregeire 04 67 77 60 55 www.ffsn.asso.fr

---

### Ex Pat heaven
**Cricket** MCC (*Midi Cricket Club*) has an artificial pitch at St Pons de Mauchiens, near Pézenas. Iin France's national league www.midicricket.com 06 21 94 40 18
**American Football** Marseillan Sète Dragons train Wed Thu in Marseillan club.quomodo.com/lesdragonsdemarseillansete 06 99 07 66 47

---

# Disabled Travellers

## Transport

### Crossing the Channel
Ferry and channel tunnel operators are very helpful. **P&0** and **DFDS** (*see page 384*) can arrange for your car to be parked onboard near flat, wheelchair access to lifts and passenger decks. Check in an hour before departure. **Eurotunnel** is easiest of all as you do not leave the car during the 35 minute crossing. Onboard wc is not wheelchair accessible, so use teminal facilities before departure.

### Flying
Let airlines know special requirements at the time of booking. All local airports are now wheelchair accessible with suitable WCs, wheelchair provision and assisted boarding service. However very few airports have airbridges for discreet access. **Béziers** has a dedicated drop off zone.

### Trains
Travelling from UK, remember Eurostar arrives in Paris at Gare du Nord, and you must cross the city by taxi to get to Gare de Lyon to continue the journey. Best option: Eurostar London to Lille, then simply change platforms for the TGV to Montpellier or Agde. Or (summer Sat only) Eurostar London to Avignon, then transfer to local trains. France's newer "doubler-decker" TGV's each have two carriages adapted for wheelchair users: elevator to raise lower decks to platform level and seats swing round for easy transfer from wheelchairs. A 19th-century railway system, with underpasses, staircases and sometimes three or four steep steps between platform and train may often prove inaccessible. Smaller stations may remain impractical for mobility-restricted travellers. However, 12 key stations in the region offer full support to disabled travellers, ranging from help crossing tracks at Agde and Sète to a dedicated team providing a comprehensive range of specialist aid accessing platforms, boarding trains and journey planning at Montpellier. Available free to registered disabled travellers connecting at Paris, Lyon and Marseille and locally at:

| Agde | Carcassonne | Narbonne |
|------|-------------|----------|
| Alès | Marvejols | Nîmes |
| Bedarieux | Mende | Perpignan |
| Béziers | Montpellier | Sète |

**Service Accès Plus**

0890 640 650 (then press 1) from France only

accesplus@sncf.fr; www.accesplus.sncf.com

*Office hours 7am-10pm*

Contact *Accès Plus* at least 48 hours before travelling to arrange assistance. Advisors help plan journeys and suggest alternative routes and facilities. Arrive at station 30 minutes before departure to be accompanied all the way to reserved seats on the train. The train manager will be informed as to your needs, and a team member waiting for at your destination. If your train is delayed or journey disrupted, you may call the helpline from your mobile phone on **0890 640 650** (then press **2**). Passengers with hearing disabilities may text to **06 10 64 06 50**.

## Buses

Marseillan will have to wait until 2014 for its buses to be upgraded. Until then, rural buses are traditional touring coaches with several steep steps and not adapted to the requirements of passengers with mobility issues. However some city shuttle buses are now accessible, including the new hoppers in **Pézenas** and low level platform buses in **Montpellier** (routes 8, 9, 12, 15, 16. and *La Ronde)*. **Béziers** has ordered 14 accessible vehicles. **Sète** has begun rolling out a fleet of adapted buses around the agglomeration (04 67 53 01 01). **Balaruc** tourist office has details of well-designed shuttles within the health spa resort.

## Trams

The Montpellier tramway (*see page 389*) is easy to use, with flat level access to and from all platforms. Key tram stations provide audio traffic info.

## Driving/Paperwork

Blue badges issued in any EU country are valid in France. You do not get free parking, but you may use designated bays. Travel with photocopies of other ID or paperwork, as some assistance requires official proof of disability status.

## Planning a trip

The national tourist office website has the usual info: **www.franceguide.com** then links: **Practical Information > During Your Stay > France for Disabled People**. Contact the CDT or CRT (*see page 371*) and ask for the *Tourisme et Handicap* brochure or listings. Montpellier's tourist office produces an excellent warts-and-all guide with honest reviews and listings for visitors with mobility, audio, visual or mental health issues. The website has useful listings at www.ot-montpellier.fr/montpellier-accessible

## Accommodation

Self-catering accommodation varies. Depending on personal mobility requirements, some ground-floor accommodation may be acceptable if flat step-free access is all you need, but for wheelchair use, accredited and approved adapted facilities should be chosen. France embraces the concept of accessibility with enthusiasm, if not always the most practical of approaches. One hotel in the region adapted a bedroom (and ensuite) to the utmost, but has no level access to the building! Other venues go beyond expectations. *Chaumière* and *Les Chambres d'Andréa* have suitable rooms. Phone to check on specific needs. Close to Marseillan, chain hotels have ground-floor rooms, with bathrooms to EU norms. Many campsites and self catering units have shower and toilet facilities. Out of town, take advantage of *Gites de France Hérault's* third wheel offer. Brilliant idea, self-catering and B&B guests get an extra front wheel for a wheelchair for rambling rough terrain. www.tourisme-vert-pour-tous.com

## Museums and sites

Of course, when Knights Templar were catapulting rocks at villages and nervous Counts building hilltop forts, universal accessibility was not always given the priority it is accorded today. Many historic sites will not be open to all. Smaller or private museums (such as the first-floor-no-lift **Résistance** display in Montpellier) will also be off the list. In listings I note major problems or decent efforts to accommodate all visitors, but, with older attractions and churches, assume the worst and phone ahead. Surprisingly, **Carcassonne's rampart tour** is fully accessible as is much of **Abbaye de Fontfroide.** There have been real efforts made recently. Newer and renovated museums, including **Musée Fabre**, with a dedicated wheelchair guide, Agde's **Ephèbe** museum, Loupian's **Villa**, Bouzigues' **Etang** museum, Nime's **Carré d'Art,** and **Serignan** and **Céret** galeries have been designed with disabled visitors in mind, as have attractions at the **Odysseum**. There is an alternative route through the Molière **Scenovision** in Pézenas. Even many vineyards and funfairs have well planned access. The excellent *Tourisme & Handicap* brochure (*see page 376*) lists no-problem addresses. Local tourist offices work hard to develop accessibility and are very helpful. If you, like me, tend to shrug and whistle at the pace of progress, do choose your tunes carefully: **Maison Charles Trenet** in Narbonne is a no-no as it has as many stairs as songs; Sète's **Espace Brassens** is completely accessible.

## Restaurants

Always phone first to check accessibility and status of lifts to upstairs venues. The regional *Tourisme & Handicap* brochure highlights venues adapted to official standards. Montpellier Tourist Office (*see page 2*00) has the very best listings, including a wider range of establishments including and indicating those that may have manageable access, if not meeting all criteria. They also provide a list of restaurants providing menus in braille. Most Marseillan restaurant terraces are accessible – but phone to check on toilets etc.

## Beaches

The long **Lido** beach from Marseillan to Sète is impractical for chair users, although there are matting paths from the *Promenade* boardwalk to the luxury beach bars at **Villeroy**. However, **Marseillan Plage** is amongst France's best adapted resorts for holidaymakers with restricted mobility: the **Plage de la Capitainerie** and **Plage d'Honneur** at the heart of the resort are very well equipped. *Faciroule* matting on the sands allows conventional wheelchairs easy access to the main Capitainerie beach and *Tiralo* beach wheelchairs are available at both beaches: special chairs that move easily on sand and float on water. Contact capitainerie or tourist office for equipment hire. There are showers by the Capitainerie and accessible toilets on both beaches. Hérault has 19 accessible beaches, many offering *Tiralo* or other floating devices, and all with access from parking to the sands. More from tourist offices and **www.handiplage.fr**

**Balaruc-les-Bains**: *plage du Poste de Secours*
**Cap d'Agde**: *La Roquille, Richelieu Ouest, Richelieu Est, Le Mole*
**Carnon**: *Centre*
**La Grande Motte**: *Levant, Rose des Sables, Grand Travers*
**Le Grau d'Agde**: *plage Centre* (first aid post)
**Mèze:** Plagette
**Palavas-les-Flots**: *Le Sarrail, Saint Pierre, Hôtel de Ville*
**Sète**: *La Corniche, Les Quilles*
**Valras**: *plage Centrale*
**Villeneuve les Maguelones**: *Prevost, Pilou*

The Plage d'Honneur at Marseillan Plage is one of the pioneering **Audioplage** beaches, adapted for blind and visually impaired visitors. Wearers of a special wristband directed sat-nav-style, via sonic posts on the beach and in the water, from their chosen place on the sand out to swim in the sea and back to their towel again. Other *Audioplage* beaches at Balaruc les Bains, *Tambourin*; Carnon, *plage du Centre*; La Grande Motte; Palavas-Les- Flots, *Le Sarrail*.

## Shopping

Some low but manageable doorsteps to village shops in Marseillan, but at older establishments in narrower streets you may still encounter tricky steps barring entry (legacy of flood defences). Staff generally relaxed and helpful about serving in the doorway. **Spar** and **Carrefour Market** supermarkets, pharmacies, most bakeries and market hall have flat or ramp access. Elsewhere, large shopping centres and supermarkets are fully accessible. There is at least one Centre Commercial on the outskirts of every town, where you may buy almost anything and remain independent. However, in city centres: **Béziers'** new **Polygone** has full access to all shops, restaurants and leisure facilities. **Montpellier**'s **Polygone** mall is also accessible, though some routes between shops and car parks are complicated. Ask at info desk. The basement **Triangle** gallery is not accessible, nor are many shops in historic city centres. Cobbled streets and high kerbs abound. For mobility equipment, *see page 373.*

# Where to Stay

The joy of Marseillan is in living the village and port lifestyle, so no wonder most visitors opt for the chance to live amongst the locals, shop for fresh fish, fruit and vegetables, inhale the inspiration of the weekly market and make morning pilgrimage to the *boulangeries*. Plenty of self-catering options: Perhaps *maisons de village* or *maisons vigneronnes*, those boulevard mansions with arched doorways to garages that once housed wine vats, now sometimes concealing a garden, and grand scale rooms upstairs. Maybe a modern house in the port, or new villa with the luxury of a private pool in a residential street. For those who prefer breakfast served by others, *Maison de Camille* on the port serves *petit déjeuner* (*see page 261*) or enjoy a *café crème* and croissant at most village bars. If you want someone else to make the bed, find hotels and *chambres d'hôtes* in village and resort.

## Self Catering
*As well as the specialist Marseillan agencies and websites, you may Google listings, webpages from private home owners and holiday agencies or visit dedicated sites such as www.creme-de-languedoc.com and the tourist office www.marseillan.com*

**www.MarseillanVillage.com**
04 67 21 75 66 (UK 0844 284 4430)
A wide selection of private houses and apartments to rent across Marseillan and beyond: many with wifi. Waterfront cottages and townhouses in Port Tabarka have views across the lagoon, from €250 per week off-peak and €570 in high season. Also find historic village houses, sprawling *maisons vigneronnes*, family homes, even luxury villas with swimming pools and gardens. Weekends to long stays.

**Port Rive Gauche** rue Suffren 04 67 00 87 65 **[2] B2**
www.garrigaeresorts.com
Contemporary-styled self-catering warehouse-conversion apartments with lagoon views. Massage and spa treatment and short-break 'hotel' option. Garage, wifi and use of laundry room. From €185/night to €1530/week in summer.

**www.beauvillage.com** village houses from UK agency.

# Hotels & Chambres d'Hôtes

*For a full list of B&B and alternative accommodation, contact the Tourist Office (see page 369)*

*See also* **Port Rive Gauche**

**Hotel le Boulevard**
2 rue Generale de Gaulle
04 67 77 21 11 **[1] B3**
The traditional budget hotel in the heart of the village is above the restaurant of the same name (*see page 268*). Nine bedrooms €30-48. Breakfast €5.50

**Petit Hotel** 5 bd Lamartine 06 85 88 95 63 www.petithotel-marseillan.com **[1] B3**
Boutique B&B by theatre roundabout. Stylish décor and swimming pool All rooms have private outside space. Rooms from €110-195 per night.

**Chambres d'Andréa** 36 bd Pasteur 04 67 11 26 37 www.leschambresdandrea.fr **[1] C2**
Smart rooms (€120-190) from Stéphanie and Philippe of the *Maison Camille* créperie on the port *(page 261)*. Breakfast in a garden of fig and tea trees. Disabled access.

**Domaine de la Bellonette** 06 13 04 41 50 www.labellonette.com (May-mid-Nov)
B&B from €99 in old wine estate on the étang, midway between Marseillan and Mèze.
**Cosy Chambres d'Hôtes** 16 Rue Capitaine Bages 04 67 31 76 75 *from € 75* **[1] A2**
**André Dautel** 17 rue Vedel 04 67 77 69 05 *from €55* **[1] B2**
**Les Muriers** 10 rue de la Paix 04 67 77 69 88 *with a pool from €80 pn*
**Hacienda** 22 av de la Zone Industrielle 06 88 60 16 35 *from €65* **[3] A3**
**Le Héron** 6 r Hérons Cendrés 04 67 77 67 41 www.chambres-hotes-marseillan.com *from €55*

# And at Marseillan Plage

**Hotel Richmont\*\*\*** allée Filliol 04 67 21 97 79 www.hotel-marseillan.com **[4] B2**
Aircon and wifi in port of Marseillan Plage, some rooms with sea views. Rooms €60-120, half board option also available. Restaurant page 276

**Hotel Les Dunes\*\*\*** rue Arc en Ciel 04 67 21 91 50 www.hotel-marseillan.com **[4] B1**
By the dunes on the beaches where Marseillan Plage meets the Lido. Rooms €55-80. Half-board available. *Restaurant page 279*

**La Chaumière** 1150 route de Sète 04 67 98 35 63 www.hotel-marseillan.fr **[4] B1**
Rooms from €43. Across the main road from the plages, a smart budget hotel with wifi. Adapted rooms for disabled guests. *Restaurant page 279*

**Domaine de Robinson** 6 quai de Plaisance 04 67 01 62 70 *B&B from €34* **[4] B2**

**Mazet de Manon** route de Sète, 04 67 01 26 71 **[4] B1**
Rooms at the restaurant on the old beach road from Marseillan Plage to Sète. €50pn

## Camping

Marseillan Plage is known for its campsites, from simple pitches for canvas and caravans to fully equipped mobile home parks; some with pools, playgrounds and wifi. The Tourist Office (*see page 369*) has constantly updated and rated listings. Some sites open from Apr / May, most close Sep / Oct.

**Les Méditerranées** av des campings 08 25 08 08 19 www.lesMéditerranées.com[4] **A3**
*Quartier Charlemagne* 04 67 21 92 49 *Quartier Nouvelle Floride* (beachside) 04 67 21 94 49
A self-contained 4* beach-resort, with waterpark, nightclub, restaurants and shopping.

**Beauregard Sud** 380 ch de l'Airette 04 67 77 18 68 www.beauregard-a-sud.com **[4] A2**
**Beauregard-Plage** 250 ch l'Airette 04 67 77 15 45 www.camping-beauregard-est.com[4]**A2**
**Beausejour** 11 chemin des Embruns 04 67 21 93 00 www.camping-beausejour.fr
**La Créole** 74 av des campings 04 67 21 92 69 www.campinglacreole.com[4] **A3**
**Europ 2000** 960 av des campings 04 67 21 92 85 www.camping-europ2000.com
**Le Galet** av des campings 04 67 21 95 61 www.camping-galet.com **[4] A3**
**La Plage** 69 chemin du Payrollet 04 67 21 92 54 www.laplage-camping.net **[4] A3**

**Le Grillon des Mers** 782 av des Campings 04 67 21 92 89 www.legrillondesmers.com
**La Jasse sur Mer** 417 chemin du Payrollet 04 67 21 92 47 **[4] A3**
**Le Nautic** av de Maldormir 04 67 21 93 40 www.campinglenautic34.com
**Le Paradou** 2 impasse Ronsard 04 67 21 90 10 www.paradou.com **[4] B1**
**Le Rieu** chemin du Payrollet 04 67 21 92 58 www.campinglerieu.fr **[4] A3**
**Le Robinson** quai de Plaisance 04 67 21 90 07 www.camping-robinson.com[4] **B2**

⁎

**La Mouette** chemin du Payrollet 04 67 21 88 92
**Les Sirènes** 04 67 21 92 83

**Municipal camp sites** (**) 04 67 21 90 58 **[4] A2**

And camping in the countryside, away from the beach resort:
**Aire Naturelle de Camping Domaine De Villemarin** (***)
Route de Mèze 04 67 77 04 62 www.camping-gites-villemarin.fr

## Self catering at Marseillan Plage

Municipal bungalows and chalets were the resort's first self catering option (*see page 73*). To book, contact the tourist office (*page 379*). The office also has lists of *Gîtes de France, Clévacances* and private homes for rent in village and resort.

Self-contained self catering holiday complexes by the beaches:
**Les Marines d'Hélios** 7 rue Georges Brassens 04 67 21 98 56 **[4] B2**
perso.wanadoo.fr/marines-helios *Shared swimming pool, private terraces, wifi*
**Les Mas de la Plage** 9 rue Georges Brassens 04 67 21 89 77[4] **B2**
**Club Wagner** 75 av des Campings 04 67 01 64 64 (*rentals agency*) **[4] A2**

# Buying property in Marseillan

## Estate Agencies

**S'Antoni** 26 ter bd Lamartine 04 67 00 00 52 www.santoni.fr **[1] B3**
**ADR Marseillan Immo** pl Guillaut 04 67 21 88 63 www.adr-marseillan-immobilier.com **[1] B2**
**Bourse de l'Immobilier** 3 pl Guillaut 04 67 00 82 22 www.bourse-immobilier.fr **[1] B3**
**Sophie Guillamat** 16 av Victor Hugo 06 84 08 14 55 www.immobilier-guillamat.fr **[3] B3**
**JP Immobilier** 34 quai Antonin Gros 04 67 77 66 77 www.jp-immobilier.com **[2] B2**
**Les Clés du Soleil** 6 bd Lamartine 04 67 77 24 77 www.clesdusoleil.com **[1] B3**
**Orpi Cabinet Anthinéa** 31 quai de la Résistance 04 67 00 05 04 www.orpi.fr**[2] A2**
**Vidal Immobilier** 19 bd Lamartine 04 67 77 23 35 www.vidal-immobilier.com**[1] B3**
**Style Immobilier** 2 ter bd Lamartine 06 99 53 40 50 www.style-immobilier.fr **[1] C3**

## Marseillan-Plage

**S'Antoni** 424 Chemin de l'Airette 04 67 01 07 77 www.santoni.fr (*rentals*) **[4] A2**
**Benoit** av de la Méditerranée 04 67 21 96 46 (*rentals*) **[4] A2**
**Bourse de l'Immobilier** 67 av Méditerranée 04 67 21 57 27www.bourse-immobilier.fr **[4] A2**
**CIM Vacances** Le Phocéa av Méditerranée 04 67 26 13 91 www.cimvacances.com **[4] A2**
**Plein Sud Immo** Phocéa av Méditerranée 04 67 21 87 91 www.pleinsudimmobilier.com **[4]A2**

## From Overseas
**www.MidiProperty.com** Has hundreds of properties online. Working directly with various agents in Marseillan, interpreting, translating and assisting through and beyond the househunting process. Based in UK.

**www.MyFrenchPA.com** Escorting non-French speakers through the language barrier. Help and assistance, from dealing with utility companies, explaining paperwork, sorting through the mail, to letter-writing, shopping and setting up home.

## Notaries
All French property transactions are handled by a state-appointed *notaire*, who handles paperwork, holds deposits and deals with taxes. The *notaire* will work with an estate agent or manage private sales. General advice in English **www.notaires.fr**
Each Marseillan partnership operates from shared offices by the allées Roques.
**Boussot, Paladel; Teisserenc, Bonestève; Teisserenc, Vidal, Boussot; Vidal, Gayral** 26 av Victor Hugo 04 67 77 22 15 **[3] B3**

**Tresor Public** 33 place du Théâtre 04 67 77 20 44 **[2] A2** *Pay taxes, rates etc*

# Getting There
## & Getting Around

## By Air

NINE AIRPORTS SERVE MARSEILLAN, with flights from more than 20 UK and Irish Airports. Newest and nearest is the misleadingly named Béziers Cap d'Agde (in truth just outside Vias), a mere 15 minutes from Marseillan. Direct UK flights from Bristol, Luton and Southampton (linking to six other regional UK/Ireland airports); domestic connections to Beauvais (for Paris). New routes serve Oslo, Stockholm, Odense and Dusseldorf.

The principal international airport in the region is Montpellier, 50 km from Marseillan. Within 75 minutes drive, Nîmes airport, at just over an hour from the village, is a far quieter affair and, out of season, you may expect to be in your hire car within 20 minutes of touching down on the tarmac. Carcassonne airport is 75 minutes from the port of Marseillan, and has a good grill for a last minute meal. Several airlines jet in from the UK regions to Perpignan airport, around 70 minutes away. Further afield, Toulouse and Marseille airports are a tad more than two hours drive away with flights by European and other national carriers, as well as the low-cost brigade.

---

### Airports

**Béziers Cap d'Agde** 04 67 80 99 09 www.Béziers.aeroport.fr
**Carcassonne** 04 68 71 96 46 www.carcassonne.aeroport.fr
**Marseille** 04 42 14 14 14 www.mrsairport.com
**Montpellier** 04 67 20 85 00 www.montpellier.aeroport.fr
**Nîmes** 04 66 70 49 49 www.nîmes-aeroport.fr
**Perpignan** 04 68 52 60 70 www.perpignan.cci.fr
**Toulouse** 01 70 46 74 74 www.toulouse.aeroport.fr
**Girona** (Spain) +34 972 186 600 www.barcelonagirona.com

### Airlines

**Air France** www.airfrance.com
**British Airways** www.britishairways.com
**Bmibaby** www.bmibaby.com
**Easyjet** www.easyjet.com
**FlyBe** www.flybe.com
**Jet2** www.jet2.com
**Ryanair** www.ryanair.com

It may be quicker from Sheffield, Bournemouth, Durham, Teeside or Blackpool to fly to Girona, just across the Spanish border, also a little over two hours away, rather than endure the long trek to London. Marseille airport also has flights from seven French regions.

From outside France, Air France connects intercontinental flights with TGV trains to Agde, Sète and Montpellier from a station beneath Paris CDG Airport. For airport transfers to city centre stations and on to Marseillan, *see page 388*

## By Train

By far the easiest way to travel to and through France: from UK, take Eurostar to Paris or Lille, and join the excellent, fast TGV national rail network. Closest station to Marseillan is Agde, although if renting a car, you might prefer Montpellier or Sète. Some Paris trains stop at Marseillan Plage station (in reality a halt – with no station facilities as such) with bus transfer to Marseillan in July and August only. From Agde station, a taxi to Marseillan should cost no more than €20-25. Otherwise, depending on the time of day, a local bus could get you to Marseillan. There are two buses a day (weekdays) from Sète station. Agde and Sète have good rail links; regular services to key cities across the country. Through-ticketing from UK regions to your final destination is also inexpensive. Bargain advance-booking options include internet-only IDTGV Paris-Montpellier from just €20 each way. First class upgrades are often good value. Validate (*composter*) tickets in platform franking machines before boarding. Disabled travellers *see pages 375-6*

**SNCF** (French National Rail Service)
08 92 35 35 35; www.voyages-sncf.com (in France)
**Rail Europe** www.raileurope.co.uk (UK); www.raileurope.com (US)

## By Car (cross-Channel)

Quickest and easiest option is Eurotunnel (**www.eurotunnel.com**), driving your car onto the train at Folkestone and off at Calais. Best value short Channel crossing is with DFDS, formerly Norfolkline (**www.dfds.com**), offering the very lowest fares (from under £15) Dover-Dunkerque (but this adds half an hour to the drive south). P&O (**www.poferries.com***)* and SeaFrance (**www.seafrance.com**) run traditional ferries Dover-Calais. LD Lines run a fast ferry route to from Newhaven to Dieppe in Normandy. Longer Western Channel crossings to Normandy and Brittany from Brittany Ferries (**www.brittanyferries.com**), taking you from Poole, Portsmouth and Plymouth to Cherbourg, Caen, Le Havre, Roscoff and St Malo, and from Cork (in Ireland) to Roscoff. Also from Ireland, Irish Ferries (**www.irishferries.com**) ply the routes Rosslare to Roscoff and Cherbourg.

# Driving to Marseillan

**From Channel ports:** *(around 1050km – 9½ hours, plus breaks),* go towards **Paris** to take the **bd Périphérique** round the capital, due south.

**From Paris** *(790km - 7 hours plus breaks):* **and Périphérique:** follow signs **Bordeaux, Orléans** then **Clermont Ferrand**, taking **A6b**, **A10** and **A71** motorways then **A75** between Clermont Ferrand to Pézenas. From exit **59** (**Sète-Pézenas-Marseillan**), follow the **D613** (signposted **Montpellier-Sète-Mèze**) through Montagnac, then **D51** to Marseillan. *Budget around €60 for tolls (including crossing world's highest bridge, Foster's amazing Millau Vidauct: €7.70 in summer, otherwise €6* **www.leviaducdemillau.com***).*

**From Béziers-Cap-d'Agde airport:** *(18km – 20 minutes):* Take **D37e** to **D612** (direction **Sète-Agde**), turn off at sign **Agde Centre**. Crossing river Hérault, at roundabout *La Belle Agathoise,* take **D51** signposted **Marseillan**

**From Montpellier airport:** *(52km – 45 minutes):* Follow signs for **A9** motorway (direction **Béziers Toulouse Barcelona**) and stay on motorway until **exit 33** (**Sète**). Then **D613** towards and through **Mèze**. At roundabout, turn left to **D51**; travel ten minutes to **Marseillan.**

**From Nîmes airport:** *(100km – 70 minutes):* Take **A54** towards **Nîmes** then **A9** direction **Montpellier** *(continue as from Montpellier, above).*

**From Perpignan airport:** *(115km – 75 minutes):* Take **D117-D900**-D83 for around 9km to **A9** motorway (direction **Montpellier**). Leave **A9** at **exit 34** (**Millau-Clermont-Ferrand-Pézenas-Agde-Vias**). Then **D13** towards **Bessan**, turning left from main road to **D28** through village of Bessan. Bear left **avenue de Marseillan**, typically French tree-lined lane crossing river Hérault, passing vineyards and continues for a good ten minutes entering **Marseillan** at a roundabout with *Carrefour Market* supermarket on your left.

**From Carcassonne airport:** *(120km – 80 minutes):* Take **A61** (signposted **Montpellier-Perpignan**) to Narbonne, join **A9** *(as from Perpignan, above).*

**From Marseille airport:** *(190km 2 hours):* Follow **Toutes Directions** signs to **A7** then **A54** and **A9** via **Montpellier** *(as above).*

**From Toulouse airport:** *(220km – 2¼ hours):* Follow signs to motorway take **A624–A61** continue to **A9** *(as from Carcassonne-Perpignan, above).*

**From Girona airport, in Spain:** *(215km – 2¼ hours):* Join **Ap7** direction **France**. At the border, motorway becomes **A9** *(as from Perpignan above).*

**From Narbonne Motorail:** *(70km - 50minutes):* take **D6009** for 10km to **A9** at **Narbonne Sud (**direction **Montpellier)** *(as from Perpignan above).*

# Customs

European Union (EU) nationals need carry only a valid identity card or passport. For nationals of non-EU countries, passports, and sometimes visas, are required. Check local embassy or consulate (taking into account the time it may take for visas to be issued). Within the EU there is officially no limitation for purchases destined for personal consumption by EU citizens, although there are recommended limits (see below Travellers from countries outside the EU must take heed of duty-free regulations and make a customs declaration and pay duty on items with a value of over €220. However, they may also claim approximately 15% tax discount on their purchases. For customs advice in France telephone 01 53 24 68 24 and in the UK 0845 010 9000.

---

## Customs Allowances from Spain

Many locals and visitors cross the frontier to Spain to take advantage of lower alcohol and tobacco prices. Be warned, despite open motorway borders, police and customs run regular spot checks on drivers returning from Spain. *Allowances are per vehicle, not per person*: **Wine** 90 litres (max 60 litres sparkling); **Fortified wine** 20 litres; **Beer** 110 litres; **Spirits** 10 litres; **Tobacco** 1000 cigarettes or 1kg loose tobacco. You may bring double quantities of tobacco if declared at motorway border control. But you must request a DSA *Attestation* for French police. NOTE Spanish motorway speed limit: 110kph.

---

# Getting Around

## Taxis

**Taxi des 7 Fonts** 04 67 01 55 12 www.taxides7fonts.com
**Taxi GT** Grégory Gamay 06 03 18 15 04 taxigt34@gmail.com
**Taxi Yves** 04 67 21 82 31

## Buses in Marseillan

A network of local buses links several villages and towns. Anyone may use these services, which usually run around the school timetable. Apart from airport shuttles, no buses run on Sundays nor public holidays. Two routes serve Marseillan's new **Gare Routière** bus station [2] **A2** (actually a bus stop on the corner of av de la Marine by the sq 8 mai 1945 and place Pradet in the main port). Buy tickets from the driver: €1.50 single; €10 *carnet* of 10 tickets. Timetables are available online (*see opposite*) or from tourist offices and the Mairie reception. Always check before travelling.

**Line 210** Five a day from the *gare routière*, serving Agde station, Vias (town, not airport) and Béziers. Journey times: 15 minutes to Agde; 50 minutes to Béziers. Departs: from Marseillan: 06.50, 07.50, 13.00, 14.00 and 17.00; Béziers: 11.15, 12.15, 16.15, 17.15 and 18.15. Agde, 30 minutes later. *See also Line 210 Aéroport (below)*.

**Line 323** The route Pinet – Sète stops at Marseillan's *gare routière* (as well as avenues Victor Hugo and Chassefière, Les Mougères, and les Onglous – for Marseillan Plage station), Marseillan Plage, various points n the beach and in Sète itself. Towards Pinet, the bus stops at the neighbouring villages of Florensac and Pomérols . Journey times 15-20 minutes. Departs Marseillan daily 11.45 and 18.40, with additional buses Wed and Sat at 12.50. Return services from Pinet at 06.55 and 13.15. Towards Marseillan Plage and Sète, buses generally leave Marseillan at 07.15 and 13.35, returning from Sète train station at 11.00 and 18.05, with Wed and Sat lunch service at 12.20; from Marseillan Plage tourist office at 11.30 and 18.35, (12.50 Wed and Sat). Journey time to Sète, 40 mins; Marseillan Plage, 10 mins.

**Line 9** *(summer only)* The Totem bus runs a circular route from the port in Marseillan, through residential areas along the étang and Les Mougères, serving Marseillan Plage station, tourist office, Marseillan Plage to The Dunes on the Lido beach. Connect with local buses linking campsites and bus stops the full length of the Lido. Services run all day, every day, July and August until late evening. Tickets from the *tabac* **Le Graffiti** 43 boulevard Lamartine. Price €1 for any journey, even if it takes 2 buses.

**Line 274** *(summer only)* Six departures a day linking Agde station with Marseillan Plage and key sites in le Cap d'Agde, including the naturist quarter. This bus does **not** serve Marseillan Ville.

**Line 210 Aéroport** (*not to be confused with the local bus bearing the same number*) runs dedicated services between Beziers Cap d'Agde airport (via Agde and Vias) to connect with all flight arrivals and departures. Unusually, regular fares/*carnets* are valid, rather than premium rate airport tarifs.

---

## Timetables and more

For connecting services to Mèze, Montpellier, Pézenas and other destinations across the Hérault departement, find bus maps and timetables at **www.Hérault-transport.fr** Should you have time on your hands, this is a delightfully lazy way of seeing the real France. If you have a long wait between buses, simply settle down at a café with a good book and a quarter pitcher of wine and enjoy the distraction of an hour or two's diversion between destinations. Information (weekdays): 04 34 88 89 99.

Totem 9 Marseillan summer shuttle: **www.thau-agglo.fr/Le-reseau-TOTEM.html**

Away from Marseillan:

# Trains

The railway line runs along the beach road across the Etang, giving the moonlight illusion of locomotives travelling across the waters of the lagoon. Agde is the closest and most practical railway station, although the halt at Marseillan Plage (formerly Les Onglous) is the only station within Marseillan's territory. The fast TGV from Brussels, Lille and Paris to Perpignan serve the station, as do regional TER services across the south of France. Béziers and Narbonne offer connecting routes to Western France, Spain and up into Lozère and Auvergne. From Sète, you may also pick up trains to Bordeaux and Marseille. The main regional hub is Montpellier, 30 minutes from Agde by TGV, 35-40 minutes on the TER. You may buy tickets online before travel: best deals are special *Prems* discount fares (non-exchangeable, non-refundable); sometimes first class seats may be found at a fraction of the cost of second class. Otherwise allow half an hour queuing at the station to buy tickets before departure. Tickets must be validated in the machines by the platforms before travel, to avoid onboard fines. You do not need a seat reservation for travel on TER services, but all TGV journeys require a reserved seat.

**SNCF** (French National Railways) 08 92 35 35 35; www.voyages-sncf.com
**Rail Europe** www.raileurope.co.uk (UK); www.raileurope.com (US)

# Airport connections

From **Béziers** airport **Bus 210 Aéroport** (*see page 387*).

Taxis from main airports (other than **Béziers**) may prove very expensive: up to 150-200 euros each way. It is often cheaper to rent a car. From Carcassonne, Nîmes, Montpellier and Perpignan, shuttle buses links airports to the nearest rail station, for the train to Agde (train tickets bookable in advance). TER trains slightly slower, but cheaper than TGV. From Agde, take bus/taxi to Marseillan.

**From Montpellier:** the airport shuttle bus (line **120**) does not go all the way to the mainline train station, but connects with Tram Line 1 at **Place de l'Europe**. Your shuttle ticket is valid on the tram. Get off at the station **Gare St Roch** for the train to Agde. See opposite for Montpellier tram services.

**From Girona:** a round-the-clock bus service connects Girona airport in Spain with Perpignan rail station in France. Timetable linked to over 70 flights. Return fare €16.50, but groups of up to five people may travel together for €80 return. Journey time 1hr20. **www.frogbus.com**

# Transport in Montpellier

## Trams & Buses
The best way to travel through and around Montpellier is by tram. 4000 **TaM** *park and ride* places offer an alternative to traffic jams. Pick up Line 1 (north-south) at the **Odysseum** by the *Ikea* exit of the A9 (montpellier Est); or Line 2 (east-west) at **St Jean de Vedas** off the old Montpellier Road or earlier A9 exit; Line 3 to the beach at Peyrol opens in 2012; and fourth and fifth cross town routes are planned. All lines meet at St Roch station, where you may transfer to buses. Each line has distinctive livery: Elizabeth Garouste and Mattia Bonetti created blue and white swallows for Line 1 and a floral Line 2. Christian Lacroix's Line 3 has a marine theme. Park and Ride for €4.20 with free return tram ticket for everyone in the car. Mon-Sat 07-20. Sun and hols: park free. Otherwise tickets from machines at tram stops: €1.40 single, €2.50 return or 10-ride pass for €11.80. Day passes €3.50 and weekly cards €13.50. Best bargain for up to 5 people travelling together is a family pass (you don't have to be a family): €5.50 for 24 hours unlimited travel. You may transfer between buses and trams. Validate your ticket in the machine each time you board - or risk a fine.

## Bikes
**Vélomagg** is an amazing bike rental scheme: 2000 bikes from 50 automatic bike stations available in and around the city, 24/7. Pay €1 for 4 hours or €2 for a day. Longer rental periods also available. Take your passport to the **Vélomagg** desk to register. Once on the books you may rent a bike from any bike station or tram ticket machine. Sign up at Central **TaM** bike station near Gare St Roch. Pick up bikes on the Esplande (by the tourist office), Antigone and Odysseum. For a day at the seaside, try **Vélomagg Plage**: €2.40 in advance, take bus 32 from place Carnot then collect a mountain bike at the end of the line to take you to the beach. Montpellier residents have a similar scheme allowing them to pick up cars as well!

**Transport info and timetables**: http://www.montpellier-agglo.com/tam

## Hiking & Biking
GR hiking trails are marked on trees and wooden posts, red/white stripes indicating directions. Local route itineraries available from tourist offices. Bring strong comfy shoes, sunblock and warm and waterproof clothes for changeable weather. Remember the country code: close gates, don't litter, no fires. Keep dogs on leads in national parks. Pack maps and GPS. Discover news and hiking itineraries on the Hérault rambler website **www.cdrp34.com** Best general map IGN 2645ET Sète/Cap-d'Agde/Etang De Thau (GPS) 1: 25,000. Cycle excursions see Sports (*page 374*). City cycling: *Velomagg* Montpellier (*above*). Planned new path around the étang: Marseillan section excellent: with safe canal/road crossing Pont du Maire.

## Bike Hire in Marseillan:
**Artimon** quai de Toulon 04 67 01 61 94 **[2] B2**
**Billy** 39 av de la Méditerranée (Marseillan Plage) 04 67 31 69 19**[4] A2**
**Domaine Robinson** 6 quai de Plaisance(Marseillan Plage) 04 67 01 62 70 **[4] B2**

# Further Reading

Allies in my research have been Jean Fayet's encyclopaedic two-volume history **Marseillan, un Village en Bas Languedoc** (ISBN 2950074200 and 2950074219) with Albert Arnaud's delightful social history **Marseillan d'Hier et Aujourd'hui** (2846470243). Twin photo-books by Jean-Vincent Molino are a must for every local coffee table: **Marseillan: Mémoire en Images** (2842549915) and **Marseillan: de la Vigne à la Table** (284910387). All these in French, but Mike and Patricia Worsam, who lead the *Marseillan Historique* guided walks (*see page 50*), researched and published their history in English: **Marseillan: Yesterday, Today & Tomorrow**. If you read and enjoy French, find second-hand copies of Maffre de Bauge's evocative poems, and Marcel Barral (*aka* Viala)'s pensive verses; peerless insights into the Marseillan mind. Planning a journey north to Lozère: take Robert Louis Stevenson's **Travels with a Donkey in the Cevennes**, with my modern eat/sleep guide to the route (imprint illyria 9780955824739). For updates to this book **www.LazyFrance.fr**

## Press

**Lo Cridaire** bi-monthly magazine from the Mairie **www.ville-marseillan.fr**
**Midi Libre** main daily regional newspaper: Montpellier, Béziers and Sète local editions and twitter feeds **www.midilibre.com**
**L'Independent** Narbonne, Carcassonne Perpignan **www.lindependant.com**
**L'Hérault du Jour** regional daily **www.lamarseillaise.fr**
**La Dépêche du Midi** regional daily, Narbonne **www.ladepeche.fr**
**Lozère Nouvelle** weekly paper for Lozère **www.Lozère -nouvelle.com**
**BBB Midi** new incarnation of bilingual monthly mag *Blablablah* **www.bbbmidi.com**
**The Herault Times** English-language quality read **www.theheralttimes.com**
**Languedoc Sun** pocket English-language mag **www.languedocsun.com**
**Olé** and **Ou Sortir** free fortnightly listings from tourist offices and bars

## Radio & TV

**France Bleu Hérault** 103.7 fm local radio station
**Radio Pays d'Hérault** 89.0 fm community radio, English language news and features by *Wow! L'Herault* Fri 18.15/Sat 8.15)
**France 3** local TV news and weather nightly at 19. **www.france3.fr**

## Online

**www.heraultwhatson.info** *Wow! L'Herault* daily updated webzine English language local and national news digest, essential travel updates and exhaustive diary of events. Edited by Robin Hicks, ex-BBC and former editor of *Blablablah*
**www.herault-tribune.com** news from Marseillan, Agde and Sète
**www.thautv.fr** video features on Marseillan and neighbouring villages and towns
**www.languedocliving.com** excellent guide to living in and visiting Languedoc by the team at www.creme-de-languedoc.com
**languedoc.angloinfo.com** exhaustive ex-pat advice site and forums
**www.the-languedoc-page.com** portal for blogs and useful info
**www.languedoc-midi.info** online business portal
**www.languedocbookshop.com** books about Languedoc and France

# INDEX

## Marseillan Village & Marseillan Plage

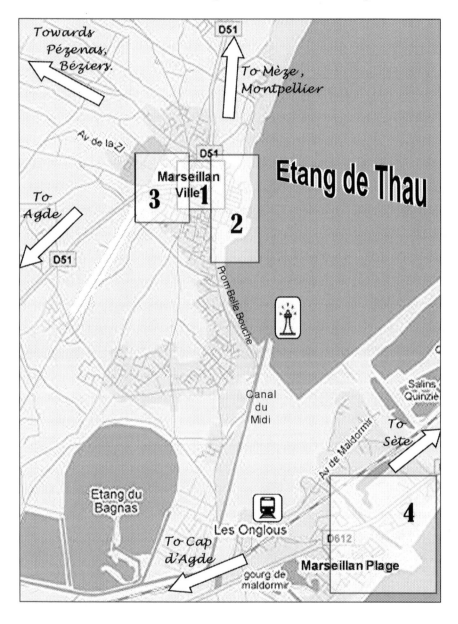

MAP 1        Marseillan (Centre)

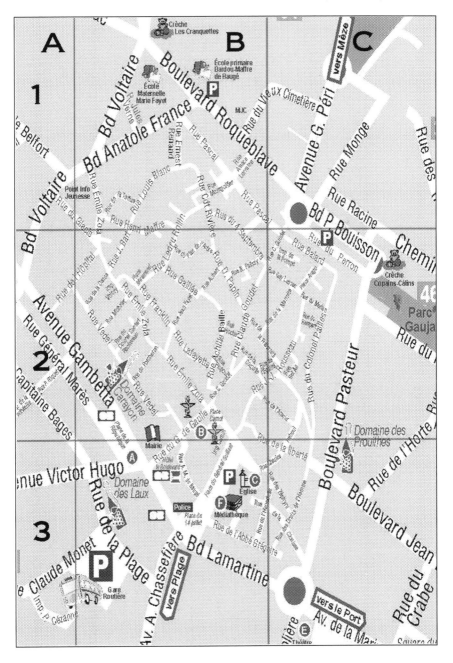

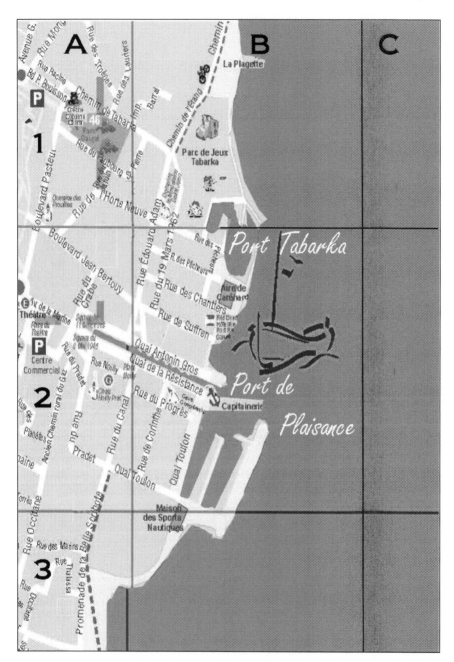

MAP 3        Marseillan (West)

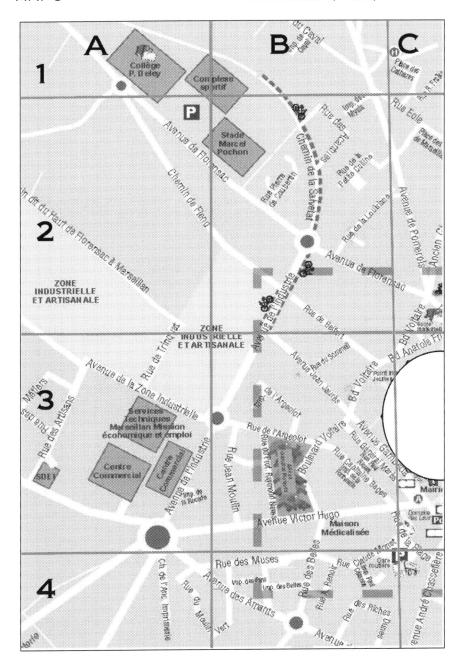

MAP 4        Marseillan Plage

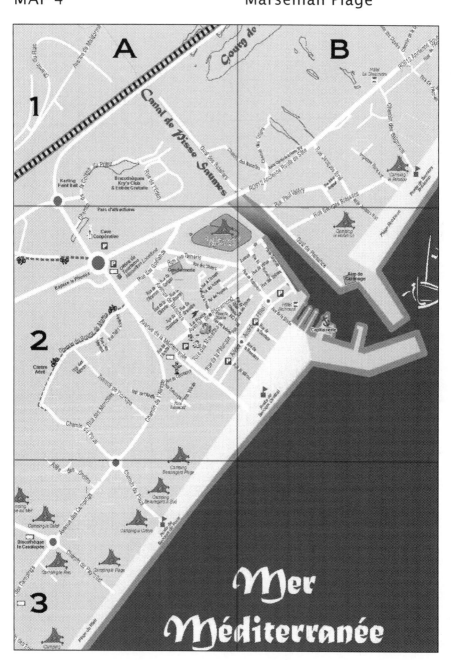

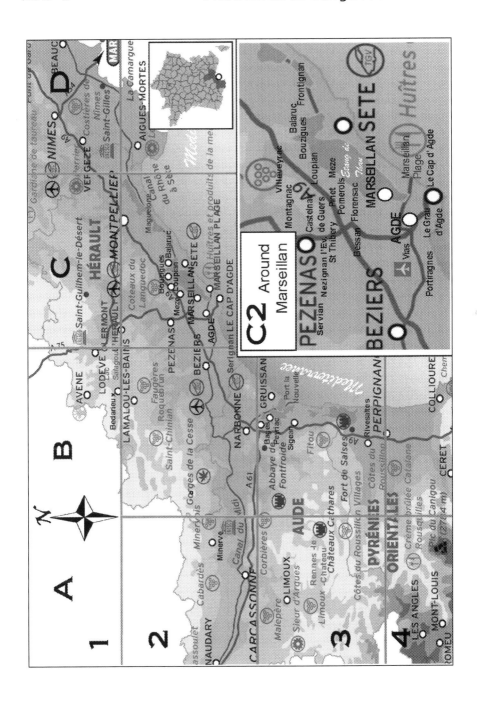

## About The Author

Smitten by Marseillan, award-winning author, Laurence Phillips has been escaping to France since boyhood and has written many and varied books on France and the French. Hailed by British critics as a witty and entertaining enthusiast; in France, his appreciation of long lunches and longer dinners was recognised when he was honoured as a member of the *Commanderie du Fromage Saint-Nectaire* and a Squire of the *Confrérie des Sacres de la Champagne* (although for the latter citation he was inscribed as 'Madame Laurence Phillips', which quite possibly makes him a Dame).

Twice winner of the prestigious Book of the Year prize from the British Guild of Travel Writers for his Bradt city guides to Lille and Paris, he combines wanderlust with a love of theatre and work as critic, playwright and songwriter, and has written for the Royal Shakespeare Company. His stage work has clocked up more travel miles than the author, performed on four continents, from the West End to the South Pacific. Closer to home, his is a familiar voice on countless BBC radio travel and arts programmes with his very personal reflections on France and the French. Most recently he followed Robert Louis Stevenson's Travel with a *Donkey in the Cevennes* – Laurence's companion piece to the classic, hailed by *Times Online* as the best read for your holiday in France, retracing the route for travelers with a donkey, a dog or a dodgy hip!

Laurence is currently working on *Rue Britannia*, a satirical tale of a British enclave in France.

## Also by Laurence Phillips

*Travel books include*
Lille (Bradt Guide)
Paris Lille Brussels (Bradt Guide)
Lille (Thomas Cook Guides)
Normandy (AA Key Guide)
Lille (AA Essential Guide)
Colours of France (AA)
France (AAA Travelbook - US)

*Fiction, plays and verse include*
Garson Lazarre's Paris Confidential (Imprint Illyria)
Poetry is Boring (Imprint Illyria)
Crumbs from my Seder Plate (Imprint Illyria)
Comings & Goings
Déja Revue at the Afterlife Café
Christmas Poppies
The Shakespeare Revue